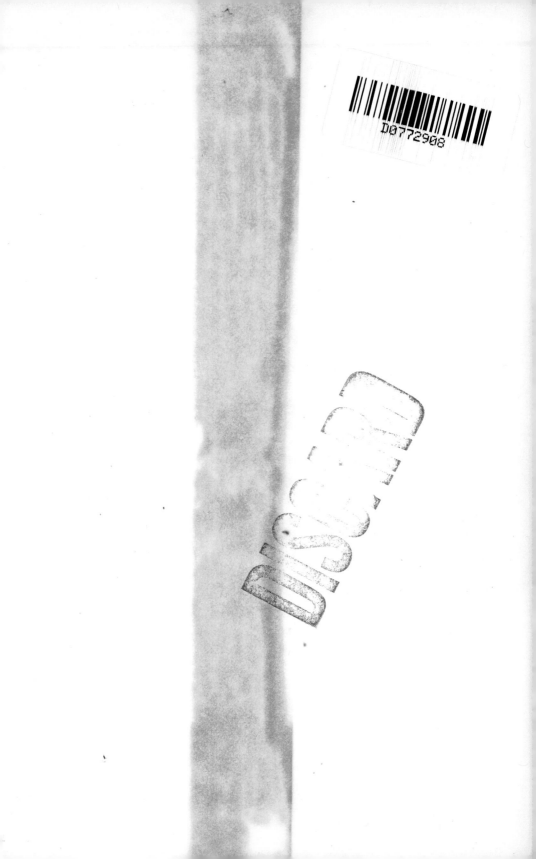

D0772908

# THE FOREIGN MINISTERS
# OF ALEXANDER I

# RUSSIAN AND EAST EUROPEAN STUDIES

Charles Jelavich,
TSARIST RUSSIA AND BALKAN NATIONALISM:
Russian Influence in the Internal Affairs of Bulgaria and Serbia, 1879–1886

Nicholas V. Riasanovsky,
NICHOLAS I AND OFFICIAL NATIONALITY IN RUSSIA,
1825–1855

Charles and Barbara Jelavich, eds.,
THE EDUCATION OF A RUSSIAN STATESMAN:
The Memoirs of Nicholas Karlovich Giers

Simon Karlinsky,
MARINA CVETAEVA:
Her Life and Art

Richard A. Pierce,
RUSSIAN CENTRAL ASIA, 1867–1917:
A Study in Colonial Rule

Jerzy F. Karcz, ed.,
SOVIET AND EAST EUROPEAN AGRICULTURE

Alex M. Shane,
THE LIFE AND WORKS OF EVGENIJ ZAMJATIN

ALEXANDER I, EMPEROR OF RUSSIA (1777–1825)
*Engraving from a Portrait by Monnier (1806)*

# THE FOREIGN MINISTERS
# OF ALEXANDER I

*Political Attitudes and the*

*Conduct of Russian Diplomacy,*

*1801-1825*

## Patricia Kennedy Grimsted

University of California Press
Berkeley and Los Angeles, 1969

University of California Press
Berkeley and Los Angeles, California
University of California Press, Ltd.
London, England
Copyright © 1969 by
The Regents of the University of California
Standard Book Number: 520-01387-5
Library of Congress Catalog Card Number: 69–11615
Designed by Steve Reoutt
Printed in the United States of America

81119

*For my mother and father*

# PREFACE

Russian foreign ministers, more in the shadows than many of their European colleagues of the nineteenth century, have been largely forgotten by history. Such neglect is justifiable, many historians would argue: since the Russian autocrat, as tsar, emperor, or party chief, has always been his own foreign minister, why spend time on mere secretaries? Such neglect is necessary, other historians would affirm: Russian diplomacy has always been based on a recognizable pattern of broad objectives — ideological, economic, or national security considerations — so why should we bother with mere individuals?

A study which looks only to the emperor as the source, inspiration, and executor of Russian foreign policy misses many complexities and fails to consider the significant contributions or alternatives offered by the men closely involved with Russian foreign relations. Under a government which lacked an efficient bureaucracy and which had few institutional and procedural controls on the executive, a minister in charge of a particular branch of government was in a unique position of power. He invariably had ideas and commitments of his own in the realm of foreign policy, for which he sought approval from his sovereign or which affected his approach or conduct of affairs. However much his expression and action may have been limited, the minister was in constant contact with the emperor, working with him closely on all phases of diplomatic activity, coordinating the activities of Russian diplomats abroad and the foreign diplomats in St. Petersburg, handling most of the business of diplomacy, editing, drafting, discussing, and redrafting. Even when the individual foreign minister was clearly an executor rather than a creator of foreign policy, he was nevertheless one of the most important officials in the Russian government.

Similar difficulties plague discussions of Russian foreign relations based primarily on sweeping geographic or ideological determinants, on an animistic conception of the state, on assumed national character, or on a metaphysic of class interest or national mission. Concentration on broad impersonal forces too often obscures the complexity of diplomatic history, superimposes ideas or rational patterns which are out of keeping with the historical milieu, overemphasizes elements of continuity, or simply reinforces prejudices. Speculation regarding Russia's centuries-old "urge to the sea" or Russia's eternal "need to stabilize her western frontier" may provide historical perspective and may have been vaguely considered by some diplomats. But as a starting point for historical research, such concepts do not provide adequate analytic tools nor do they lead to adequate explanations of the particulars of specific diplomatic situations.

Fundamental to understanding the determinants of prerevolutionary Russian foreign relations is a careful study of the men who formulated and carried out policy. This book analyzes the political attitudes and functions of the eight men who served Alexander I in the capacity of foreign minister in an effort to understand their views and how they may have affected the formation and implementation of Russian foreign policy during the first quarter of the nineteenth century. Since the reign of Alexander I represents the apogee of Russian international power and prestige in the prerevolutionary period, and since Alexander I himself was diplomatically among the most successful prerevolutionary leaders, his reign and the men who served him make one of the most intriguing case studies of the conduct of Russian diplomacy.

Initially I had intended to write a more narrowly administrative analysis of the conduct of Russian diplomacy, but such an approach seemed incongruent with the historical situation of the early nineteenth-century. Russia remained an autocracy, and in diplomacy, as in most other affairs, individual considerations of the autocrat and his advisers outweighed institutional patterns. Personal predilections were often more important than generalized considerations of economics, domestic politics, social pressures, or even broadly defined "national interests." Bureaucratic procedures were less significant than the personal role and interpersonal relationships of individuals. For example, the institutional office of foreign minister existed, but its real function and significance depended on the intellectual and psychological relation to the emperor of the individual who — with or without the official title of Foreign Minister — occupied the office and served as spokesman for the emperor's policies. As situations and the emperor's attitudes changed, so changed the men with whom he dealt.

During the twenty-five years that Alexander I governed Russia, eight different men with sharply contrasting backgrounds, personalities, and ideas held the position of Russian foreign minister. As a carry-over from the reign of Paul I, Count Nikita Petrovich Panin occupied the office only briefly, during the first six months of the reign. He was followed in the fall of 1801 by Count Victor Pavlovich Kochubei, one of Alexander's young friends on the Secret Committee who was later the interior minister. An elder statesman from the days of Catherine the Great and brother of Russia's long-time ambassador to England, Count Alexander Romanovich Vorontsov assumed the position in September 1802 and held it until his retirement in January 1804, when his functions were taken over by Alexander's boyhood Polish friend, Prince Adam Jerzy Czartoryski. Czartoryski lasted until mid-1806, at which time the office was assumed, for a little more than a year, by Baron Andrei Gotthard Budberg, one of the emperor's childhood tutors. The elderly and distinguished minister of commerce, Count Nikolai Petrovich Rumiantsev, was the effective foreign minister during most of the Napoleonic alliance, from the fall of 1807 until the Napoleonic invasion of 1812. On the eve of campaigns in Europe, Count Karl Robert Nesselrode was appointed secretary to the emperor; he functioned as foreign minister until Alexander's death in 1825 and continued in the office through most of the reign of Nicholas I. During the years 1815 to 1822, however, Nesselrode served, usually as a subordinate, with Count Ionnes Antonios Capodistrias, a native of Corfu in the Russian service, better known for his later role as the first president of the Greek republic. The actual titles of these men varied considerably; only three of them held the official designation of Foreign Minis-

ter. All, however, functioned in that capacity and that is how
they are considered here.

My object in treating all the men is not primarily biographical.
Rather, to the extent sources have been available, I have analyzed
their personal commitments, political attitudes, and intellectual
framework, in an effort to illuminate the assumptions behind the
particular policies they advocated or for which they served as
spokesman. In particular, their personal and political relationships to the emperor are probed to determine what part they
played in specific diplomatic developments. Although I believe it
desirable to focus on the men themselves, I also tried to abstract
and define the function, powers, and limitations of the office of
foreign minister. The fact that Alexander I had so many ministers
illustrates the importance of the personal dimension of the situation and at the same time helps expose the institutional patterns
of the office.

My study does not, however, provide a comprehensive treatment of Russian foreign relations during the period, even if it
may expose some of the diplomatic complexities and suggest
many important aspects of foreign policy. Indeed, work remains
to be done on crucial phases of the period's diplomacy, and many
of the men covered here are deserving of more extensive biographical treatment, particularly when a more thorough investigation in the Russian foreign ministry archives and other related
papers becomes possible. The chief problem in generalizing about
Russian foreign policy and diplomatic history is the dearth of
monographic studies through which to test methodological insights and generalizations. I hope that my study will help fill this
important gap, while at the same time suggesting some of the
complexities of political attitudes and aims which were involved
in the formulation and implementation of Russian foreign policy.

# ACKNOWLEDGMENTS

The preparation of this book owes much to the financial generosity of several institutions. I am particularly grateful to the Center for Slavic and East European Studies at the University of California at Berkeley for a Senior Research Fellowship, which enabled me to carry out much of the early archival research in Western Europe while preparing my doctoral dissertation, and for several subsequent grants which supported further research and preparation of the manuscript for the press. The acquisition of archival microfilms and other research expenses were aided by grants from the Woodrow Wilson Foundation and the American Philosophical Society. The final stages of revision and publication were undertaken during my two years as a Scholar of the Radcliffe Institute, to which I am greatly indebted both for its financial support and for the access to Widener Library and the other resources of Harvard University which it provided; my association with the Russian Research Center was most helpful during that period.

I was greatly aided by many librarians in the location of research materials. I gratefully acknowledge the assistance of members of the staffs of the Library of Congress, the New York Public Library, the British Museum, the Bibliothèque Nationale, the Leningrad Public Library, the Lenin Library in Moscow, and the libraries of the University of California at Berkeley, Columbia University, and Harvard University.

Archivists in the many repositories in which I worked deserve a hearty word of thanks; my research owes much to their efforts in uncovering documents and arranging for microfilms. I am accordingly grateful to the staffs of the Public Record Office in London, of the French Foreign Ministry Archives at the Quay d'Orsay, and of the Hof-, Haus-, und Staatsarchiv in Vienna, particularly Dr. Anna Coreth. Unpublished Crown-copyright materials in the Public Record Office have been microfilmed and cited by permission of the Controller of Her Majesty's Stationery

Office. I am further grateful to the Massachusetts Historical Society for making available *The Adams Papers on Microfilm*.

I am particularly indebted to the directors and staffs of the following institutions who offered their knowledge and assistance
during my research in the Soviet Union: The Central State Archives of Ancient Acts (TsGADA), the Central State Archives
of the October Revolution (TsGAOR), and the Central State
Historical Archives of the USSR (TsGIA), all under the Main
Archival Administration; The Institute of Russian Literature
(Pushkinskii Dom) and the Leningrad Branch of the Institute of
History, both of the Academy of Sciences of the USSR; and the
manuscript divisions of the Lenin Library, the Leningrad Public
Library, and the State Historical Museum in Moscow.

I also wish to thank the following individuals for their kind assistance in connection with my use of specific manuscript collections: Mr. Roger Ellis, Secretary of the Royal Historical Manuscripts Commission, for his help in locating various private papers
in Great Britain; the Keeper of Manuscripts in the British Museum for arranging for my use of the uncataloged Lieven Papers; Mademoiselle Hembert at the Bibliothèque de Victor
Cousin of the Sorbonne for arranging for my use of the Richelieu
Papers; the director and members of the staff of the Czartoryski
Museum in Cracow for their help in connection with my use of
the Czartoryski Papers; Princesse de Robech, Comtesse de Levis-
Mirepoix, for permitting me to use the Lebzeltern Papers in her
family archives at her Eure estate of Brûmare; Colonel the Earl
Cathcart for permitting my use of his ancestral papers in London
and Cornwall; Professor John M. P. McErlean of York University, Toronto, for arranging microfilms for me of manuscript correspondence from the Pozzo di Borgo Papers in Paris.

The University of Chicago Press kindly permitted me to reprint
sections from my article on Capodistrias which appeared in the
June 1968 *Journal of Modern History*.

This book benefited greatly from the careful reading and critical comments of several scholars at various stages of the manuscript's completion. For their time and efforts in this direction, I
owe great appreciation to Professor Paul Seabury of the Univer-

sity of California, Father G. de Bertier de Sauvigny, professor at the Institute Catholique de Paris, Professor Franco Venturi of the University of Turin, Professor Allen McConnell of Queens College of the City University of New York, and Professor Firuz Kazemzadeh of Yale University. I particularly appreciate the constant assistance and constructive criticism of Professor Nicholas V. Riasanovsky, of the University of California at Berkeley, who has so encouragingly followed my study since its inception.

Pamela Cocks at the Russian Research Center of Harvard University deserves much praise for her assistance during the final preparation of the manuscript for the press.

I owe a special word of gratitude to my husband David, who so graciously put down his own work to contribute his keen criticism, and who so cheerfully bore the domestic inconveniences of my academic endeavors.

P.K.G.

# CONTENTS

# NOTE ON ANNOTATION

In an effort to reduce the number of textual footnotes, references for multiple short quotations have often been gathered into a single note indicated at the end of a paragraph or a major section of a paragraph. In such instances, individual references, which appear in the order of the citations in the text, have been separated by periods. References to secondary sources, to countervailing interpretations, and to additional bibliographical data have been kept to a minimum in the footnotes. To the extent feasible, such information is covered in the chapter bibliographies at the end of the book; these accordingly should be read in conjunction with the footnotes for more complete textual annotation.

Descriptions and evaluations of the most frequently cited sources and archival collections appear in the bibliographical note and in chapter bibliographies.

In citations from Soviet archival sources, the name of the collection of papers (fond) is usually given in English; the three numbers separated by virgules indicate, respectively, the fond, *opis* [inventory], and *dela* [item] numbers, or, when there are only two numbers, the fond and the item numbers.

Citations from British Foreign Office files in the Public Record Office (PRO/FO) are by file number (FO 65 is the number for diplomatic correspondence between the Foreign Office and the British embassy in Russia); a virgule divides file and volume numbers. Diplomatic correspondence (AE/CP) from the French Foreign Ministry Archives is listed by country followed by volume number; or in the case of materials from the "Mémoires et Documents" (AE/MD) series, by section and volume numbers. For diplomatic correspondence in the Austrian files, citation is by carton number in the second or third Russian series (HHS/Russ. II or Russ. III). Folio numbers (fol(s).) are usually given for longer works or memoranda but not for short letters and diplomatic correspondence.

Throughout the work, the transliteration of Russian names and titles has been based on the Library of Congress system, with such slight modifications as the omission of ligatures, and the apostrophe rendition of the Russian soft sign at the ends of words. Russian names have usually been transcribed from the originals, except where close English equivalents such as Alexander and Nicholas have become customary in historical writing. Names of non-Russian origin have been spelled according to the originals, except where they occur in book titles, and with the notable exception of Capodistrias, where the more familiar English form has been used in preference to the Greek and Russian "Kapodistrias" or the French "Capo d'Istrias." In listing prerevolutionary publications and terms, orthography has been modernized. Spelling has not been changed when Russian words or names appear in an English-language quotation or in book titles in languages other than Russian.

Postrevolutionary Soviet or New Style dating, according to the Gregorian calendar in use in the West, has been used throughout. The Julian or Old Style calendar was twelve days behind the Gregorian calendar in the nineteenth century. Where diplomatic documents of the period bear both dates — as they frequently do — only the New Style date has been given in citation. Where only one date is available, the citation has been updated only if it can be presumed to have been according to the Old Style Russian calendar.

# Abbreviations Used
## in Footnotes and Bibliography

AE

Archives du Ministère des Affaires Etrangères (Quai d'Orsay), Paris.

AE/CPR

Correspondance Politique: Russie. In AE (above).

AE/MD

Mémoires et Documents. In AE (above).

Adams, *Memoirs*

*Memoirs of John Quincy Adams Comprising Portions of His Diary from 1795 to 1848.* Ed. Charles Francis Adams. 12 vols. Philadelphia, 1874–1877.

Adams, *Writings*

*Writings of John Quincy Adams.* Ed. Worthington C. Ford. 7 vols. New York, 1913–1917.

*AKV*

*Arkhiv kniazia Vorontsova* [The Archive of Prince Vorontsov]. Ed. P. I. Bartenev. 40 vols. Moscow, 1870–1897.

*ASEER*

*American Slavic and East European Review.*

AVPR

Arkhiv vneshnei politika Rossii [Archives of the Foreign Policy of Russia], Ministerstvo Inostrannykh del SSSR [USSR Foreign Ministry], Moscow.

BM/Add. MSS.

British Museum, Manuscript Division, Additional manuscripts.

*British Diplomacy*

*British Diplomacy, 1813–1815: Select Documents Dealing with the Reconstruction of Europe.* Ed. C. K. Webster. London, 1921.

CA

Czartoryski Papers, located in Muzeum, Archivwum i Bibljoteka Czartoryskich [Czartoryski Museum, Archives and Library], part of the National Museum, Cracow.

Capodistrias, "Aperçu"   Ionnes Capodistrias. "Aperçu de ma carrière publique, depuis 1798 jusqu'à 1822 (Mémoire presentée à S. M. l'Empereur Nicholas)" Dec. 24, 1826. In *SIRIO* (see below), III, 163–292.

Castlereagh,             *Correspondence, Despatches and other Pa-*
Correspondence           *pers of Viscount Castlereagh, Second Mar-*
                         *quess of Londonderry.* Ed. Charles W. Vane. 12 vols. London, 1848–1853.

Chichagov, *Mémoires*    Pavel V. Chichagov. *Mémoires de l'amiral Tchitchagoff, commandant en chef de l'armée du Danube, gouverneur des principautés de Moldavie et de Valachie en 1812 (1767–1849).* 3 vols. Leipzig, 1862. "Bibliothèque russe," n.s., VII.

Chodzko, *Pologne*       L. J. B. Chodzko (Comte d'Angeberg). *Recueil des traités, conventions et actes diplomatiques concernant la Pologne, 1762–1862.* Paris, 1862.

Czartoryski, *Essai*     Adam Jerzy Czartoryski. *Essai sur la diplomatie.* Paris, 1864.

Czartoryski, *Mémoires*  *Mémoires du prince Adam Czartoryski et sa correspondance avec l'empereur Alexandre Ier.* Ed. Charles de Mazade. 2 vols. Paris, 1887.

Czartoryski, "Système"   Adam Jerzy Czartoryski, "Sur le Système politique que devroit suivre la Russie" (1803). Published from the manuscript in CA 5226/IV in "Principles for Russian Foreign Policy: An Early Nineteenth-Century Version of Prince Adam Czartoryski," edited text with notes, introduction, and analysis by

Patricia K. Grimsted. *California Slavic Papers*, Vol. 5, Berkeley, in process.

*DSRF*
*Diplomaticheskie snosheniia Rossi i Frantsii po doneseniiam poslov Imperatorov Aleksandra i Napoleona, 1808–1812.* Ed. Grand Duke Nikolai Mikhailovich. 7 vols. St. Petersburg, 1905–1914.

Edling, *Mémoires*
Roxandra [Sturdza] Edling. *Mémoires de la Ctesse Edling (née Stourdza).* Moscow, 1888.

Fournier, *Châtillon*
August Fournier. *Der Congress von Châtillon. Die Politik im Kriege von 1814.* Leipzig, Vienna, and Prague, 1900.

*Friedrich Wilhelm*
*Briefwechsel König Friedrich Wilhelm's III und der Königin Luise mit Kaiser Alexander I nebst ergänzenden fürstlichen Korrespondenzen.* Ed. Paul Bailleu. Leipzig, 1900. "Publicationen aus den K. Preussischen Staatsarchiven," LXXV. The collection simultaneously appeared in French.

GBL
Gosudarstvennaia biblioteka SSSR imena V. I. Lenina [V. I. Lenin State Library of the USSR] Moscow, Manuscript Division.

Gentz, *Briefe*
*Briefe von und an Friedrich von Gentz.* Ed. F. C. Wittichen and E. Salzer. 3 vols. Munich and Berlin, 1909–1913.

Gentz, *Dépêches*
Friedrich von Gentz. *Dépêches inédites aux hospodars de Valachie pour servir à l'histoire de la politique européenne (1813 à 1828).* Ed. Anton Prokesch von Osten. 3 vols. Paris, 1876–1877.

Goriainov, *1812*
*1812. Dokumenty Gosudarstvennogo i S. Peterburgskogo Glavnogo arkhivov, izdanie Ministerstva Inostrannykh del* [1812: Documents from the State and St. Petersburg

Main Archives, published by the Ministry of Foreign Affairs]. Ed. S. M. Goriainov. 2 parts. St. Petersburg, 1912.

GPB

Gosudarstvennaia Publichnaia biblioteka imena M. E. Saltykova-Shchedrina [M. E. Saltykov-Shchedrin State Public Library], Leningrad, Manuscript Division.

Hardenberg, *Denkwürdigkeiten*

*Denkwürdigkeiten des Staatskanzlers Fürsten von Hardenberg.* Ed. Leopold von Ranke. 5 vols. Leipzig, 1877.

HHS

Hof-, Haus-, und Staatsarchiv, Österreichisches Staatsarchiv, Vienna.

HHS/Russ.

Staatskanzlei: Russland. In HHS (above).

Kukiel, *Czartoryski*

Marian Kukiel. *Czartoryski and European Unity, 1770–1861.* Princeton, 1955.

Lebzeltern, *Doneseniia*

Ludwig von Lebzeltern. *Doneseniia avstriiskogo poslannika pri russkom dvore Lebtselterna za 1816–1825 Gody* [Diplomatic reports of Lebzeltern, Austrian minister at the court of Russia, 1816–1826]. Ed. Grand Duke Nikolai Mikhailovich. St. Petersburg, 1913.

LOII

Leningradskoe otdelenie Instituta istorii, Akademiia Nauk SSSR [Leningrad Branch of the Institute of History of the Academy of Sciences of the USSR], Manuscript Division.

*LPN*

Karl Robert Nesselrode. *Lettres et papiers du chancelier comte de Nesselrode, 1760–1850. Extraits de ses archives.* Ed. A. de Nesselrode. 11 vols. Paris, 1904–1912.

Maistre, *Correspondance*

*Correspondance diplomatique de Joseph de Maistre, 1811–1817.* Ed. A. Blanc. 2 vols. Paris, 1860.

| | |
|---|---|
| Maistre, *Mémoires* | *Mémoires politiques et correspondance diplomatique de Joseph de Maistre.* Ed. A. Blanc. Paris, 1858. |
| Martens, *Recueil* | Fedor Fedorovich Martens. *Sobranie traktatov i konventsii zakliuchennykh Rossieiu s inostrannymi derzhavami/Recueil des traités et conventions conçlus par la Russie avec les puissances étrangères.* 15 vols. St. Petersburg, 1874–1909. |
| Metternich, *Mémoires* | *Mémoires, documents et écrits divers laissés par le prince de Metternich, chancelier de cour et d'état.* Ed. Richard Metternich. 8 vols. Paris, 1880–1884. |
| NM, *Alexandre* | Grand Duke Nikolai Mikhailovich. *L'empereur Alexandre Ier. Essai d'étude historique.* 2 vols. St. Petersburg, 1912. |
| *NPP* | Nikita Petrovich Panin. *Materialy dlia zhizneopisaniia grafa Nikity Petrovicha Panina (1770–1837)* [Materials for the biography of Count Nikita Petrovich Panin]. Ed. A. Brückner. 7 vols. St. Petersburg, 1888–1892. |
| Pasquier, *Histoire* | Etienne Denis Pasquier. *Histoire de mon temps. Mémoires du chancelier Pasquier.* Ed. duc d'Audiffret-Pasquier. 6 vols. Paris, 1894–1895. |
| PD | Institut russkoi literatury (Pushkinskii Dom), Akademiia Nauk SSSR [Institute of Russian Literature (Pushkin House) of the Academy of Sciences of the USSR], Leningrad, Manuscript Division. |
| Pozzo, *Correspondance* | *Correspondance diplomatique du comte Pozzo di Borgo et du comte de Nesselrode depuis la restauration des Bourbons jusqu'au congrès d'Aix-la-Chapelle, 1814–1818.* Ed. Charles Pozzo di Borgo. 2 vols. Paris, 1890. |

PRO                             Public Record Office, London

PRO/FO                          State Papers of the Foreign Office. In PRO (above).

Prokesch-Osten,                 Anton Prokesch von Osten. *Geschichte des*
Geschichte                      *Abfalls der Griechen vom Türikischen Reiche im Jahre 1821 und der Gründung des Hellenischen Königreiches aus diplomatischem Standpunkte.* 6 vols. Vienna, 1867.

*Razoumowski*                   A. A. Vasilchikov (Wassiltchikow). *Les Razoumowski.* Ed. A. Brückner. Halle s/Salle, 1893–1894. Vol. II: *Le Comte André Razoumowski*, 4 parts.

*SEER*                          *Slavonic and East European Review*

Schilder, *Aleksandr*           N. K. Schilder. *Imperator Aleksandr Pervyi, ego zhizn i tsarstvovanie* [Emperor Alexander the First, his life and reign]. 2nd ed. 4 vols. St. Petersburg, 1904–1905.

*SIRIO*                         *Sbornik Imperatorskogo russkogo istoricheskogo obshchestva* [Collection of the Imperial Russian Historical Society]. 148 vols. St. Petersburg, 1867–1917.

*Starhemberg*                   A. Thürheim. *Ludwig Fürst Starhemberg. Ehemaliger K. K. A. O. Gesandter an den Höfen in Haag, London, und Turin etc. Eine Lebensskizze.* Graz, 1889.

Stedingk, *Mémoires*            *Mémoires posthumes du feld-maréchal comte de Stedingk rédigés sur les lettres, dépêches et autres pièces authentiques laissées à sa famille par le général comte de Björnstjerna.* 3 vols. Paris, 1844–1847.

Stein, *Briefe*                 Heinrich Friedrich Karl von Stein. *Briefe und amtliche Schriften.* New ed. Walther Hubatsch. 6 vols. Stuttgart, 1957–1965.

| | |
|---|---|
| *Stroganov* | Grand Duke Nikolai Mikhailovich. *Graf P. A. Stroganov (1774–1817). Istoricheskoe issledovanie epokhi imperatora Aleksandra I* [Count P. A. Stroganov (1774–1817): A historical study of the epoch of Emperor Alexander I]. 3 vols. St. Petersburg, 1903. |
| Sturdza, *Oeuvres* | Aleksandr Skarlatovich Sturdza. *Oeuvres posthumes, réligieuses, historiques, philosophiques et littéraires d'Alexandre de Stourdza.* 5 vols. Paris, 1858–1861. |
| Talleyrand, *Mémoires* | *Mémoires du prince de Talleyrand, publiés avec une préface et des notes par le duc de Broglie.* 5 vols. Paris, 1891. |
| TsGADA | Tsentral'nyi gosudarstvennyi arkhiv drevnikh aktov SSSR [Central State Archives of Ancient Acts of the USSR], Moscow. |
| TsGAOR | Tsentral'nyi gosudarstvennyi arkhiv Oktiabrskoi revoliutsii, vysshikh organov gosudarstvennoi vlasti i organ gosudarstvennogo upravleniia SSSR [Central State Archives of the October Revolution, Supreme Organs of State Power, and Organs of State Administration of the USSR], Moscow. |
| TsGIA | Tsentral'nyi gosudarstvennyi istoricheskii Arkhiv SSSR [Central State Historical Archives of the USSR], Leningrad. |
| *VPR* | Ministerstvo Inostrannykh del SSSR. *Vneshniaia politika Rossi XIX i nachala XX veka. Dokumenty rossiiskogo Ministerstva Inostrannykh del* [The foreign policy of Russia in the 19th and the beginning of the 20th centuries: Documents of the Russian Ministry of Foreign Affairs]. Moscow, 1960–1967. Series I, Vols. I–VI. |

Wawrzkowicz, *Sprawa*      Eugenius Wawrzkowicz. *Anglia a sprawa*
*Polska*                   *Polska, 1813–1815* [England and the Polish
                           question, 1813–1815]. Cracow and Warsaw,
                           1919. "Monografie w zakresie Dziejow no-
                           wozytnych."

Webster, *Castlereagh,*    C. K. Webster. *The Foreign Policy of Cas-*
*1815–1822*                *tlereagh, 1815–1822: Britain and the Euro-*
                           *pean Alliance.* 2nd ed. London, 1934.

Weil, *Congrès*            Maurice-Henri Weil, ed. *Les dessous du*
                           *Congrès de Vienne d'après les documents*
                           *originaux des archives du Ministère Impérial*
                           *et Royal de l'Intérieur à Vienne.* 2 vols.
                           Paris, 1917.

Wellington, *Despatches*   *Despatches, Correspondence and Memo-*
                           *randa of Field Marshall Arthur, Duke of*
                           *Wellington, K. G.* New series. 7 vols. Lon-
                           don, 1867–1880.

Wellington, *Supplemen-*   *Supplementary Despatches, Correspondence,*
*tary Despatches*          *and Memoranda of Field Marshal Arthur,*
                           *Duke of Wellington, K. G.,* edited by his
                           son. 15 vols. London, 1858–1872.

# THE FOREIGN MINISTERS
## OF ALEXANDER I

"The conduct of Russia necessarily has the greatest influence on general politics and consequently must be the object of careful scrutiny. Anything which could give some indication of the views, projects, and even mental disposition of the Emperor is of the highest interest. Although it may always be difficult to penetrate the secret intentions of a cabinet, they may often be surmised by gathering all manner of suggestive information and by keeping an attentive eye on the proceedings and activities which, meaningless in themselves, might really have secret connections and might be indicative of important plans. I must accordingly request that you devote yourself to gathering and transmitting to me as much information as possible, not only on general activities in Russia, but also on the personal dispositions of the Emperor and those who surround him and on the system which he might presumably have the intention of pursuing."

From Richelieu's ministerial instructions to a French ambassador departing for his post in Russia, August 21, 1816

"I would like to have the present epoch in which I have taken such an active part withdrawn from the premature judgment of my contemporaries, who would not know how — however hard they may try — to place it in proper perspective. Providence reserves to posterity the fruit of our works, and it is posterity alone who is their true judge."

Alexander I to Madame de Stael,
June 25, 1815

## Chapter 1

# THE CONTEXT OF DIPLOMACY

Russia reached a point of power and prestige in Europe during the reign of Alexander I which was unequaled until World War II. Russia proved to be the one continental power capable of standing up to Napoleonic France, and, symbolically, Alexander I led the European armies across the continent to the French capital, forcing the abdication of Napoleon. Such diplomatic and military achievements were no mere aberration; during the first quarter of the nineteenth century, Russian diplomacy was more predominantly linked to general European developments than it was at any other time in history. Russian leaders sensed themselves and their country as part of a cosmopolitan aristocratic European community, because the nationalistic reaction which posited the intellectual and political divorce between Russia and the West had not yet set in. Indeed, Russia's stature as a great European power reached its zenith because the economic, social, and political developments which were to transform the European continent in the next hundred years had not, by 1800, separated Russia from Western Europe to the extent that would be so evident in the Crimean War at mid-century. The late-nineteenth-century paradox of the largest and one of the most backward countries of Europe trying to maintain an international position as a great power had not yet become apparent during the reign of Alexander I.

The eighteenth century had firmly established Russia as a member of the European community and one of the most important nations to be reckoned with in the European system of states. The extension of Russian boundaries through Poland in the west and to the Black Sea in the southwest during the expansive reign of Catherine the Great magnified but left unsolved the thorny problems of Russia's relationship to Poland and to the Ottoman

Empire, which carried over to become the most immediate problems for Russian diplomacy in the nineteenth century. In addition to such specific problems, the expansion of Catherine's period had a tremendous strategic impact on the European balance of power, for it signified Russia's decisive importance as a great power on the continent. The diplomatic problems resulting from such a position were to be felt fully during Alexander's reign; Russia was too deeply committed to Europe and to its position as a great European power to be able to withdraw easily. Cultural and intellectual developments went hand in hand with diplomatic ones, for as Catherine brought western Enlightenment ideas to Russia — and an "Enlightened" education to her grandson, Alexander — she committed Russia more decisively to the European cultural community. The Russian government was as severely challenged by the French Revolution as most other governments in Europe. Alexander came to the throne at a time when Russia had to respond, not only to the revolution, but to the Napoleonic regime which succeeded it.

When Alexander took power in March of 1801, Russia was on the verge of a far-reaching rapprochement with France and, allied with the northern courts, was on the brink of naval war with England. Some of the specific peculiarities of this diplomatic situation, most notably the abortive expedition of 23,000 Cossacks dispatched early in the year "to conquer India," may well have resulted from the questionable mental state of Alexander's father, Paul I. Despite such far-fetched schemes, which were quickly called off after Paul's assassination, Russia remained clearly a European power, intricately involved in European politics. European leaders may have had some reservations, supported by some of the diplomatic follies of Paul I, about how deeply European civilization had penetrated the Potemkin facades of Catherine's Russia. But in the person of Alexander I the Russian monarch was indeed considered one of their rank — courted or feared, but above all involved in the major diplomatic maneuvers of the next quarter-century.

The diplomatic world for Russia in the early nineteenth century was definitely Europe-centered. Although Russian embassies were dispatched to, or permanent legations established in, such areas as the United States, Persia, Japan, and China, these were clearly of subsidiary interest. The only important power in Russian foreign relations outside continental Europe was the Ottoman Empire, and it, in many ways, was considered part of the European system. Indeed, Russia's own predominant concern with the "Eastern Question" immediately became a problem that European powers were unwilling to let Russia solve alone. A subject of conflict with Napoleon at the beginning of the period, it became one of the most embroiled issues of general European diplomacy in the years following the Congress of Vienna. The increasingly global scope of international affairs which was to widen Russia's diplomatic field later in the century had barely become apparent during Alexander's reign.

Along with the concrete manifestations of Russia's involvement in Europe went political attitudes through which Alexander and his diplomatic advisers shared a sense of a European community of nations. They shared with their Western counterparts a concern about any threats to that community; and they readily joined in efforts to protect it when those threats materialized. Traditional eighteenth-century concepts of balance-of-power diplomacy were being questioned somewhat in the period, but it was still those concepts on which most contemporary diplomatic decisions were predicated. The dichotomy of "Russia" and "The West" was raised to new levels of significance through intellectual currents which were developing in Russia in the early nineteenth century; but such currents had barely manifested themselves in the upper echelons where foreign policy decisions were made. The eighteenth-century world of aristocratic cosmopolitanism remained the diplomatic context for Russian leaders during the reign of Alexander I.

Russian diplomacy was cosmopolitan in another sense in the early nineteenth century, in that it was motivated primarily by a response to external concerns. The French Revolution and the Napoleonic imperium cast heavy shadows over Europe; the diplomacy and political developments of the period were dominated by the issues they raised. Napoleon threatened the European community and the balance of power in which the Russian political entity functioned. He threatened the traditional great powers of England, Prussia, and Austria, thereby threatening to isolate Russia from its most needed allies. He posed a direct threat to the newly won Russian lands of Poland, to Russia's recently acquired passageway to the Mediterranean, and to the presumed right of Russia to arbitrate the destinies of the Ottoman Empire. Such strategic threats to Russia linked the empire more closely with the fate of Europe than it had ever been before. England and the continental powers outside of France were forced to suppress their divisive quarrels in the interest of the Europe-wide effort for survival. Russia immediately assumed a crucial position in the power balance with Napoleon. Even by 1800, when he sought a rapprochement with Paul I, Bonaparte seemed to realize that Russia was the most important power with whom he would have to deal. And indeed Alexander's alternating decisions for war and peace with Napoleon largely determined the destinies of the entire continent. Symbolically enough, Napoleon at the head of a European army first faced defeat in the Russian capital in 1812, and two and a half years later it was Alexander who led the armies of Europe in their final triumphal march through Paris.

War may have been an extension of diplomacy, but too often in Napoleonic Europe, politics went hand in hand with war, obscuring the line between military and diplomatic decisions. The military concern to rid Europe of the Napoleonic armies was intricately related to the political concerns of restoring peace and the balance of power. Because at the highest level of imperial power the key military and diplomatic decisions came from the same man, pressures from the military establishment sometimes had as much effect as pressures from the foreign ministry. This is not to suggest that the Russian generals usually made political decisions or the foreign ministers military ones, but military realities clearly played their part and often did determine the course of diplomacy. The generals may have pressured Alexander to make peace with Napoleon in 1807, but they mostly opposed Alexander's decision to extend the war into Europe at the end of 1812. Many of Russia's top diplomats had some military experience or education; and from the emperor down, there was a great deal of interchange in personnel, with high military leaders often serving in diplomatic capacities, not to mention that the emperor's closest associates — his aides-de-camp — were military men. It was still the age when "the glory of Russia" was most frequently conceived in military terms, when the very concept of sovereign carried with it the traditional image of the military commander-in-chief, and when the office of emperor involved Alexander personally as leader of the Russian army to the extent that he sought glory for his country through his personal role as a great military hero. Indeed, Alexander I, however unmilitary many of his attitudes may have been, was the last of the Romanovs who could be so pictured with any degree of realism.

The military developments also had significant social and economic dimensions, as historians of the period have often mentioned. Russia, no less than other parts of Europe, experienced the ravages of war and the deprivations of a society at war. This experience lay deep in the motivation of the diplomatic settlement following the defeat of Napoleon, for it had affected the lives and attitudes of the men who made that settlement. At the same time the extent and nature of wars in the period, contributing as they did to social change, affected the problems with which the diplomats had to deal. Patriotic war to liberate or preserve the fatherland augmented both the popular dimension of foreign relations and the spiritual dimension of national consciousness, however much European leaders might have wished to overlook these elements.

The strategic and military challenge of the Napoleonic empire went hand in hand with important political issues. France as a military power had to be resisted, but France as a nation was not so much the enemy as was Napoleon or as were the abstract issues of revolution and empire that challenged the European social and political order and disrupted the so-called balance of power. Even constitution-minded British statesmen or a ruler like Alexander, who cherished hopes of reform, came to fear the overthrow of the established social and political order and the tyranny of revolutionary dictatorship. This vision of a revolutionary challenge to

the existing order brought the European issues immediately home
to Russia. Whether or not Alexander and his advisers fully understood the issues, they came to sense the fundamental challenge
to the government and social structure of the Russian Empire.
However sympathetic these men may have been toward the need
for reform and the implications of that challenge for the future,
they were all members of the established ancien régime and clearly
had a personal, economic, and social stake in its preservation.

This long-range threat to the political and social structure with
its only implicit economic dimensions was much more significant
than any purely economic threats to trade routes or commerce —
at least it was in the minds of those who framed diplomatic
policies. Certainly, the commercial threat to Russia's newly won
passage to the Mediterranean cannot be denied, but at the time of
the Napoleonic wars, that threat was rarely conceived in economic terms. The commercial development of Odessa and its surrounding region was beginning under the governorship of the
French émigré statesman Richelieu, and exports through Black
Sea ports were increasing rapidly; Russians, however, still had
only a small stake in the commerce, and only a few of the minor
entrepreneurs there were actually Russian. Vociferous as they
were about "Russian glory" and Russian claims to control in the
Black Sea area, government and high society were only gradually
becoming aware of the commercial potential of the region. Although a few leaders who had been urging aggression against
Turkey recognized the economic dimension of the Eastern Question, there was no actual economic motivation for the Russo-
Turkish war which started in 1806, nor did economic considerations play a part in the 1812 settlement at Bucharest. It was not
until after the Congress of Vienna and the threat of war with Turkey in the 1820's that the political repercussions of economic developments there slowly became apparent, but these had no direct
relationship to major foreign policy decisions. Russia's adherence
to the Continental System and its relatively uneconomical commercial break with England after 1807 brought more severe political pressures, but even these could not determine political decisions. Thus the Napoleonic threat came on military, political, and

social levels, and, except for long-range implications barely fore-
seen at the time, economic factors had little effect on diplomatic
decision-making.

In fact, domestic developments or internal concerns generally
had much less impact on Russian foreign policy than did the military challenges and political pressures from abroad during the period. By virtue of the fact that the Russian emperor ruled auto-
cratically and simultaneously conducted both domestic and
foreign affairs, a certain correlation between the two realms was
always apparent. His own interests and attitudes gave a personal
cast to most phases of government during his reign; most
particularly — as will be discussed in the next chapter — his
vague, counterbalancing concerns for the promotion of "enlightenment" and the preservation of order were as important for foreign as for domestic developments. However, partly because of
the exceedingly vague nature of the emperor's political concerns
and the curious blending in them of rational and irrational elements, there was very little practical correlation between domestic
and foreign policy. Too often foreign policy decisions were made
with no regard for their immediate domestic effects or repercussions, and the concept of "national interest" could hardly be said
to be operative in foreign policy. To be sure, the defense of Russia against the Napoleonic empire — a definite element of national security — was an operative goal in the determination of
Russian foreign policy for much of the first half of Alexander's
reign; but the emperor tended to regard this, aside from the immediate military situation, more as part of a general problem of the
European balance of power or of the preservation of traditional
forms of government, than as a uniquely national goal. For even
when Napoleon was on the retreat from Russia and the country
needed anything but further war, Alexander was more concerned
about a grand coalition to pursue his enemy to the gates of Paris
than with the rebuilding and development of his own war-ravaged,
backward nation.

Foreign policy for imperial Russia during the first quarter of
the century — as at the end — proved to be more often an escape than an integral extension of domestic needs or problems.

And it was in this respect that there was the greatest carry-over
between domestic and international affairs. Throughout Alexander's reign there was a vacillation between active involvement in
general European politics and a withdrawal to concentrate on domestic affairs; the emperor often attempted to pursue these rival
paths simultaneously, or at least to leave adequate room to maneuver freely between them. During a short period at the beginning of his reign he appeared ready to ally himself with the policy
of his acting foreign minister Kochubei to withdraw from active
European policies in favor of thoroughgoing reform at home. But
that policy was short-lived, and the unsatisfactory results of the
1802 reform efforts apparently left the emperor more ready to become active abroad. Again, from 1808 to 1811, an official policy
of peace abroad corresponded with Speranskii's great reform efforts on the domestic scene, while Napoleon's invasion of Russia
in 1812, correlating as it did with the end of the Speranskii era,
brought a renewed commitment to foreign campaigns. Thus, periods of peace or relative inactivity abroad did seem to coincide
with some periods of attempted domestic reform, while renewed
efforts abroad and concentration on foreign affairs often appeared
to be in direct response to failures or frustrations on the domestic
front. But such responses derived more from the personal inclinations of the emperor than from any serious domestic political
pressures or any calculated requirements of national economic
development. And more often than not, the responses also
stemmed from external pressures which seemed to the emperor to
demand more active attention.

The sense of international community with Europe, to which
Russia was intricately bound both politically and culturally, was
felt by the top foreign policy decision-makers, and it naturally affected the procedures and institutions of diplomatic conduct. The
forms and methods of Russian diplomacy, if not directly bor-
rowed from those of other countries of Europe had much in common with them. And in the case of Russia particularly, many of
these institutional elements had much to do with the divorce of
foreign policy from domestic policies and internal developments.

Diplomacy in the early nineteenth century remained basically court-centered. With few exceptions, absolute monarchy was the form of government in Europe. In France during the Bourbon Restoration, political factions often had more effect than the king in choosing the foreign minister and determining his role, and in England the crown assumed a less important role in foreign affairs than in the eastern monarchies; but these situations were exceptional, and even there diplomatic instruments bore the king's name. A powerful minister like the Austrian chancellor Metternich in reality may have been in complete control of both the formulation and the execution of foreign policy, but Hapsburg foreign relations were still conducted in the name of the emperor and only with his full approval. On the whole, diplomacy continued, and was reaffirmed after the fall of Napoleon, as "classical" or even "monarchical" diplomacy.

The form and basic monarchical principles of government in Russia made Alexander's position similar to that of other European sovereigns, particularly those of Prussia and Austria, in the conduct of affairs. Yet the Russian autocrat, in the eyes of many observers, assumed a more important position than his European counterparts. Metternich's ambassador to St. Petersburg, Lebzeltern, could rightfully be surprised to find "how absolute the will of the sovereign is in this empire." [1] Especially in respect to foreign policy and the actual conduct of diplomacy, Russia stood somewhat apart; no other sovereign of the period, with the exception of Napoleon, took such a personal interest and played such an important role in the foreign relations of his country. Alexander, the tsar-diplomat par excellence, was prone to believe that some matters were "of such a nature that ministers can be of no help" and that "sovereigns alone are capable of deciding." [2]

State decisions were not made by nations as a whole, so that it is often misleading to speak of purely Russian foreign policies with emphasis on an animistic conception of the state. Only to the extent that the positions of those individuals who formally represented the state are recognized, can a holistic conception of Rus-

[1] Lebzeltern to Metternich, May 6, 1817, HHS/Russ. III, 22.
[2] Quoted by Metternich, "Autobiographie," *Mémoires*, I, 210.

sian policy be meaningful. State decisions were made by individuals; they may have reflected a particular sociopolitical milieu or
outlook, but they were not dictated by party or by any pervasive
ideology. Government bureaucracy and cabinet government were
better established in Western Europe than in Russia, but even
there, in the diplomatic realm, decisions were principally dependent on individuals rather than upon institutions. In Russia the
Council of State hardly functioned in the diplomatic field, and the
Senate, while it had a few formal discussions of items relating to
foreign affairs, played almost no part in the formation or implementation of policy. The Unofficial — or Secret — Committee of
the early years of Alexander's reign was perhaps Russia's closest
approximation to cabinet government before 1905, but it was an
irregular and informal group whose importance depended more
on its personnel as individuals than on any institutional function.
What N. I. Panin had said about the reign of the empress Elizabeth less than a century earlier was still true in the Russia of the
early nineteenth century: "Russia was governed not by 'the authority of state institutions,' but by 'the power of persons.'"[3]

Public opinion and popular aspirations counted for little in the
diplomatic developments of the early nineteenth century. Only in
England, where Castlereagh and later Canning had to account to
Parliament, was the conduct of foreign affairs starting to show the
influence of public opinion. Secrecy and lack of publicity were
the hallmarks of the period. Foreign relations were conducted by
the cosmopolitan brotherhood of reigning monarchs and their
ministers, while nationalism and growing liberal popular movements were of mainly negative concern.

What "public opinion" did exist in Russia in the first quarter of
the nineteenth century was limited to gentry or court circles. Gentry complaisance with the status quo may have been largely responsible for the failure of efforts at domestic reform, but in foreign affairs, their pressures counted for little. They may have
closed their homes to the French ambassador or, like Karamzin in

---

[3] Quoted in Michael T. Florinsky, *Russia: A History and an Interpretation*
(2 vols.; New York, 1953), I, 456.

his "Memoir on Ancient and Modern Russia," they may have openly expressed their opposition to the French alliance in the years following Tilsit, but their pressures had no more effect on Russian foreign policy than they did fifteen years later when many groups desired war with Turkey in support of the Greeks. Alexander may have been affected personally by the opposition to his policies, but rarely did such feelings affect his diplomatic decisions. Napoleon's envoys and their staff were well and honorably received at court, as Alexander scoffed at the public pressures. "It would be criminal on my part, if I were to stop what I think useful to the interest of the empire," he explained in a letter to his mother, "as a result of the idle gossip which the public permits itself without any knowledge of the circumstances." [4]

Not only that, but the public was kept poorly informed about diplomatic developments. The modern newspaper was barely developing in the West, but in Russia current news in the modern sense was virtually nonexistent. The minimal international news that got into the Russian press was frequently out of date and was strictly censored. Current information from abroad was even further garbled as it spread through the grapevines of society. "You know as well as anyone," the Russian foreign minister wrote to the ambassador in Vienna in 1802, "that secrecy is the soul of business." His words were well applicable to diplomatic proceedings throughout the period. "The impenetrable secrecy with which important matters are decided," which was criticized by foreign diplomats, was taken for granted by Russian officials, even those in high positions. [5]

The reign of Alexander I could well be characterized as a period of "conference diplomacy," which, in Metternich's words, was "unique in the annals of the world." There was no other span of twenty-five years which included so many important international conferences where "the chief personages in the great drama found themselves together in the very same place." Châtillon, Vi-

[4] Alexander to Maria Feodorovna, Sept. 1808, "Nakanune Erfurtskogo svidaniia 1808 goda," ed. N. K. Schilder, *Russkaia starina* XCVIII (April 1899), 23.
[5] Kochubei to A. K. Razumovskii, May 28, 1802, *Razoumowski*, II, Part 4, 306. La Ferronnays to Pasquier, April 10, 1820, *SIRIO*, CXXVII, 360.

enna, Paris, Aix-la-Chapelle, Troppau, Laibach, and Verona overshadowed the smaller gatherings at Memel, Tilsit, Erfurt, and
Carlsbad. In fact, conference diplomacy was continuous during
parts of the period, most notably from the time of Napoleon's retreat from Russia until the settlements in Paris after the battle of
Waterloo. "The most difficult affairs, and the arrangements most
complicated in their nature, were, so to speak, negotiated from
one room to another." And because the negotiators were sovereign, these conferences resulted in major decisions. Even in the
more formal congresses, as Metternich remarked, "the most important affairs were always discussed in confidential conversations
between the three monarchs, as well as between the heads of cabinets." Later, out of the formal ministerial conferences, came the
protocols; but these were routine, their components having been
discussed and drafted in advance.[6]

Aside from the effects of such procedures on the current diplomatic forms, an unusual intimacy developed among the statesmen
of Europe out of their common experiences around the battlefield, the conference table, and the salons of European centers,
which gave diplomacy an additional cosmopolitan dimension and
enhanced the sense of a European community. It further widened
the gulf, particularly in the case of Russia, between domestic developments and foreign policy. And it often meant that personal
interaction between heads of state had an important bearing on
foreign policy. For as emotional a leader as Alexander I, his personal relations with Napoleon had as crucial an importance in
state decisions as did his personal feuds and later reconciliations
with Metternich. Conference diplomacy assumed a more relaxed
quality than in earlier periods, presenting, in the words of a contemporary French diplomat-historian, "the aspect of amicable
conversations entirely devoid of the etiquette, precautions, and
pretensions of former years."[7] Such remarks may have indicated a
change from the past, but in comparison to the future, the conferences of the early nineteenth century appeared as highly formal

---

[6] Metternich, "Autobiographie," *Mémoires*, I, 152, 173. Webster, *Castlereagh, 1815–1822*, pp. 63–64.
[7] Edmund Boislecomte, "Aix-la-Chapelle," AE/MD: France, 714.

and stylized affairs. Yet the style was clearly that of the great age of aristocratic government. The "dancing congress," by which name the Vienna meetings of 1814 to 1815 are so often mocked, remains an apt phrase for characterizing much of the conduct of European foreign relations in the period.

The sense of brotherhood among the sovereigns had its counterpart in the cosmopolitan friendships and esprit de corps among diplomats. Through their common use of the French language, their similar social and cultural values, wealth, and usually aristocratic blood or titles, Russia's diplomats belonged to the socioculturally homogeneous European *corps diplomatique*. Foreigners served as Russian foreign ministers for more than half of Alexander's reign. A great many ambassadors, ministers, and lesser diplomats were not of Russian extraction, had been educated and trained outside of Russia, and had served other monarchs before entering the Russian service. And many important diplomats from established Russian families were much more at home in the West than in their native land. For example, the long-time Russian ambassador in London S. R. Vorontsov, although he was self-consciously Russian, felt very much at home in England; he was a great admirer of Pitt, and a large part of his wealth was tied up in British holdings. Of Alexander's suite at the Congress of Vienna, only one of his major advisers, A. K. Razumovskii, was of Russian parentage. Even he, for many years the Russian ambassador in Vienna, was "cosmopolitan in every sense of the term"; unable to write a dispatch in Russian, he successively married two Germans and converted to Roman Catholicism before his death.[8]

Most Russian diplomats had traveled and lived abroad a great part of their lives, as foreign assignments, particularly on the ambassadorial or high ministerial levels, were much more permanent than they are today. And it was quite common for a diplomatic career to pass down through a family. Most diplomats of Alexander's day who had not had some education abroad had been schooled by foreign tutors — especially French. Through travel,

[8] Grand Duke Nikolai Mikhailovich, *Russkie portrety XVIII i XIX stoletii* (10 vols.; St. Petersburg, 1905–1909), V, 158; Caulaincourt to Napoleon, Dec. 31, 1807, *DSRF*, I, 42.

conferences, and ties of blood and friendship, they knew their foreign colleagues personally and were as at home in the salons of Paris as French diplomats were in St. Petersburg. With their Western colleagues, they frequented the spas of Carlsbad, Aix-la-Chapelle, and Baden. Like their colleagues, Russia's diplomats could look to Callières or to the *Manuel diplomatique* by the French diplomat Martens for their professional instruction. Whether addressed to Vienna, Copenhagen, Berlin, or St. Petersburg, the dispatches and most of the personal correspondence of all diplomats were in French.

Although the prevalence of French eased diplomatic communication during the early nineteenth century, travel time impeded it. The fastest courier might make the journey from Paris to St. Petersburg in twelve or thirteen days, but the more normal time would range from eighteen to twenty-four days, depending on the season and route. Joseph de Maistre, the conservative publicist who served as the Sardinian minister to Russia, complained that in 1803 it took from two to three months to consult his home cabinet and receive an answer. John Quincy Adams, the American minister from 1809 to 1813, was at greater disadvantage; it usually took two and a half months for a letter to reach him from Washington, while in winter a private letter might require as long as seven months.[9] No wonder things moved faster in international conferences where negotiations could proceed and decisions could be taken almost instantaneously.

Yet even at congresses the home office or diplomats in the field were consulted, with resultant delays; accordingly, many congresses lasted for several months. Negotiations were timed to the rate of production of scribes or copyists, when the many required copies of a single document had to be prepared individually by hand. "Let it not be supposed that midnight closes the day's work, for then at all such busy times, then commences the laborious duties of a diplomatic chancelerie," recalled a British diplomat in the early 1820's. "If a courier is to be sent off he seldom is

⁹ Maistre, *Mémoires*, p. 78. J. Q. to T. B. Adams, May 11, 1811, "Letterbooks," *The Adams Papers on Microfilm* (MSS), Reel 135, fols. 158–159; J. Q. to Abigail Adams, March 30, 1814, in Adams, *Writings*, V, 22–23.

despatched till day light has dawned upon the methodical confusion of red tape and calf skin bags, sealing wax — candles expiring in their sockets, and weary attachés intrenched behind piles of protocols and dispatches not to mention a stray pack or two of the Devil's books to beguile with a game at ecarte the interval between the copying of one dispatch and the arrival of another draft hot from the Anvil of the industrious chief." [10] Problems of communication gave foreign relations a very different pace in the early nineteenth century.

Travel time was only part of the diplomat's communication problem. More significantly, the post and even many diplomatic couriers were extremely unreliable, while intelligence activities were extensive and highly organized. The frivolous aspects of the "dancing congress," for example, had their counterpart in Metternich's intelligence networks, the records of which are almost as voluminous as all the protocols and official dispatches put together. Almost every country had its systems of censorship and interception of diplomatic communications. The most honest and resourceful courier often found it difficult to get his dispatches through, while the most trusted secretary or faithful mistress was frequently subjected to the temptations of a few gold pieces for a pertinent bit of information. The Austrian ambassador Lebzeltern wrote Metternich: "Here is one of Count Nesselrode's letters, of which he vowed I would never know the contents." [11] There is evidence that in St. Petersburg a register was kept of interesting parts of letters, particularly those written in invisible ink, to be presented daily to the emperor. "Every letter is opened and read, with no other distinction than in degrees of care in the making them up for delivery or transmission after perusal," complained Lord Cathcart, the British ambassador in St. Petersburg, as he requested additional private couriers. Rewards abounded for fathoming the ciphers of foreign governments.[12]

[10] George Cathcart, Vienna, 1823, "Record of the Principal Events of My Life Commencing with My First Appointment as Aide de Camp to the Duke of Wellington in 1815 to the end of 1837," Cathcart Papers, Box 21, No. 49.

[11] Lebzeltern to Metternich, Jan. 31, 1825, HHS/Russ. III, 72. Maistre, note with letters of Feb. 15, 1806, *Mémoires*, pp. 12–13.

[12] Cathcart to Castlereagh, Dec. 28, 1815, Castlereagh, *Correspondence*, XI,

One of the most important effects of these difficulties was the relative independence of diplomats at foreign posts. When assuming a post, they were given explicit but generalized instructions, setting bounds to their powers and guidelines for their negotiations; additional instructions were sent from time to time, but much of the day-to-day conduct of affairs had to be left to the discretion of the ambassador or minister. "Pay close attention to what I have written, and make your decisions with reflection," Alexander warned an envoy in 1812. "I am too far away to be able to direct you at every moment; your own wisdom must supplement." Ambassadors were often conscious of the difficulties of their position. "At the distance which we are from one another, much indulgence is necessary, it being impossible to ask orders before deciding . . . when it is necessary to act at once," wrote Pozzo di Borgo from Paris to the foreign minister, Nesselrode.[13]

Russian diplomats shared this problem with their foreign counterparts, but many of them were criticized for undue independence. "Their only desire was to be on good terms with the governments to which they were accredited," complained the foreign minister, with particular reference to the ambassadors in Berlin and Vienna, "and they often nullified the effect of our communications by attenuating them at their pleasure." [14] One of the most observant statesmen of the period, Metternich's assistant Friedrich von Gentz, noted with surprise and alarm the *"attitude of independence* which the Russian ministers and agents assume everywhere in their opinions, in their language, and very often in their actions, even in regard to the most important affairs." These attitudes frequently seemed diametrically opposed not only to one another but also to professed attitudes of the Russian court. Ac-

---

102. S. R. Vorontsov to N. P. Panin, Aug. 21, 1801, *NPP*, VI, 509; *AKV*, XI, 226–227. Cathcart to Castlereagh, June 14, 1816, PRO/FO 65/104. Toward the end of the reign, Alexander increased the censorship to include personal letters, which had usually been respected previously. He required in 1825 that one in six, instead of one in twenty, be read (e.g. Disbrowe to Canning, April 20, 1825, PRO/FO 65/148).

[13] Alexander to Chichagov, 1812, quoted by Chichagov, *Mémoires*, p. 89. Pozzo di Borgo to Nesselrode, May 20, 1817, personal, *SIRIO*, CXIX, 191.

[14] Czartoryski, *Mémoires*, I, 366; see also Nikolai Ivanovich Turgenev, *La Russie et les russes* (3 vols.; Paris, 1847), I, 50–51n.

cordingly, Gentz explained that "one must never attach too much importance to what is said by Russian agents to foreign courts, even the accredited ones." Rather, he said, it was most important to determine "how the emperor himself envisages the matter." [15] The most successful diplomats nevertheless found that they had to deal with both. There was no strict party line or official ideology during this period to counteract the web of complex personal and political relationships.

In an effort to countermand this independence and also to ease communications, the Russian court made constant use of special emissaries. These might be secret agents, ordinary couriers who had been given secret — often verbal — instructions, or even special ambassadors or ministers extraordinary, most of whom were accountable directly to the emperor. While successful in important individual cases, such a system provided scant overall regulation of the complex problems of diplomacy.

Foreign diplomats accredited to the court of the tsars felt relatively at home in the "society" of St. Petersburg and on the surface had much in common with their Russian counterparts; however, they faced some problems they did not experience in other capitals. "There is no other foreign court where the diplomatic corps is less informed on political dispositions and proceedings than here," the French ambassador complained in 1804. "The simple and retiring life of the emperor and the isolation of all the ministers from each other, the distrust that is held for agents of foreign powers, and the order given to all the employees of different ministries not to associate with them, render information indeed uncertain." The actual extent of the distrust may be questionable, but the other problems indeed existed. A regulation dating from a ukase of Peter the Great forbade all lesser officials of the department of foreign affairs to associate with foreign diplomats. Since this order, sanctioned by official etiquette, also forbade contacts with officials of other ministries, the punctilious John Quincy Adams was hesitant to take matters directly to the finance minister, even when the latter assured him that by so

[15] Gentz to Soutsos, Nov. 16, 1819, Gentz, *Dépêches*, I, 443–445.

doing, "the business will be more expeditiously settled than by a note to Count Rumiantsev."[16]

The foreign diplomats suffered, too, from the general secrecy in which so many of the affairs of state were conducted. Newspapers and periodicals were of little help in keeping them posted on events either within Russia or abroad. One of the most important papers of the time published a German-language edition for a limited period, the *St. Petersburgischer Zeitung*, which was read by many in the foreign colony; but its political sections also were strictly controlled by the foreign ministry. Starting in 1806 the foreign ministry sponsored the *Journal du Nord*, which after 1813 was published as the *Conservateur impartial*; printed in French and intended particularly for diplomatic consumption, it contained little of what might be considered either foreign or domestic news.[17]

However unreliable a source it was, the diplomatic corps were very much attuned to the hearsay or gossip of St. Petersburg society. Social activities occupied an inordinate amount of time and occasioned tremendous expenses. Regular evening gatherings in the salons of prominent families were a must on the diplomatic circuit. During the later part of the period, for example, Madame Nesselrode, daughter of the finance minister, often presented impressive spreads, and diplomats were often critical of ministers like Panin or Czartoryski who failed to entertain. At congresses abroad, Madame Lieven, wife of the Russian ambassador to England and sister of an important court official, held her usual soirees, which often "formed the point of reunion for all errant diplomats who did not allow public affairs to interfere with that part of the evening which is legitimately due to digestion and

[16] Hédouville to Talleyrand, Jan. 4 and 19, 1804, *SIRIO*, LXXVII, 451–452, 458–459. Adams, *Memoirs*, II, 277–278.

[17] In 1825 this paper assumed the better-known title *Journal de St. Petersbourg, politique et littéraire*. The extent to which these papers were controlled by the foreign ministry was revealed by Rumiantsev to J. Q. Adams (diary entry for Feb. 1, 1814, *Memoirs*, II, 573), by Budberg to Divov in two letters of October 1806 (TsGIA, 1409/1/201), and by Capodistrias to Sturdza (Nov. 11, 1819, Sturdza Papers, PD, 288/1/186). The *Zeitung* was the German-language counterpart of the important St. Petersburg paper, *Severnaia pochta ili novaia Sanktpeterburgskaia gazeta*.

society." [18] If lesser diplomats attended for relaxation, most felt obligated to attend, hoping to meet and visit with members of the court, the ministers, or other diplomats, to pick up all hints of forthcoming activities that might be of some concern. "If I refuse only two or three invitations, I would be regarded as a Trappist monk and be overlooked; then I would see no one and know nothing," wrote Joseph de Maistre. Maistre's complaints to his sovereign, however, were accompanied by a request for an extra secretary, who, he specified, should be a young man, a good dancer and musician with a good sense of humor: "I should have — in a milieu of the most futile and the most immoral society in the world — a man who would serve me as an informer with the women to learn the secrets of their husbands." Many complained about the pervasive punctilious superficiality, which caused a British ambassador to remark, "If one makes a bow too little, it is an immediate matter of observation, and there is something quite absurd in the mysteriousness with which one is told that a Courier is arrived from Berlin or Vienna." [19] Although some of the diplomats appeared to enjoy this social life, for many the expense of maintaining an embassy in St. Petersburg and the hectic pace of festivities were hardships equaled only by the rigors of the Russian climate. The fortune, if not the health, required for this post caused many ambassadors to demand recall or, at least, further subsidies.

The diplomatic corps was included peripherally in the life of the court. Diplomats were invited to certain court dinners, receptions, and festivals; and although it was not the general practice, some were invited to presentations at the court theater in the Hermitage at certain periods of the reign. Such occasions were extremely formal, permitting little opportunity for the business of diplomacy. Even when Alexander was residing in St. Petersburg, access to the emperor and conduct of business with his ministers were often extremely difficult. "More and more, the court and

[18] George Cathcart, 1823, "Record of the Principal Events of My Life," Cathcart Papers, Box 21, No. 49.

[19] Maistre to Victor Emmanuel I, Aug. 19, 1803, Maistre, *Mémoires*, pp. 383–385. Leveson-Gower to Lady B[essborough], Jan. 13, 1805, Lord Granville Leveson-Gower, *Private Correspondence, 1781–1821*, ed. Castalia Countess Granville (2 vols.; London, 1916), II, 37.

ministers stay away from foreign agents as much as they can,"
complained a French chargé d'affaires early in the reign. "The
emperor avoids rather than seeks opportunities to see the diplomatic corps," reported an ambassador in 1820.[20]

Alexander, however, did have a way of singling out individual
diplomats, who, for personal or political reasons, might be established in positions of unusual intimacy. Thus Napoleon's envoys
after the Tilsit peace, General Savary and Caulaincourt, frequently dined at court and were admitted to intimate conversations with Alexander. The British ambassador, Lord Cathcart,
and the French ambassador, La Ferronnays, both formed closer
friendships with the emperor than many of their colleagues. "Etiquette and all its ceremonies may accompany you to the door of
my reception room," Alexander once remarked to La Ferronnays,
"but it will await you at the threshold to reaccompany you back to
your lodgings." [21] Despite such friendly gestures, even these favored diplomats often felt exasperated at not being able to see the
sovereign to discuss matters with him personally, especially when
negotiations with a minister of questionable responsiblity bogged
down in the red tape of the bureaucracy.

Foreign diplomats and their home offices were constantly
trying to find ways to keep themselves better informed. John
Quincy Adams often timed his afternoon walks so that he would
meet Alexander, who frequently strolled virtually unattended and
would willingly converse with him, at least briefly, on matters of
current interest.[22] Some diplomats found military parades to be
important for contacts with the emperor in the early years of the
reign; and after 1815, with Alexander's increased military preoccupations following the Napoleonic wars, such parades became
an even more important meeting place. Thus, the French ambassador donned a military uniform in attempt to meet the sovereign: "The usages of the St. Petersburg court rarely place the dip-

[20] Rayneval to Talleyrand, Aug. 10, 1804, *SIRIO*, LXXVII, 687. La Ferronnays to Pasquier, Jan. 9, 1820, *SIRIO*, CXXVII, 285. See also Maistre, *Mémoires*,
p. 78.
[21] La Ferronnays to Damas, Feb. 22, 1825, AE/CPR 167.
[22] Adams recorded many of these conversations in his diary (Adams, *Memoirs*,
II, *passim*).

lomatic corps in direct relations with the emperor at least those who are not also attired in military uniform. . . . It is to the tastes of the day that I must bow; it is these parades which I must attend. . . . This method of gaining information is practically the only one."[23] Often foreign governments sent official visitors or extraordinary ambassadors who, because of the special nature of their missions, gained entrée to the imperial chambers and participated in the activities of the court. Before 1812, for example, St. Julien of Austria and Stedingk of Sweden were frequent palace visitors; lacking official accreditation, they escaped the questions of diplomatic etiquette or the precedence of the French ambassador at the time. The visits of Colonel Stutterheim in 1804 and 1805, of General Steigentesch in 1816, and of General Clam-Martinez in 1818, all supplied the Austrian government with well documented first-hand reports of the emperor, his immediate entourage and activities.[24]

The periods when the emperor was away from St. Petersburg were the most difficult for foreign diplomats who were not invited to accompany the official party. "The departure of the emperor leaves political affairs in complete stagnation," reported the French chargé d'affaires in 1819; "nothing is done in this respect during his absence; hardly anything is spoken of them." During the absence of the emperor in 1805, the British ambassador wrote, "M. de Weydemeyer, who is appointed to communicate with the foreign ministers residing here, seems to be in complete ignorance of everything that is transacting." No wonder the American consul in 1814 advised his government, "Nor ought it to be thought of less consequence to us, in our general relations with Russia, considering the character of its Government, to at-

[23] Noailles to Richelieu, May 21, 1816, *SIRIO*, CXII, 514–515.
[24] Stedingk, *Mémoires*, II and III, *passim*. See also the letters and reports of St. Julien to the foreign ministry in HHS/Russ. III, 10 and 11, portions of which are published as an appendix in NM, *Alexandre*, I, 374–504. Colonel Baron Karl von Stutterheim, "Journal du Colonel Baron de Stutterheim pendant sa mission à St. Petersbourg," HHS/Russ. II, 138; reports of General Steigentesch, Russ. III, 19; reports of General Clam-Martinez, Russ. III, 26. Gentz described the unusual attentions given to General Steigentesch in a letter to Karadja, Sept. 13, 1816, Gentz. *Dépêches*, I, 259–270.

tend always to our representation near the person of the sovereign." [25]

While most foreign diplomats aimed at access to the emperor himself, they found that they had to conduct most business with the foreign minister. Diplomatic affairs had to follow the slow, formal procedure of notes and applications through the foreign ministry; replies were almost invariably subject to long delays. "The absolute impossibility of hurrying the Petersburg cabinet, even on the most ordinary and least significant communications has always stopped me from one day to the next," explained an exasperated Austrian ambassador in 1805.[26] The long waiting period while the emperor was consulted on a given matter and while scribes copied or recopied a simple rescript was only part of the problem. Continuity was broken by changes in personnel, with different methods and orientation. In short, the administrative backwardness of the Russian foreign ministry combined with Alexander's personal role in diplomacy to make the routine conduct of diplomatic business extremely cumbersome and aggravating to foreigners.

Although the Russian diplomatic service may have shared the forms, style, and language of other great powers, it was beset by many such distinctive problems. At home, the centralized bureaucracy was more limited and poorly developed. The College of Foreign Affairs, the executive organ charged with the administration of diplomacy, which followed the organization and nomenclature established by Peter the Great in the early eighteenth century, was not transformed into the more modernized "ministry" until 1802. In many ways, the 1802 reform act brought only titular change; throughout Alexander's reign the term "college" continued in use, and organizational changes proved insignificant. In

---

[25] Hulot d'Osery to Dessolle, Aug. 22, 1819, *SIRIO*, CXXVII, 168. Note that "political" referred in that period most often to foreign affairs. Leveson-Gower to Mulgrave, No. 44, Oct. 12, 1805, PRO/FO 65/59. L. Harris to James Monroe, Sept. 16, 1814, U. S. Department of State, Consular Letters, St. Petersburg, Vol. 2 (National Archives microfilm). The reports of the English, French, and Austrian envoys at the same period were similar: Noailles to Talleyrand, Oct. 17, 1814, *SIRIO*, CXII, 103; Provost to Metternich, July 4, 1815, HHS/Russ. III, 18; Walpole to Castlereagh, No. 30, July 16, 1814, PRO/FO 65/94.

[26] Report of Stadion, No. 107, Jan. 15, 1805, HHS/Russ. II, 106.

practice, during the century after Peter established the *kollegia*, the principle of group or collegiate direction had been modified so that usually one person was principally responsible for the direction of the foreign department. By the end of the eighteenth century one individual generally functioned as minister. Usually holding the title of state chancellor and the highest rank of civil servant, he was generally seconded by a vice-chancellor and several other ranking members of the college. Thus Ostermann, Bestuzhev-Riumin, N. I. Panin, or Bezborodko, could be singled out as having been effectively in charge of the conduct of Russian diplomacy.

Even after the ministry was formally established in 1802, there were variations in the official title of the directing position. Of the eight men who directed foreign relations during Alexander's reign, only three — A. R. Vorontsov, A. Budberg, and N. P. Rumiantsev — held the title Minister of Foreign Affairs; only two of these were chancellor for part of the period. In some cases the titular ranking member of the department was not the effective "minister," as in the cases of both N. P. Panin and V. P. Kochubei who were outranked in their department, or when Vorontsov held the titles of Minister and Chancellor of the Empire from the fall of 1802 to his death in 1805, while Czartoryski conducted the business after 1803 with the title of "assistant" or "acting" minister. However, although function did not always correspond to title, there was always an effective "minister" to whom the emperor turned for assistance not only in dealing with foreign diplomats, but also in corresponding with Russian diplomats abroad, in preparing or editing diplomatic papers, and in formulating, implementing, and interpreting Russian foreign policy.

The ministry was subdivided into several departments, handling such matters as diplomatic correspondence with legations abroad, protocol, financial affairs, and relations with other parts of the government, as well as a records department associated with the Moscow archives. There was a separate Asian department, which became more important in the nineteenth century as it became the organ for administering newly acquired lands in the East. Such arrangements may have spelled organization on paper,

but in practice in some cases adequate functional distinctions between offices were lacking, and in other cases lines of authority
were crossed by meaningless or excessive distinctions of rank and
function. Backwardness and inefficiency were paramount. "Such
as it is at present, this unfortunate department is unique in the
world" complained one vocal critic. The Russian ambassador in
London, S. R. Vorontsov, taking the British for his ideal, believed
that the Russian foreign service and the ministry at home were
in a "terrible state of disorganization." [27] This comparison of the
Russian ministry with those of other countries is difficult to substantiate, but such comments and criticism were frequent enough
then to suggest validity, coming as they did from Russian and foreign diplomats who were well acquainted with administrative organs abroad.

Compared to the smaller and more efficient foreign offices of
many other European powers, the Russian ministry counted on its
rolls an extraordinarily large number of officials, from those of
higher rank to clerks, codifiers, translators, and copyists. The exact number of men functioning at a given time is almost impossible to ascertain because the rolls listed many persons who rarely
or never served. Kochubei estimated roughly three hundred, not
including those serving abroad and in the Moscow archives,
which is probably not far wrong.[28] To compare, the British foreign office functioned with a staff of twenty-eight, including the
librarian, in 1822. In 1794 the staff of the French foreign ministry had risen to the high total of eighty-five, but by 1800 it had
been reduced to fifty-five, where it remained through the first
quarter of the century. It is thus no wonder that Vorontsov com-

[27] S. R. to A. R. Vorontsov, Nov. 15, 1802, *AKV*, X, 177; Nov. 11, 1802,
*AKV*, XV, 435.
[28] Kochubei to S. R. Vorontsov, Nov. 21, 1801, *AKV*, XVIII, 252. Two reg-
istries for the foreign ministry, one for the end of 1801 and the other dated
April 3, 1803, found among the Vorontsov Papers (TsGADA, 1261/1177:
"Generalnyi spisok gospodam Prisudstvuiushchim v Kollegie Inostrannykh del
Ministram, Konsulat i drugim chinam zdes, v chuzhikh kraiakh i v Moskve
nakhodiashchimisia") list 560 names for 1801, and 700 for 1803, including some
of the personnel abroad and in the Moscow archives; this number is misleading,
however, because the register includes retired persons, children, and some who
were not actually employed.

plained that the Russian ministry "contained more people than the offices of all the secretaries of state in Europe combined." [29]

The overstaffing and the inefficiency of the Russian service were symptomatic of the dearth of reliable and well trained personnel. It would be hard to confirm the allegation of the French ambassador in 1820 that corruption was so extensive and so seemingly organized that "there was perhaps no government employee who did not have his price"; but Russian high officials themselves were so mindful of the corruption that they readily admitted that it was "necessary to hide the addresses from the codifiers." [30] Despite attempts at reform, state secrets were often compromised. Russian foreign ministers frequently complained about "the dearth of talents in the diplomatic line of this country," while foreign diplomats were quick to point out that "perhaps no court is as poor in able men as that of Russia." The extent of the problem was demonstrated on one occasion when an official of the foreign ministry who had been banished was ordered back to the ministry to work all one night, because no one else could be found to complete some urgent dispatches.[31]

The problem stemmed largely from the recruitment policies and the lack of a training program, but even those who recognized the difficulties had little success in trying to institute reforms. As in most branches of the Russian government in the early nineteenth century, placement continued to be largely by favor — commonly, imperial favor. The diplomatic service was generally one of the highest prestige appointments and therefore did not often attract the most qualified individuals. A few men

[29] Harold Temperley, *The Foreign Policy of Canning, 1822–1827: England, the Neo-Holy Alliance, and the New World* (London, 1925), p. 259. Emmanuel de Lévis-Mirepoix, *Le Ministère des affaires étrangères. Organisation de l'administration centrale et des services extérieures (1793–1933)* (Angers, 1934), pp. 35–74. S. R. to A. R. Vorontsov, Nov. 8, 1803, *AKV*, X, 223.

[30] La Ferronnays to Pasquier, April 10, 1820, *SIRIO*, CXXVII, 360. Tatishchev to S. R. Vorontsov, June 6, 1804, *AKV*, XVIII, 379.

[31] Charles Stuart to Fox, Aug. 9, 1806, private, PRO/FO 65/63. Talleyrand, Circular to French ambassadors, Aug. 14, 1804, *SIRIO*, LXXVII, 690; see also Metternich to Lebzeltern, June 5, 1820, HHS, Gesandtschaft Archiv: St. Petersburg, 39. The story of the dismissal of André Gervais, at the time of the banishment of Michael Speranskii in March 1812 was recounted by Lebzeltern to Metternich, No. 115, April 12, 1812, HHS/Russ. III, 12.

came from families important in the diplomatic service and could profit from the experience of their fathers, but more of them were little qualified. The diplomatic service drew its personnel from the gentry, most of whom had had home educations of varying thoroughness, "grand tours" or some foreign visits, and some training in the cadet schools or the principal military regiments. A period as copyist or office apprentice which may or may not have been taken seriously was their only training until Capodistrias attempted to introduce a more extensive program after the Congress of Vienna. But even the best education program proposed was predicated on attracting and training Russians of *gentry birth*, and even the foreigners brought into the service boasted some mark of noble blood.

From the eighteenth century there was a strong tradition of employing many foreigners in the diplomatic service. This was due both to the lack of Russian talent and to the desire to "Westernize" diplomacy and thus bring Russia closer to the European nations. The upheavals of the French Revolution and Napoleon brought many French émigrés into the Russian service to join a host of men from a variety of European nations. Non-Russians predominated among Alexander's foreign ministers and close advisers in the foreign service abroad and in the ministry in St. Petersburg. Alexander justified this: "Unless I use the help of foreigners who are known and whose talents are proved, the number of capable men, already so small, would further diminish. . . . What would Peter the First have done had he not employed foreigners? At the same time, I sense that it is an evil, but . . . how can we adjourn events until the time when our nationals are at their best?" [32] The practice was not uniquely Russian, but it would be hard to find another diplomatic roster so crowded with foreign names. The many complaints leveled at the system failed to produce a real remedy.[33]

[32] Alexander to P. V. Chichagov, March 21, 1806, quoted in Schilder, *Aleksandr*, II, 351. Earlier in the reign, Alexander's tutor, Laharpe, had recommended the use of foreigners to improve the caliber of the Russian service, but Alexander was hesitant in his reply (Alexander to Laharpe, July 19, 1803, NM, *Alexandre*, I, 337).

[33] An example of such complaints was the letter of S. R. to A. R. Vorontsov,

While the use of foreigners as diplomats and foreign ministers may have increased the competence in the conduct of Russian diplomacy, and while it did much to promote and strengthen Russian ties with the European community, it did little to make Russian foreign policy more responsive to the needs of the country. Certainly, during Alexander's reign the men who did most to promote and assure Russian involvement in general continental politics were non-Russian, as — surprisingly enough — were those who did most to promote Russian expansionism. Neither of Alexander's two most talented and creative foreign ministers — Czartoryski and Capodistrias — was Russian, nor was Nesselrode, who served him longest. Czartoryski and Capodistrias were both devoted to enlightened political reform, but their activities in this direction while they were under Russian auspices were mostly divorced from the problems of the Russian state, and their strong patriotic commitments to Poland and Greece, respectively, led to their outspoken efforts to extend Russian protectorates to their native lands. The nationalist reactions of the Restoration years did little to increase the participation of Russians in the highest echelons of Russian diplomacy. Even during the reign of Nicholas I, when the ideology of "Official Nationality" held so much importance in the government, the foreign-born and -educated Nesselrode remained in charge of Russian diplomacy and rose from the rank of foreign minister to that of state chancellor.

Attempts to insist on having more Russians in the diplomatic service combined with the intensive military activities of the period to increase the reliance on military figures for diplomatic missions. An apparent upsurge of this tendency in the later years of the reign brought strong criticism and claims — probably not too well founded — that qualified, experienced diplomats were forced to stand aside for those "amateurs in diplomacy," as they were dubbed. Military men were used, nevertheless, largely because Russia lacked an effective, responsible, well educated civil

---

Nov. 15, 1802, *AKV*, X, 177. See also the critical comments of A. I. Mikhailovskii-Danilevskii, "Predstaviteli Rossii na Venskom kongresse v 1815 godu (Iz vospominanii A. I. Mikhailovskogo-Danilevskogo)," *Russkaia starina*, XCVIII (June 1899), pp. 627–650.

service from which to staff its diplomatic missions and its central
bureaucracy.

Alexander's foreign ministers were themselves not all well
trained diplomats, but this did not lessen their role. In a government which lacked an efficient bureaucracy, executive procedures
gave much more responsibility to the man in charge of each ministry. A government which lacked institutional or procedural
means to control the executive functions of government gave
more power to those in executive positions. The minister, then,
largely controlled the vast and vastly inefficient foreign ministry.
With no cabinet or executive council, the only control on the
minister was the emperor. With an emperor who characteristically lacked an ability for the practical, much responsibility for
the elaboration and implementation of vague policies fell to the
ministers. The emperor, of course, remained at the apex of the
pyramid as the chief diplomatic decision-maker for the state, but
his almost daily sessions with his foreign ministers resulted in the
delegation of a tremendous amount of political control and the
joint formulation of policy. "It is always in these tête-à-tête sessions that all the decisions are made or the private favors granted,
which fear the light of day." [34] All-important in the formation of
Russian foreign policy, as in the day-to-day conduct of foreign relations, was the interplay of attitudes and personalities between
the emperor and the men who served him as foreign minister.

While the French ambassador may not have been telling the
whole story when he claimed that in Russia "the really essential
things remain secret, because it is the emperor alone who decides
them," [35] he was underlining an important component in the conduct of Russian government. Thus the study of the role of the foreign ministers must be predicated on a clear understanding of the
personality and political attitudes of the emperor with whom they
dealt. Under the absolute and only partially bureaucratized Russian autocracy in the early nineteenth century, foreign policy and
the diplomatic decisions which guided its implementation lay un-

---

[34] Buturlin to S. R. Vorontsov, Jan. 28, 1803, *AKV*, XXXII, 328.
[35] La Ferronnays to Pasquier, April 10, 1820, *SIRIO*, CXXVII, 360.

der the strong shadow of Alexander I. He worked within the given diplomatic context. He had to deal with the problems arising from developments of the late eighteenth century. He had to meet the external pressures that threatened Russia and the European community, within which Russia had assumed a paramount position. But in so doing, Alexander gave the Russian foreign relations of his reign the strong impress of his own personality and political outlook.

## Chapter 2

# THE TSAR-DIPLOMAT

When Alexander I led the European armies to rout Napoleon from Paris, he brought Imperial Russia to the highest point of its prestige and power on the continent. Yet this moment of triumph masked Alexander's essential failure, which had serious consequences for Europe and tragic ones for Russia. The brilliant flash and glamor of a Russian-led triumph contrasted starkly with the hardships of wartime devastation and the failure of crucial domestic transformation within Russia. Alexander's success abroad was real enough, but in retrospect it appears artificially exaggerated, largely because his failure to improve the domestic bases for international power rendered similar achievements impossible for his successors. At the same time, the example of his military achievements and his high level of commitment to great-power status in the European community set an increasingly difficult goal for later Russian sovereigns. Their efforts to recover this position further widened the gap between domestic potential and foreign commitment, which eventually proved disastrous for their nation.

Military success and the failure to respond to domestic problems were not as unrelated as they might seem. Curiously enough, military success itself partly explained the general failure; for in a country and in an age which were willing to measure the success of a sovereign in terms of the military glory he brought to the country, domestic reform resulted more often from military disaster than from foreign triumphs. The impressive "Great Reforms" of the 1860's, for example, came in the wake of military defeat, and the reforms of Peter the Great were precipitated by immediate defense needs and by the desire to enhance Russia's position in Europe. Initially Alexander had started his reign with intentions for extensive domestic reforms, but the time and circumstances were not ripe; the relative stability of Russian society of the period, the self-perpetuating nature of the autocracy, and the absence of widespread pressures for reform within Russia's traditionalistic social structure had a stagnating effect. The failures of the Russian armies in 1805 and 1807 gave no real incentive for reform, although the 1807 alliance with Napoleon was followed by significant projects for change. But those efforts were cut short as external pressures mounted for renewed war; and the triumphs of 1812 and 1814 seemed to crown Alexander's reign and make the need for fundamental change less apparent. The great success of Russia abroad bolstered the regime even in the eyes of its critics. It obscured the administrative problems which had been increased by the further extension of Russian frontiers and the economic problems which had been magnified by the high costs of the continental power struggles. Domestic ills appear to have been neglected in proportion to the increase in involvement abroad.

On closer examination, even Russia's success abroad proves illusory. On the international front, political leadership did not follow military triumph. Rational conduct of government dissolved in the face of the emperor's emotional excesses and withdrawal. Russian prestige was unmistakably established abroad; but Alexander's imperious demands for a Russian kingdom of Poland — the emperor's most important diplomatic aim following his 1814 victory — resulted more from his personal whims than from a rational calculation of Russia's national interest or the balance of European power. The Congress of Vienna may have brought Europe almost a century without major war, but Russian leadership deserved little credit for that, although the settlement corresponded to many of the emperor's ideals. Alexander hardly compares to Castlereagh as the architect of "the Concert of Europe." In fact, long before the end of Alexander's reign effective continental leadership had passed to Austria's Metternich, paralleling the almost total eclipse of serious plans for reform within Russia. During Alexander's reign, orderly, progressive change seemed more viable than it would at any time in the succeeding years of the nineteenth century. But, with tragic irony, by the time of Alexander's death Russia clearly was moving toward increased social stagnation, diplomatic isolation, and the demise of its power in Europe, which was so dramatically symbolized in the disastrous defeat of the Crimean War a quarter of a century later.

In a country where the sovereign's word was law and the sovereign's whim was foreign policy, much of the cause of failure — like some of the hopes for success — must be sought in the character and attitudes of the autocrat. It is no mere coincidence that the superficial brilliance and underlying failures of his reign were paralleled in his own complex personality. In the great age of monarchical diplomacy, Alexander's "imposing air of grandeur and nobility" and his "persuasive and captivating eloquence" gave him the appearance of the imperial diplomat par excellence. The charismatic quality of his personality affected those who came in contact with him, "won him the hearts of the Russian people," and "instantly inspired confidence" among his associates. After the difficult years of his mentally unbalanced father's despotic rule, the gentry welcomed him to the throne and felt it "an inexpressable happiness to serve such a prince." The epithet "angel," with which he was frequently addressed, had a real significance for his family and court associates. Even the crusty John Quincy Adams described him as "the darling of the human race." Superficially, to his contemporaries at home and abroad, Alexander I appeared as one of the best-loved and most brilliant sovereigns in Russian history.[1]

Had such qualities predominated in Alexander's personality, his success as diplomat and sovereign would have been much greater. But "the admiration which some of the sovereign's brilliant qualities had inspired in almost all his contemporaries" was too often "cooled" by disturbing revelations of emotional imbal-

---

[1] General Savary, duc de Rovigo, *Mémoires du duc de Rovigo, pour servir à l'histoire de l'empereur Napoléon* (8 vols.; Paris, 1828), II, 175; Stein to Alexander, June 10, 1813, Stein, *Briefe*, IV, 180. Hédouville to Talleyrand, April 19, 1802, *SIRIO*, LXX, 724n; Countess de Choiseul-Gouffier, *Historical Memoirs of the Emperor Alexander I and the Court of Russia*, tr. M. B. Patterson, 2nd ed. (Chicago, 1901), p. 82 (the French edition was originally published in Paris, 1829). S. R. to A. R. Vorontsov, June 19, 1801, *AKV*, X, 97; J. Q. to L. C. Adams, July 2, 1814, Adams, *Writings*, V, 55.

ance. "His daily explosions of rage and frenzy" at the Congress of Vienna were but one indication of "the most astonishing incongruities" in his personality, which impaired so much of his diplomatic conduct.[2] The man who could not make up his mind to go to war at one moment, would be eager to show himself as a dazzling military hero in the fight against Napoleon at the next; and a few months later he could be found in daily seances with the religious mystic Baroness de Krüdener. And the man who could spend hours with his advisers working out plans for the rationalization of the Russian government or be in tears at the plight of ill-treated peasants or wounded soldiers, could later appoint Count Alexis Arakcheev, one of the most inconsequential of his childhood friends, to be a virtual prime minister and continue to sanction his friend's political scheming and unjustified brutalities.

The appearance of "something wanting," as Napoleon phrased it,[3] was really basic to Alexander's character. His partial deafness and growing myopia had their emotional counterparts, as the emperor seemed constantly to be searching for inner peace and security. Behind the charm, the benevolence, and outward duplicity, Alexander was a sensitive, deeply disturbed individual striving to come to terms with himself, his family, and his surroundings. Such epithets as "the sphinx" or "the enigmatic tsar," which abound in the historical accounts of his reign, understandably stem from "the flagrant contradictions" which made it difficult for more ordinary, practical men to understand and deal with Alexander and which hardly fitted him for the role of statesman.[4]

[2] Gentz to Karadja, Feb. 5, 1817, Gentz, *Dépêches*, I, 286; Gentz, "Le Congrès de Vienne: Mémoire," Feb. 12, 1815, in Metternich, *Mémoires*, II, 477; Gentz to Karadja, Jan. 1, 1816, Gentz, *Dépêches*, I, 219.

[3] "With so many intellectual advantages and dazzling qualities . . . there is something always wanting in him," Napoleon remarked to Metternich in a conversation in 1810. "The most singular thing is, that one cannot foresee, in a given case or special affair, what will be wanting, because that which is wanting changes perpetually" (Metternich, "Alexandre Ier, Empereur de Russie [Portrait tracé en 1829]," Metternich, *Mémoires*, I, 315). Cf. Metternich to Esterhazy, Aug. 28, 1817, in "Alexandre Ier jugé par ses contemporains: Une dépêche inédite de Metternich," ed. Louis de Voinovich, *Revue d'histoire diplomatique*, XXV (March 1911), 336–337.

[4] See, for example, Metternich, "Alexandre Ier, Empereur de Russie (Portrait tracé en 1829)," Metternich, *Mémoires*, I, 315–332. Metternich himself both in

The crises of Alexander's youth, while not sufficient to explain his character, certainly affected his emotional stability and his later political attitudes. The stresses attendant on his having to cater to both his grandmother and his father, themselves mutually antagonistic, was compounded by his own ambivalence to each of them. The young grand duke was the idol of his grandmother, Catherine the Great, to the extent that she took him away from his father, Paul, and even had plans to disinherit Paul in his favor. Yet, although he outwardly returned her affection and adopted many of her ways and attitudes, he always harbored resentment against her, and he always remained deeply critical of her reign. Although Alexander abhorred the tyrannical despotism with which he felt Paul conducted the government and although he resented the years his father forced him to spend on the military grounds of his estate at Gatchina, the mutual fear of the father and son never entirely obliterated affection. The sense of guilt from his foreknowledge of the plot against his father increased his own sense of insecurity on a throne that all too frequently had been overturned by palace revolution.

The early years of his marriage to Elizabeth provided a confidante who, he felt, shared his sentimental hopes and idyllic dreams; but his amorous attentions soon turned to a variety of feminine diversions until the final years of his reign. Most of his involvements with women betrayed emotional stress — the estrangement from his mother, the dowager empress Maria Feodorovna, the unusual intimacy and childlike devotion to his sister Catherine, and the curious spiritual rapport with religious luminaries such as Madame de Krüdener — but none had any real political importance during his reign. Even Madame Naryshkin, the wife of a high court official and the mother of Alexander's children, who remained the chief object of his attentions for most of his reign, had no real influence, unless his devotion to her may have aroused a deeper concern for the fate of her native Poland.[5]

---

this portrait and in active life, despite his claims to the contrary, was an example of the type of person who never could adequately understand Alexander's personality.

[5] John Quincy Adams noted (*Memoirs*, II, 94): "Some little place or trifling

Alexander's unhappy youth established in him a deep sense of alienation from the life at court; with prophetic irony, he wrote in 1796 that he was "in no way cut out for the position which I occupy, and even less for the one for which I am one day destined." The state of mind which led to his adolescent desire to retire from the responsibilities of his destiny and settle in America, along the banks of the Rhine, or on an idyllic farm in Switzerland[6] was basic to Alexander's character. It revealed a man deeply concerned with his own identity, self-consciously insecure about his personal and political situation. He soon abandoned his early wishes to surrender the throne, but his youthful desire for withdrawal showed the same quality of mind that sought solace from the abuses which surrounded him in dreams of political reform and escape from the impossible backwardness of his own administration in the type of religious exultation associated with his final years. His refusal of medication on his deathbed and the legend that he retired to the life of a wandering monk as Feodor Kuzmich, which has shrouded the details of his death in 1825, are indicative of tendencies in his complex personality.

The Hamlet analogy, so often advanced in accounts of Alexander's reign, is not without some use in understanding this introspective man, plagued by doubts and suspicions and deeply frustrated with both his political dreams and the reality within which he was fated to operate. But, if detached withdrawal from government was one course which Alexander frequently chose, he also went through periods of great activity and emotional commitment. His involvement was often with important political causes, but it also centered sometimes on rather trivial activities such as the dissipations of "Congress society," or the pomp and

---

favor for any person she might patronize perhaps might be accepted, but the Emperor makes it a point of honor to allow no political influence to the woman by whom he has children because she is beautiful and he is young and fond of pleasure." See also Caulaincourt, "Nouvelles et on dit de Saint-Petersbourg," Report of April 4, 1808, *DSRF*, VI, 15.

[6] Alexander to Kochubei, May 22, 1796, Schilder, *Aleksandr*, I, 277; see also Edling, *Mémoires*, pp. 35–36. In conversations with Czartoryski, Alexander expressed a hope to retire after his country had been liberated from the ill effects of despotism and a constitutional regime had been established (Czartoryski, *Mémoires*, I, 103–105, 149–150).

minutiae of military display, in which his interest at times drew
the charge of "paradomania." Even in periods of withdrawal Alexander seemed to be seeking commitment or the type of emotional
exultation which accompanied his religious quests.

Alexander's unusual absorption in religion was one indication
of psychological problems which often struck his contemporaries.
Finding little spiritual satisfaction in the Orthodox church, Alexander's stress was on direct, personal religious experience through
mystical communication with the Deity. Particularly after his supposed "conversion" before the politically humiliating Napoleonic
invasion of Russia in 1812, these concerns led him into association with a variety of religious luminaries. His absorption in the
Russian Bible Society movement was an important domestic re-
percussion of these interests, and the Holy Alliance was the most
renowned outcome on the international front. Disappointments
and frustrations in personal and political affairs seemed to increase his religious involvement. The gap between his hopes for
his country and the political realities contributed to Alexander's
extreme religiosity in his last years, with his consequent "satisfaction in the total isolation" in which he found himself and with his
politically disastrous withdrawal from the responsibilities of government. "Far from being occupied only with temporal affairs, as
you might expect," Alexander wrote to one of his spiritual advisers in 1818, "my principal occupation, by Divine Mercy, is the
advancement of His order with great application on my part in
this unique goal." By 1825, according to one account, "he had almost become a monk. . . . No one went near him, he saw his
ministers seldom; . . . preoccupied with pious readings . . . he
was so isolated from all contact with men." [7]

Alexander's political role was also influenced by a deep emotional commitment to his destiny as Russian monarch, which

[7] Alexander to Catherine, Feb. 9, 1817, *Scenes of Russian Court Life: Being
the Correspondence of Alexander I with his Sister Catherine*, ed. Grand Duke
Nikolai Mikhailovich, tr. Henry Havelock (London, n.d.), p. 251. Alexander
to Koshelev, April 7, 1818, NM, *Alexandre*, II, 9; see also M. I. Posnikova to
A. I. Arkharova, Jan. 22, 1818, *Russkii arkhiv*, V (1867), 1037–1038. Dorothea
Lieven, *Unpublished Diary and Political Sketches of Princess Lieven*, ed. Harold
Temperley (London, 1925), pp. 87–89.

seemed to give identity and meaning to his life, once he had abandoned the idea of renouncing the throne. The sense of personal mission, so often noticed by contemporaries and so openly revealed in his correspondence, was at times dominated by his secular goals for enlightened reform and the obliteration of tyranny. And it could be infused with religious overtones, as when he might picture himself in the Christlike mission of establishing a Christian commonwealth in Europe or ridding the continent of the Satanic forces of revolution and despotism. At times the mission assumed paranoiac dimensions, with himself as the persecuted savior of an evil world which seemed to be conspiring against him and his high ideals. "In this period it is a question of fighting against the reign of Satan," he wrote in 1820; "only those whom Our Lord has placed at the head of Nations, in His Great Pleasure, are able to persevere in this struggle, and not yield themselves under the ever increasing Satanic power." He continued, "I feel that I am the depository of a Sacred, Holy Task, and I neither must nor can compromise it." [8] Interestingly enough, Alexander's own sense of mission appears to have coincided with the charismatic aura with which he impressed his contemporaries. The traditional bases of imperial power in his case were hence augmented by this high degree of charismatic authority.

Nevertheless, the vacillations and uncertainties which so deeply imbued Alexander's personality provided a poor basis for the conduct of government. He came to power at the age of twenty-three, inexperienced and unprepared to face the difficulties of the Russian sociopolitical environment, the backward and corrupt administration, and the virtually unenlightened society, let alone to reform them. With his great sense of personal mission, Alexander had much difficulty in administering a country; and the emotional excesses of his personality did not at all suit the type of rationalized government he wanted to see introduced. The scarcity of capable subordinates was not the only aspect of the problem. When anyone proved too capable or independent, Alexander grew distrustful and suspicious. Partly because of his own suspi-

[8] Alexander to Golitsyn, Feb. 8–15, 1821, NM, *Alexandre*, I, 526.

ciousness, and partly because of the feeling that others did not share his goals, he wanted to supervise everything himself. Complaints were many about the disorganization and inefficiency that resulted from Alexander's desire "to deal himself with all types of matters from the most important to the most insignificant." [9] Difficulties arose, too, on the diplomatic front from his frequent insistence on dealing personally with foreign heads of state or their representatives rather than pursuing matters through established diplomatic channels. "Conference diplomacy" well suited Alexander, who was thoroughly at home in the personalized diplomatic context of his age. This meant also that Alexander's emotional reactions to individuals often had an overbearing effect on the affairs of state.

The difficulties of dealing with subordinates were complicated further because he preferred having affairs in the hands of a personal friend rather than in those of a capable administrator. "I must esteem those with whom I work," he told Czartoryski; "it is only on this condition that I can give them my confidence." [10] For him the degree of personal confidence was often the prime determinant of the degree of influence of a given subordinate. Relations with his ministers or advisers were always conducted on an extremely personal basis, but at the same time Alexander expected a high degree of subordination. "He has not, as far as I know, any Minister who would venture to persist in opposing cool reflections to his declared will," reported one ambassador, "and I do not know any to whom he would allow opportunities of giving such opposition." [11] He wanted the close friendship of his subordinates, but he wanted his close friends to agree with him and be themselves committed to his ideals.

Alexander carried on political relations — as he did personal — with a high degree of insecurity and outward duplicity. His needs

[9] Lebzeltern to Metternich, Sept. 13, 1825, HHS/Russ. III, 68; Maria Feodorovna to Alexander, April 30, 1806, ed. Nikolai Mikhailovich, *Russkii arkhiv*, XLIX (1911, No. 1), 142.

[10] Alexander to Czartoryski, 1806, Czartoryski, *Mémoires*, II, 159.

[11] Cathcart to Castlereagh, July 13, 1816, Castlereagh, *Correspondence*, XI, 263. This attitude was very apparent in Alexander's penciled notes to his finance minister, Gur'ev (1818–1824), Gosarkhiv V, TsGADA, 5/230.

to please both his mutually antagonistic father and grandmother in his youth gave him a legacy of insecurity in personal relations and may well have forced him to develop the duplicity with which he extended his confidence to diverse or even rival individuals and approaches with so much apparent sincerity. His highly personal concept of government, where personal esteem or youthful association could bring a friend to power, did not, however, guarantee that friend long tenure in office, nor the sovereign's full confidence. Characteristically, Alexander would have several men, frequently unknown to each other, in whom he would confide at the same time, turning from one to another with his changing moods or in an effort to keep several possible lines of action open simultaneously. His ideas and confidences could change quickly and completely, for even when he had built up an unusual amount of trust in a given individual, he might — as he did with Speranskii — turn against the man. Yet, despite the power of his position and his frequent shifts in confidence, Alexander had unusual difficulty in getting rid of an adviser. He never accomplished smooth transitions from one to another; and nowhere was this problem more apparent than with the foreign ministers. Whether out of personal consideration for a man's feelings or whether he thought he might again want that man's services, Alexander hated to dismiss one with whom he had been working closely, even when he had already shifted his confidence.

The ambivalence and shifts between commitment and abandonment, so basic to his character, carried over into complete and often unexplained reversals in manner or attitude, revealing "a disconnectedness in his action, an irregularity in his determinations which troubles and totally disappoints those who by position must follow him." One who worked with him complained, "You often meet at close hand an abandon, letting things go their own way, which seems to be a facility and unlimited confidence in the gravest cases, and the next moment, in regard to a completely futile matter, you meet a resistance and obstinacy which is often insurmountable." [12] Many of Alexander's governmental affairs

[12] Buturlin to S. R. Vorontsov, March 6, 1803, *AKV*, XXXVII, 332–333. See also La Ferronnays to Chateaubriand, May 19, 1823, François-René de Chateau-

may have been characterized by irresolution, but once a decision was taken, even one based on whim or fancy, he could not be swayed by any advice or logic from his most trusted associates, or by violent public opposition. His subordinates had to fit themselves into this framework.

As emperor, responsible for the conduct of Russian diplomacy, Alexander I was bound to deal with current problems facing his country, and his foreign policy was necessarily responsive to the issues they raised. The specific problems of Poland and the relations with the Ottoman Empire, rendered more complex by the expansion of Russian boundaries under Catherine II, demanded solution. Most important, the relationship to Napoleonic France had already become a major problem in the reign of Paul I. On a more general level, Russia's relationship to the other great powers of the European states-system brought many problems which could not be easily overlooked, committed as Alexander was to maintaining Russia's stature and prestige in the European political scene.

Alexander dealt — or had his ministers deal — with the practical diplomatic problems which arose, but his policies and solutions were rarely based on a practical or realistic sense of his country's "national interest." He more often approached foreign relations, as he approached many domestic issues, with vague, theoretical concerns. He gave the foreign policy of his reign an idealistic, utopian cast which reflected much more his own personal, impressionistic — and at times whimsical — way of looking at the world, than a clearly formulated set of aims related to his country's interest. For the very concept of Russian national interest or *raison d'état* was hardly meaningful to him, unable as he usually was to separate state interests from his personal interests as monarch.

The suggestion that at times of revolutionary stress such as the early nineteenth century "theoretical objectives" took precedence over more traditional and practical "security objectives" in Rus-

briand, *Congrès de Verone; Guerre d'Espagne; Negociations; colonies espagnoles,* 2nd ed. (2 vols.; Paris, 1838), II, 17–18.

sian foreign policy is borne out by a consideration of Alexander's reign.[13] Alexander's personality and the revolutionary ferment of the period interacted to produce a much more coherent and theoretically oriented foreign policy than most analysts of his reign have recognized. Alexander's foreign policy cannot be explained simply in terms of such traditional Russian "security objectives" as economic development or trade, imperial aggrandizement or the stabilization of frontiers, or coordination with the European balance of power.

Alexander rarely considered foreign policy in economic terms. For a short period toward the beginning of his reign he was willing to endorse a policy of withdrawal from major European affairs in order to concentrate efforts on Russian internal development. However strongly he may have recognized the great need for such an emphasis, economic development had scant influence on practical policy after 1802. His participation in European affairs in reality had no economic goals; in fact many of his policies, the 1807 alliance with Napoleon, for example, hardly took Russian economic interests into account. Alexander encouraged the development of Odessa under the governorship of the Duke of Richelieu, but he himself never conceived programs to achieve long-range economic goals, responsive as he subsequently became to the possibilities of promoting Black Sea trade. Trade developed in the area without real government initiative. Although some of his ministers argued for the economic benefits of a more aggressive Eastern policy, Alexander never argued for war with Turkey in terms of protecting or promoting trade. Similarly, in other areas he was usually sympathetic to plans and proposals which would enhance trade and commerce, but never did his policies develop primarily from economic motives.

Neither did Alexander promote aggressive policies in order to

[13] The suggestion is voiced by Cyril E. Black, "The Pattern of Russian Objectives," in *Russian Foreign Policy: Essays in Historical Perspective*, ed. Ivo J. Lederer (New Haven, 1962), p. 3. Black's formulation of "security objectives" and "objectives based on considerations of a theoretical character" is not entirely adequate for analyzing Alexander's theoretical concerns; however, his four categories of "security objectives" serve to point up some traditional aims of Russian foreign policy which were scarcely operative in Alexander's policies.

extend the Russian Empire, although ironically Russian boundaries were greatly extended during his reign. Even in the dramatic
peace settlement with Napoleon at Tilsit in 1807, Alexander
made peace out of eagerness to end the war on the continent
rather than to initiate any grandiose plans of "dividing the world."
In fact, the tsar was basically more indifferent than his foreign
minister, Rumiantsev, to Napoleon's discussions of dividing the
Ottoman Empire; he left it to this expansionist-minded foreign
minister to carry on such negotiations after the Tilsit peace.
"What need have I to increase my empire?" he asked Chateaubriand in 1823. "Providence has not put eight hundred thousand
soldiers at my order to satisfy my ambition, but to protect religion, and justice, and to preserve those principles of order on
which human society rests." [14] His words can be taken as quite
sincere, for there is no evidence that he ever actively sought Russian expansion, however much his policies might have contributed to the extension of the frontiers of the empire. Even in the
tragic case of Poland, where he was dramatically devoted to establishing himself as constitutional monarch, his aim was strongly
idealistic — the rectification of his grandmother's partitions and
the realization of his ideals of government — more than mere
crass concern about stabilizing the western frontier. He had no
idea of unification of territories which through historical prece-
dent he considered to be Russian; and, especially in the case of
Poland and Finland, he was quite opposed to any Russification
measures in border areas.

War for Alexander was a justifiable extension of diplomacy;
but he resorted to war reluctantly, usually when he felt it necessary for defense, when he became convinced that "peace can be
acquired only at the point of the sword," or occasionally when he
believed he had a great cause, such as ridding Europe of Napoleon. As early as 1801 he stated a line of policy to which he was
to revert on later occasions: "If I make use of arms . . . it will
only be to repulse an unjust aggressor, to protect my peoples or
other victims of an ambition which is alarming for the safety of

---

[14] Recorded in Chateaubriand, *Congrès de Vérone*, I, 222.

Europe." [15] He inherited some of his father's taste for military affairs but refused to see war as an instrument of expansion, because expansion and conquest were far from his goals for Russia.

Similarly, Alexander lacked any fundamental geographical concerns which might have influenced Russian policy. He had no "urge to the sea," although he was sympathetic to his commerce minister's plans for canal development and was intrigued by plans for steamship navigation. He did not think of European diplomacy in geopolitical terms, although he may have sympathized with some of Czartoryski's policies which were tinged with such concepts. Nor did he have real sympathy for the notions of Slavic solidarity which were beginning to be voiced during his reign, even by close advisers.

The one area where traditional "security" concerns strongly affected Alexander's diplomatic thinking was Russia's relationship with the European balance of power. Alexander was much more an eighteenth-century cosmopolitan than a nineteenth-century nationalist in his view of international relations: he enthusiastically looked to the West for economic, political, and moral enlightenment, and, in the tradition of his grandmother Catherine, he sought the respect of European statesmen. Among nineteenth-century Russian sovereigns he was personally the most deeply committed to Russia's community with Europe, accepting fully "the heaviness of the obligations that weigh on me in my quality of member state of the European Republic." [16] Paradoxically, although the intellectual dichotomy of "Russia" and "the West" was unlikely to be raised during his reign because he clearly considered Russia one with Europe, it was his failure to keep Russia politically and economically abreast of Europe that caused the dichotomy to assume such absolute metaphysical proportions soon after his death.

While acutely responsive to changes in the balance of power,

[15] Alexander to Frederick William III, March 15, 1804, *Friedrich Wilhelm*, p. 44. Alexander to S. R. Vorontsov, July 17, 1801, *AKV*, X, 265; the last statement was also made to Krüdener, July 17, 1801, *VPR*, I, 43; to Morkov, July 9, 1801, *SIRIO*, LXX, 216; and to Razumovskii, Sept. 22, 1801, *VPR*, I, 78.

[16] Alexander to Alopeus, Dec. 19, 1806, Benckendorff Papers, TsGAOR 1126/461.

Alexander diverged from most of his predecessors and successors, in being less concerned with particular diplomatic systems or alliances with particular states and more concerned with a general community of Europe and a theoretical balance of power. At times his foreign policy showed concern for traditional diplomatic and military alliances with individual nations, but these he saw as short-range necessities rather than long-range security goals. Indeed, it is impossible to understand his policies adequately if they are seen as the result of a preference for one or another country. He may have tended to favor individual nations at particular junctures, not because he was an anglophile devoted to English trade, nor because of his admiration for France under Napoleon or for Metternich's Austria or for the Prussian queen, but because alliances with those countries tended to serve his more general purposes at particular times. In fact, from Alexander's standpoint his practical "security" efforts to promote alliances were hardly divorced from his theoretical concerns. More than other Russian rulers, Alexander was genuinely devoted to a stable, peaceful, well coordinated community of Europe, which gave his foreign policy an idealistic slant scarcely related to more traditional security aims.

Alexander's foreign policy can best be understood in terms of the vague theoretical concerns which dominated his political attitudes. These did not add up to a consistent ideology, even in a vague pre-twentieth-century use of the term. Alexander's political theory had none of the systematic, functional elements, which in a limited sense made the doctrine of "official nationality" operative in the foreign policy of Nicholas I. Yet running through Alexander's policies were two main ideals to which he was deeply committed emotionally — the encouragement of enlightened reform and the maintenance of social order and political stability. At first glance these ideals seem basically incompatible, and indeed there were inherent contradictions in them which Alexander was never able to resolve. But the very contradictions seemed to provide a pivot for Alexander's apparent vacillations; his attempts to reconcile them largely explain his approach to many specific issues.

The formation of Alexander's political attitudes owed as much to his personal reactions to his surroundings during his formative adolescent years as it did to the intellectual influence of his liberal Swiss tutor Frédéric César de Laharpe. He was impressed by the injustice of Catherine's Polish partitions and was horrified by his father's despotism; hence, he was unable to identify fully with either of his predecessors. Overcoming his initial plans to escape his destiny in idyllic retirement, he resolved "to sacrifice all my efforts and my life" to the goal "of rendering Russia free and of guaranteeing for her the extinction of despotism and tyranny." Alexander's whole political outlook was predicated on this early abhorrence of despotism, whose extinction he came to believe was his mission. The young Alexander who wanted "to work to render my country free and so prevent for the future its serving as the plaything of madmen" later extended his concerns beyond Russian frontiers. He identified the same abhorrent tyranny with the reign of Napoleon, assuming for himself the role of champion against "one of the most infamous tyrants that history has ever produced." Despotism, Alexander came to realize, could come from the left as well as the right. Too easily the "inert and passive" masses could be led to "suffer and groan from the passions and despotism of factions . . . always submitting to the one which triumphs." The threat of revolutionary tyranny and violence seemed as pernicious to him as the despotism of Bonaparte, which led us surely to his concern for social stability as to his ideals for humanitarian reform.[17]

The antidote for tyranny and despotism from individuals or factions in Alexander's view was the promotion of enlightened reform. The fascination which the young Alexander found in the French Revolution and Enlightenment concepts of "the general welfare" was — as it was for many of his aristocratic compatriots — a type of spiritual compensation for his emotional reaction of horror at conditions in Russia. Unfortunately these concepts did not include the intellectual means of reconciling or

---

[17] Alexander to Laharpe, Oct. 20, 1797, Schilder, *Aleksandr*, I, 281–282. Alexander to Laharpe, July 19, 1803, NM, *Alexandre*, I, 336. La Ferronnays to Pasquier, March 8, 1820, *SIRIO*, CXXVII, 329.

even rationalizing the incongruities of his position. The friendships he formed with a group of wealthy aristocrats his own age —
N. N. Novosiltsev, P. A. Stroganov, V. P. Kochubei, and the
Polish prince A. J. Czartoryski — tended to reinforce his own
sense of isolation and despair at the situation in Russia. These
young friends, who were to constitute the Secret Committee for
reform after Alexander came to power, had all spent a good
many of their formative years abroad at the time of the French
Revolution. Relatively free personally and representing differing
degrees of political concern or alienation, they were as progressive in their hopes as they were impractical in their understanding of how such hopes might be implemented in Russia without
threatening their own families' positions of social and political
preeminence.

Given the early-nineteenth-century option between progress
and the reinforcement of the status quo, Alexander in theory embraced the idea of progress. Progress, he assumed, through proper
enlightenment and guidance, would lead to the realization of
optimistic humanitarian goals, and particularly to the obliteration
of the despotism which beset his native land. His life ideal "to
make his subjects happy" was reinforced by rational convictions
that progress was both necessary and possible because of man's
capacities for enlightenment and moral improvement. "A more
virtuous man, I believe, does not exist, nor one who is more enthusiastically devoted to bettering the condition of mankind,"
wrote Thomas Jefferson in 1807. The American President was so
impressed by "the rare qualities of a philanthropic" Russian ruler
that he kept a bust of Alexander in his office and urged America
to initiate formal diplomatic relations with Russia.[18] Alexander's
views had many other international ramifications, from his financial support for education in Greece to his outspoken condemna-
tion of the slave trade in 1818 because he believed that Africans

---

[18] Leveson-Gower to Lady B[essborough], May 9, 1805, Lord Granville
Leveson-Gower, *Private Correspondence, 1781–1821*, ed. Castalia Countess
Granville (2 vols.; London, n.d.), II, 78–79. Jefferson to William Duane,
July 20, 1807, "Tsar Alexander I and Jefferson: Unpublished Correspondence,"
ed. N. Hans, *SEER*, XXXII (Dec. 1953), 225. F. P. Pahlen to Rumiantsev,
May 15, 1811, *VPR*, VI, 109.

were "men capable of being brought to as high a degree of proficiency as any other Men." [19]

Alexander's profound emotional involvement with his mission makes it impossible to dismiss his loudly proclaimed "liberal ideas" as mere sham or exotic hypocrisy. He may not have been able to resolve the contradictions in his position which prevented the realization of those ideals, but his sense of mission as a liberal reformer was so important to him that, after he was frustrated by the failure of reform efforts in his own country, he began proclaiming his liberal goals abroad. This caused great astonishment among foreign statesmen, who were baffled at the incongruity of a Russian despot who could "speak of the rights of man, and of nations, [and] the duties of a sovereign . . . as the pupil of a *philosophe*." His great wish "to see liberal ideas reborn in Europe . . . to find happiness for oppressed humanity," as he wrote Bernadotte in 1812, was, in his mind, as real an incentive for the struggle against Napoleon as was the retribution due the man who had led the Grand Armée to Moscow.[20] The connotations of his often-repeated phrase, "liberal ideas," were neither precise, comprehensive, nor systematic; he had neither adequate plans for their practical implementation, nor sufficient understanding of such a possibility. When faced with the necessity of applying these ideas, he was usually fraught with vacillation, hesitations, and basic fears. But the ideas themselves held an attraction for him throughout his life, leading him to sympathize with several different, if not contradictory, reform movements in Russia and abroad, and hence deeply influencing his policies and actions on the foreign and the domestic scenes.

Russia was hardly a model of good government, but so concerned was her sovereign with constitutional reform that when his efforts failed in Russia, he turned to a variety of foreign constitutional projects. The promotion of constitutional government

[19] *Thomas Clarkson's Interview with the Emperor Alexander I of Russia at Aix-la-Chapelle as told by himself* (Wisbech, n.d.), p. 13.

[20] La Ferronnays to Pasquier, April 10, 1820, *SIRIO*, CXXVII, 363. Alexander to Bernadotte, March 10, 1812, *Correspondance inédite de l'empereur Alexandre et de Bernadotte pendant l'année 1812* (Paris, 1909), p. 3.

abroad, in fact, became one of the cardinal points of Alexander's foreign policy. It was largely through his insistence that constitutions were drawn up for the Ionian Islands in 1803, for Finland in 1809, and for France and Poland in 1815; he insisted on a constitution for Switzerland and urged constitutions for many of the German states during and after the Congress of Vienna; and he recommended constitutions for Spain and Naples.

The meaning of "constitution" for Alexander was vague, and it varied considerably in different contexts. In many instances Alexander implied the goal of a rationalized, legalized administration; in recommending a constitution, he meant a written body of laws and the establishment of institutions which would provide safeguards against the exercise of arbitrary authority by a sovereign or by mob rule. But his vision of a constitution frequently went beyond the provision of mere "legal authority" to suggest a strong interest in representative government and a real concern for the guarantees of popular rights and privileges. In his early years he had dreamed of "republics everywhere and considered this form of government as the only one conforming to the wishes and rights of humanity"; America, Switzerland, and England stood out as models. But later, like many liberal-minded European statesmen, he entertained increasing doubts about the readiness of most nations for complete self-government, although his espousal of "constitutions" frequently implied a definite support for representative institutions, more or less liberal as he believed the nation merited or required. "The emperor has always recognized the utility and even the necessity of institutions which maintain the support of national representation for the power of the sovereign," explained his foreign minister, Capodistrias, in 1820. "His Majesty always remains convinced that with the aid of this system . . . governments will triumph over all obstacles and will be able to fulfill the great mission that Providence has confided to them." [21] Like many liberal spokesmen in Restora-

---

[21] Czartoryski, *Mémoires*, I, 102–103, 96–98. Capodistrias to Sturdza, Oct. 17, 1820, Sturdza Papers, PD 288/1/186b. Capodistrias was outlining the views Sturdza was to present in an article or memorandum he was to write for the emperor.

tion Europe, he came to believe that constitutional monarchy — often with the monarch supplying the constitution — was the most satisfactory form of government.

However great might be the aim of human welfare or "the happiness of the people," in Alexander's view the great mission of government would be accomplished only if it promoted and preserved social order and stability. Constitutions were fine, in Alexander's mind, to the extent that they guarded society against tyranny from both left and right. He could admire the American Revolution when it resulted in a well ordered government; but the excesses of the French Revolution revealed the dangers of too radical attempts to change the social and political order. He could admire Napoleon's early efforts at governmental reform, but when he sensed that Napoleonic tyranny was threatening the social and political structure of Europe, his concerns turned to real alarm. The frightening upheavals which brought devastation to the heart of Russia had their effect on the sensitive and not entirely stable mind of Alexander I. He continued to advocate constitutions and representative institutions, but the threats of revolution across the continent presented more serious challenges from the "general enemies of all order," who, he feared, wanted "the ruin of all thrones and the overthrow of social order." He never lost his admiration for the American republic, but he adamantly opposed movements for self-government in Latin America. There, he believed, the people were "torn by factional struggles . . . , motivated by passions," and "lacked the enlightened leadership" necessary for stable self-government. The principle of revolution was not good, he had come to believe, but at least in North America, "there was one sole party revolting against a suppression which had become insupportable: one could see a united people, leaders, estimable leaders." But he saw "no analogy" in the case of South America. "Where are the Franklins, the Washingtons, the Jeffersons of South America?" he asked.[22]

[22] Quoted by Bagot to Castlereagh, No. 32, June 20, 1820, PRO/FO 65/127; La Ferronnays to Pasquier, July 19, 1821, AE/CPR, 162. La Ferronnays to Chateaubriand, No. 36, confidential, Nov. 28, 1823, AE/CPR, 165.

That very tyranny which in some cases demanded liberal institutions in other cases limited their applicability, particularly in countries where the population was not "enlightened" and where political leadership was inadequate. Alexander became convinced that enlightened leadership was the key to bettering the condition of humanity within the context of social order. He concluded that reform could best be effected by those enlightened heads of state, who, like himself, had the best interests of humanity at heart. With many liberal leaders of Restoration Europe, he looked to constitutional monarchy as the most satisfactory political solution, but unlike many conservative leaders, he came to the principle of "legitimacy" slowly and hesitantly.

His attitude toward the French Restoration demonstrates well his central political stance. In 1813 Alexander passively assured French royalist representatives that "the reestablishment of legitimacy everywhere is the only base on which the peace and tranquillity of Europe can be assured." [23] However, his lack of confidence in the future Louis XVIII made it clear that in his view legitimacy connoted more allegiance to political stability than to any particular strain of royal blood. In fact, the "legitimacy" of the Bourbon monarchy was so uncertain to Alexander that, contrary to the recommendations of his advisers and allied statesmen, he insisted on calling an assembly to allow the French people to choose their new sovereign, giving some indications that he favored the candidacy of Bernadotte. Only when he came to believe that the French people really wanted Louis XVIII was he willing reluctantly to support the Bourbon Restoration, and then only with the constitutional safeguards of the Charter, which granted the country a limited representative assembly. As he liked to express it, he "envisaged the reestablishment of royalty [in France] as the only way to preserve European civilization against revolutionary exaggerations and immoralities, and [the Charter] as the only proper way of reconciling the spirit of

[23] Auguste de La Ferronnays, *En émigration, souvenirs tirés des papiers du Cte A. de La Ferronnays (1777–1814)*, ed. Costa de Beauregard (Paris, 1900), p. 396.

the times with the conservative principle of the legitimacy of thrones."[24]

Alexander's solution for France brought together the two strands of his political outlook, reflecting his own development in face of the experience of the early part of his reign. The emperor could rightfully pride himself as the magnanimous restorer of peace and order on the continent, while demonstrating his sincere liberal sympathies by providing France with a constitution. Establishing in France "the liberal institutions that she owes partly to the Revolution" was not for Alexander merely a liberal gesture, but it also resulted from his fear that "to destroy [the liberal institutions] . . . would provoke a second revolution a thousand times more frightening than the first."[25] During the French Restoration, Alexander became increasingly concerned about the viability of those "liberal institutions," because he came to believe — and was so encouraged by Metternich — that France was haunted by the specter of further revolution and mass violence. But his concerns went deeper, because France represented to him a testing ground for his own political attitudes, even as it had in his youth during the early years of the First Republic. The degree of his personal commitment to France was apparent in the extent to which "he watches the course of her government as an object for which he was responsible and which he is particularly called upon to regulate."[26] France always remained a key focus for his foreign policies, because his reactions to the French political scene directly affected his general political orientation. For example, when revolution struck Naples in 1820, Alexander argued strongly for a constitution following the model of the French charter to be granted that country in conjunction with the restoration of the king. He retreated from these liberal demands only in the face of strong opposition from Metternich and other

[24] Alexander to Richelieu, April 29, 1816, *SIRIO*, LIV, 473.

[25] Alexander to Maria Feodorovna, April 3, 1814, in N. K. Schilder, *Imperator Nikolai Pervyi, ego zhizn i tsarstvovanie* (2 vols.; St. Petersburg, 1903), I, 566; *Russkaia starina*, CLVII (March 1914), 486–490.

[26] Lebzeltern to Metternich, Dec. 31, 1816, HHS/Russ. III, 20.

statesmen and from a discouraging sense that all was not well with his constitutional experiment in France.[27]

Poland was another testing ground, closer to home both geographically and personally, where the ideals and incongruities of the emperor's view are clearly revealed. From an early age, Alexander was disgusted at his grandmother's Polish partitions; and he considered the restoration of Poland to be one of his "favorite ideas."[28] Yet Alexander's imperious demands for a reconstituted Kingdom of Poland with himself as constitutional monarch aroused the strong opposition of most of his own advisers, much of public opinion in Russia, and many Polish leaders, and it brought the Congress of Vienna to the brink of war. But for all the obstinacy with which he insisted on assuming the Polish crown, he believed that his motives were purely humanitarian. His arguments were based on "his moral duty" to provide for "the happiness of the people."[29] He saw himself as the enlightened king advancing the interests and well-being of his Polish subjects by granting them a constitution and a representative assembly, with the liberal aim, as he said in a speech at the opening of the Polish diet, "to unite the power of the Sovereign to intermediary powers, to the rights, and to the legitimate interests of society." He further hoped that the diet would produce "laws destined to guarantee the most precious things: security of your persons, of your property, the liberty of your opinions." Alexander saw Poland as the proving ground for "the salutary influence of such liberal principles," which he sincerely hoped "to extend . . . to all the countries that providence has confided to my care" when, he explained, "the basis for a work of such importance has attained the necessary development."[30]

[27] This point is well established in the transcripts of his conversations with the French ambassador in the reports and personal letters of La Ferronnays; see especially La Ferronnays to Pasquier, personal, Feb. 27, 1821, AE/MD: France, 719.

[28] Czartoryski, *Mémoires*, I, 96; Edling, *Mémoires*, p. 35; Alexander to Czartoryski, April 13, 1812, *VPR*, VI, 351.

[29] Castlereagh to Liverpool, No. 3, Oct. 2, 1814, and No. 9, Oct. 14, 1814, *British Diplomacy*, pp. 197–199, 206–207. See also, report to Hager, Oct. 3, 1814, Weil, *Congrès*, I, 206.

[30] Alexander I, *Adresse à la Diète de Pologne, 13/1 septembre 1820* (Warsaw,

Although Alexander found satisfaction in his paternal role of constitutional monarch and talked openly to the Poles of his high hopes for a liberal constitutional regime, he was increasingly apprehensive about the license and the abuse of power which might result from the freedoms he had advocated. As he came under fire from conservative leaders and as new upheavals threatened Europe, he began to fear that his ideal of a conjunction between liberty and order might not be possible. He admitted to Metternich's ambassador in 1819, "I believed it necessary to give the Poles a liberal constitution, but I created besides repressive means sufficient to make them know that they must not abuse it or exceed certain limits." Once again his liberal goals were checked by his fears of social instability. "Following my private opinions," he explained about the situation in Poland, "I owe it to God and my conscience to satisfy the rights of all, but responsible for the public order and anything that could upset it, I am there, and at the least excess . . . the strong arm of authority will make itself felt." [31]

Alexander had not really turned from liberal to conservative, as many commentators have argued. Elements of both these strands were apparent throughout his reign in his conception of the delicate balance of right-ordered government, which he could never work out in practice. The basic liberal dilemma between freedom and order in its early-nineteenth-century guise was in a sense Alexander's. Indeed, Poland came to represent the tragic paradox of his reign. It gave Alexander a chance to "put into practice the principles of those liberal institutions which have not ceased to be the object of my solicitude," [32] while at the same time it symbolized the negation of the hopeful pronouncements of the "constitutional monarch." By the end of 1825 the strong arm of authority exercised by Alexander's brother Constantine

---

1820; republished in Chodzko, *Pologne*, pp. 741–745). Alexander I, *Adresse à la Diète de Pologne, 15/27 mars 1818* (Warsaw, 1818; republished in Chodzko, *Pologne*, pp. 734–737); Schilder believed that this latter speech was "one of the most liberal pieces to come from the pen of the emperor" (*Aleksandr*, IV, 179–180).

[31] Lebzeltern to Metternich, Oct. 10, 1819, HHS/Russ. III, 28.
[32] *Adresse à la Diète de Pologne*, March 27, 1818; Chodzko, *Pologne*, p. 734.

and his other agents in Poland had all but obliterated liberal institutions and denied "the salutary influence of such liberal principles."

Alexander's dual commitment to the preservation of political order and the encouragement of enlightened reform can be seen clearly in his concern for international relations. In a period when the French term *politique* connoted foreign as well as domestic affairs, domestic and international politics were not arbitrarily separated in his thought. Alexander had seen too much turmoil resulting from the French Revolution to be unconcerned about the international repercussions of domestic unrest; intervention in the internal affairs of other states was a crucial standard procedure for him. The most significant aim of his policy throughout his reign was international stability; as in his fight against Napoleon, his goal was "the reestablishment in Europe of a political equilibrium, without which the tranquillity of nations rests on a very uncertain basis." [33]

Alexander grew up in a period when the concept of equilibrium or "balance of power" dominated diplomatic thinking, and he himself was thoroughly convinced of the necessity of such a balance. Yet commitment to the balance of power was not merely a practical means of insuring European security, but a theoretical commitment to an ideal order or equilibrium. The enlightenment that Alexander wanted to bring to the European scene involved not only his hopes for representative assemblies, constitutions, and constitutional monarchs, but embraced also the means for the stabilization of the European community, which would prevent future Napoleons from dreaming of hegemony and would promote the Kantian ideal of perpetual peace. A mere reversion to an eighteenth-century states-system was inadequate in Alexander's view; the "balance of power" had to be transformed into a new order for Europe.

[33] Alexander to Frederick William, June 15, 1804, *Friedrich Wilhelm*, p. 51. Alexander made frequent references to "the equilibrium of the continent" and "the Balance of Europe," e.g. to Frederick William, Dec. 22, 1804, *ibid.*, p. 55; and to Francis, Dec. 17, 1812, HHS/Russ. III, 46. A. R. Vorontsov, quoted by Warren to Hawkesbury, No. 47, Sept. 16, 1803, PRO/FO 65/53.

Early in his reign, in reaction to Napoleon, Alexander stressed the need for legal and institutional safeguards to preserve the balance of Europe. The best guarantee, he thought, would be a "union between the great states," which "alone could save Europe." [34] With a view to the post-Napoleonic restoration, in 1804 he firmly endorsed the ideals spelled out by his foreign minister, Czartoryski, in the famous secret instructions to Novosiltsev, for "a league . . . to which . . . most governments would want to belong" and a "new code of international law . . . which would become the immutable rule for cabinets." [35] The legal and institutional requirements became vaguer in later pronouncements, but he remained convinced of the need to establish for Europe "a concert of views and measures which alone can guarantee it against new disorder." [36]

By the time of the Congress of Vienna, Alexander was more concerned with irrational religious ideals stemming from an organic conception of a European community and reinforced by visions of a Christian commonwealth. The pietistic currents in which Alexander became so absorbed after 1812 deepened his earlier concern for European order and provided the intellectual background for the Holy Alliance of September 26, 1815. In a period of intense religious exaltation Alexander wrote the text and insisted it be signed as a treaty, rather than merely a proclamation or statement of faith. The curious document, based on the emperor's "profound conviction that the policy of the powers, in their mutual relations, ought to be guided by the sublime

[34] Alexander to Francis, July 19, 1801, HHS/Russ. II, 212; also in Adolf Beer, *Zur Geschichte der Oesterreicher Politik in den Jahren 1801 und 1802* (Vienna, 1874), pp. 13–14.

[35] Secret Instructions of Alexander I to Novosiltsev, Sept. 23, 1804, *VPR*, II, 141–142; the text which appears in Czartoryski, *Mémoires*, II, 27–45, is identical with the Soviet version, but lacks the secret additions; in the English edition of the memoirs it is highly abridged. Although scholarly opinions differ about the authorship of the instructions, it would appear that Czartoryski played the major part; the document, nevertheless, clearly reflects Alexander's own views at the time and was delivered under his signature and with his full approval.

[36] Alexander to Francis, April 25, 1804, text in Adolf Beer, *Österreich und Russland in den Jahren 1804 und 1805* (Vienna, 1875), p. 187. The provision for a concert was included in the convention between England and Russia of April 11, 1805 (Martens, *Recueil*, II, 433).

truths taught by the eternal religion of God our Saviour," affirmed that the conduct of foreign relations be based on the brotherhood of sovereigns, "united by the bonds of a true and indissoluble fraternity," who were to regard themselves as "compatriots . . . of one great Christian nation." Their "sole principle of conduct, be it between the said governments or their subjects," was to be "that of rendering mutual service and testifying by unceasing good will, the mutual affections with which they should be animated." [37]

However strong were the reinforcing intellectual currents of the period, the document still reads, as Gentz said at the time, as "a monument to the eccentricity of men and princes in the diplomatic code of the nineteenth century." But for Alexander this was far from a "loud-sounding nothing" or awkward "piece of sublime mysticism and nonsense," as it was described by Metternich and Castlereagh.[38] The statement clearly fits the moralistic, idealistic cast of his political outlook at that period. Just as he had found meaning for his own life in religious absorption, he believed that adherence of governments to Christian precepts could save Europe from the evil forces menacing it and — as he stated a few years later — provide "the means of salvation to which Europe attaches all its hope." [39]

After the terrible series of wars that disrupted Europe, the alliance system, together with the moral sanctions Alexander sought to give it, was associated in his distraught mind with his goal of peace and stability for the continent. He may have found tremendous satisfaction in the exploits and glory of the successful military commander and even great delight in the rational perfection

[37] The text of the Holy Alliance is available in many published collections, including an English translation in Edward Hertslet, ed., *Europe by Treaty, Showing the Various Political and Territorial Changes which have Taken Place Since the General Peace of 1814* (4 vols.; London, 1875–1891), I, 317–319.

[38] Gentz to Karadja, Feb. 25, 1816, Gentz, *Dépêches*, I, 222–224. Metternich, *Mémoires*, I, 212; Castlereagh to Liverpool, Sept. 28, 1815, *British Diplomacy*, p. 383.

[39] Alexander to Frederick William, Sept. 12, 1820, *Friedrich Wilhelm*, p. 308; see also his justifications written to Pozzo di Borgo, April 11, 1816 (*SIRIO*, CXII, 456), to Lieven, April 11, 1816 (NM, *Alexandre*, I, 171–173), and to Frederick William, Jan. 27, 1816, *Friedrich Wilhelm*, p. 269.

of parade-ground drills, but he sustained a deep abhorrence of war. He loathed the suffering engendered by armed violence and the disruption of the social order, which he knew as the political accompaniment of war. Too often for his liking, war represented the personal ambitions of a military leader like Bonaparte or the selfish expansionism of a particular nation. The personal peace he sought assumed political implications through his sense of his mission to achieve the Enlightenment — and, for him, the Christian — goal of world peace.

Alexander's utopian emphasis on the moral and religious sanctions for international relations seems to betray a certain disrespect for the "alliance system" as formalized in the treaties of Paris in 1815. His overzealous religious concern often led him to disregard practical political problems, but it did not prevent him from remaining a steadfast defender of the "congress system" and the European order that it guaranteed. Alexander was in full sympathy with the treaty provisions for periodic congresses and consultation among the allies, and he was ready to take up arms personally to help carry out punitive measures against any threats to the political order. He thoroughly agreed with the other leaders about the right to intervene in the internal affairs of other states when a threat to the established order was apparent. However, he was not always in agreement with the practical political goals of the other great powers; for example, concerned lest the Quadruple Alliance of Russia, Prussia, Austria, and England maintain itself as an anti-French coalition, he urged the recognition of France as a fifth power of equal stature. His reservations about the chief architect of the "congress system," Castlereagh, and its chief defender, Metternich, were accompanied in both cases by emotional malice and serious differences of opinion. Alexander, nevertheless, personally assumed a major role in the settlement of 1814 and 1815 and, to his death, was extremely intent on joining the allies in the maintenance of the European political structure as established by the treaties.

Alexander intended his treaty of the Holy Alliance to be a reinforcement of these political ties. Often when he used the term "Holy Alliance," he did not differentiate between the more concrete political guarantees of the alliance system and the moral overtones of his own religious "treaty." Even when Alexander later came to stress the need for a revitalized *alliance générale*, he thought of it as an amalgamation of political guarantees with the religious concerns which preoccupied him toward the end of his reign.

Many have suggested that Alexander's active support of the alliance system represented a shift from liberal ideas to conservative reaction; and indeed his adherence to it had the same result when Metternich's rise to diplomatic leadership brought the dominance of Austria-centered reactionary policies. Such, however, was far from Alexander's idealistic intent; he took great pains to deny such "vain and sterile" charges, affirming that the pact was intended as "the surest guarantee of a well-ordered liberty, the true safeguard of law, and the most implacable enemy of arbitrary power." [40] The term "conservative" was used in the justification, but here, as in other aspects of his thought, the terms "conservative" and "liberal" were not really mutually exclusive opposites. Alexander did not intend his "liberal ideas" to be understood as radical, as Metternich accused, nor did he base his political reasoning on an a priori affirmation of "policies or administration based on absolute power." In 1819 he emphasized that "it is neither one nor the other. It is sound reasoning, composed of pious and religious sentiments, nourished by the experience of all time and even more by that of our century." [41] Such phrasing may have shown the influence of his then favorite foreign minister, Capodistrias, who was charged with defending Alexander's position, but its denial of the liberal-conservative

---

[40] *Conservateur impartial*, No. 36 (May 16, 1817). The article quoted is an unsigned defense of the Holy Alliance; Lebzeltern claimed Capodistrias was the author in a letter to Metternich (May 26, 1817, HHS/Russ. III, 22), but the author may well have been Alexander Sturdza, who, under Capodistrias' supervision, was writing many similar pieces for the foreign office. For example, his "Considerations sur l'acte de l'alliance fraternelle et chrétienne," dated 1815 (Sturdza Papers, PD, 288/1/21), was typical of many such justificatory pieces. The supporting manifesto published in St. Petersburg on Christmas day, 1815, is printed in Walter Näf, *Zur Geschichte der Heiligen Allianz* (Bern, 1928, "Berner Untersuchungen zur allgemeinen Geschichte," Vol. 1), pp 33–34.

[41] Capodistrias to Sturdza, Nov. 11, 1819, Sturdza Papers, PD, 288/1/186.

dichotomy is important to understanding Alexander's view. The emperor was all for "conserving" peace, order, and social stability; Christianity and the morality of the Holy Alliance were "conservative" insofar as they might accomplish these ends. At the same time, however, Christianity and the alliance system, he hoped, would provide the legitimate basis for the development of civil liberty and liberal institutions, and the promotion of prosperity and human welfare.

The Holy Alliance was clearly opposed to what Alexander called the revolutionary and anti-Christian movements, but he hoped his own brand of constitutionalism, particularly his "liberal institutions" in Poland, could withstand the radical forces and the "subversive doctrines which today menace the social system with a terrifying catastrophe." He sincerely hoped that the "sacred principles" of his liberal ideas and their institutional manifestations would not prove to be "in any way a dangerous illusion." [42] Before the Congress of Troppau in 1820 he was still insisting to the Austrian emperor that, while the alliance could provide the best and only safeguard against the growing dangers from "the criminal audacity of misguided men" with "their subversive doctrine," it was nonetheless the great "protector of all legitimate rights and interests," including those of constitutions and representative assemblies as well as the stability of thrones.[43]

Despite his hopes, Alexander was never able to reconcile his contradictory ideals of reform and order. The compromise had remained uneasy in France, had been plagued by difficulties and eventual failure in Poland, and was hardly more successful in regard to the alliance system. After strong opposition movements in the Polish diet of 1820, came the mutiny of his own Semenovskii regiment in the autumn of that year. The mutiny had no real political overtones; nevertheless, despite the efforts of his most trusted advisers to convince him otherwise, Alexander insisted on linking it with a Europe-wide revolutionary conspiracy. Metternich, who conveniently had been the one to inform the tsar of the

---

[42] Alexander, *Adresse à la Diète de Pologne* (March 27, 1818); Chodzko, *Pologne*, pp. 734–737.
[43] Alexander to Francis, Sept. 10, 1820, HHS/Russ. III, 46.

mutiny, knew well how to encourage such fears, which were rapidly gaining paranoid dimensions in Alexander's mind. Fears of "the *empire of evil* which extends itself with rapidity and by all the *occult means* used by the *Satanic spirit* which directs it" were magnified in his mind in a period of renewed religious exaltation. As he had felt called upon to vanquish the earlier menace from Napoleon, he came to believe a new crusade was necessary, because, he wrote, the evil revolutionary conspirators, "even while being enemies of thrones, are even more directed against the Christian religion." [44]

It was in this spirit that Alexander turned to Metternich, more in despair and discouragement than in real trust or conviction that Metternich's policies for defending the status quo held the most righteous or satisfactory answer. Alexander became convinced that his own more liberal solutions to the political problems of the period — supported as they were by his foreign minister Capodistrias — had to be sacrificed to the preservation of the alliance system on which he believed the hope of political order was predicated. Peace and order had to be maintained at all cost, even the sacrifice of constitutions, national self-determination, or other progressive projects.[45] Not always sympathetic to Metternich, Alexander lacked the will or political initiative to oppose the Austrian chancellor's resourceful arguments. "I am still not quite clear whether the emperor knows what he wants," wrote Metternich from Troppau, "but his language is as plain as mine . . . we talk for hours together without ever disagreeing." [46] The alliance itself became more important to Alexander than the cause of the Greeks or the aspiration of the Poles.

[44] Alexander to Princess Meshcherska, Oct. 22, 1820, "Pis'mo imperatora Aleksandra Pervogo k kniagine Soffi Sergeevne Meshcherskoi," *Russkii arkhiv*, XXIV (1886, No. 3), 406. Alexander to Golitsyn, Feb. 20–27, 1821, NM, *Alexandre*, I, 521. In his discussion of this letter and Alexander's attitude at this time, the Grand Duke Nicholas suggested (I, 234) the neurotic elements present as the product of some psychological crisis.

[45] This view was well developed in conversations with the French ambassador, e.g. La Ferronnays to Richelieu, Oct. 15, 1820, AE/MD: France, 716; Nov. 20 and Dec. 10, 1820, *ibid.*, 717; Feb. 27, 1821, *ibid.*, 719. Such ideas make it clear that he was not so completely "sold out to Metternich" as the Austrian chancellor and some of his supporters liked to believe.

[46] Fragment of a personal letter, Nov. 15, 1820, Metternich, *Mémoires*, III,

"To maintain peace, to combat the revolutionaries and attack them everywhere, there is my ambition, and the only glory to which I aspire," he assured the French ambassador.[47] Alexander's surrender to the repressive policies of Metternich in the final years of his reign was not wholehearted, nor did it imply full support for Metternich's principles. He still cherished the hope for enlightenment and liberal reform, even as he decried the "tyranny" of revolutionary conspirators and the unenlightened masses. He felt that for the moment he had to sacrifice his hopes to preserve peace and order, but he lacked the strength of character to carry on the government of his country. In his final years, when he became more uneasy about Metternich's solutions, it was too late, because he had withdrawn himself too much from an active role in governmental affairs and because through neglect he had condoned in Russia the type of arbitrary despotism he had vowed to eradicate. As one sympathetic friend remarked, in an effort to find spiritual consolation for the emperor's political failure: "Alexander withdrew at the thought that it was for him to open the fatal Pandora's box which was placed within his grasp." Instead he surrendered to a tendency noted in his personality from the beginning, "seeking more and more isolation in quest of spiritual peace": "Time, instead of diminishing the difficulties, only augmented them, and Alexander, discouraged and unhappy, found consolation in that solitude which drew him closer to a superior order of things, a stranger to this earth filled with misery and discontentment."[48]

In the nineteenth century Alexander was the Russian ruler most deeply committed to Westernization and enlightened reform, but his commitment came not out of a realistic sense of Russia's needs, but out of eighteenth-century humanitarian ideals, which he was incapable of transforming into a nineteenth-

---

377–378. Metternich has usually been given excessive credit for changing Alexander's attitude; Sturdza suggested an important angle, contending it was "not really the eloquent insistence of Metternich which caused Alexander to favor the alliance," but rather the emperor's own fears and anxieties (Sturdza, "Souvenirs de la vie et carrière du comte Jean Capodistrias," Sturdza Papers, PD 288/2/36).

[47] La Ferronnays to Villèle, July 24, 1824, AE/CPR, 166.

[48] Edling, *Mémoires*, pp. 253–254.

century program of action. The intrinsic contradiction between his ideal of enlightened reform and his dedication to the stabilization and preservation of social order involved a deeper divorce between his political visions and the reality of contemporary social structure and his own supreme personal authority. Difficulties were compounded, too, because, despite his brilliant and noble appearance, Alexander was never able to rise above the severe emotional tensions and the profound psychological imbalance in his personality. He had too deep a tendency to remain the alienated prince who sensed that the times and his country were "out of joint," self-consciously sensing his incapacities and cursing the fate that had designated him to attempt to set things right. Intellectually, Alexander remained strongly committed to his "liberal ideas" of Western constitutionalism and his moralistic ideals of a new order for Europe which would efface despotism and establish a new reign of enlightened humanitarianism. But as a ruler he had neither the ability to adjust his ideals to reality nor the statesmanship to adjust that reality to his ideals. Once established in a position of supreme power, he appeared alternately too anxious to retain his personal control of government or too willing to withdraw in despair and let others carry out the despotic possibilities of his authority. He never developed the trust in people necessary for the delegation of responsibility, and for all his abstract concern for popular welfare, he never felt real confidence in "the people." In sharp contrast to his brother Nicholas I, Alexander gave early-nineteenth-century Russia a welcome breath of reform; but the breath failed to penetrate the organism. Again in contrast to Nicholas, Alexander's ideas lacked rigor and precision as his character lacked the determination and hard-headed practicality to bring them to life. Alexander was too enlightened to decree reform despotically as had Peter the Great, especially as he realized how ill-prepared he was to carry it through and how unprepared his world was to receive it. Yet he was too despotically committed to personal authority and political stability to rationalize change toward effective enlightened Westernization.

The young man of high ideals who thoroughly questioned the assumptions underlying his nation's government reluctantly acquiesced to the tradition of his grandmother Catherine, the tradition of eighteenth-century enlightened despotism, amidst the changing world of the nineteenth century where despotism could only stifle enlightenment. The very inner contradiction of the concept "enlightened despotism" was involved in his own failure, because the realization of enlightenment was still as incompatible with the practice of despotism as it was for Catherine the Great, even given his deeper commitment to enlightenment. When Alexander resigned himself to the position that despotism was the only, if not the best, way to enlightenment at home and abroad, he did more than he realized, or would have wanted to do, toward paving the way for the bureaucratic conservatism of his brother Nicholas. It was thus little wonder that social critics such as Alexander Herzen could look back with nostalgia to the reign of "the man who had crushed Napoleon," but with regretful contempt for the emperor who "was himself crushed under the burden of glory and of helpless, hopeless autocracy." [49] For in Herzen's youth, enlightenment had been driven from being a creative force on the throne into the secret societies of the Decembrists, into the salons of Westernized gentry, whose only use for it could be to oppose the throne and the vast bureaucracy which developed afterward under Nicholas to rationalize and perpetuate his despotism.

Alexander's reign, like any in Russia under the prevailing personal monarchy, bore the strong impress of the man. Because the political and personal were so intricately related in Alexander's own policies and actions, he looked for a similar commitment in the men to whom he delegated authority or with whom he discussed his plans and programs. He chose his ministers not because they were particularly capable administrators, but because their attitudes and personal commitments corresponded to his own vague ideas or to the specific policies he wanted implemented at a given time. His character and his political ideas established both the opportunities and the limitations of the role at home and abroad of his ministers for foreign affairs.

---

[49] *My Past and Thoughts: The Memoirs of Alexander Herzen*, tr. Constance Garnett (6 vols.; London, 1924–1927), V, 278.

## Chapter 3

# PANIN, KOCHUBEI, AND VORONTSOV: GRAND POLITICS, ISOLATION, AND MODERATION

Alexander's first formal utterances on ascending the throne thrilled the gentry with the promise of a return to the "spirit and laws" of Catherine the Great.[1] It was soon apparent, however, that just as his domestic reform projects were not in keeping with Catherine's traditions, so her grand manner in foreign affairs hardly suited Alexander's world perspective. Alexander's choice of his first three foreign ministers might suggest a wish to connect his reign with hers. Two were nephews of Catherine's most illustrious foreign ministers, and the third was a leading diplomat and statesman of her day. But the ties to Catherine's traditions were more nominal than real; what little success these ministers had did not depend on their support of her policies. Ironically, the only one who ostensibly endorsed some of her ideas soon found his aims to be incompatible with Alexander's.

During the first three years of his reign, Alexander I focused much of his attention on domestic issues. Once the impending crises growing out of Paul's short-lived Franco-Russian rapprochement had been overcome, there were no major crises on the continent to draw the emperor's immediate attention from his hopes for internal reform — hopes for which implementation still seemed possible. While the general direction of Alexander's policy favored noninvolvement on the continent (the most successful of the three ministers was a major spokesman for this view), Alexander's diplomacy during these years betrayed the hesitancy of a young emperor new to the intricacies of world power, feeling

[1] Imperial manifesto quoted in Schilder, *Aleksandr*, II, 6.

his way amidst the growing turmoil of Napoleonic Europe and the intrigues of his own court.

Alexander's initial moves on the foreign scene betrayed a desire for less active involvement on the continent than under either Catherine or Paul. He immediately abandoned the extensive rapprochement with France which had led Paul to launch an expedition to conquer India, to break diplomatic relations with England, and to bring Russia so clearly to the side of France that a naval war with England was imminent in early 1801. Much to Napoleon's distress, Alexander recalled Orlov and his band of Cossacks from India, denying any further Russian interest in such excursions; renewed diplomatic relations with England; and proceeded with plans for a commercial treaty with England and the northern courts. When simultaneous assurances to Napoleon that his aim was for peace on the continent were not taken as sincere, Alexander authorized negotiations for a more thorough treaty of friendship with France (signed in October 1801), a prelude to the more extensive Anglo-French accord in the Treaty of Amiens of March 1802. Prussia, too, was brought more closely into the orbit of Russian friendship, as symbolized by the personal meeting between Alexander and King Frederick William III at the East Prussian city of Memel in the spring of 1802.

The general continental pacification showed signs of strain even before it had been achieved. Napoleon's assumption of the position of Consul for life in August 1802 added fuel to the fires in French royalist and émigré circles. His continued bellicosity toward England appeared to dissolve the Treaty of Amiens, his massing of French troops near the Channel was a threat England could not ignore, and the invasion of Hanover seemed to portend further French expansion. Alexander I was still holding Russia aloof when the British declared war on France in May 1803, but his ambassador in Paris demonstrated sufficient royalist and anglophile sympathies to cause Napoleon to demand his recall in November. Continental developments seemed to be forcing Alexander to reconsider Russia's role.

Alexander's desire for world peace suited the drift of continental politics in the first few years of the new century, but it resulted from different considerations than had Paul's acceptance of Napoleon's bid for an accord. Alexander's conciliatory policies toward his European colleagues, despite their superficial contradictions, had the beneficent and consistent effect of leaving all paths open for maneuver, while giving him time to concentrate on domestic reform. Yet the Russian emperor found it increasingly difficult to follow the paths of friendship in all directions simultaneously, in face of the struggles for power and survival on the continent. The devious course of his foreign relations and the difficulty of finding a competent man willing to follow his gestures of friendship from the English, to the French, to the Prussians, and back to the English helps explain the short tenure of his earliest foreign ministers.

The functions and ideas of Alexander's first three foreign ministers are of interest not because those men were particularly influential, but because their experiences illustrate many of the problems of the office. Their failures are significant because the reasons behind them underscore the difficulties which were to beset their successors, difficulties growing out of their personal relationships to the emperor as well as out of the political situations and the policies they advocated.

Nikita Petrovich Panin, both in name and in his professed goals for Russian foreign policy, recalled the reign of Alexander's grandmother and suggested the sharp break the young monarch sought to make with the advisers and policies of his father and immediate predecessor, Paul I. Panin's family ties had initially put him in a position of favor in Paul's reign, since he was son of an important general who had been one of Paul's childhood friends and was nephew of Catherine's influential diplomatic adviser, Nikita Ivanovich Panin, who had also served as the much-admired tutor of Paul I. When only twenty-seven, Nikita Petrovich was given the prestigious appointment of Russian minister to Berlin; two years later, in 1799, he was recalled, made a member of the College of Foreign Affairs, and raised to the rank of vice-chancellor. When Paul turned to a policy of rapprochement with France, however, Panin's violent disagreement with the emperor brought earlier clashes to a head. Generally embittered about

COUNT NIKITA PETROVICH PANIN (1771–1837)
*Engraving from a Portrait by Voille (n.d.)*

PRINCE VICTOR PAVLOVICH KOCHUBEI (1768–1834)

*Engraving from a Portrait by P. Sokolov (n.d.)*

COUNT ALEXANDER ROMANOVICH VORONTSOV (1741–1805)
*Engraving from a Portrait Found on the
Vorontsov Estate (unsigned, n.d.)*

PRINCE ADAM JERZY CZARTORYSKI (1770–1861)

*Engraving from a Portrait by Oleshkevich (n.d.)*

GENERAL ALEXANDER GOTTHARD BUDBERG (1750–1812)
*Engraving from a Portrait by Greff (n.d.)*

COUNT NIKOLAI PETROVICH RUMIANTSEV (1754–1826)
*Engraving from a Portrait by G. Dawe (1828)*

COUNT KARL ROBERT NESSELRODE (1780–1862)
*Engraving from a Portrait by Robert (n.d.)*

COUNT IONNES ANTONIOS CAPODISTRIAS (1776–1831)
*Engraving by M. A. Bouvier from a Sketch*
*by Mme Munier-Romilly*

Paul's administration, Panin became one of the leaders in the conspiracy which eventually resulted in the emperor's assassination
in March 1801. Paul may well have caught wind of Panin's involvement when he banished him to his estates in November
1800.[2]

Deeply shocked by the violent death of his father, insecure
himself in his new position of autocratic power, and somewhat
fearful of the men who had engineered the coup, Alexander
initially turned to one of the ringleaders, Count Peter Alekseevich
Pahlen, as one of his close advisers during his early months on the
throne, particularly because his "young friends" who were later to
form the Secret Committee were all abroad at the time. Among
Pahlen's other functions, he was in charge of the College of
Foreign Affairs and hence nominally in charge of diplomacy before his dismissal in June. Alexander's attitude toward Pahlen and
basic lack of confidence in him, however, prevented a constructive
relationship and kept him from making a significant contribution
during this period to either foreign or domestic affairs.

In titular rank Panin was actually the third member of the
college, but the emperor explained to him in their initial interview
at the beginning of April that he wanted Panin to serve as "the
exclusive director of the department of foreign affairs."[3] Panin
was preceded by his cousin and vice-chancellor, Prince A. B.
Kurakin, and, until June, by Pahlen.[4] But, as was often the case
in the Russia of Alexander I, rank did not determine function.
From most reports, it was Panin who, "charged with editing as
well as executing [His Majesty's] orders," became the emperor's

[2] For a discussion of the circumstances of his banishment under Paul, see the
letter of I. M. Muraviev-Apostol to S. R. Vorontsov, Feb. 16, 1801, *AKV*, XI,
161–167; *Russkii arkhiv*, XIV (1876, No. 1), 121–126.

[3] Panin was quoting Alexander's designation in their initial interview: Panin
to Krüdener, April 3, 1801, *NPP*, VI, 3; Panin to his wife, April 3, 1801, *NPP*,
VI, 8.

[4] Panin claimed he was offered the title of Vice Chancellor, which, in deference to his cousin, he did not accept. Alexander Borisovich Kurakin (1752–
1818) had been important in the College of Foreign Affairs under Paul and
retained his position until September 1802, although he was definitely in a subordinate role; he served as ambassador to Austria from 1806 to 1808 and to
France from 1808 to 1812.

right-hand man in the conduct of diplomacy — "the soul of the department, the hub around which everything revolves." [5]

Panin's relationship to the conspiracy which brought Alexander to power left him in a very awkward position, vis-à-vis the emperor throughout his six months in the foreign ministry. Alexander never forgave the conspirators for taking his father's life, since apparently he had been assured and had hoped (however unrealistically) that the plot could succeed without assassination. Panin had actually been the one to inform Alexander of the plot in advance and seek his approval. Since he was not in St. Petersburg on the fateful night, Panin was not directly implicated himself. Nevertheless, his close association with the group made for a difficult relationship with Alexander.

Panin was as far from Alexander in attitude as in friendship. Quick to complain about "Alexander's obstinacy in following the false principles and the most dangerous sophisms which he owes to the perfidious instruction of Laharpe," [6] Panin was disgusted at Alexander's enthusiasm for the French Revolution and shared none of his hopes for basic constitutional reform. Panin's principal experience abroad had been limited to Prussia, where he had become acquainted with Gentz, whose antirevolutionary orientation and defense of the established order he greatly admired.[7] Panin was ready to support administrative reform, particularly the creation of individually controlled and efficiently organized ministries for the various branches of government; he had drafted such a plan for the foreign ministry himself while he had been in office under Paul.[8] However, like many influential leaders of the gentry at the time, the only basic limitation of the emperor's authority which he envisaged was in the direction of providing a larger role for the gentry, particularly for advisers like himself who had the best conservative interests of Russia at heart. Alexander's "liberal opinions or the prejudices which Laharpe in-

[5] Panin to Krüdener, April 3, 1801, *NPP*, VI, 3; Rogerson to S. R. Vorontsov, spring 1801, *AKV*, XXX, 133.

[6] Panin to S. R. Vorontsov, June 23, 1801, *NPP*, VI, 484; *AKV*, XI, 133–136.

[7] E.g., Panin to Paul, Feb. 23, 1799, *NPP*, IV, 73.

[8] Panin, "Zapiska o reforme departmenta vneshnikh del," July 1800, *NPP*, V, 24–25.

spired in his youth" Panin saw as a severe threat to the Russian tradition he cherished. "If [Alexander] does not abandon them and if he refuses to recognize the danger which menaces all thrones," Panin wrote at one point, "there will be no possibility of establishing a system of government such as Russia should have." [9] In contrast to some of the other men around the emperor at the time, Panin evidenced no real interest in constitutions.

Panin betrayed in all his attitudes a strong national consciousness and a strong belief in Russia's great historical mission. In terms of foreign policy, this meant an active, power-oriented leadership in diplomatic affairs. His opposition to Russian isolationism dated back many years. He believed in 1801 as he had in 1798 that Russia "was called by her greatness to assume a leading role in Europe." [10] He had a great admiration for Catherine II, especially for her diplomatic and military achievements for Russia. Suspicious of Austrian desires for expansion, he thought that Russia must do her best to consolidate the gains Catherine had made to the south, and accordingly wanted to see a strong expansionist role in the Balkan area.

Central to his foreign policy was the demand for a renewed anti-French coalition in conjunction with the major powers of Europe, particularly England and Prussia, with the aim of restoring the French monarchy. Panin regarded the French Revolution and the French republican regime with typical conservative scorn — "with the eyes of a French émigré." [11] Many of his reports from Prussia under Paul reveal his contempt for Bonaparte and his early support for a strong Russian policy against France. Europe could not be safe, he believed, until legitimate government was reestablished in France. Other diplomatic considerations were all secondary to this prime goal which must be the major concern for all of Europe.

He was enraged at Paul's desire to pull Russia out of an anti-

<hr>

[9] Panin to S. R. Vorontsov, July 28, 1801, *NPP*, VI, 500; *AKV*, XI, 141–144; Panin to S. R. Vorontsov, Sept. 26, 1801, *NPP*, VI, 529; *AKV*, XI, 151–160.

[10] Panin to Krüdener, No. 70, secret and confidential, May 3, 1798, *NPP*, III, 241.

[11] Rostopchin to S. R. Vorontsov, July 12, 1801, *AKV*, VIII, 286; a selection of his letters and reports from Prussia is published in *NPP*, Vols. II and III.

French coalition. At the height of his clash with Paul over a
Franco-Russian accord, he declared that his "hand would never
sign a treaty of peace with France until after the reestablishment
of the monarchy." A general pacification including Russia's allies
might be viable, he admitted in October 1800, but only as an expedient to provide "time to prepare for a renewed struggle." [12]
He was thus exceedingly eager for Alexander to turn his back on
the French-oriented foreign policies of Paul's final year, especially the quixotic schemes for military expeditions to India or
naval wars with England, when Russia was ill-prepared for such
ventures. He was therefore pleased to find Alexander ready to call
Orlov and his band of Cossacks back from India and was satisfied with the reestablishment of diplomatic relations with England, particularly since such moves implied a break with what he
believed to be the disastrous policy of rapprochement with France.

Although he was no real friend of England, Panin believed extended cooperation with the British to be the most satisfactory
policy for Russia in the spring of 1801. Foreseeing the long-term
advantages of such a policy for the renewed struggle against
France, he was well fitted for his role as key Russian negotiator
for the new convention with England, signed on June 17, which
essentially abandoned the policy of "Armed Neutrality" and initiated real cooperation. The situation continued to be awkward
because Pahlen was still nominally in charge of the College
of Foreign Affairs, but Alexander apparently had more confidence in Panin. Although the British were also dealing with
Pahlen and did not exactly understand Panin's formal position
as "the third, but efficient member of the department," they
found Panin easy to work with.[13] Panin's general ideas on foreign
policy were therefore suitable enough for Alexander's early diplomatic maneuvers. Only when Alexander turned to a more con-

---

[12] Panin to Krüdener, Feb. 11, 1800, *NPP*, V, 254; to Krüdener, Nov. 1, 1800,
*NPP*, V, 493–494.

[13] St. Helens to Hawkesbury, private, May 24, 1801, PRO/FO 65/48. His role
in these negotiations can be followed in the reports of Garlike and (particularly)
St. Helens, found in FO 65/48, and in protocols, dispatches, and correspondence
contained in *NPP*, VI, 31–105; for a discussion and the texts of the agreement,
see Martens, *Recueil*, XI, 10–49, and *VPR*, I, 28–41.

ciliatory policy towards France later in the summer of 1801 did Panin's position become more difficult.

Besides his initial superficial agreement with Alexander's foreign policy, Panin had the minimal qualification of being experienced in the College of Foreign Affairs. Alexander's friend and later his foreign minister, Adam Czartoryski, stated early in Alexander's reign that Panin "more than others seemed destined to play an important role in the affairs of the empire"; he credited Panin with "the necessary prerequisites: a celebrated name in Russia, unusual talents, and much ambition." The British ambassador, undoubtedly pleased with Panin's policy orientation, confirmed Czartoryski's appraisal by reporting Panin's "uncommon talents for business, added to great uprightness and integrity." In fact, Panin had adequate ability at editing diplomatic dispatches and made some attempts at making the conduct of business within the foreign department more orderly.[14] His abilities seemed unusual, however, only against the meager background of the Russian foreign office, where even technical competence was rare.

Whatever Panin's talents for the routine of diplomatic business, his major failing was his inability to get along with people. As a supervisor, he soon succeeded in antagonizing most of his subordinates, his colleagues, and the foreign diplomatic colony. His "dry, imperious character and little affability," were targets of much scorn; even many who were quite ready to support him recognized that "pride and self-esteem are his great faults." The count usually kept to himself and was soon quite isolated. "He goes nowhere, sees no one," noted one close observer; "his outward manners are anything but welcoming."[15] The diplomatic world had little place for a man unwilling to make friends and possessed of a forbidding, self-righteous character.

Panin's imperiousness toward colleagues and subordinates in-

---

[14] Czartoryski, *Mémoires*, I, 231. St. Helens to Hawkesbury, No. 33, secret and confidential, Sept. 10, 1801, PRO/FO 65/49. For example, see Panin's circular to Russian ambassadors and ministers abroad, July 1, 1801, *NPP*, VI, 28–29; *AKV*, XI, 137–138; *SIRIO*, LXX, 187–189.

[15] Czartoryski, *Mémoires*, I, 232; Morkov to S. R. Vorontsov, Jan. 25, 1802, *AKV*, XX, 100. Rogerson to S. R. Vorontsov, July 28, Aug. 29, 1801, *AKV*, XXX, 160, 167–168.

creased as the months progressed. He evidenced a strong tendency "to govern all the ministry himself with no advice from any
council or individuals" and, according to some contemporaries,
to concentrate his efforts on "low intrigue and the advancement
of his personal views." Defensively, but revealingly, he wrote the
emperor, "The portfolio of foreign affairs cannot be in several
hands at one time." [16] The unusual extent to which he carried
censorship was but one of the more distasteful aspects of his bid
for power. Panin's "distrustful curiosity" is "indecent and contrary to the virtuous principles of our adorable sovereign," complained the Russian ambassador in London, Count Simon, to his
brother A. R. Vorontsov. Panin blamed his procedures on the in-
eptitude of his subordinates: "Unfortunately there is no one here
in whom I can have confidence, [or] who has the necessary
knowledge and firmness to second me with any success," he
explained.[17] This may have been somewhat true, but it was
equally true that he became jealous of all who threatened his supremacy, particularly as he increasingly feared losing it.

Despite their political differences, Panin had high praise for
Alexander, commenting, for example, on his "rectitude of judgment and the most magnanimous intentions, besides his angelic
patience and great ardor for work." However, although throughout the spring months Alexander entrusted Panin with much responsibility and "seemed very satisfied with his work," [18] he never
really returned Panin's praise and remained uneasy about working with him. Insecure himself during his initial months of power,
Alexander was plagued by remorse about his father's death and
by a fundamental distrust toward the men who had engineered it.
After the important negotiations with England, he entrusted

[16] S. R. Vorontsov to Novosiltsev, Oct. 8, 1801, *AKV*, XI, 407–409; Rostop-
chin to S. R. Vorontsov, July 12, 1801, *AKV*, VIII, 286. Panin to Alexander,
June 9, 1801, *NPP*, VI, 381.
    [17] S. R. to A. R. Vorontsov, Aug. 14, 1801, *AKV*, X, 117–118; see also, S. R.
Vorontsov to Panin, Aug. 14, 1801, *AKV*, XI, 223–226; *NPP*, VI, 503–506.
Panin to S. R. Vorontsov, July 28, 1801, *NPP*, VI, 500.
    [18] Panin to S. R. Vorontsov, June 23, 1801, *NPP*, VI, 483; *AKV*, XI, 134.
Rogerson to S. R. Vorontsov, April 17, 1801, *AKV*, XXX, 139; see also Panin
to his wife, mid-April 1801, *NPP*, VI, 10–11; and Muraviev-Apostol to S. R.
Vorontsov, April 18, 1801, *Russkii arkhiv*, XIV (1876, No. 1), 128.

Panin only with the routine conduct of business and the correspondence of the diplomatic chancellery. "In the beginning, when he did not have that experience which he increasingly acquired in succeeding days," Panin's successor Kochubei said, Alexander's "extreme distrust of himself may have often caused him to give in" to Panin, even when he "often saw things differently than his minister." But as Alexander gained confidence, Panin's importance quickly waned. The observers who thought after the banishment of Pahlen in June that "Panin gained much credit and a major influence" were deluded.[19] The dismissal may have slightly eased Panin's situation, as it eliminated one of his titular superiors in the department, but it did not perceptibly increase his influence. As the emperor's own foreign policy came into sharper focus, revealing that an accord with England was only part of a larger pacification effort, Alexander's differences with Panin became more pronounced. The major issue on which they clashed was Alexander's unwillingness to close the door on further understanding with France.

While distressed by some of Bonaparte's aggressive and despotic designs, Alexander was impressed with his reform program and foresaw no immediate danger from France to Russian security. Moreover, Alexander, together with his friends of the Secret Committee, did not want foreign involvements to interfere with their domestic reform efforts. Whereas Panin favored a strong Russian policy against France, Alexander wanted to establish peace. It was in this context that Panin complained, "Sometimes the emperor pays attention to my advice, but often his decisions follow his own opinions or the prejudices which Laharpe inspired in his youth." [20]

In fact, Alexander was turning more often to the sympathetic counsel of his "young friends" of the Secret Committee, Czartoryski, Novosiltsev, Stroganov, and Kochubei. By early July he

[19] Kochubei to S. R. Vorontsov, Nov. 21, 1801, *AKV*, XVIII, 250. Stedingk to Gustav IV, July 26, 1801, quoted by Brückner, in *NPP*, VI, 394. The report of Schwarzenberg, No. 11, July 9, 1801, HHS/Russ. II, 95, discusses the background of Pahlen's dismissal.

[20] Panin to S. R. Vorontsov, Sept. 14, 1801, *NPP*, VI, 529; *AKV*, XI, 154.

had initiated periodic group meetings, in addition to frequent informal individual conferences. The Secret Committee spent relatively little time on foreign affairs during the summer, although
Alexander was becoming more attentive to their diplomatic advice, particularly their strong desire to keep Russia out of European war. The emperor's "young friends" were opposed to Panin
personally and politically, and their forceful criticism of his policies had its effect. By the meeting of September 7, Alexander admitted his strong discontent with Panin, "saying that he was always obliged to quarrel with him . . . and to correct the count's
proposals." [21]

Alexander also listened to the Vorontsov brothers, who were
friendly and sympathetic with the Secret Committee. Count Simon, the Russian ambassador in London, was vocal against Panin's conduct of negotiations with the British. Later his criticism
became more general: he differed with Panin's views and methods, especially his censorship proceedings; he felt that Panin did
not keep him adequately informed of developments and that
Panin was "more prone to intrigue" than "to the uncompromising
service of his country." "It is a great misfortune that this man,
placed so far above his proper position, works directly with the
emperor and leads him into error, not by deliberate intent, I suppose, but because he is ignorant himself and presumptuous beyond measure," wrote Count Simon to his brother.[22] Alexander
approved of Count Simon's frankness and the general tenor of his
reports regarding Panin, although in retrospect it would appear
that much of his criticism was excessive or unjust. Yet, however

[21] Minutes of the Secret Committee, Sept. 7, 1801, *Stroganov*, II, 96–97. The
need for a general plan for foreign relations was discussed in the meetings on
July 22; further discussion of other plans took place August 25 (*ibid.*, pp. 68–71,
94–95).

[22] S. R. to A. R. Vorontsov, Aug. 24, 1801, *AKV*, X, 124–125. His complaints increased, and by fall he resolved to bypass Panin and write directly
to the emperor: S. R. to A. R. Vorontsov, July 24, Aug. 14, Oct. 9, 12, 26, and
30, 1801, *AKV*, X, 107–145; S. R. Vorontsov to Kurakin, Oct. 19, 1801, *AKV*,
XXX, 494–497; S. R. Vorontsov to Panin, Aug. 21, 1801, *NPP*, VI, 508–520;
*AKV*, XI, 226–237; Sept. 25, 1801, *AKV*, XI, 238–239; S. R. Vorontsov to
Alexander, Oct. 10, 1801, *AKV*, X, 276–295. Morkov labeled Vorontsov's criticism excessive (to S. R. Vorontsov, Jan. 25, 1802), *AKV*, XX, 100; Martens
(*Recueil*, XI, 24, 29–64), called it "unjust and uncalled for."

much ill will may have been mixed with the advice of Panin's critics — the dowager empress among them — it is clear that their words served only to intensify the emperor's own feelings against Panin and to strengthen his resolve to install a more congenial foreign minister.[23]

The basic disagreement between Panin and the emperor came to a head over the new negotiations with France which, with the approval of most of the Secret Committee, were proceeding in September. The British ambassador reported with some distress that "the members of the Emperor's Council, with whom he is particularly connected . . . had been . . . zealous in promoting the intended peace with France; it being their professed System to endeavor to disengage the Emperor from all foreign Concerns as well as connections and induce Him to direct His principal attention to the Affairs of the Interior." The ambassador continued with sympathy for Panin's view, "Count Panin on the other hand is anxious that His Majesty should take the leading part in the affairs of Europe which belongs to His Situation, and which in truth He could not forego without the most essential detriment to the interests and dignity of His Crown."[24]

Panin continued to be very critical of the negotiations. He was distressed to find that he was actually being bypassed, while the most important discussions were being carried on in Paris by the Russian ambassador, Count Morkov. He did his best to interfere. "The emperor of Russia wanted peace at all costs," explained the Prussian envoy in St. Petersburg, while "Count Panin had taken it on himself to order Morkov to differ his signature." Despite

---

[23] Criticism of Panin came from all directions. See, for example, Locatelli to Trautmansdorff, No. 27, Aug. 25, 1801, HHS/Russ. II, 95; see also the letters of Novosiltsev in *AKV*, XVIII, 440–450, and Sergei S. Tatishchev, *Iz proshlogo russkoi diplomatii; istoricheskie issledovaniia i polemicheskie stat'i* (St. Petersburg, 1890), pp. 291–295. The dowager empress was especially vocal because of Panin's involvement in the plot against Paul, although she was more tolerant of Panin than of Pahlen. Muriaev-Apostol warned Panin of the extent of opposition in a letter Aug. 23, 1801, *NPP*, VI, 614–617.

[24] St. Helens to Hawkesbury, No. 33, secret and confidential, Sept. 10, 1801, PRO/FO 65/49. A full statement of Panin's system for diplomacy was presented in his partially preserved memorandum of June 28, 1801, "Du système politique de l'Empire de Russie," *VPR*, I, 62–68; *NPP*, VI, 17–28.

Panin's firm opposition, he had virtually no influence over the course of proceedings.[25]

If Panin's opposition to the French negotiations was, as one observer saw it, "one of the principal reasons which accelerated his fall," the outspoken nature of that opposition was equally important. For what galled Alexander more than Panin's basic divergence from him in foreign policy was the manner in which Panin conducted his opposition. Panin clearly wanted an active and responsible role as foreign minister and was not content to be "only an instrument" of an all-powerful autocrat. "I regard it as my first duty," he wrote during the reign of Paul, "not to let myself be intimidated by the fear of displeasing, when it is a question of the glory of my master and the interests of the most sacred cause." Panin was extremely zealous in presenting his recommendations to Alexander on all matters and gave the impression that he "never wanted to follow the views of His Majesty" when they disagreed with his own.[26] For example, during the summer of 1801 he had begged Alexander not to invite Laharpe to Russia, confiding to Vorontsov that "if that scoundrel comes here as I fear, and is listened to, you will soon learn . . . that I have renounced all service whatsoever." He then proceeded, according to one report, to take it upon himself to send a circular to Russian legations asking them to refuse Laharpe passports.[27] Laharpe did come to Russia, but it was hardly on his own initiative that Panin renounced his service.

Alexander was not content with the independence of a foreign minister who apparently "wanted to make everyone yield to his own ideas," particularly as the emperor began

[25] S. de Lusi to Prussian Foreign Office, Nov. 1801 (copy), Papers of the Imperial Russian Historical Society, LOII, 113/17/90. See also Panin to S. R. Vorontsov, Sept. 26, 1801, *NPP*, VI, 526–535; *AKV*, XI, 151–160, and F. Saurau to Starhemberg, Oct. 10, 1801, in *Starhemberg*, p. 79.

[26] Lusi to Prussian Foreign Office, Nov. 1801 (copy), Papers of the Imperial Russian Historical Society, LOII, 113/17/90. Panin to Kurakin, secret and confidential, No. 70, May 3, 1798, *NPP*, III, 245. Minutes of the meeting of the Secret Committee, Sept. 7, 1801, *Stroganov*, II, 96–97.

[27] Panin to S. R. Vorontsov, June 23, 1801, *NPP*, VI, 484; *AKV*, XI, 135. Charles Monnard, *Notice biographique sur le général Frédéric-César La Harpe, précepteur de l'empereur de Russie, Alexandre Ier* (Paris, 1838), p. 60; Schilder, *Aleksandr*, II, 269n.

to assume more control in the conduct of foreign relations. Panin became distressingly aware that Alexander wanted his services only as a secretary and in most major matters was turning to other advisers. Alexander could have issued an order and rid himself of Panin as he had earlier with Pahlen, but he hesitated to do so. The emperor was clearly dissatisfied and readily admitted that "in truth he often differed in opinion with Count Panin over affairs," yet he oddly claimed that he "had not intended to dismiss him." [28] Although he had lost confidence in his minister, he was not willing to force his resignation, procrastinating until a bitter dispute between Panin and his cousin, Kurakin, brought matters to a climax.

The situation in the foreign office was exceedingly awkward because, while Alexander had assigned the major role to Panin, he retained Kurakin with a superior rank. Particularly when Panin came to disagree with Kurakin over policies toward France, he tried to exclude his cousin from many aspects of business in the department. As Kurakin found his position more and more tedious, he complained, first to Panin, and, when that had no effect, to the emperor. In the course of a violent argument with the emperor over this in October, Panin suggested that his services were not appreciated and requested leave. The emperor, more ready for a pretext to change his foreign minister than he was willing to admit or than Panin suspected, did not hesitate to grant his request, believing that "it was impossible for him not to accept the resignation without compromising himself." [29]

Panin's bitterness about his dismissal and his total exclusion

[28] Kochubei to S. R. Vorontsov, Oct. 18, 1801, *VPR*, I, 103–107; *AKV*, XVIII, 244–247. Morkov to S. R. Vorontsov, Jan. 25, 1802, *AKV*, XX, 100. See Panin's complaints quoted by Schwarzenberg to Coblenz, Aug. 12, 1801, HHS/Russ. II, 95. Alexander to S. R. Vorontsov, Nov. 12, 1801, *AKV*, XXVIII, 455 and X, 302; *VPR*, I, 130.

[29] Kochubei to S. R. Vorontsov, Oct. 18, 1801, *VPR*, I, 103–107; *AKV*, XVIII, 244–247. Several of the letters from Kurakin to Panin and the replies are printed in *NPP*, VI, 588–611, 628–637. Alexander explained the incident of the dismissal in his letter (edited by Kochubei) to S. R. Vorontsov, Nov. 12, 1801, *AKV*, XXVIII, 451–455; X, 299–302; *VPR*, I, 128–131. See also Stedingk to Gustav IV, quoted by Brückner, *NPP*, VI, 632; Caulaincourt to Talleyrand, Nov. 20, 1801, *SIRIO*, LXX, 294; and St. Helens to Hawkesbury, No. 42, Oct. 10, 1801, PRO/FO 65/49.

from affairs left him with nothing but criticism for Alexander's diplomacy: "I hope that I will be able to forget the fatal error which led me into affairs in a time of semi-confidences, of semi-measures, of semi-alliances, and of the most entire political nullity," he wrote several years later. "It was great foolishness on my part to hope that the system of Catherine the Second could amalgamate itself with such elements." [30]

Panin's grand politics, reminiscent as they were of Catherine's reign, may have appealed to Alexander in the early days of his rule because he was anxious to turn away from his father's policies. Panin was a capable enough negotiator to restore Russian ties with England. But Panin's support for a grand and aggressive foreign policy, his conservative attitude, and most particularly the firmness with which he presented his views soon diminished and eventually dispelled the imperial favor. Personal factors were as important as political ones; Alexander, from remorse and distrust if not actually from fear, was never fully at ease with a man who had been so deeply involved in the plot against his father. Holding views which were in fundamental conflict with those of the emperor and failing to secure the emperor's trust and friendship, Panin was not able to exert any significant influence on Alexander or even to maintain his confidence. It is little wonder that his foreign ministry lasted only six months and proved so basically unsuccessful, except for its stopgap function.

The appointment of Victor Pavlovich Kochubei to replace Panin in mid-October 1801 brought to the direction of Russian diplomacy a man who shared many of the emperor's views and who was much more willing than Panin to bow to Alexander's wishes. A member of the Secret Committee, he had the initial advantage of being a personal friend of the emperor. Born in 1768, Kochubei was the nephew of Catherine's illustrious diplomatic adviser, Bezborodko, but, unlike Panin, he had no illusions about

---

[30] Panin to Razumovskii, July 6, 1805, in *Razoumowski*, Vol. II, Part 4, 119. Initially Panin was given a three-year leave, but when he had been offered no other post by the end of 1804, he sent in his resignation and was banished from St. Petersburg (Panin to Alexander, Jan. 7, 1805, *NPP*, VII, 84–85). The official circular, dated Oct. 14, 1801, stated that Panin had requested a three-year leave for reasons of health (AVPR, Administrativnye dela, IV, 4, No. 3).

a return to the diplomacy of her reign. As with many of Alexander's younger friends, much of Kochubei's life had been spent abroad, more in Western Europe than in Prussia. In 1784 he had been placed in the Russian mission to Sweden, and, while a subordinate there under Count Morkov, he had studied at the University of Uppsala. He made a long visit to London in 1788 and 1789, where, under the tutelage of Simon Vorontsov, he spent some time studying the embassy archives. He was in Paris during the early period of the French Revolution and made lengthy sojourns in Lisbon, Madrid, and Vienna before assuming a post in the Russian embassy in Constantinople in 1793. In 1798 he was promoted to vice-chancellor and was placed in the College of Foreign Affairs. Finding that he did not get along well under Paul, he again went abroad, returning to Russia only after Alexander had assumed power.

Kochubei was "very well liked in the department" and was noted for his "kindness and affability" toward his colleagues. Most persons associated with him attested to "his zeal, his talents, and his honesty." Even Panin, who later became quite bitter toward the man who replaced him, felt when he worked with Kochubei under Paul that he "could not have been more content with his procedures, his outlook, conduct of business, and the nobility of his feelings." [31] Although Kochubei possessed the attributes of diplomatic congeniality, his "certain European varnish and grand manner which made him a favorite in society" did not particularly qualify him for his political function. "His zeal for the public good is recognized, but his application is more doubtful," noted a perceptive Saxon diplomat. Like many of the contemporary gentry in the Russian service, it could be said of Kochubei "that he finds work difficult and is more disposed towards civil and social virtues than towards those associated with public office." [32] Such failings, however, hardly stood in the way of his

[31] Rogerson to S. R. Vorontsov, Dec. 23, 1801, *AKV*, XXX, 179. F. V. Rostopchin to S. R. Vorontsov, Oct. 8, 1794, *AKV*, VIII, 102. Panin to his wife, Oct. 5, 1799, *NPP*, V, 10–11.

[32] Czartoryski, *Mémoires*, I, 268. "Imperator Aleksandr Pavlovich i ego dvor v 1804 g.," ed. F. F. Schiemann, *Russkaia starina*, XXIX (Dec. 1880), 815. For other similar appraisals, see Caulaincourt to Napoleon, June 17, 1808, *DSRF*,

service, particularly since his friendship with the emperor gave him such a great advantage over his predecessor.

Alexander's personal ties with Kochubei dated back many years; they had shared an enthusiasm for Western European political developments and a distaste for many of the practices of the reign of Paul I. When Kochubei went abroad in 1796 and 1797 with Alexander's blessing to renew contacts with Laharpe in Switzerland and to study "constitutions" and "liberal ideas," the two friends maintained an avid correspondence, with Kochubei as the confidant of many of Alexander's personal and political concerns. The strong mutual regard which developed was heightened by Alexander's hope that Kochubei would assist him in bringing Enlightenment ideas into Russia. Kochubei felt as much responsibility for the personal interests of his friend as for the public interest of Russia. "I believe that all honest men must unite about him and make their best efforts to heal the wounds which his father brought to his country." [33]

Soon after Alexander ascended the throne, Kochubei returned to Russia, full of praise for the new emperor and eager "to do my best in His service." "All the actions of our new master strike to the heart of wisdom and moderation in an extraordinary degree for his age," he wrote in May 1801. Kochubei had no official post before being appointed to the foreign office in October, but by August the Prussian ambassador had noted that "Prince Kochubei is one of the ministers who is in the greatest intimacy with the emperor. . . . Everywhere this prince meets him, he takes him by the hand and converses for a long time with him in the most friendly and confidential manner." [34] Throughout the summer, in addition to his important role in the Secret Committee,

---

II, 191–192; Morkov to S. R. Vorontsov, April 19, 1796, *AKV*, XX, 69; Nesselrode to his wife, June 10, 1812, *LPN*, IV, 41; and S. R. Vorontsov to N. P. Panin, Oct. 23, 1798, *NPP*, III, 629.

[33] Kochubei to S. R. Vorontsov, April 8, 1801, *AKV*, XVIII, 236. Their early correspondence is discussed and extracted in T. Bogdanovich, "Iz perepiski Aleksandra I s V. P. Kochubeem," *Russkoe proshloe* (1923, No. 5), pp. 101–111. See also Rostopchin to S. R. Vorontsov, July 18, 1793, *AKV*, VIII, 75.

[34] Kochubei to S. R. Vorontsov, April 8 and May 13, 1801, *AKV*, XVIII, 236, 238. Report from Lusi to Prussian Foreign Office, Aug. 19, 1801 (copy), Papers of the Imperial Russian Historical Society, LOII, 113/17/90.

Kochubei worked closely in frequent conferences with the emperor about both domestic and foreign problems. Panin, fearing Kochubei's closeness to Alexander, proposed the young prince for the post of ambassador to Paris, but Kochubei declined on the grounds that financial and family affairs required him to remain in Russia. "As for a diplomatic career," he had explained soon after his return to Russia, "I renounce it willingly and forever." [35]

However sympathetic Kochubei may have been to Alexander's hopes for Russian reform, his intellectual and political capacities were hardly those of a reformer. As a friend observed, "his intelligence was clear but not deep," and "he showed an extreme readiness to adopt any opinion that might be in fashion." His flirtations with Western ideas stemmed more from the dilettantism of a fashionable eighteenth-century aristocrat than from the emotional commitment of a nineteenth-century reformer, alienated from his social or political background. He showed concern for peasant reform and the eventual abolition of serfdom in Russia, but when it came to implementation he was all too ready to bow before the difficulties of changing the system. His self-imposed "exile" during the final years of the reign of Paul I showed opposition to an "unreasonable despot," but Kochubei had enough faith in Alexander I not to want to change the fundamental political system of the empire. Occasionally critical of the emperor's irresolution in domestic reform, he generally praised Alexander's "moderation." His participation in the Secret Committee revealed his own ideas to be somewhat more moderate than those of the emperor's other "young friends." Czartoryski came to feel that Kochubei's liberalism was often "professed with a certain reserve, as though it was not to be reconciled with his real opinion." [36] While such flexibility helped make him a successful assistant for Alexander, it did not generate a thoroughgoing reform effort.

[35] Kochubei to A. R. Vorontsov, July 11, 1801, *AKV*, XIV, 152. Kochubei to S. R. Vorontsov, May 13, 1801, *AKV*, XVIII, 238.

[36] Czartoryski, *Mémoires*, I, 268. Czartoryski's view may be somewhat exaggerated as it was written later, when Kochubei was supporting more reactionary ideas.

Kochubei's experience in office and his knowledge of procedures abroad made him extremely critical of the backwardness of Russian bureaucracy: "Dispatches, letters, forms — everything has to be done by the minister, a situation without example in other countries," he complained. "Anywhere else a minister thinks, orders, dictates, corrects, confers, discusses, and attends council meetings; but in Russia he also has to be a clerk, and yet we have three hundred employees in the College of Foreign Affairs, not including foreign missions and the Moscow archives." Kochubei was one of the firmest members of the Secret Committee in support of administrative reform, but the 1802 enactments regarding the Senate and executive organs were indeed meager. The reform of the Senate which attempted to define its powers and function was never fully carried out. And the executive reform whereby the colleges were replaced by ministries, while it gave Kochubei's department the modern-sounding title of Ministry for Foreign Affairs, offered no real change in the administration or conduct of government.[37]

Kochubei, even after the dismissal of Panin in mid-October, was reluctant to accept the post of foreign minister because of "his aversion to a diplomatic career." [38] He was willing to serve the state, he said, but he preferred to work on the domestic scene; and throughout his year as director of the College of Foreign Affairs, he was openly discontented with the position. The ambiguities of his situation augmented his original qualms, because the

---

[37] Kochubei to S. R. Vorontsov, Nov. 21, 1801, *AKV*, XVIII, 252. Kochubei's active role is apparent in the minutes of the Secret Committee, *Stroganov*, II, 148–228; see especially the meeting of Jan. 15, 1801, *ibid.*, II, 161–162, the meeting of March 22, *ibid.*, pp. 180–184, Kochubei's project for the ministries presented on April 5, *ibid.*, pp. 197–199, and his 1802 letter to Stroganov, *ibid.*, pp. 298–300. The employee registers for the years 1801 to 1803 (Vorontsov Papers, TsGADA, 1261/1177) demonstrate that there was no immediate organizational change after the reform. Czartoryski (*Mémoires*, I, 311–316) in emphasizing the importance of the reform, however, gave inadequate supporting evidence regarding the foreign office.

[38] Kochubei to S. R. Vorontsov, Oct. 18, 1801, *VPR*, I, 103; *AKV*, XVIII, 244. See also Kochubei to A. R. Vorontsov, Oct. 1801, *AKV*, XIV, 157, and Kochubei to S. R. Vorontsov, Nov. 21, 1801, *AKV*, XVIII, 253. Cf. Novosiltsev to S. R. Vorontsov, Dec. 12, 1801, *ibid.*, p. 448, and S. R. Vorontsov to Czartoryski, Feb. 12, 1802, *AKV*, XV, 154. Czartoryski (*Mémoires*, I, 316) noted Kochubei's pleasure at leaving the office in 1802.

role he assumed did not carry with it the title of Foreign Minister. Like Panin, throughout his term he was outranked in the college by Kurakin, who as vice-chancellor was nominally in charge of many of the routine conferences with foreign diplomats despite Kochubei's complaints and the open denunciation of Kurakin by the Secret Committee. Finding that Kurakin "has no idea of affairs at all" despite his "involvement in everything," Kochubei had to be present at all conferences and oversee the work of the department.[39]

Alexander was naturally eager to have him as foreign minister because, in addition to their personal friendship, Kochubei had become the spokesman for a foreign policy which was completely congenial to the emperor's current views. As early as July 1801 Kochubei had presented a memorandum outlining a system for Russia which gave an alternative to the plan being suggested by Panin. Kochubei's prime goal was to keep Russia as isolated as possible from Europe and its wars, so that the efforts of state could be turned to domestic reform: "We need peace to heal the enormous ills of the country. . . . Those who want to plunge us into further wars . . . are the real enemies of Russia. . . . Peace and internal reform — those are the words which should be written in golden letters in the offices of our statesmen." [40] Thus Kochubei's preoccupation with internal affairs became the cornerstone for the foreign policy he continued to advocate throughout his year in office.

Alexander had been following this policy in effect, particularly in the rapprochement with France which Panin had so adamantly opposed in September. The Austrian ambassador in St. Peters-

[39] Kochubei to S. R. Vorontsov, Nov. 21, 1801, *AKV*, XVIII, 254; see also St. Helens to Hawkesbury, No. 40, Oct. 15, 1801, PRO/FO 65/49; minutes of the Secret Committee meetings of April 12 and May 3, 1801, *Stroganov*, II, 206, 213. Regarding the background of Kurakin's later displacement, see the report of Lusi to the Prussian Foreign Office, Sept. 1802 (copy), Papers of the Imperial Russian Historical Society, LOII, 113/17/90.

[40] Kochubei to S. R. Vorontsov, May 24, 1801, *AKV*, XVIII, 241. His views were outlined by St. Helens to Hawkesbury, No. 33, secret and confidential, Sept. 10, 1801, PRO/FO 65/49. Reference to his memorandum on diplomacy was made in different letters and can be verified in the minutes of the Secret Committee for the meetings of July 22 and August 25 (*Stroganov*, II, 68–71, 94–95). Unfortunately the text of this memorandum could not be located.

burg correctly sensed that the only change to be expected with
the new minister was that Kochubei "will act with even more circumspection on occasions when it might be a question of energetic measures." Kochubei did not deny that a more active policy
against France might be required in the future, but he felt that
for the present Russia should maintain as passive a system of diplomacy as possible. His aim of reconciliation with France, however, betrayed none of the schemes for Russian expansion often
attributed to those who wanted an alliance with Napoleon. Russia should have no eyes for expansion, he affirmed, even regarding the Eastern Question. He firmly believed that a weak Turkey
made a good neighbor for Russia and that Russia should prevent
dismemberment of the Ottoman Empire, having no need to increase her territory to the south.[41] When Kochubei took over the
office, then, his "system" was in complete conformity with the
outlook of Alexander and his other intimate advisers, which
placed him in a good position to elaborate and implement foreign
policy decisions with more influence than his predecessor.[42]

Kochubei's active participation in the Secret Committee at the
time he was foreign minister meant that diplomatic affairs were
given wider discussion than during any other part of Alexander's reign. The composition of the group, lack of legal sanction,
and the informality of its meetings hardly qualified it as a cabinet
government, but in the realm of foreign policy decisions, particularly during the winter of 1801/1802, it certainly had a similar
effect. Several of the recorded sessions were devoted to discussing

[41] Saurau to Starhemberg, Oct. 17, 1801, *Starhemberg*, p. 80. Kochubei to
S. R. Vorontsov, Nov. 21, 1801, *AKV*, XVIII, 248–249. Sergei Goriainov, *Bosfor
i Dardanelly. Issledovanie voprosa o prolivakh po diplomaticheskoi perepiske,
khraniashcheisia v Gosudarstvennom i S. Peterburgskom Glavnom arkhivakh*
(St. Petersburg, 1907), p. 38. Kochubei's appraisal of both present and future
requirements of Russian foreign policy was outlined in his memorandum drawn
up at the end of 1801 and presented to the Secret Committee (meetings of
February 3 and 8, 1802, *Stroganov*, II, 169–170, 172–173; Czartoryski,
*Mémoires*, I, 292–293, 316); Stroganov noted that this memorandum did not
differ much from the one presented during the previous summer. Unfortunately,
neither text is available.

[42] Kochubei sensed the emperor's agreement in his initial conference after his
appointment, as he reported to S. R. Vorontsov, Oct. 18, 1801, *AKV*, XVIII,
244–247; *VPR*, I, 103–105.

general plans of foreign policy, and Kochubei often raised specific issues. The group as a whole basically agreed with the "system" of Kochubei; discussion was open and the advice of the others was often sought.[43]

The willingness and frequency with which Kochubei sought advice on matters of diplomacy contrasts markedly with the practices of his predecessor. In addition to the Secret Committee, Kochubei also frequently consulted such sympathetic advisers as the Vorontsov brothers. He had a particularly deep respect for Alexander Vorontsov, who, he felt, should actually be occupying his office. Although the Austrian diplomat who reported that "he does nothing without consulting Count Vorontsov," was certainly exaggerating, there is ample evidence to show the great extent to which Kochubei consulted both Alexander and his brother Simon on policy and appointments.[44] Kochubei's conduct resulted in part from his ability to work with others, but also from the insecurity which he felt in the office. He had worked out the general lines of his policy, but was often unsure how best to maintain the delicate equilibrium which would keep Russia on the periphery of European affairs.

There were many attributes which might have made Kochubei a relatively successful foreign minister under Alexander I. Yet, despite his friendship and intellectual compatibility with the emperor, Kochubei found that his role and influence decreased after his first six months in office. In effect, Alexander was becoming disenchanted with the Secret Committee as viable plans for domestic reform failed to materialize, and concomitantly — if not as a result — he found less appeal in the policy of withdrawal from continental affairs. By the spring of 1802, he was ready to adopt a more independent attitude and act more as his own min-

---

[43] For at least a partial account of these discussions, see the minutes in *Stroganov*, II. After the meeting of May 23, 1802, just before the emperor's departure for Memel, the committee apparently did not meet again until Nov. 7, 1803. See also Czartoryski, *Mémoires*, I, 292.

[44] Unsigned, "Mémoire sur la Russie," Nov. 1801, HHS/Russ. II, 96. See Saurau to Starhemberg, Oct. 17, 1801, *Starhemberg*, p. 80; Hudelist to Starhemberg, Jan. 20, 1802, *Starhemberg*, pp. 93–94; Kochubei to A. R. Vorontsov, Nov. 5, 1801, *AKV*, XIV, 163, and succeeding letters.

ister for foreign affairs. At the end of March "the emperor appeared very determined in his outlook" in a meeting of the Secret
Committee, standing in opposition to most of the group over a
question in the negotiations with Sweden, then under way. A
week later in a discussion about an alliance between France,
Prussia, and Russia, Alexander disagreed sharply with the reasoning of the committee and even suggested the possibility of a
more active policy of alliances.[45] The practical results of the emperor's views did not come immediately, but the group was conscious of his growing independence and that he was starting to
abandon the policy of withdrawal, which Kochubei and the others were still advocating.

The most striking example of Alexander's independence was
in regard to his Memel interview with King Frederick William III
of Prussia in June 1802, which was to result in a personal alliance that lasted for most of his reign. The plans for such a meeting originated in the personal correspondence between Alexander and the Prussian monarch and were not even discussed with
Kochubei until mid-April, when the arrangements were well under way. "Imagine a minister for foreign affairs who had no
knowledge at all of this escapade," Kochubei wrote disgustedly
a few weeks later. Hardly sympathetic to the idea of a Prussian
alliance, Kochubei was strongly opposed to the meeting. "I see
no utility whatsoever and many inconveniences in this trip," he
admitted, but "it was not my place to prevent it." [46] The Secret
Committee heard of the journey on the eve of the emperor's departure, when Alexander assured them that the visit was merely
one of friendship and that no business would be discussed. Kochubei's presentation of a memorandum — with the emperor's
permission — to the committee on the policy Alexander should

[45] Meetings of March 28 and April 5, 1802, *Stroganov*, II, 188; 199–201;
*VPR*, I, 188–189.
[46] Kochubei to S. R. Vorontsov, May 19, 1802, *AKV*, XVIII, 272; Kochubei
to Razumovskii, May 28, 1802, *Razoumowski*, II, Part 4, 305. Frederick William
first suggested the possibility to Alexander in his letter of Oct. 15, 1801 (*Friede-
rich Wilhelm*, p. 11), and more precisely in his letter of Jan. 13, 1802 (*ibid.*,
p. 14). Alexander expressed his interest in such a meeting in his reply Feb. 8,
1802 (*ibid.*, p. 15).

follow during the interviews proved to be little more than a formality.[47] Not enthusiastic about accompanying the emperor, Kochubei found his position more difficult during the visit because, for the most part, "The two sovereigns settled matters personally." Kochubei's attempts to advise the emperor had little effect, and in several instances caused Alexander to become annoyed with him. "In such a state of affairs, I am often reduced to silence," Kochubei complained.[48]

Unfortunately such was the state of affairs for most of the rest of his term as foreign minister. Although certainly not pleased with the situation, he adapted himself to the emperor's views and methods. Occasionally, when Alexander did not take a personal interest, Kochubei was left to make decisions and, with the emperor's approval, to execute them. Sometimes he found that Alexander would listen to his advice, but in other cases, Kochubei confided to a friend, "I find that, as in the time of Paul I, I am in the position of executing the orders which I am given, when those from whom I received them are not concerned whether or not they are reasonable." "What is more," he complained, "I am still reduced to saying, 'The emperor wants it thus.' And to the question, 'Why?' I am forced to reply: 'I know nothing about it; such is his supreme will.'"[49]

Continued disagreements over basic foreign policy heightened the difficulties, as Alexander inclined more toward an active involvement abroad. Further discouraged by the lack of progress in domestic reform, he was ready to turn his attention to foreign affairs. His bond of friendship with the Prussian monarch and their joint concern over the Napoleonic advances reinforced this, as did overtures from the British government. Kochubei, however, remained firm in his proposals for noninvolvement and continued to advocate a passive system of diplomacy. As an able administrator and a friend of Alexander's, Kochubei retained an important role in the conduct of Russian diplomacy, but his dis-

---

[47] Minutes of meeting of May 24, 1802, *Stroganov*, II, 229–230.
[48] Czartoryski, *Mémoires*, I, 294–295. Kochubei to S. R. Vorontsov, June 14, 1802, *AKV*, XVIII, 275–276.
[49] Kochubei to S. R. Vorontsov, July 30, 1802, *AKV*, XVIII, 281–282.

content with his position mounted. He had long been asking for transfer from the foreign ministry, and the emperor was growing more amenable to his request. "If you find that I am no longer in foreign affairs, do not be surprised," he wrote his friend Razumovskii, the Russian ambassador in Vienna; "for a long time this grace has been promised me and I have been pressing more than ever to have it effected." [50]

When Kochubei was finally relieved of his position in the foreign office after the ministerial reform of September 1802, he retained sufficient respect and confidence to be given the important post of Minister of the Interior, where he hoped to occupy himself with "reforms useful for the interior." In contrast to his feeling about the foreign office, he admitted, "I am happy enough in my place. It satisfies the soul by the good that one can often do for the Russian humanity, who suffers more than other peoples." [51] However high Kochubei's expectations may have been, his role in internal affairs proved to be of little more significance than in the College of Foreign Affairs.

Serving slightly less than a year as foreign minister, Kochubei's impact on the office was meager, although he was in a much more influential situation than his predecessor, Count Panin. Through his friendship with the emperor and his membership in the intimate circle of close advisers, Kochubei held a key position in the Russian government in the early years of the new reign. He shared some of the emperor's enthusiasm for liberal innovations and his zeal for reform measures, as he shared the responsibility for their failure. As the most vocal proponent among the emperor's young advisers of a foreign policy of isolation, Kochubei seemed to Alexander the natural spokesman for its implementation in the College of Foreign Affairs. And in general terms his policy prevailed throughout his year as foreign minister. But as the specific policies of the emperor and his chief diplomatic spokesman diverged, Kochubei was eclipsed. Satisfied

[50] Kochubei to Razumovskii, July 22, 1802, *Razoumowski*, IV, Part 4, 311–312.

[51] Kochubei to Razumovskii, Oct. 15, 1802, *Razoumowski*, IV, Part 4, 313–314.

neither with Panin's course of active involvement in European affairs at a time when domestic issues had loomed large, nor with Kochubei's proposals for passive withdrawal when the affairs of Europe seemed to beckon, Alexander was ready for a different policy and a different minister who would better conform to his current diplomatic outlook. The propitious occasion for change was the enactment of the ministerial reform of September 1802, which formally established the office of minister for foreign affairs. The simultaneous appointment of Count Alexander Vorontsov to the highest state office — that of state chancellor — and to the office of foreign minister portended an increased concern with European developments.

Alexander Romanovich Vorontsov brought to his new position the reputation of distinguished state service in the days of Catherine the Great. A member of one of Russia's most distinguished gentry families, he had begun his diplomatic career as minister to England during the brief reign of Peter III. Recalled to St. Petersburg by Catherine, he was named senator and later was made president of the College of Commerce. Disagreement with many imperial policies toward the end of Catherine's reign led to his retirement after the treaty of Jassy in 1791. In Czartoryski's words, "The length of his wise retirement," which lasted during Paul's entire reign, "added luster" to his reputation.[52] Unassociated with any of the difficult developments of Paul's reign, Vorontsov was quickly given a place in the Council of State when he returned to St. Petersburg in 1801.

Although praised for his "pre-eminence in knowledge, abilities, and zeal for public service" and for his combination of "a fine mind and wide knowledge with great industry," Vorontsov achieved his great reputation more from his general background and character than from any specific contributions to governmental administration of policy. Because it was "the time-honored experience of Count Vorontsov more than the intimate confidence of the emperor" that was "the real reason for his appointment as chancellor," Vorontsov was not in a position to exert

[52] Czartoryski, *Mémoires*, I, 300.

any significant influence over the course of Russian foreign relations during his term.[53]

Aptly described as a "bewigged figure from the age of Louis XV," embodying for some "the spirit and manners of a bygone era," Vorontsov at sixty nevertheless had the sympathy of the younger generation.[54] The emperor, almost forty years his junior and surrounded by young advisers, realized that the elder count Vorontsov lent dignity and respect to the regime. Never regarding Vorontsov as a close friend and often hesitating to consult him, Alexander became "entirely convinced, and with reason, that the presence" of Vorontsov in the senate, council, and committee meetings "maintained order and justice there more than his own." While many older courtiers and gentry saw him alone as "the true witness of the state," Czartoryski and the emperor's other young advisers felt Vorontsov to be definitely superior in knowledge and judgment to most of the older members of the government, perhaps because he was friendly and supported some of their ideas. "While he may be old, his ideas are young," Czartoryski remarked, "and he in no way holds on to old prejudices." [55]

In some ways, Czartoryski was right when he recognized that Vorontsov "was not at all opposed to certain liberal ideas" and "was prepared to accept and sustain them by his own disposition." Vorontsov had demonstrated his liberal tendencies through his close friendship with and protection of Radishchev. Disgusted by the policies of Paul I, he was closely associated with the Charter for the Russian People, which he hoped Alexander would issue on the occasion of his coronation; the Secret Com-

[53] Rogerson to S. R. Vorontsov, 1803, *AKV*, XXX, 204. "Imperator Aleksandr Pavlovich i ego dvor v 1804 g.," ed. F. F. Schiemann, *Russkaia starina*, XXIX (Dec. 1880), 809–810. Hédouville to Talleyrand, Nov. 28, 1802, *SIRIO*, LXX, 563.

[54] David Marshall Lang, *The First Russian Radical: Alexander Radishchev 1749–1802* (London, 1959), p. 253.

[55] Buturlin to S. R. Vorontsov, July 15, 1803, *AKV*, XXXII, 359; Stroganov set forth Czartoryski's remarks made in a meeting of the Secret Committee (July 27, 1801, *Stroganov*, II, 74). Alexander's hesitancy to entrust Vorontsov with great responsibility is also apparent in the minutes of this meeting. See also Czartoryski, *Mémoires*, I, 300–301.

mittee and the emperor, however, decided against it, proving Vorontsov to be more liberal in some respects than the young friends.[56]

Vorontsov's liberal leanings, however, hardly challenged the basic autocratic nature of the state or the institution of serfdom. He was all for overhauling the backward legal system and for reform that would obviate many of the administrative abuses in Russia, but his charter advocated liberties only for the gentry. He dreamed not of republics or popular rights, but of the rights, privileges, and economic protection of the Russian upper classes. With his eye on the proclamation of Peter III and Catherine's Charter of the Nobility of 1782, his ideal was a progressive monarchy limited by the powers and privileges of a cosmopolitan aristocracy, secure in their persons, property, and opinions, and free from the service requirements of Peter the Great's service state. Czartoryski recalled his saying that "he could imagine nothing wiser, or happier for himself and the country, than to be a grand seigneur such as had existed formerly in Poland, with the same rights and privileges." [57] During the first year and a half of Alexander's reign, Vorontsov was active in promoting such reforms, laying stress on strengthening the senate to provide a greater voice and political role for the gentry.

Despite his sympathy for such proposals as the never-promulgated Charter for the Russian People, Vorontsov often provided a moderating or restraining influence in the early years of the reign. As the Prussian representative aptly reported, "this minister, knowing the character, and even more the danger of changes or reforms accumulated too rapidly, has scant taste for novel innovations and favors principles sanctioned by time and by experience." [58] In his ideas, as in his actions, he seemed to pro-

---

[56] Czartoryski, *Mémoires,* I, 302–303. A brief account of some of the Secret Committee discussions of the Vorontsov-sponsored charter (July 27 and Aug. 4, 1801) is found in *Stroganov,* II, esp. 73–79. An English translation of the charter, edited by Marc Raeff, is printed in *Plans for Political Reform in Imperial Russia, 1730–1905* (Englewood Cliffs, N.J., 1966), pp. 75–84.

[57] Czartoryski, *Mémoires,* I, 300–303.

[58] Lusi to Prussian Foreign Office, Feb. 24, 1803 (copy), Papers of the Imperial Russian Historical Society, LOII, 113/17/90; Vorontsov's reform activities were also described in a dispatch sent by Lusi dated September 1802.

vide a stabilizing link between the young emperor and his immediate friends and the older, more conservative traditions of
Russia, a link which unfortunately could only strengthen the uncertain legacy from Catherine of enlightened despotism.

With regard to foreign policy, Alexander Vorontsov was
strongly concerned with upholding the dignity of Russia vis-á-vis
Europe, but was vague enough about what this entailed to es-
pouse a policy of moderation. "He had not approved of Catherine's ideas and inclinations to meddle in all the European affairs"
nor was he sympathetic to "those of Paul I to give himself without measure or calculation to adventurous enterprises." Vorontsov had not agreed with Panin's idea that Russia should play
"the grand role" in Europe; neither had he fully supported Kochubei's system of keeping Russia withdrawn. He did not want to
get Russia unduly involved in the struggle with Napoleon, but at
the same time did not want to sacrifice the honor of the empire.[59]

During the early months of his ministry, Vorontsov supported
a foreign policy quite similar to that of Kochubei; the British envoy reported that the Russian leaders were still strongly supporting the system of "withdrawing from all European connections,
and confining themselves entirely, for the present, to their internal concerns."[60] Very conscious of the economic, fiscal, and administrative problems in Russia, he wanted to keep the country
out of costly or disastrous wars on the continent. And with the
enactment of the ministerial and senatorial reforms of 1802, he
was eager to attend to their implementation rather than become
immediately involved in foreign enterprises. Like Kochubei he
had been suspicious of Alexander's apparent alignment with the
Prussian emperor at the Memel conference; the Prussian envoy
was concerned lest he turn out to be "nothing less than an enemy
of the common cause." But the truth of the matter, as the same
envoy perceptively sensed, was that Vorontsov was "a great patriot without any real dominating system." Fixing his attention

---

[59] From a statement of principles to the Austrian diplomat Hudelist, Hudelist
to Colloredo, No. 5, Nov. 9, 1802, HHS/Russ. II, 98; Lusi to Prussian Foreign
Office, Dec. 22, 1801 (copy), Papers of the Imperial Russian Historical Society,
LOII, 113/17/90.

[60] Warren to Hawkesbury, Nov. 27, 1802, PRO/FO 65/61.

"on the essential interests of Russia," although not always clear what those interests were, "he would like to assign an important and decisive role to his country in foreign affairs, but he wants to combine it with his love of peace and tranquillity." [61] Such a policy left adequate room for the hesitant moves the emperor was contemplating toward increasing Russia's involvement in European affairs.

The impasse reached in the efforts at domestic reform and the growing menace of Napoleon abroad worked together to turn Russian eyes toward Europe. As time went on and Napoleon advanced across the continent, Vorontsov perceived that the policy of withdrawal from European entanglements was not giving adequate "force and dignity" to Russian diplomacy.[62] The threat of French expansion diminished the hope of peaceful containment; Vorontsov, like the emperor, became more convinced of the necessity of war and abandoned his earlier hopes for rapprochement with France. For Vorontsov, the key to an anti-French coalition lay in a strong defensive alliance with England; in this he was strongly influenced by his brother Simon, then Russia's ambassador in London, and further backed by the emperor's young friends, who all looked to England rather than Prussia as Russia's staunch defender. In the early period of his ministry and in his previous advisory role, Vorontsov had not been any more responsive than Kochubei to English overtures for an alliance.[63] Renewed war between France and England in the summer of 1803 brought his anglophile sympathies to the fore, encouraged as they were by the commitment of his brother. Yet in the early fall, his strong feelings against Napoleonic France remained counterbalanced by the desire for moderation, making him hesitant about full-scale Russian involvement.[64]

[61] Lusi to Prussian Foreign Office, Oct. 22, 1802 (copy), Papers of the Imperial Russian Historical Society, LOII, 113/17/90.

[62] Czartoryski, *Mémoires*, I, 332–333.

[63] Harold Beeley, "A Project of Alliance with Russia in 1802," *English Historical Review*, XLIX (July 1934), 497–502, documents the early Russian rebuffs to English initiative.

[64] Goltz to Prussian Foreign Office, Oct. 1, 1803 (copy), Papers of the Imperial Russian Historical Society, LOII, 113/17/90. Vorontsov has often been associated with the so-called English party, although the French ambassador,

When Napoleon's demand for the recall of the Russian ambassador, Morkov, from Paris was accompanied by increased French threats in the Balkans and the Near East, Vorontsov in December 1803 more openly recommended an alliance with England, a move interpreted by some as the first step toward the Third Coalition.[65] By January 1804 there was no question about his position. He was prepared for Russian involvement in a new Europe-wide coalition against France and stressed the need to follow up overtures Russia had made to Denmark and Austria regarding their reactions to further French invasions. The failure of the royalist coup against Bonaparte, followed by the innocent slaying of the Bourbon prince, the Duke of Enghien, which put the Russian court into official mourning, reaffirmed Vorontsov's resolve against France. Continuing his pleas for a strong alliance with England during the summer of 1804, he spoke of such a policy as "giving soul and vigor to the coalition" which he believed Europe should form against Napoleon. In 1805 he was one of the most important supporters of the convention with Britain and firmly advised strengthening the Third Coalition.[66]

Although Vorontsov remained officially the foreign minister during the formation of the Third Coalition and strongly defended it until his death, he cannot be seen as its architect or engineer. By the fall of 1803 he was clearly only a figurehead in the foreign ministry. Indeed, even during his first year in office, he lent his name and prestige to the office more than he acted as an effective decision-maker. In part, Vorontsov's ineffective-

---

for example, reported that he was not "so completely sold out to the English" as his brother Simon (Hédouville to Talleyrand, April 24, 1803, *SIRIO*, LXXVII, 120–121).

[65] A. R. to S. R. Vorontsov, Dec. 2, 1803, *VPR*, I, 557–558; this letter was first published by John Holland Rose, *Napoleonic Studies* (London, 1904) pp. 364–367. See A. M. Stanislavskaia, *Russko-angliiskie otnosheniia i problemy sredizemnomor'ia, 1798–1807* (Moscow, 1962), pp. 339–340.

[66] A. R. Vorontsov, "Notices sur differens sujets-II," Jan. 26, 1804, CA 5531/IV. A. R. Vorontsov, "Rassuzhdeniia i primechaniia gosudarstvennogo kantslera grafa A. R. Vorontsova o nastoiashchikh obstoiatelstvakh Evropy i pokoliku oni Rossii kasatsia mogut, 1804," Aug. 4, 1804, *AKV*, XI, 474 (the original French text of this memorandum is preserved in TsGADA, 1261/1270). Czartoryski to S. R. Vorontsov, April 16, 1805, *AKV*, XV, 290; A. R. Vorontsov to Czartoryski, July 2, Aug. 5, and Sept. 25, 1805, *SIRIO*, LXXXII, 81–90, 97–102, 146–155.

ness resulted from his failing health. By the winter of 1803 his associates could suggest that "his health was better than it had been for the past couple of years," yet it was obvious that, despite his zeal and conscientiousness, he could not keep up the full routine which the job required, even with his great reliance on assistants.[67]

Unable to keep up with the basically slow pace of diplomatic life, he was not an effective reformer. Vorontsov had been active in drafting the reform of the ministries in 1802, but once in office after its enactment, he contributed little or nothing to its implementation. His brother Simon constantly urged him to try to effect major reform and innovations, and his nephew, Dmitrii Tatishchev, pressed for reorganization, definition of departmental functions, and limitation of the number of employees. Both had to conclude sadly that "the Chancellor is not interested."[68]

Vorontsov was not an innovator, nor did he attempt to impose any system on the course or methods of Russian diplomacy. Not afraid to express his ideas or recommendations, he might often press for their adoption, but with his weakened health and advanced years, he was rarely outspoken. Eager "to conserve his position and influence," suggested the Austrian ambassador, "he did not fear complying to assure one or the other."[69] His actual influence was mostly indirect and usually related to the means or details of handling a specific issue. By character and approach, he was a conciliator. Just as he tried to reconcile the youthful views of the emperor and his young advisers with Russian diplomatic traditions, so he tried to modify their impractical dreams. His strength — and in the long run his weakness — lay in his moderate resistance to change. As the Prussian envoy — himself suspicious of the radical tendencies of some of the rumored

---

[67] D. P. Buturlin to S. R. Vorontsov, March 6, 1803, *AKV*, XXXII, 330; D. P. Tatishchev to S. R. Vorontsov, March 25, 1803, *AKV*, XVIII, 356–357.

[68] Tatishchev to S. R. Vorontsov, April 23, 1803, *AKV*, XVIII, 358. In the memorandum on the reform of the ministry dated Berlin, Nov. 11, 1802, Simon Vorontsov outlined the program for a proposed eight-year institute to train young Russians of gentry origins and Orthodox faith for the diplomatic service (*AKV*, XV, 433–440); the covering letter, dated Nov. 15, 1803, is included in *AKV*, X, 177–178.

[69] Stadion to Colloredo, Sept. 10, 1803, HHS/Russ. II, 102.

projects — explained, Vorontsov was "perhaps the only one with
enough firmness and experience to maintain the edifice of which
the foundations are being undermined." [70] Socially content with
Alexander's restoration of the gentry's rights and privileges and
without the will to push for further reform, he only moved when
the system was threatened from without by the advances of Napoleon, and then he lacked the vigor to move effectively.

Vorontsov's personal failings contributed directly to the emperor's attitudes toward him, and they in turn further curtailed
his effectiveness. Like others who were associated with the chancellor, Alexander showed a measure of respect for Vorontsov, although he never regarded him as a close friend. Diplomats could
report with some authority in 1803 that "he was always consulted," even though his advice might not always be followed.[71]
Aside from his regular biweekly conference sessions, Alexander
often summoned him for advice, evidencing varying degrees of
confidence in his opinions.

To a large degree, Vorontsov's failure was the failure of an
older generation. Despite the praise of many admirers and the respect of the emperor, he was never able to make an effective
bridge with the younger generation. Vorontsov himself became
increasingly aware of how much "things were really being run by
the younger groups," [72] to whom Alexander listened more closely
than he did to his foreign minister. Most particularly, the emper-
or's close friend, Prince Adam Czartoryski, as assistant foreign
minister was as active in the conduct of diplomacy as the chancellor and was much closer to the emperor in confidence. While
Alexander continued handling the bulk of diplomatic affairs with
Vorontsov when the latter's health permitted, the emperor admittedly preferred working with Czartoryski.[73]

---

[70] Czartoryski, *Mémoires*, I, 300–301. Lusi to Prussian Foreign Office, Feb. 24,
1803 (copy), Papers of the Imperial Russian Historical Society, LOII,
113/17/90.

[71] Lusi to Prussian Foreign Office, Feb. 24, 1803 (copy), Papers of the
Imperial Russian Historical Society, LOII, 113/17/90.

[72] Rogerson to S. R. Vorontsov, 1804, *AKV*, XXX, 208–209.

[73] Buturlin to S. R. Vorontsov, July 15, 1803, *AKV*, XXXII, 359–360;
Czartoryski, *Mémoires*, I, 354–355.

Sensing the situation and conscious of his declining health, Vorontsov started pressing for leave before he had been in office a year. Yet Alexander, valuing the dignity that Vorontsov gave to his office, was reluctant to allow the retirement of such a respected and virtually irreplaceable chancellor. By character hesitant in such matters, Alexander procrastinated, preferring to ignore Vorontsov's requests. He wanted Czartoryski as his foreign minister but was aware of the opposition that the appointment of the Polish prince would arouse and the respect that the elder Vorontsov commanded. By the end of 1803, however, the chancellor's health definitely required his release from his duties. Yet, rather than let him retire completely, the emperor granted him "temporary leave" to return to his estates near Moscow. Retaining his post as chancellor and accompanied by several assistants from his office, Vorontsov remained the titular Minister for Foreign Affairs; important matters, and even many of the routine affairs, were to be referred to him.[74]

Before leaving St. Petersburg, Vorontsov dictated several memoranda for Czartoryski, who assumed the direction of the ministry — "ideas on the future, instructions of all kinds for Prince Adam, materials for important pieces in case they are necessary, and so forth." Czartoryski admitted, however, that he never had time to read all these instructions or the voluminous correspondence that Vorontsov sent him.[75] Vorontsov continued to have a great deal of respect for Czartoryski and wanted to maintain close ties with him even though he did not always approve of the measures recommended or adopted by the Polish prince. Sometimes Vorontsov's advice was both sought after and considered; but for the most part Vorontsov was quite justified

[74] Buturlin to S. R. Vorontsov, Nov. 25, 1803, and Feb. 25, 1804, *AKV*, XXXII, 386–388. Tatishchev (to S. R. Vorontsov, Nov. 28, 1803, *AKV*, XVIII, 362–364) noted the public's relief that Vorontsov was remaining as chancellor. The official circular announcing Vorontsov's leave was dated Feb. 10, 1804 (AVPR, Administrativnye dela, IV, 2, No. 3 [1804]).

[75] Buturlin claimed that he spent every evening for three weeks taking dictation from Vorontsov (to S. R. Vorontsov, Feb. 25, 1804, *AKV*, XXXII, 388); some of these memoranda are preserved among Czartoryski's family papers, C⁄ 5531/IV. Czartoryski, *Mémoires*, I, 352.

in his complaints that he was not always kept up to date on diplomacy and that his "recommendations, judging by the indifference with which they are received, are not really appreciated." [76]

In fact, when Vorontsov left St. Petersburg in February 1804, he retained little more than his title. "The chancellor on his estates imagines that he governs the foreign policy of our cabinet," wrote Kochubei. "He writes to Prince Adam, who, undoubtedly, writes him the most wonderful things in the world in reply, but does not really listen to him." [77] Although he continued to be consulted and although there were some rumors of his return toward the end of 1804, Count Vorontsov, until his death at the end of 1805, had little to do with the course of diplomacy.

Vorontsov's retirement brought considerable distress to contemporaries who were full of praise "for the success of our diplomacy since it has been in his hands." But such success, if indeed it can be called success, was only in the moderation with which the transition was made from a policy of withdrawal to a more active participation in European affairs. Foreign relations had been conducted with dignity and there was some truth in the claim of Vorontsov's nephew and assistant in his chancellery that credited him with preparing "the empire for a role which would cover it with glory and save Europe from the domination" of Napoleon.[78] But the credit goes for little beyond the preparation, for Alexander Vorontsov's importance as Russian foreign minister was relatively minor. The Prussian ambassador remarked with some foresight in January of 1804, "If formerly we could complain of too much slowness and irresolution, perhaps now there will be too much determination to fear." [79] With Vorontsov's retirement, Czartoryski was in a favorable position to try

[76] A. R. Vorontsov to Czartoryski, Sept. 25, 1805, *SIRIO*, LXXXII, 153. A. R. Vorontsov to Czartoryski, June 5, 1805, *SIRIO*, LXXXII, 38; see also Tatishchev to A. R. Vorontsov, June 22, 1804, *AKV*, XVIII, 381–383, and Czartoryski to S. R. Vorontsov, April 16, 1805, *AKV*, XV, 290.

[77] Kochubei to Razumovskii, April 15, 1804, *Razoumowski*, II, Part 4, 316.

[78] Buturlin to S. R. Vorontsov, July 15, 1803, *AKV*, XXXII, 361. Tatishchev to S. R. Vorontsov, Nov. 16, 1803, *AKV*, XVIII, 364.

[79] Goltz to Prussian Foreign Office, Jan. 19, 1804 (copy), Papers of the Imperial Russian Historical Society, LOII, 113/17/90.

his hand at bringing strength and determination to Russian foreign relations.

The rapid turnover of men directing Russian diplomacy in the early years of Alexander's reign in part reflects the hesitations and vacillations of a young sovereign in dealing with men and affairs for which he was unprepared. But the nature of the changes also suggests underlying patterns which are indicative of difficulties which beset the foreign ministry throughout the first quarter of the century.

On the level of policy, a casual observer might note that the shifts of foreign minister seem to coincide with changes of principal allies or commitments to specific major powers. Panin, who came into office at a time of reconciliation with England, had opposed Paul's Franco-Russian rapprochement and hence was a favorable negotiator for the Anglo-Russian convention. He left office after the convention with Napoleon in September 1801, which he heartily disapproved. Kochubei, much more a Francophile, who came into office on the heels of the French agreement, had been eager for a reconciliation with France and was in full sympathy with the September accord. He, in turn, left office a few months after the Memel interview, where he had outspokenly opposed Alexander's bid for friendship with the Prussian king and queen; at the same time he was reluctant about making firmer commitments to England. Vorontsov, brother of the long-term Russian ambassador to England, came into office ready and eager to strengthen the ties across the Channel. His premature retirement did not really break the pattern because his physical infirmity and death did not prevent the realization of his policy which was clearly continued by his successor.

Such a pattern of matching his minister to his current alliances is only one facet of his policy-making relationships. Throughout his reign Alexander was only superficially concerned with particular allies. More fundamentally, in this period he was shifting between active and passive involvement in foreign affairs and reacting to major domestic and international developments. He supported ministers not so much because of their sympathy or aversion to France, England, or Prussia, but because of their general accord and sympathy for his fundamental approach to foreign affairs at the time.

The ministerial changes do follow a pattern of shifts in general orientation towards continental involvement. Panin suited the early months of Alexander's reign because of his strong opposition to the potentially devastating foreign policies of Paul I. He symbolized a return to the grand policies of Catherine the Great for an energetic involvement in European affairs which seemed to coincide with the spirit of Alexander's first address after ascending the throne. But Panin's orientation soon proved to be quite out of step with the emperor's more developed views, as Alexander tried to steer a flexible middle course between France and the more determined anti-Napoleonic forces on the continent. Kochubei's appointment coincided with Alexander's determination to keep Russia from entangling continental involvements while concentrating on domestic reform; and Kochubei's interest in reform projects and his association with the Secret Committee established an appropriate and convenient relationship between the foreign and domestic aspects of this policy. Kochubei accordingly kept the position until the promulgation of the half-hearted reform measures of September 1802. In response to renewed pressures from abroad and to the disappointing outcome of the early reforms at home, Alexander again shifted toward increased involvement in continental affairs. That shift brought the appointment of a man who at once had been instrumental in the reforms and who was also eager for Russia to play a greater role in European affairs. Vorontsov's appointment, then, well fit the new Russian orientation toward moderately active continental politics.

While major shifts in policy were certainly crucial in determining appointments and tenure in the Russian foreign ministry, the experience of the first three men in the office also demonstrates problems of the personal nature of government at that time. Panin and Vorontsov were both hampered because they were not personally close to the emperor. Specific policy differences could also curtail the general effectiveness of foreign ministers who were unwilling to silence their divergent views. Panin found himself cut off from the emperor at the beginning of his disagreement over France; Kochubei was cut off after his objection to the Memel interview. In the former situation the disagreement was evidence of a more basic divergence of political attitudes, but in both cases Alexander was quite ready to turn to more sympathetic advisers. Yet even when Alexander was ready to appoint a new minister, the transition plagued him, and several months of activity were often lost while he vacillated and hesitated. Institutional difficulties, such as the lack of effective personnel, poor organization, and curious anomalies of rank and function — none of which were changed by the 1802 reform — were problems in themselves. More important, they magnified the personal dimension of the difficulties of any foreign minister.

Panin, Kochubei, and Vorontsov were all brought to power by their appropriateness or their willingness to serve as spokesmen for particular policies or approaches to foreign policy with which the emperor sympathized at particular times. They lasted as long as the policy lasted, but the successful implementation of a policy had scant reward. What success they had derived from their personal and intellectual accord with Alexander and their compliance with his political concerns. Their failures point the way to their successor: With Czartoryski, Alexander for the first time found a man whose personal and intellectual qualities suited him for success in the Russian foreign office.

## Chapter 4

# CZARTORYSKI: A SPOKESMAN FOR CONCERTED ACTION

The question of how much Russia should be involved in continental affairs continued to plague those responsible for Russian foreign policy. In 1804 and 1805 the issue was greatly affected by the growing challenge of Napoleon and by the rise to power in the Russian foreign ministry of a man completely committed to full-scale involvement on the continent.

Alexander's hopes for a pacified Europe, which would permit Russia to remain relatively uninvolved, had dimmed well before England abandoned the Treaty of Amiens and declared war on France again in May of 1803. Simultaneously, Alexander's hopes for thoroughgoing reform at home were being dashed by his country's seeming social and political intransigence. Hesitantly, his eyes were turning westward. The imperial interviews in Memel in 1802 had warmed ties of personal friendship and increased his emotional commitment to the fate of Germany; therefore, Napoleon's advances into Germany, with the occupation of Hanover, brought considerable alarm. Alexander was not fully sympathetic to the English refusal to surrender Malta and remained aloof when England met Napoleon's threatened invasion with a declaration of war. But when Russian interests in the Mediterranean were threatened — especially the recently consolidated protectorate of the Ionian Islands — Alexander became more alarmed. He was suspicious of Napoleon's grand plan to carve up the Ottoman Empire and had little sympathy for the grandiose fantasies of dividing the world with Russia which had won the approval of his father, Paul I.

Morkov, the Russian ambassador to France, had never been a close favorite of Alexander, but Napoleon's demand for his recall in the fall of 1803 appeared to be a direct insult. More serious, however, was the political murder of the Bourbon Duke d'Enghien in March 1804, which sent the Russian court into official mourning and made court circles more sympathetic to the cries of French émigrés. The proclamation of Napoleon as Emperor of the French in May further changed Alexander's earlier impression of him as a constructive reformer of European political systems. Clearly Alexander's cherished "balance of Europe" was threatened. The foreign stage beckoned to Alexander at a time when he was discouraged at the impasse in his domestic reform.

Alexander moved slowly toward involving his country in continental struggles, and most of his advisers at court were still opposed to such entanglements. The European political order was truly amiss, but he was not yet fully committed to the responsibility of righting it. The challenge of Napoleon remained remote from Russia, but foreign battles became a possibility in his mind as he came to realize that Napoleon's bids for continental hegemony must be contained. A grand coalition and visions of a reconstructed Europe had allure, but he was unwilling to commit Russian troops to the field if containment could take place through the encouragement of allies who were closer at hand. Alexander did not plan his moves in advance with experienced calculation, but the hesitations and vacillations with which he did move betrayed his feeling that war should result only if diplomacy failed. Even if it were necessary, it should not be a war of adventure or conquest, but a defensive war to restore order, stability, and peace to the continent.

From the standpoint of the continental powers which did at last join forces in 1805 against Napoleon, the Third Coalition was a disastrous failure. The British enjoyed an astounding victory at Trafalgar in October 1805, but this did little to prevent Napoleon's sweep across the continent. The battle of Austerlitz that December, one of Napoleon's greatest military triumphs, forced Russia to withdraw and made Austria accept the costly Treaty of Pressburg. A second round of hostilities the following year involving Prussia and Russia was to prove equally calamitous, and by 1807 Alexander himself felt forced to the conference table.

While the Third Coalition proved to be a military disaster, by its very existence it was a diplomatic success. The continental powers were neither eager nor prepared for joint action when it was formed. England was the nation which most wanted a coalition in the years immediately preceding it, but even William Pitt, who is sometimes viewed as the architect of the alliance, was not interested in deploying British military forces on the continent. However important British diplomatic support and subsidies were to be, undoubtedly Russia was the motive force in forming the coalition in 1804 and 1805. Yet even Alexander was only partly committed to joint military action. Alexander's acting foreign minister, Prince Adam Jerzy Czartoryski, stands out as the most important architect of the Third Coalition. The commitment of this Polish prince was more responsible than that of his sovereign for Russia's deep involvement in the continental struggle against Napoleon in 1804 and 1805. Czartoryski's plans for a reconstructed Europe were the starting point for negotiations; his attitudes developed the long-range aims of the coalition, and his diplomatic activity did most to unite the continental powers.

Prince Adam Czartoryski possessed all the most important attributes of a successful foreign minister under Alexander I: close personal friendship with the emperor, commitment to his general political views, and plans for Russian diplomacy which coincided with the emperor's current outlook. He presented a developed system for Russian foreign policy, which, however deep its fault of vague idealism, gave substance to the hopes and aims of his imperial protector. Because of the emperor's high personal regard and confidence in him, and because the emperor himself remained uncertain about the course of coalition, Czartoryski was given a degree of responsibility unusual under the government of Alexander I. But that much responsibility could quickly make its practitioner a scapegoat in time of failure. With the defeat of the coalition armies at the Battle of Austerlitz, Czartoryski became only a figurehead in the foreign office, with the emperor's confidence decisively revoked. Czartoryski's policy was later revived and vindicated, but by that time he was no longer in that office. Because of his major role in forming the Third Coalition,

he was one of the most significant foreign ministers to serve
Alexander; and because his ideas became so extensively incorporated into Russian foreign policy both at the time and later,
he was one of the most important diplomatic advisers of the
period. Hence, the implications of his ideas and the ambiguities
involved in his role reveal much about the central dilemmas of
Alexander's foreign policy and the conduct of Russian diplomacy.

Cosmopolitan reformist sentiments and strong Polish patriotism, the two most important elements in Czartoryski's political
outlook, were already apparent when he first went to Russia in
1795 at the age of 25. The very circumstances of his arrival suggested the latter, for he and his brother were there as hostages on
the order of Catherine II, following her final partition of Poland.[1]
Scion of one of the oldest, most prominent, and most patriotic
Polish families, which had been deeply involved in the struggle to
establish an independent constitutional government in Poland, he
was filled with malice by Catherine's treatment of his country
and by the impending confiscation of his family properties and
fortune.

Supplementing his education by private tutors, who included
the physiocrat, Dupont de Nemours, Czartoryski's wide travels
abroad gave him the varnish of a socially prominent, cosmopolitan aristocrat. They also imbued him with strong constitutional
hopes and reformist zeal. A winter "in close attendance at the
[French] National Assembly in the most brilliant days of Mirabeau" filled him with enthusiasm and left him "full of great expectations of happy changes in society." His lengthy sojourns in
Germany and Vienna had less effect on him than his year in
England, where as "a close attendant on the debates in . . .
Parliament," he had become a great "idolater of Fox," and a
strong admirer of the British system.[2] Whatever suspicions were
to arise later about his reformist views and his position as a

[1] As Czartoryski claimed in his *Mémoires*, I, 38–39.
[2] Dr. Currie to Thomas Creevey, Oct. 31, 1803, CA 5452/IV, printed in the
English edition of *Memoirs of Prince Adam Czartoryski and His Correspondence
with Alexander I* . . . , ed. Adam Gielgud (2 vols.; London, 1888), I, 50–51.

Roman Catholic and a Pole in the Russian foreign office, when he arrived in the final year of Catherine's reign he was welcomed by St. Petersburg society as befit such a prominent and attractive young prince.

Born in 1770, the young Prince Adam developed as a product of the European Enlightenment. His political attitudes were very much an outgrowth of the whole intellectual climate of late eighteenth-century Poland. The Polish milieu then was much enriched by the enthusiasm for Enlightenment ideas and the search for European learning by such political leaders as Czartoryski's cultured father in their desperate attempts to bolster the failing Polish political structure. Rousseau, for example, had sent the manuscript text of his *Considérations sur le gouvernement de Pologne* to the elder Czartoryski long before it was published, and undoubtedly Prince Adam was familiar with it. The penetration and discussion of Enlightenment ideas was furthered by the activities in Masonic circles, by the private circulation of texts of important writers, and the patronage or support of devotees of the Enlightenment as tutors for wealthy aristocratic youths and as unofficial advisers for Polish political leaders. Scippione Piattoli was such a figure; he had a large advisory role in Polish government circles in the early 1790's, served as tutor for a cousin of Czartoryski, and then accompanied the latter to Paris. Czartoryski formed a close attachment to him and credited Piattoli with having an extensive intellectual influence on him. It is not surprising that Piattoli was back at Czartoryski's side from late 1804 in St. Petersburg, as a political adviser and secretary.

Czartoryski's appointment as aide-de-camp to Grand Duke Alexander at the end of 1796 gave another dimension to his personal political outlook. "A devoted attachment was formed," wrote Czartoryski later, "which was never extinguished despite the many causes and sad misunderstandings that could have destroyed it." [3] Catherine favored their friendship, little suspecting the liberal sentiments and Polish sympathies that united her favorite grandson with Czartoryski. The personal dimension of the

[3] Czartoryski, *Mémoires*, I, 98.

relationship was complicated by Czartoryski's infatuation with Alexander's young wife, Grand Duchess Elizabeth, whom some biographers consider the first and only great love of his life. Suspicions of an affair between them were not relieved by the noted resemblance of Elizabeth's daughter, Maria Alexandrovna, to the Polish prince; the emperor, Paul, who considered Czartoryski a bad influence on his son anyway, banished him from Russia in 1799 by appointing him minister to the exiled Sardinian king. That the affair existed is well confirmed. The extent to which Alexander, who was beginning to turn his own amorous attentions elsewhere, actually gave his blessing to the liaison is more open to question; but undoubtedly it had important implications for the relationship between Alexander and his future foreign minister.[4]

The historical debate about the relative strength of the two friends in the course of their relationship, while not amenable to easy resolution here, points up the significant political dimension of their complex friendship. Alexander's personal regard and respect for Czartoryski were great. As grand duke and later as emperor, the young Alexander, who had never been abroad, was impressed to the point of envy by Prince Adam's learning and first-hand political experience, both of which were much more extensive than his own. He thought from the first that Czartoryski would be particularly helpful to him in bringing enlightened ideas to Russia. He admired Czartoryski's verbal ability and his capacity for developing and giving substance to vague political aims and was deeply influenced by his ideas. He depended on Czartoryski as a mentor in his most cherished projects, as an adviser for his reform efforts, and later as a capable diplomat to develop and implement his foreign policy. He counted on Czar-

[4] Varvara Nikolaevna Golovina, *Souvenirs de la comtesse Golovine, née Princesse Galitzine 1766–1821*, ed. K. Waliszewski (Paris, 1910), pp. 112–116; Alexander Sturdza, "Souvenirs du règne de l'empereur Alexandre Ier," *Oeuvres*, III, 98; Kukiel, *Czartoryski*, pp. 21–23. Although some of Czartoryski's letters to his family are destroyed, there are many references to his love affair in his letters from his sister Marie (esp. Feb. 19, Feb. 29 [1800], and July 4, 1800, CA ew XVII/823). Elizabeth's daughter, Maria Alexandrovna, was born May 29, 1799, and died Aug. 7, 1800, before Czartoryski returned to St. Petersburg.

toryski's support for his policies at home and abroad, and most particularly for his "favorite idea" of the regeneration of Poland.

Czartoryski, too, had a deep respect for Alexander and was greatly influenced by him. His regard for the emperor is apparent in the extent to which he considered Alexander "the only man in his empire capable up to a certain point of understanding the scope of [my] system and adopting its principles by conviction . . . or even by conscience."[5] In several instances, and particularly with reference to Poland, Czartoryski's faith in the benevolence and righteousness of Alexander's intentions went so far as to dull his political judgment. However well meaning Czartoryski's aims, his willingness to make Alexander the repository of his most important hopes for his country brought personal anguish and disastrous political consequences for Poland. Yet even later, when writing his memoirs of the period, Czartoryski was still unable or unwilling to tone down his deep admiration for the emperor whose personal friendship meant so much to him. The wholehearted sincerity with which he responded to the confidence Alexander often showed in him tended to blind him to the dissimulation with which Alexander might be following counterproposals behind his back; and it left him unprepared for the apparently swift reversals of policy with which the emperor was to act.

Czartoryski's devotion was returned by Alexander to a large extent, particularly in the early years when he was greatly dependent on Czartoryski's political help and guidance. Recalled to Russia as soon as Alexander took the throne, Czartoryski immediately became "the intimate and most confidential friend of the present Emperor of Russia." Although he held no official post before September 1802, he was one of the most active members of the Secret Committee and one of those most directly responsible for the early reforms. In retrospect he believed that he "more than all others" possessed "the full confidence of the emperor."[6]

Czartoryski's active participation in the foreign ministry began

---

[5] Czartoryski, *Mémoires*, I, 371–372.
[6] Warren to Hawkesbury, Jan. 4, 1803, PRO/FO 65/52. Czartoryski, *Mémoires*, I, 289–290, 156–158.

well before his appointment as assistant foreign minister in September 1802. Throughout his "apprenticeship" under Alexander Vorontsov, his own influence was often predominant; he took part in official conferences, edited protocols, and prepared dispatches and instructions.[7] Czartoryski sensed that the emperor actually preferred working with him and was often glad for the excuse of Vorontsov's illness. His idealistic plans for Russian diplomacy, which were set forth in his extensive memorandum "On the Political System to Be Followed by Russia (1803)," impressed the emperor, strengthening Alexander's "secret wish" to see Czartoryski "in charge of the department of foreign affairs." This wish was realized after Vorontsov retired to Moscow in February 1804, telling the emperor "that my adjunct, Prince Czartoryski, is in a fine position to direct the Department of Foreign Affairs during my absence; I recognize his capacity, knowledge, and zeal for your service." In deference to the elder statesman and perhaps also in response to the loud public outcry against his appointment, Czartoryski retained the title of Assistant Minister.[8] By the time of Vorontsov's death in December 1805, Czartoryski's fortunes were on the wane, what with the military reverses of the Third Coalition; although he remained in office until July 1806, he was never formally promoted.

The public protestations against him as a Pole and a Roman Catholic in charge of the Russian foreign office or against other aspects of Czartoryski's role and policies sometimes made his life difficult, but never in themselves limited his influence. Alexander assured him that he was "little bothered by clamors [which] are ordinarily only the effect of party spirit." He had no intention of letting critics who gossiped about Czartoryski's relations with

[7] For indications of Czartoryski's influence in the period see: Hédouville to Talleyrand, Jan. 20, 1803, *SIRIO*, LXXVII, 9–11; Nov. 28, 1802, *SIRIO*, LXX, 563–565; Kochubei to S. R. Vorontsov, Feb. 1, 1803, *AKV*, XVIII, 283–284; and Warren to Hawkesbury, Jan. 4, 1803, PRO/FO 65/52.

[8] Czartoryski, *Mémoires*, I, 355, 360–361, 323–324, 331–332. A. R. Vorontsov to Alexander I, Jan. 1, 1804, CA 5529/IV. Although some writers have claimed that Czartoryski was promoted to the rank of minister in February 1804, his signature on official documents remained "assistant," "adjunct," or sometimes "acting" minister.

the empress, about his suspected aspirations to the Polish throne, or about his supposed Jacobin tendencies and Anglophile sentiments deter him from working with a man who shared many of his views, enjoyed his friendship, and inspired his confidence. "It is necessary that I like those with whom I work," Alexander assured him; "only then can I give them my confidence." [9]

Alexander's respect for Czartoryski was not exceptional, for, from all reports, he was able to draw "the confidence of all the people who have had to deal with him." Some critics complained that he was "one of the most false and haughty men that exist," that he spent too little time at social functions, and that his reserve was indicative of a character as "cold as an icicle." [10] Personally, Czartoryski did have a certain contempt for the dissimulation of diplomatic life, and diplomats who came to deal regularly with him found him "in general more candid and open than many of the members of the Russian Administration." Even an ambassador who for political reasons was glad to see him leave the foreign ministry could not "refuse to recognize his talents, his straightforwardness, and his integrity." [11] His aristocratic style, his cosmopolitan manner and background, and his circumspection, which united "much learning with sound judgment" with the sensitivity of "a well-placed heart," gave contemporaries reason to believe he had "all the qualities requisite to the direction of the foreign ministry." [12]

Undoubtedly, Czartoryski was one of the ablest and most in-

[9] Alexander to Czartoryski, 1806, Czartoryski, *Mémoires*, II, 159. For a sample of the opposition to Czartoryski, see Maria to Alexander, April 30, 1806, *Russkii arkhiv*, XLIX (1911, No. 1), pp. 138–140; Hudelist to Colloredo, Jan. 7, 1803, HHS/Russ. II, 100; and "Journal du Colonel Baron de Stutterheim pendant sa mission à St. Petersburg," Nov. 11, 1804, and Jan. 13, 1805, HHS/Russ. II, 138.

[10] Stedingk to Baron d'Ehrenheim, June 20, 1806, Stedingk, *Mémoires*, II, 179. Hudelist to Colloredo, Jan. 7, 1803, HHS/Russ. II, 100; Maistre to Rossi, March 1807, Maistre, *Mémoires*, p. 268.

[11] Warren to Hawkesbury, No. 66, Dec. 2, 1803, PRO/FO 65/53. Merveldt to Stadion, June 28, 1806, HHS/Russ. II, 110. For an example of Czartoryski's biting contempt for diplomats, see his *Essai*, p. 6.

[12] Rogerson to S. R. Vorontsov, April 30, 1804, *AKV*, XXX, 214; Stedingk to King Gustav IV, April 21, 1806, Stedingk, *Mémoires*, II, 163; "Imperator Aleksandr Pavlovich i ego dvor v 1804 g.," ed. F. F. Schiemann, *Russkaia starina*, XXIX (Dec. 1880), 811.

fluential ministers to serve Alexander I. Despite his active interest
and proposals for further administrative reform, he was not the
man — if such a man existed then — to overcome the difficulties
of the Russian bureaucracy.[13] His contributions came rather from
the intellectual stance and creativity he brought to Russian foreign policy. Like Alexander I, Czartoryski was a sensitive individual with strong personal commitments and high ideals, with
great pride and self-righteous indignation toward many of his
contemporaries and the political developments of his period.
And, like the emperor, he had a great difficulty in combining
those ideals with the realities of political life.

Czartoryski's general political attitudes were exceedingly
vague and eclectic; in general they were based on an abstract
strain of rational moralism, apparent in some of his early memoranda and developed later in the 1820's in his more extensive
and reflective *Essai sur la Diplomatie.* The political systems he
wanted to introduce on both domestic and international fronts
were predicated on that morality and justice — "the eternal type
given to our soul" — which were within reach of all men and nations, provided there would be the necessary "augmentation and
dispersal of enlightenment and civilization." Such enlightenment,
it followed, was to be one of the prime functions of government
along the road toward the progressive perfection of man, nation,
and international society. The object, he admitted in 1803, might
never be attained, but "we must be capable of conceiving such an
object in order to progress." Too often "in our imperfect society," he explained, "the general well-being is continually forgotten." But men, no less than nations, must come to realize that
"individual self-interest demands working for the good of all."

---

[13] Czartoryski to S. R. Vorontsov, Aug. 18, 1804, *AKV*, XV, 248. Tatishchev
reported to A. R. Vorontsov that "the first weeks showed [Czartoryski] his mis-
take [in relying heavily on the chancellery]. Seeing that he was obliged to redo
three-quarters of their work, he came to me, not being able to get along alone;
since then we have divided everything that is of some importance" (March 16,
1804, *AKV*, XVIII, 369). Czartoryski's suggestions for reform include "Projet
d'organisation d'une Chancellerie pour le ministre des affaires étrangères"
(1804), CA 5226/IV, and "Vues sur la formation d'un conseil privé de cabinet
qui ont été presentés à S. M. I. et discutés avec Elle" (1806), CA 5228/IV.

Czartoryski and the young emperor shared common "faith in the final success of justice and liberty." [14]

Czartoryski believed domestic reform and economic modernization to be a prerequisite to international stability. "The general well-being of the inhabitants" he considered to be the "supreme law" for internal politics in all states and the only real guarantor of "perpetual peace." More practically, he believed that eventually every country needed "a free constitution founded on a solid basis." [15] Czartoryski's constitutionalism, like the emperor's, remained exceedingly amorphous, sometimes amounting to little more than a vague alternative to despotism. He was much more an "enlightened" or "liberal" aristocrat than a thoroughgoing democrat and was quite ready to admit the advantages of enlightened constitutional monarchy. In fact, he never really questioned the desirability of preserving the Russian imperial autocracy or the traditional Polish kingship. Republics — especially aristocratic republics — he reasoned, might eventually be possible in some instances, but his and Alexander's republican dreams of the 1790's suffered "a cruel deception" as "the cycle of empire chilled and turned away the warmest partisans" of the revolution that had shaken France. Regarding England as "the model nation" with respect to its "domestic constitution" and its commercial development, he was very critical of the inadequacies of the Russian government. He believed, however, that Russia was not ready for the popular, elective government of which Alexander had dreamed. In the early days, he was one to "moderate the extreme opinions of the grand duke"; later, however, it was Czartoryski who was disappointed by the lack of content in Alexander's liberal declarations and his abandonment of reform projects.[16]

Something of a political relativist, Czartoryski stressed that the form of government had to vary according to the nation in-

[14] Czartoryski, *Essai*, p. 121. Czartoryski, "Système," fol. 24. Czartoryski, *Mémoires*, I, 99.

[15] Czartoryski, "Système," fols. 23–24, 129.

[16] Czartoryski, *Mémoires*, I, 99. "La politique de Grande Bretagne, mémoire presenté au cabinet anglais en faveur de la Pologne," Puławy, Sept. 9, 1813, Wawrzkowicz, *Sprawa Polska*, p. 324. Czartoryski, *Mémoires*, I, 102–103, 344–345.

volved. Just as he thought the Poles "must be granted a government conforming to their wishes and ancient laws," so he made it clear that the future forms of government in those states subjected to Napoleon were "to conform to their own wishes and best interests." In his Novosiltsev instructions, however, there was no guarantee that the individual countries would, or even should, have the final word in determining "their best interests," since England and Russia together were to assume advisory, if not actually supervisory, roles.[17]

Political stability was extremely important to Czartoryski. The social upheaval of the French Revolution remained strong in his mind, and even his early admiration for Mirabeau waned. "It is a question of the struggle between peoples and governments; and what is most important for any government is its own conservation." [18] Reform and constitutional safegards would be a stabilizing force, but change must come gradually under careful supervision and must be dictated by reason, he believed.

Czartoryski's rationalist ideals extended to his conception of international order. His proposals, far-reaching and futuristic as they might seem, came as a direct response both to Napoleon's empire and to the eighteenth-century partitions of Poland, as he sought immediate ways to rectify these wrongs and to prevent similar developments in the future. He thought of Europe in terms of a cosmopolitan society of nations whose individual strivings could and should be held in check by a rational balance of power. In his reflective writings about European politics he espoused the Enlightenment ideal of perpetual peace and regarded the European community abstractly in geopolitical terms. Just as civil government had removed indviduals from the "state of Nature," so he hoped for the day when the triumph of reason in diplomacy would remove the individual nations from the mutually distrustful and hostile "state of Nature" which characterized in-

[17] "Mémoire sur la nécessité de rétablir la Pologne pour prévenir Bonaparte," Dec. 5, 1806, Czartoryski, *Mémoires*, II, 153–154; "Instructions secrètes à M. de Novosiltzow," Sept. 23, 1804, *VPR*, II, 140–142; Russian direction of new constitutions in other countries was also suggested in the 1803 memorandum, "Système," fol. 129.

[18] Czartoryski, "Système," fols. 95–96.

ternational relations. Although only sketched out there in a few lines, his proposals are most often discussed on the basis of the famous "Novosiltsev instructions" of 1804, in which he spoke in terms of a "European federation" and recommended the formation of "a league, the stipulations for which, so to speak, would form a new code of international law, which, sanctioned by most of the states of Europe, would become without difficulty the immutable rule for the conduct of cabinets" and which would "guarantee the highest possible degree of peace and security to governments."

He singled out Russia and England — since an alliance between them was being considered in 1804 — as the paternalistic guides for the rearrangement of Europe after the defeat of Napoleon. An avid spokesman for national self-determination, he nevertheless believed that a multitude of small nations would be unable by themselves to maintain their viability within the general European power structure. Accordingly, he recommended that they be organized into regional federations, for example in the Balkans, Italy, and Germany, and that they be given the protection of larger states. Specifications for these regional groupings varied in different memoranda and changed somewhat with European developments. In some cases, as in a Russian protectorate for the Balkans, he recommended that the entire federation be put under the protection of a neighboring great power. Such attempts to overcome power vacuums in Europe, he argued, would help reestablish a "natural equilibrium" among the great powers. In connection with these rearrangements, he also stressed the need for establishment of national boundaries on natural frontiers, freedom of commerce, political liberalization, and economic development, particularly in the more backward nations.[19]

Czartoryski developed his ideas for international reorganiza-

---

[19] "Instructions secrètes à M. de Novosiltzow," Sept. 23, 1804, *VPR*, II, 138–146. Many of these ideals were originally set forth in 1803 in his "Système," *passim*. He presented additional plans for regional federations in a memorandum at the end of 1806, "Article pour l'arrangement des affaires de l'Europe à la suite d'une guerre heureuse," Czartoryski, *Mémoirs*, II, 62–66 (this published version misdated the memorandum 1804; see the explanation by Kukiel, *Czartoryski*, pp. 80–81, and *VPR*, II, 665, n. 79).

tion more fully much later in his almost forgotton *Essai sur la Diplomatie*, published anonymously in 1830. The rambling treatise shows all the signs of his profound discouragement and bitterness at his own ineffectiveness and at the conservatively repressive aftermath of the Vienna settlements. His proposals to remedy what he termed "the deplorable state of international relations" were presented through an idealized discussion of the "Grand Design of Henry IV," a seventeenth-century French proposal usually attributed to Henry's minister Sully which had been revived and discussed by several eighteenth-century writers with whom Czartoryski was acquainted. Czartoryski looked forward to compulsory arbitration of international disputes by a permanent and responsible deliberative assembly to whose decisions nations would be morally obliged to submit voluntarily. He concluded that the Grand Design would produce such beneficial results that "Christian morality would thus establish itself on earth and inaugurate a diplomacy founded on justice, constant in its principles and its relations." [20]

Alexander was profoundly influenced by Czartoryski's ideals and shared his hopes for a morally regulated European community in his own plans for the reconstruction of Europe after Napoleon. But the emperor's mystical leanings at the time of the 1814/1815 settlements and the Holy Alliance gave his proposals a religious cast and transformed Czartoryski's early plans in such a way that they had little effect in the arena of power politics. Yet the similarity in aims of the Holy Alliance and Czartoryski's later version of the Grand Design shows a common advocacy of a Christian commonwealth and a basic strain of utopianism which they were unable to translate into meaningful political action. Czartoryski has often been taken out of his early-nineteenth-century context and praised as a forerunner of Woodrow Wilson and an apostle of twentieth-century attempts at international organization; but it is doubtful that Wilson had ever heard of Czartoryski's plan or that the League of Nations owed more to Czartoryski than it did to their common eighteenth-century an-

---

[20] Czartoryski, *Essai*, p. 328, *passim*.

cestors. In many ways, Czartoryski's ideas appear to be eclectic borrowings from a variety of intellectual currents of his day, poorly synthesized into constructive proposals for the contemporary international realities.

Although moralistic cosmopolitan ideas were important in Czartoryski's foreign policy, his views were impregnated, too, with a developed national consciousness. Czartoryski may have had altruistic ideals for Russian foreign policy and visions of a rational international order, but his emotional commitment to the Polish cause put him in an extremely vulnerable position as Russian foreign minister and left him historically a most controversial figure. At the time and since, his Polish background aroused Russian uneasiness. Obversely, among the Poles his service to a Russian tsar immediately made him an object of suspicion. Subsequent historians have both used him as a convenient scapegoat for the hardships of the Russian annexation and eulogized him as a legendary hero in the tragic struggle for Polish independence. The ambiguities of his position and his ideas give a grain of truth to both interpretations.

Czartoryski believed, as he wrote in 1803, "Every individual nation has its own language, its mores, its habits, its manner of seeing and feeling; real mutual knowledge of understanding is impossible between them. Hence foreign domination is unsuitable for any nation . . . and is contrary to the natural equilibrium of things." The guarantee of national self-determination, he stressed, was a crucial element in the improvement of society and the attainment of permanent international peace and welfare. In the abstract, he condemned that form of patriotism that might degenerate into national egotism or aggressiveness and deplored "the self-aggrandizing tendencies that had been the pattern of many strong nations in the past and present." Nevertheless, national feelings and national pride were so important that "government, being in charge of public education, must especially try to mold character, to form national self-esteem, to form a sacred respect and an inalterable attraction for the national heritage and practices," he wrote in 1805, echoing Rousseau's proposals for the extension of Polish national consciousness.[21] But Czartoryski went beyond Rousseau's appeal or his own Polish patriotism. His very criticism of the Polish partitions as being "contrary to the fundamental laws of European society" suggests the rationalist basis for his ideas of the right of national self-determination. Later his legalistic basis was phrased in terms of divine law, as he suggested that "the division of nations is, so to speak, of divine institution, because it took place under the pure and spontaneous reign of natural law." [22]

Czartoryski's general sympathy for national aspirations grew directly from his devotion to the Polish cause, which throughout his life was central to his political motivation. "My first duties toward my country are evident, and when a choice is necessary, that must take priority," he admitted to Russian friends in 1812; and there is no doubt that he felt that way throughout his Russian service. He wrote in 1810, "No one, I believe, loves his country with more fervor than I. . . . To do good for my country is the only glory that can satisfy me." [23] From the first, he clearly believed that accepting service to Alexander and the Russian state would advance the interests of his own people. His earlier ties of friendship with the grand duke were founded on Alexander's assurances of his deep sympathy for the Poles and his indignation about his grandmother's partitions. Czartoryski's own reaction to the lot of Poland strengthened Alexander's resolve, and there is no doubt that Alexander gave Czartoryski good reason to hope for the improvement of Polish affairs to the point of eventual restoration of independence.[24] Czartoryski's ex-

[21] Czartoryski, "Système," fols. 123–124. Czartoryski, "Dangers des innovations à introduire," 1805, CA 5227/IV. Czartoryski's familiarity with Rousseau's treatise, "Considérations sur le gouvernement de Pologne," is noted in an introduction by the editor, C. E. Vaughan, *The Political Writings of Jean Jacques Rousseau* (Oxford, 1962), II, 424.

[22] Czartoryski to Stroganov and Novosiltsev, July 4, 1812, draft, CA 5516/IV; Czartoryski, *Essai*, pp. 157, 175.

[23] Czartoryski to Stroganov and Novosiltsev, July 4, 1812, draft, CA 5516/IV, fols. 105–106. "Zapiska kniazia Adama Chartoryzhskogo," June 20, 1810, *Russkii arkhiv*, XIV (1876, No. 1), p. 427. Some of the pro-Polish passages in his memoirs (e.g., *Mémoires*, I, 208) can be seen as attempts at self-justification against the criticism that he had done little for the Polish cause in Russia.

[24] Czartoryski, *Essai*, p. 86. *Mémoires*, I, 96.

pectations are shown in his 1803 memorandum on Russian foreign policy, where he argued on humanitarian grounds that the regeneration of Poland, "assured by justice," was "in the interest of the general peace and welfare." He further argued that the partitions were against what he saw as the Russian national interest. The basic principles which he advocated for Russian diplomacy would not "allow for Poland to remain partitioned as it is at present under foreign domination and with its commerce in the hands of the King of Prussia." At that point he suggested that Grand Duke Constantine be made king of an independent, reintegrated, and constitutional Poland, much to his regret later when Constantine actually did become Alexander's Polish viceroy.[25] Alternatively he hinted at a Russian protectorate or eventual annexation.

Czartoryski soon gave up the hope of complete independence for Poland and turned to the eventually disastrous policy of the reunification of Poland under a Russian protectorate, with Alexander I assuming the Polish crown. "Russia alone, through the goodness of her sovereigns and by enlightened policies, will be able to render domination decidedly preferable to the two other [partitioning powers]." [26] Czartoryski's proposal had little to do with self-interest; he undoubtedly hoped for a high office under the Russian kingship, but his political future in Poland hardly needed Russian support. His policy — the policy Alexander firmly adopted — stemmed on one hand from his fear that Poland would not prove strong or politically stable enough to win or to maintain its independence. "Complete independence is without a doubt the greatest good which can come to a nation," Czartoryski explained to Stroganov in 1811, "but when it is probable that it could never be attained, an intermediary existence such as an associated kingdom with its own laws and constitution should be readily accepted, especially when through this means many of the evils, calamities, and difficulties could be avoided

---

[25] Czartoryski, "Système," fol. 128, fols. 83–84. The proposal for Constantine's kingship had been discussed in Poland at the end of the eighteenth century.

[26] Czartoryski, "Idée sur l'avenir de la Pologne vis-à-vis de la Russie" [1806], CA 5231/IV, fols. 37–40.

and the major aspects of its goals could be obtained on a sounder and more assured basis." [27]

Second, and with equal importance, Czartoryski's policy stemmed from his sincere faith in Alexander's beneficent intentions towards the Poles. "Indeed, gentlemen," he wrote in a circular letter to Polish leaders in 1807, "the hope of placing Poland once again among the nations, which seemed entirely a lost cause, can now be revived. Its greatest support is in the sentiments that lead our August Monarch. For a long time he has nourished in the depths of his heart the desire to spread among the Polish nation, this illustrious and interesting branch of the great family of Slavs, all the prosperity for which it has the right to hope." His proposal was made with an eye also to the Russian advantage, however, and he rightly sensed that the plan was much to Alexander's liking. As he explained to his father after leaving Russia in 1806, all his efforts were directed toward arousing support for the reunion of Poland with Russia, because this project "is the only one that all my compatriots could rationally desire, because it is the only one that is possible in the present and sound for the future. . . . It combines the glory of the emperor and advantages for Russia with the welfare of poor Poland." [28]

The extent to which Czartoryski was actually pursuing Polish interests during his service in Russia has always been debated. Although his hopes for Poland were the single strongest element in his political motivation, Czartoryski's Polish concerns were never any real detriment to his service to the Russian emperor. Czartoryski himself, aware of the possible division of his loyalties, had been extremely hesitant to accept the ministerial post in the first place. Once in office, he went out of his way to consider policies from a Russian or even a general European standpoint. Czartoryski never used the negotiations for the Third Coalition

[27] Czartoryski to Stroganov, April 2, 1811, Stroganov Papers, TsGADA 1278/162.

[28] Czartoryski, "Circulaire du Prince à quelques personnes éminentes de Pologne," 1807, CA 5231/IV, fol. 127. Czartoryski to his father, July 16, 1807, CA ew XVII/819.

merely to advance the reunification of Poland. He had reason to suspect that such a development could most easily result from a successful war against Napoleon. He would have liked to see a Polish kingdom proclaimed in 1805, but his political motivation for anti-Napoleonic campaigns went deeper. His Polish goals had only marginal effect on the success — or, rather, failure — of the Third Coalition. It was really only after the defeat of the allies in the battle of Austerlitz, when he realized that his days in the Russian foreign office were numbered, that Czartoryski started pressing openly for Alexander's proclamation of a kingdom of Poland. At that time neither Prussia nor Austria was strong enough to object, and Czartoryski rightly feared that Napoleon's move across the continent might result in a French effort to gain the support of the Poles against Russia. In case of further war, he queried, "Must not the sovereign of Russia immediately declare himself King of Poland, in order to increase his forces and prevent further means to Bonaparte" [29] Despite Czartoryski's hopes and entreaties, Alexander failed to follow his advice on any of the likely occasions which arose before the Congress of Vienna.

Czartoryski's contributions toward political independence for Poland were negligible before 1815. With tragic irony, the growing pressures he exerted on the emperor resulted finally in Alexander's ill-fated demand for the Polish crown in 1815. Czartoryski's faith in Alexander's benevolent intentions proved to be politically naïve; for "benevolent intentions" figured little in the subsequent Russian government of Poland. The Kingdom of Poland which emerged from the Congress of Vienna was a sad tribute to Czartoryski's hopes; it brought more limitations of Polish

---

[29] Czartoryski, "Questions," May, 1806, CA 5228/IV (another copy is in the Stroganov Papers, TsGADA 1278/1/41, dated May 4, 1806). See also "Mémoire sur les déterminations à prendre d'après les dernières ouvertures de l'Angleterre," June 4, 1806, CA 5228/IV, fols. 201–202; "Mémoire sur les mesures à adopter dans la position actuelle de la Russie," Nov. 23, 1806, CA 5229/IV; and "Mémoire sur la nécessité de rétablir la Pologne pour prévenir Bonaparte," Dec. 5, 1806, Czartoryski, *Mémoires*, II, 148–158. Elsewhere Czartoryski counseled holding off the declaration until the end of the war or until steps could be taken to prepare the Poles: Czartoryski, "Mémoire representant le tableau de l'Europe et proposant la marche à suivre," Part 2, Sept. 3, 1806, CA 5229/IV, and "Mémoire sur les mesures à adopter relativement aux provinces çi-devant polonaises," 1806, Czartoryski, *Mémoires*, II, 178–182.

liberties and more repressive measures against nationalist sentiment than it did constructive steps toward a reconstituted nation.
His well-intended political efforts brought only personal disappointment and the severe criticism of man of his countrymen,
whose suspicions of their Russian neighbor confirmed time and
time again by the policies and practices of Alexander's administrators and even more by those of his successors.[30] Czartoryski's
contributions to Polish interests in the educational and cultural
realm in his concurrent position as curator of the University of
Vilna, and as director of educational policies in the Polish western provinces of the Russian Empire, proved much more successful. But he could well lament that "the consolation of having
done some good" for his people was offset by the deeper regret of
"never seeing the realization of the object of all my hopes." [31]

The difficulty with Czartoryski's Polish policy stemmed from
his willingness to make a conjunction between Polish welfare and
the Russian national interest inherent in a Russian protectorate.
It stemmed from his failure to differentiate between the emperor's
benevolent concerns and the realities of Russian government or
to recognize the explosive potential of a Russian-controlled Poland. That he thought reason and justice could overcome the
emotional strife between Russian and Pole, the absolutism of
Russian government, or the expansionist tendencies in Russian
foreign policy showed him to be a child more of the eighteenth
than the nineteenth century. His Enlightenment idealism was out
of tune with his Polish patriotism; and his background of cosmopolitan aristocracy set him apart from the militant nationalism
of the later nineteenth century. It is little wonder that his policy
was satisfactory neither to aggressive Russian expansionists nor
to ardent Polish patriots.

Czartoryski's general foreign policy showed the same unsuccessful floundering between abstract ideals and political realities.
His concepts of Christian morality, justice, and perpetual peace
were closely in keeping with the hopes of Alexander I, who

[30] See especially his letters to Alexander from 1815 to 1823 in Czartoryski,
*Mémoires*, II, 331–394, and his comments in his *Essai*, pp. 215–219.

[31] Czartoryski, *Mémoires*, I, 289.

prided himself on humanitarian and pacifist sentiments and nurtured a sense of his own mission, but they were out of step with the political passions of the early nineteenth century. What could be more politically appealing than Czartoryski's proposal that Russia "adopt great, just, benevolent, and peaceful diplomatic policies, conforming to both her position and power . . . forming a system in which the necessity of employing the force of inertia or action would be regulated by coordinating the principles of her own defense with that of the general welfare of nations"? Russia in Czartoryski's expression was thus to serve as "the arbitrator of peace for the civilized world"; Alexander's reign, he hoped, "would inaugurate a new era in European relations"; the aim of her sovereign was to be none other than "to give peace, happiness, and independence to the states of Europe and to assure his empire of the primary glory of having been the source and the instrument of advantages accorded to all." [32] Czartoryski believed that "a country accustomed to the continual success of Catherine and the irregularities of Paul could not be content with an inferior or insignificant role," despite the internal advantages which might thereby accrue; but "the Russian craving for glory and supremacy" should be used "for the general benefit of mankind." [33] Czartoryski really was criticizing Kochubei's system and advocating a more extensive Russian involvement in continental politics than under Kochubei or even Vorontsov. The high-sounding but basically sincere moralistic phraseology of his proposals made them infinitely appealing to Alexander I.

The basic difficulty in Czarotryski's foreign policy stemmed from the ambiguities which arose in the implementation of his idealistic statements. His whole foreign policy seems to have rested on the questionable premise that a great role for Russia would or could be a moral role. It may have conformed to the emperor's own hopes, but it was dangerously utopian, especially in the face of the Russian expansionism advocated by those very circles most critical of having a Pole in the Russian foreign office.

[32] Czartoryski, "Système," fols. 51, 122.
[33] Czartoryski, *Mémoires*, I, 367–370. His lofty ideals were also developed in his "Projet d'une instruction générale à donner au Ministère des Affaires Étrangères," 1803, CA 5226/IV.

While annexation and subsequent repressive Russification was the sorry result of his utopian scheme for a great and moral role for Russia in Poland, in his views on the Balkans lay the seeds of Russia's century-long, disastrous embroilment in the Eastern Question.

The premises of his Balkan policy were similar to those of his Polish policy, combining all the usual arguments for Russia's assuming a predominant role with moralistic concern for the liberation of suppressed nationalities. His consideration of policies toward the Ottoman Empire involved him in a common Russian ambivalence. On one hand he argued that "the Turks must indeed be chased out of Europe. . . . Humanity demands it with loud cries; the cause of civilization requires it, and they themselves are not in a state to prevent it." And yet he recognized the political advantages of avoiding the complete dismemberment of Turkey. Even if the Ottoman Empire were to be maintained, however, Russia still had legitimate grounds for offering protection to her coreligionists in the area. But Czartoryski was not content just to advocate the carrying out of existing treaty provisions for religious protection; he favored carving out a far-reaching Russian protectorate over the Balkan areas, not unlike a Russian kingdom of Poland. "What is certain," he argued, "is that no other European power must establish posts there."[34] His idealistic reasoning was clear when he recommended that the Danubian principalities of Moldavia and Wallachia should no longer be subject to Turkish rule; but his ideals too obviously camouflaged selfish Russian interest, as he argued that these areas be incorporated directly into the Russian Empire. Czartoryski regretted that during his ministry he could not see the realization of this project whereby "so many people who suffer under the weight of tyranny and misfortune, notably the two principalities," might be rescued in a way "so happy for humanity and advantageous for Russia."[35]

[34] Czartoryski, "Système," fols. 85–89, 122–128. He did add (fols. 88–89) that Austria might have to be given compensation for the Russian protectorate.

[35] Czartoryski to C. Ypsilanti, July, 1806, *Corespondenta lui Constantin Ypsilanti cu guvernul rusesc 1806–1810, pregătirea eteriei și a renașterii politice românești*, ed. P. P. Panaitescu (Bucharest, 1933; Aşezământul cultural ion C.

The same conjunction of idealism and Russian expansionism characterized his arguments for a Russian protectorate for Greece and a South Slavic federation. In 1803 his goal sounded benign enough when he suggested that "the sovereign of Russia must be the Protector of all these little states, their assured refuge, the creator of their union and of their strength, and when they have attained these, their constant friend." [36] But by 1806 his proposals for Russian inroads sounded more menacing: in the event of a dismemberment of European Turkey, he explained in one of his many memoranda on the subject, "the mass of the Turkish countries in Europe must be divided into separate States, governed according to their localities and joined by a common federation, over which Russia could assure itself of a decisive and legal influence by means of the title of emperor or protector of the Slavs and of the Orient to be granted to His Imperial Majesty." This exclusive influence would be established, Czartoryski continued, through "the part which the Russians will have taken in the deliverance of these countries, through their common religion and common origin, through the able choice of posts which would be occupied by our troops, and through well understood policies." [37]

Although this type of statement has led some scholars to claim that Czartoryski "initiated the first Panslavist policy of Russia in the Balkans" and although he did use many of the arguments later associated with that movement, Czartoryski was not a real Panslavist.[38] His plans are much more in line with the grandiose

---

Bratianu, Vol. 20), p. 27; see also, "Mémoire sur les moyens qui peuvent concourir à terminer la guerre actuelle entre la Russie et la Porte," April 5, 1806, CA 5229/IV, and Czartoryski to Alexander, April 1806, in Czartoryski, *Mémoires*, II, 105.

[36] Czartoryski, "Système," fol. 127.

[37] "Article pour l'arrangement des affaires de l'Europe à la suite d'une guerre heureuse" [late 1806], Czartoryski, *Mémoires*, II, 65. See also Czartoryski's Balkan proposals in, for example, "Questions," May 1806, CA 5228/IV and TsGADA, 1278/1/41; and three separate memoranda dated Jan. 23, 1806, *SIRIO*, LXXXII, 252–278.

[38] Marceli Handelsman, *Adam Czartoryski* (3 vols.; Warsaw, 1948–1950, "Rozprawy historyczne," Vols. 23–25), I, 329; Kukiel, *Czartoryski*, p. 35. Frank Fadner, *Seventy Years of Pan-Slavism in Russia, Karazin to Danilevskii, 1800–1870* (Washington, 1962), pp. 89–92, by contrast emphasizes Czartoryski's pre-

designs for Russian expansion in the East current in the last part of Catherine's reign, particularly those associated with her "Greek project," than with later nineteenth-century Russian Panslavism. They are typical, too, of strains of national feeling expressed in many parts of Europe in the early nineteenth century in reaction to the Napoleonic bid for European hegemony.

In fact, many of Czartoryski's recommendations were expressed in terms of the immediate defensive need to arouse "a formidable mass opposition" to Napoleon in the Balkans and the Near East, to "prevent the French from any hope of succeeding in their projects of expansion." Even in his specific plans for the new Balkan federations of Greeks and Slavs, he intended that "both . . . would have as their first obligation to use all of their resources to prevent the French from penetrating Turkey." [39] After the defeat at Austerlitz and in response to Napoleon's further penetration in the eastern Mediterranean, Czartoryski began to argue more extensively for a southern front of defense against Napoleon. This necessity, as expressed in his arguments, meshed appropriately with his long-range plans for the political reconstruction of southeastern Europe.

Underlying Czartoryski's concern about the Eastern Question was his recognition of the commercial importance of the area to the Russian economy. His own family had been involved in Polish trade through southern Russian ports before Catherine's partitions, which may well have first opened his eyes to the economic potential of the region. Czartoryski was one of the first in the nineteenth century to stress the economic importance of the Black Sea trade route for Russia. He was convinced of the need for further industrialization and the extension of commerce, particularly in order to lessen Russia's commercial dependence

---

occupation with geopolitics and Russian expansionism and suggests that any Panslavic elements in his proposals were definitely "adulterated."

[39] "Zapiska Chartorizhskogo," Jan. 23, 1806, *SIRIO*, LXXXII, 246. Czartoryski to Stroganov, Feb. 18, 1806, *Stroganov*, III, 10–11 (*VPR*, III, 54–56). Even as early as 1804 his Balkan proposals emphasized the need for defense against Napoleonic penetration of the area, for example, Czartoryski to Alexander, Feb. 29, 1804, *VPR*, I, 619–627 (*SIRIO*, LXXVII, 486–498), and Czartoryski to S. R. Vorontsov, March 9, 1804, *VPR*, I, 630–640.

on England. To a much greater degree than the emperor, who usually ignored economic issues, Czartoryski often phrased his fears of penetration of the eastern Mediterranean and the Black Sea by other nations in economic terms. He was eager to cooperate with England in the area — although the extent of cooperation varied in different statements — because he saw the mutually profitable and well established commercial relations between the countries as a sound basis for political cooperation. But the French occupation, he argued, posed a definite threat to established commerce, while the admission of other rivals into the area would prove disastrous for Russia's economic interests.[40]

With his high purposes and his sincere devotion to the cause of national self-determination and his long-range political plans for the area, he had no intention of merely exploiting movements of national independence, as has sometimes been said. Yet his high-minded intentions usually were inadequate dressing for the explosive Russian expansionism inherent in his projects. Regardless of his idealistic humanitarian terms and his real concern for the Poles and the southern Slavs, his proposals clearly laid the ground for Russia's economic and political penetration of Poland and the Balkans. His plans all too thinly masked basic expansionist premises, which went far beyond any Alexander himself was willing to adopt. While Czartoryski believed that Russia had a prime responsibility to insure a European equilibrium and to safeguard the general welfare, he nevertheless constantly reminded the emperor that Russia "must not forget her own interests." [41] Alexander had little interest in increasing the Russian Empire and hence showed scant sympathy for Czartoryski's argument in the spring of 1806 "that the need to extend and assure our influence, to enlarge the limits and extent of the empire, could become more and more urgent, not only for the maintenance of Russia in

---

[40] His economic argument is particularly explicit in his memorandum to the emperor dated Feb. 29, 1804, *VPR*, I, 619–627 (*SIRIO*, LXXVII, 486–498), but was expressed also in the earlier "Système," *passim*. His family interest in early trade in the Black Sea area is mentioned by Jan Reychman, "Le commerce polonais en mer noire au XVIII$^e$ siècle par le port de Kherson," *Cahiers du Monde russe et soviétique*, VII (1966, No. 2), 245.

[41] Czartoryski, "Système," fols. 122–128.

the position she must occupy, but for the establishment of a real and lasting peace." Not surprisingly, Czartoryski's views for the Balkans, robbed of their humanitarian intent, were welcomed by his expansionist colleagues.[42] Czartoryski's arguments for Russian interests in the Eastern Question in one way or another were to embroil European diplomats throughout the nineteenth and into the twentieth century. Their influence on negotiations with Napoleon during the Tilsit years is hard to document. During his own tenure in the foreign office, however, he did much to prepare the ground for support of the Russo-Turkish war, begun in 1806 under his successor, who was deaf to any of the more humanitarian aspects of Czartoryski's proposals.

If the great and moral role Czartoryski had in mind for Russia in the Balkans had questionable implications and unfortunate consequences, the role he envisioned in western Europe in the early nineteenth century was much more constructive and much more to the emperor's immediate taste. Alexander himself, discouraged by early difficulties in his reform projects and alarmed by the Napoleonic menace, was beginning to turn more of his attention to the international scene. He sensed with Czartoryski that by 1803 "the passive system of peace and tranquillity adopted by Kochubei," to which Vorontsov "had added assurance and dignity," had become "difficult to sustain." Moreover, Czartoryski argued, this passive policy "does not provide any well-thought-out system that can be followed when action becomes necessary." The lack of system in foreign affairs, he continued, "was not befitting a great power such as Russia."[43]

At the heart of Czartoryski's "system" was a grand coalition against France. "The insatiable and revolting ambition of her present chief makes any real liaison with him impossible," he wrote in 1803, at which time he was already recommending a co-

---

[42] Czartoryski, "Mémoire sur les determinations à prendre d'après les dernières ouvertures de l'Angleterre," June 11, 1806, CA 5228/IV (TsGADA, 1278/1/41); Czartoryski to Alexander, April 1806, Czartoryski, *Mémoires*, II, 106. Czartoryski (*Mémoires*, I, 372–373) complained that in welcoming his views his colleagues too often overlooked his underlying humanitarian principles.

[43] Czartoryski, *Mémoires*, I, 367; "Système," fols. 122, 50–51.

alition and other steps to influence public opinion against Napoleon.[44] The assassination of the Duke d'Enghien early in the spring of 1804 was followed by Napoleon's proclamation of the French Empire in May; these moves, his occupation of Naples and Hanover, and the increasing threat to Turkey and the Dalmatian coast all confirmed Czartoryski's recommendations for Russian action. "It is for her dignity and in her own interest not to neglect the occasions that offer themselves to restore Europe's lost equilibrium and reassert it on more stable footing by rendering to states that independence without which their existence will only be precarious." [45] By the end of the summer of 1804, Alexander was ready to give his backing to Czartoryski's recommendations for concerted European action against Napoleon, to be initiated through an alliance with England into which other continental powers would be drawn. Such an alliance had been under consideration in Russia and England for some time, but the Novosiltsev mission to England in the fall of 1804 was the first decisive action toward it during Czartoryski's ministry.

The Third Coalition was the most important diplomatic development of Czartoryski's term, and in connection with it Czartoryski had a more important role in initiating and carrying out a major policy than any of Alexander's other foreign ministers were to assume during his reign. Throughout the negotiations the emperor worked closely with his minister, and, assured of Czartoryski's abilities and commitment to the coalition, he gave the prince great responsibility in seeing it through. Even when Alexander made constant and crucial use of his own special emissaries, bypassing regular Russian diplomats, Czartoryski's role was never diminished. In dealing with England, for instance, the emperor worked through his special envoy, Novosiltsev, whom he sent in the fall of 1804 with special secret instructions for the negotiations, circumventing the established Russian ambassador in England, Simon Vorontsov. Czartoryski drafted both the initial secret instructions and the later dispatches which the emperor

---

[44] Czartoryski, "Système," fols. 63–69.
[45] Czartoryski to Alexander, May 17, 1804, *VPR*, II, 58.

sent to Novosiltsev. As a close political associate, Czartoryski also maintained a personal correspondence with Novosiltsev during his stay in London. In addition, and often in an effort to keep an eye on Novosiltsev, Czartoryski corresponded privately with Vorontsov during the period, thus keeping closely abreast of the different strands in the negotiations. Both Alexander and Czartoryski, despite their regard for Vorontsov, were suspicious of his strong pro-English sympathies, and especially of his high regard for Pitt. Vorontsov, informed of the general intent of the mission, participated in certain aspects of the talks and, because of his often unfriendly attitude toward Novosiltsev, whom he resented, reported on the latter's activities.[46]

Novosiltsev, who bore the responsibility for most of the actual negotiations in London, was hampered by the vague idealism and futuristic emphasis of his instructions; Pitt, who was much more concerned about securing Russian support for present war than about the future reconstruction of Europe, was therefore able to have the last word on many of the specifics leading to the preliminary treaty of alliance.[47] Alexander and Czartoryski were not pleased with the treaty Novosiltsev brought back. He had won British support, but it was obvious that the allies were far apart in their aims and reasoning. Subsequent delays were costly to the cause of the coalition. A preliminary treaty, signed in April 1805, gave British approval of the allied war aims on the continent, but provided for subsidies rather than troops. The final convention, ratified in July, bore few traces of Czartoryski's future plans for Europe. Its ratification, despite the many divisive forces working to split the powers, owed much to Czartoryski's perseverance. In retrospect, however, his insistence that a British-Russian alliance was paramount to the success of the

[46] Czartoryski, *Mémoires*, I, 301–303, 365–367; Czartoryski to S. R. Vorontsov, Aug. 30, 1804, *AKV*, XV, 245–246; Alexander to S. R. Vorontsov, Sept. 22, 1804, *VPR*, II, 131–138; Novosiltsev to Czartoryski, Nov. 20, 1804, Stroganov Papers, TsGADA, 1278/1/40. See also, Czartoryski to Novosiltsev, Feb. 16, 1805, and Feb. 17, 1805, *VPR*, II, 310–320.

[47] See Novosiltsev's minutes of his conversations with Pitt, Dec. 25, 1804, *VPR*, II, 219–246, and Novosiltsev to Alexander I, no. 3, Jan. 5, 1805, *VPR*, II, 257–260.

coalition seems questionable in light of continental developments.

A preliminary agreement was signed with Austria in November 1804; Sweden allied itself with Russia in January 1805, but the prospects for a real continental coalition faded. Czartoryski again was most important in securing Austrian participation; and the emperor saw to it that he was not eclipsed. For example, when Czartoryski first took over the correspondence pertaining to the negotiations with Austria, the Russian ambassador in Vienna, Alexander Razumovskii, was very disdainful of him. But when Razumovskii started sending his most important comments in secret dispatches directly to the emperor, Alexander protested and, according to Czartoryski's account, ordered that all communications pass through his minister's hands.[48] As with Vorontsov in England, Alexander and Czartoryski did not have entire confidence in the reports of Razumovskii. The emperor's personal envoy, General Wintzingerode, was dispatched ostensibly to deal with military relations, but he actually had a key role in the diplomatic negotiations between the two countries. Close in politics and friendship to Czartoryski, he kept the prince well informed. The special Austrian envoy in St. Petersburg, Colonel Stutterheim, was in particularly close contact with the emperor, but even he usually had to deal through Czartoryski. Hard political bargaining and the actual preparations for war, however, were much more important than future plans for a reconstructed Europe in obtaining Austrian accession to the coalition in August 1805.[49]

Czartoryski's policies and role in regard to the negotiations with Prussia were among the most difficult and controversial aspects of his diplomacy. The continued adherence of Prussia to its neutrality proved the greatest stumbling block to the formation of the Third Coalition; the lack of Prussian support substantially contributed to the failure of the coalition, and these negotiations

[48] Czartoryski, *Mémoires*, I, 364.
[49] *Razoumowski*, II, Part 2, 60–297; "Journal du Colonel Baron de Stutterheim" (e.g. entry for April 15, 1805), HHS/Russ. II, 138; Martens, *Recueil*, II, 421–433.

also resulted in the failure of Czartoryski's personal relationship with Alexander. Although Czartoryski personally thought of Prussia as "a natural enemy of Russia," bent only on "continual aggrandizement," he recognized the crucial importance of bringing Prussia into the coalition. "Nothing will be neglected to obtain the cooperation of Prussia," he assured Vorontsov,[50] but Czartoryski was ill-suited for the task. To no avail, he constantly urged the Prussian court through established diplomatic channels and special emissaries to stand firm against the French advances. General Wintzingerode, a friend of Czartoryski's and a strong partisan of the coalition, was sent to Berlin in February 1805; he confirmed the intransigence of Prussian neutrality in reports which "gave little hope for the expectation of cooperation from Prussia." Novosiltsev, who visited Prussia in the summer of 1805, made a similar appraisal.[51] Czartoryski never came up with an adequate inducement to turn Prussia from the neutral path so cleverly supported by Prussian court circles and so strongly encouraged by French counterthreats. Czartoryski was certainly well aware of Alexander's feelings of friendship toward King Frederick William which would work against a break between their countries. He sensed that "in spite of the marked differences of opinion and principles between the cabinets" such differences "do not really exist between the sovereigns." [52] He may have hoped that rational political necessities would overcome

---

[50] Czartoryski, "Système," fols. 70–71. Czartoryski to A. R. Vorontsov, Aug. 22, 1805, CA 5533/IV.

[51] See, Czartoryski to M. M. Alopeus, Nov. 15, 1804, *VPR*, II, 193–195; Dec. 17 and 22, 1804, *VPR*, II, 213–219; Czartoryski, *Mémoires*, I, 366; Czartoryski to S. R. Vorontsov, Feb. 16, 1805, *AKV*, XV, 167; Novosiltsev to Alexander, July 10, 1805, *VPR*, II, 470–472. See also Leveson-Gower to Harrowby, No. 4, Feb. 17, 1805, PRO/FO 65/57, in J. H. Rose, ed., *Select Dispatches from the British Foreign Office Archives Relating to the Formation of the Third Coalition Against France, 1804–1805* (London, 1904), pp. 103–104; *The Diaries and Letters of Sir George Jackson, K. C. H. from the Peace of Amiens to the Battle of Talavera*, ed. Lady Jackson (2 vols.; London, 1872), I, 269; Metternich, *Mémoires*, II, 38–45.

[52] Czartoryski to Alopeus, Oct. 9, 1804, *VPR*, II, 158–159. There seem no grounds for Albert Sorel's assertion (*L'Europe et la Révolution française*, 4th ed. [8 vols.; Paris, 1897–1906], VI, 375–376) that Czartoryski was trying to prevent the Prussian alliance while Alexander was promoting it in personal correspondence with the king.

this personal element, yet the only plan he devised was a highly bellicose and basically unsatisfactory procedure for trying to force Prussia to join the allies.

As early as the spring of 1804, Czartoryski put forth the plan of forcing Prussia into the coalition by declaring war on Prussia.[53] At the time Novosiltsev was dispatched to England in September 1804, he was informed that the emperor was disposed to keep some forces "ready on the frontier in case the need arose for action against Prussia"; in February 1805 Czartoryski confidentially asked Novosiltsev to try to determine the English position with regard to such action.[54] Since both England and Austria, realizing the importance of Prussian support, appeared willing enough to back such action if Prussia could not be swayed otherwise, Czartoryski continued to press his plan, convinced that "the court of Berlin will not make a decision unless forced to do so." [55]

Given Czartoryski's strong patriotic commitment to Poland, the most attractive aspect of the plan for him — which he lost no time in preparing in the summer of 1805 — was inciting the Poles to rise up and join with the Russian armies against Prussia. Alexander would not have to start war in Prussia proper, Czartoryski suggested, but could merely enter Warsaw (then under Prussian rule), where he would be welcomed as a liberator by the Poles, who would want to oppose Prussia and assist in the coalition war efforts. In so doing, he would put sufficient pressure on Prussia to induce the king to give his full support to the allies. In the diplomatic interchanges of the perod, Czartoryski was rel-

---

[53] According to the remarks of Razumovskii to Sir Arthur Paget in Paget to Hawkesbury, April 2, 1804, Augustus B. Paget, ed., *The Paget Papers: Diplomatic and other Correspondence of the Right Hon. Sir Arthur Paget, G. C. B. 1794–1807* (2 vols.; London, 1896), II, 110. Vorontsov's support of the plan was indicated to Czartoryski, April 13, 1804, CA 5529/IV.

[54] "Notes additionnelles à l'instruction donnée par Sa Majesté Imperiale à M^r de Novossiltzoff," Sept. 23, 1804, *VPR*, II, 151–154 (this secret addition to the Novosiltsev instructions was here published for the first time). It was evident that Czartoryski had carefully discussed the plan with the emperor because he wrote to Novosiltsev (Feb. 17, 1805, *VPR*, II, 319) that Alexander did not want him to mention it in his dispatch to S. R. Vorontsov.

[55] Czartoryski to S. R. Vorontsov, May 15, 1805, *AKV*, XV, 298–299; Czartoryski to A. R. Vorontsov, June 14, 1805, CA 5583/IV.

atively silent about his further plan: He hoped that in the course of his entry into Prussian Poland, Polish enthusiasm would be great enough to provide an occasion which might induce Alexander to proclaim himself king of a reunited Polish state. Rumors to this effect circulated widely, particularly as Czartoryski did take measures to gain the sympathy of Polish leaders for the Russian war effort and the eventuality of Russian-sponsored restoration. If the support of Polish leaders was not sufficient for Alexander to name himself king immediately, Czartoryski reasoned (and he had cause to suspect it might not be), at least such moves would bring Warsaw and the Prussian section of Poland closer to the Russians. Then, a victorious war might result in a reunification of Poland under Russian auspices.[56]

Ostensibly Alexander had much earlier approved Czartoryski's plan to force Prussia into the coalition, although he remained more confident that it would not have to be put into operation.[57] Prussia had been informed of early parts of the plan, much to Czartoryski's distress, but still made no move during the summer to cooperate with the allies. Alexander then prepared for more threatening action, and at the beginning of September he moved Russian troops into Austrian-occupied Poland, established headquarters at the Czartoryski family home at Puławy, and allowed further preparations to win Polish support for a declaration of war on Prussia.

A year later, castigating the emperor for not going through

[56] Inadequate documentation makes it difficult to reconstruct the exact aims and date the shifts in Czartoryski's proposals in autumn 1805. Czartoryski described his Polish project most completely, including the possibility of Alexander's kingship, in a confidential letter to Razumovskii, [ca. Oct. 10, 1805], printed in *Razoumowski*, II, Part 2, pp. 247–250. That he had been awaiting a suitable occasion for a Russian-sponsored restoration is apparent in his 1803 memorandum ("Système," fols. 74–84), where he suggested that a rupture between the partitioning powers could be a good time for Russia to move in; or if a Russian-Prussian split occurred, Russia should try to win the support of the Prussian Polish provinces by promising independence or some similar alternative.

[57] E.g. Alexander to Razumovskii, May 10, 1805, *VPR*, II, 396 (*Razoumowski*, II, Part 2, 197–199); the plan and Alexander's hope of not having to force passage in Prussia were also explained by Alexander to S. R. Vorontsov, May 11, 1805, *VPR*, II, 403, but neither Polish support nor Polish restoration was mentioned.

with the whole plan, Czartoryski claimed that "all Poland was ready to rise in mass and demand that the sovereign of Russia add to his titles that of King of Poland." [58] But evidently Alexander had not really endorsed the idea of proclaiming a Polish kingship at that point. Nor did Polish support for the Russian war effort necessarily in his mind imply an immediate restoration. That the emperor actually did "persist in the idea," as Czartoryski claimed in his memoirs, appears to have been more a projection of Czartoryski's hopes — and the fears of allied diplomats — than a fact of imperial decision. There is no question, however, that such a proclamation was considered. The emperor spoke of the Polish project, reportedly vowed "to make the Poles rise against Prussia," and was flattered by apparent Polish support. [59] But however much he may have liked the idea, Alexander later denied the possibility of a Polish restoration in 1805, because "we would have had the whole Prussian army against us." And other indications from the period appear to support his denial. Even in the most specific discussions of possible operations against Prussia, even in Czartoryski's drafts of his manifestos against Prussia, there is no definite plan for an immediate Polish kingdom. Military instructions prepared for use in the event of war against Prussia called for proclamations to the Polish people, particularly the armies, exhorting them to support Russia and promising future privileges, but they carried no suggestion of an immediate restoration and made no mention of a Russian kingship. [60]

Although Alexander had entertained his minister's plan for war against Prussia with the help of the Poles, and apparently had even toyed with declaring himself King of Poland, he did so largely

[58] Czartoryski, memorandum of April 5, 1806, *Mémoires*, II, 143.

[59] Czartoryski, *Mémoires*, I, 398; see also II, 143, 230. Alexander's remark was quoted in a dispatch by the Austrian envoy Stutterheim from Puławy, Oct. 4, 1805 (in Eduard Wertheimer, *Geschichte Oesterreichs und Ungarns im ersten Jahrzehnt des 19. Jahrhunderts* [Leipzig, 1884], I, 275).

[60] Alexander, quoted in a conversation with Czartoryski on April 5, 1810, Czartoryski, *Mémoires*, II, 230. See for example, Czartoryski, "Projet de manifeste contre la Prusse." CA 5227/IV, fols. 297–327, and "Extrait de l'instruction de S.M.I. au général Michelson," 1805, in Nikolai Mikhailovich, *Kniazia Dolgorukie, spodvizhniki imperatora Aleksandra I v pervye gody ego tsarstvovaniia. Biograficheskie ocherki* (St. Petersburg, 1902), pp. 146–152.

to counter French threats and dubious Prussian maneuvers. He still had little intention of putting the plan into full-scale operation. When he moved troops into Poland, he was simultaneously trying to renew ties of friendship with Prussia and seeking an accord through his ambassador Alopeus and his aide-de-camp, Czartoryski's archenemy Peter Dolgorukii. On several occasions he wrote begging the Prussian king to meet with him, insisting only on the free passage of Russian troops.[61] Czartoryski's hopes and the emperor's confidence in him seemingly blinded the young prince to Alexander's basic indecision and his unwillingness to risk a Prussian war for any cause, let alone to restore Poland at that time.

Czartoryski's hope for entry of Russian troops into Prussian Poland with the possibility of a Polish restoration explains much of his extreme bitterness when Alexander accepted instead what proved to be a useless proclamation of friendship from the Prussian king. But the coalition on which Czartoryski had concentrated such great efforts was also at stake, and he was enough of a diplomat to realize that the allies might have had much to fear from such a Polish proclamation at that point. A letter he drafted to Razumovskii in the autumn of 1805 indicated his recognition that it was "neither expedient, nor advantageous, nor even permitted, to pursue such a project, or even to instigate it, especially without full discussion and the agreement of an ally as necessary and faithful as Austria," even while he admitted, "It is honorable to gain unto a sovereign a country that burns with the desire to belong to him." He knew that Austria, however strong its support for the war effort, was not prepared to agree to a Russian kingdom of Poland at that juncture. Furthermore, once Alexander had notified Prussia of the impending invasion and Prussia had started to prepare for war, Czartoryski recognized the diffi-

[61] Alexander's correspondence with Frederick William from August 7 to October 7, 1805, is very revealing of his attitude (*Freidrich Wilhelm*, pp. 68–83). Alexander expressed his sincere hope to reach an understanding with Frederick William in a letter to the Austrian emperor, Francis, Sept. 26, 1805 (Adolf Beer, *Zehn Jahre oesterreichischer Politik, 1801–1811* [Leipzig, 1877], p. 460).

culty of going through with the plan, particularly without the complete support of Austria. Yet Czartoryski still hoped.[62]

Although Czartoryski's eagerness to use the opportunity to bring the Poles closer to Russia did not make him an appropriate individual to bring about close accord with Prussia, he can hardly be accused of trying to mislead Alexander about Prussian attitudes. He believed that Prussia's wholehearted support for the coalition should be secured, not just the minimal agreement to the free passage of Russian troops through Prussian territories. His antagonism to Prussia was not conducive to warmer relations, for he believed that "even if [King Frederick William] totally cedes, we will have gained only a detestable ally of whom it will always be necessary to beware." [63] Yet from the point of view of the coalition there was good reason for Czartoryski's contempt. Even when the Prussian monarch did cede, he only granted free passage to Russian troops; Prussia failed to join or decisively support the strong actions which Czartoryski had been urging against Napoleon in 1805. Czartoryski was also justified in his dissatisfaction with the conduct and reports of the Russian ambassador in Prussia, Maxim Alopeus, who, he believed, was "preoccupied beyond measure with preserving good relations" between the countries rather than pressing the interests of the coalition.[64] Czartoryski's assessment of the intransigence of Prussian neutrality was even initially confirmed by Dolgorukii, who was himself eager to avoid war with Prussia. Alexander had dispatched Dolgorukii in September as a last-minute effort to avert war; in early October Dolgorukii was returning with Frederick William's refusal of passage for Russian troops, when the news of Napoleon's violation of the territory of Amsbach led the Prussian monarch to change his mind. Dolgorukii was overtaken

[62] Czartoryski to Razumovskii ([early autumn] 1805), draft, CA ew XVII/605; Czartoryski to Razumovskii, Oct. 10, 1805, *VPR*, II, 602–604.
    [63] Czartoryski to Razumovskii, [early autumn] 1805, draft, CA ew XVII/605.
    [64] Czartoryski, *Mémoires*, I, 366; II, 113; Czartoryski to Razumovskii Oct. 10, 1805, *VPR*, II, 602–606; Stadion to Colloredo, Jan. 15, 1805, HHS/Russ. II, 106; Stedingk to King Gustav IV, Jan. 15, 1805, Stedingk, *Mémoires*, II, 23–24.

en route and given the message that the king wanted to meet Alexander and would agree to Russia's final moderate demands.

So committed was Czartoryski to his Polish plan that he grew bitter when Alexander avoided war with Prussia. It is small wonder that the emperor turned away from his recommendations and resisted virtually all his advice. "This personal liaison contracted with the sovereign of a power whose interests are most often opposed to those of Russia influenced considerably the conduct of our cabinet," he complained to the emperor, "and finally prevented the development of those rigorous measures at the beginning of the campaign which had been well thought out and decided." Friendship was reaffirmed when the two sovereigns met in Potsdam, swore a weird ceremonial oath of Prussian-Russian solidarity in the underground tomb of Frederick the Great, and signed the Treaty of Potsdam on November 3. "I will always reproach myself for having been compelled by circumstances to put my name to such a calamitous treaty," Czartoryski wrote after having participated in the negotiations more as the emperor's secretary than as his foreign minister.[65] It is doubtful, however, that Prince Adam's plan or even Prussian military support, would have prevented defeat. But as it was, with Alexander's blessing, Prussia remained neutral in this initial stage of the Third Coalition, while the allied armies were routed by Napoleon on the battlefield of Austerlitz in one of the greatest triumphs of the French emperor's career.

Austerlitz was a sorry tribute to Czartoryski's vision of a grand coalition against Napoleon, but the allies were ill-prepared for war. When it was time for battle, Alexander impatiently and imperiously wanted to try out his military prowess. While his own military tactics contributed to the disaster, his earlier indecision and vacillation about the war had left the allies in a weak position and too often had left Bonaparte to profit from the delays. "The assurance and frankness necessary for a well-taken decision are not to be found in him," Czartoryski complained. "On

---

[65] Czartoryski to Alexander April 1806, Czartoryski, *Mémoires*, II, 112–113, 116–118. See also Czartoryski to S. R. Vorontsov, Feb. 18, 1806, *AKV*, XV, 363.

the contrary, I often notice worry and the reticence of indecision. . . . The idea of a war burdens and torments him." On one hand, Alexander looked forward to leading his armies, which, as Czartoryski explained, "would give him the relief that he needs here and which he will not acquire in other ways." [66] But Alexander also sought to avoid war; and he found much support for this, particularly from the so-called Russian party, led by the ministers of commerce and finance and seconded by the minister of the interior and members of influential court circles who criticized both the prospective war and the warlike sympathies of the foreign minister. In 1804 and 1805 Alexander had none of the patriotic zeal or sense of religious mission which were to motivate him in the formation of the Fourth Coalition after the French invasion of Russia in 1812. "I know, on good authority, that Prince Czartoryski would wish for more vigor on the part of his sovereign," an Austrian diplomat reported, "while the sovereign on this occasion seems to want to listen only to his heart, the minister listens only to his head." [67] That the Third Coalition even became a reality owed much to the enterprise of Czartoryski.

Up to the last moment, Alexander hoped that war might be avoided, that the coalition might be more of a deterrent than a prelude to battle. He never fully committed himself to any policy which would have precluded that possibility. He was in that frame of mind when he sent Novosiltsev to Paris in the early summer of 1805 to give Napoleon a final chance to come to a settlement and avoid a general war. Czartoryski saw little point in the mission, but suggested "this measure fits the emperor's view too well to allow him to be dissuaded." [68] Alexander still hoped that the formation of the Third Coalition could be used to force Napoleon to a more reasonable line of conduct. Later Alexander admitted that the mission "must be approved less on the

---

[66] Czartoryski to Novosiltsev, Feb. 17, 1805, *VPR*, II, 319. Czartoryski to A. R. Vorontsov, Aug. 28, 1804, CA 5533/IV.

[67] "Journal du Colonel Baron de Stutterheim," Nov. 23, 1804, HHS/Russ. II, 138. The hesitations at court were well presented in a letter from Stroganov to Novosiltsev, Dec. 6, 1804, Gosudarstvennyi istoricheskii muzei [State Historical Museum] (Moscow), 316/2.

[68] Czartoryski to A. R. Vorontsov, April 16, 1805, *AKV*, XV, 290.

hope of obtaining an immediate settlement than on the effect it will produce in Europe," but he did not want to neglect any possibility of avoiding armed conflict. Although the tsar was forced to justify the mission as a demonstration of his peaceful intentions which clearly put the blame for war on Napoleon, the whole episode was marked with indecision. In fact, the mission was never carried through; Novosiltsev got as far as Berlin at the end of June, but he was recalled after Napoleon's seizure of Genoa.[69]

With the failure of Novosiltsev's "peace" mission, a last-gasp attempt to come to terms with Bonaparte, Alexander was more resolved on war. But his indecisiveness came to the fore again in the face of the difficult problem of Prussian neutrality. A year earlier, Czartoryski had written prophetically, "the personal and cordial union that reigns between the two sovereigns could, in the most difficult circumstances, easily deceive political calculations that fail to take it into account." [70] Had he taken his own remark to heart, he might not have pushed the particular plan he did; but at least he would have been less perturbed when Alexander's desire to avoid a war against Prussia brought him to the abandonment of the Polish aspect of Czartoryski's plan. Alexander turned away from Czartoryski when the threat of his movement into Poland did not bring Prussia to arms. The emperor was ready to find hope in the dispatches of Alopeus and to listen to the urgings of his aide-de-camp Prince Dolgorukii only because they corresponded to his own attitudes and his fundamental desire to avoid war with Prussia.

While Alexander vacillated about the specific plans for war, he was more firm regarding general principles and plans for future peace. Along with the disagreements on concrete political issues which divided Alexander and his allies, there was an effusion of

[69] Alexander to S. R. Vorontsov, April 15, 1805, *VPR*, II, 379. See also: Czartoryski to Novosiltsev, Feb. 16, 1805, *VPR*, II, 312–313; Alexander to G. A. Stroganov, May 24, 1805, *VPR*, II, 418–419. The indecision of the Russian government was especially apparent in the explanations for Novosiltsev's recall: Czartoryski to Novosiltsev, June 21, 1805, *SIRIO*, LXXXII, 75–77, and Czartoryski to S. R. Vorontsov, June 22, 1805, *AKV*, XV, 332–336.
[70] Czartoryski to Alopeus, Oct. 9, 1804, *VPR*, II, 159.

grandiose plans for restructuring the European political system, restoring the independence of subject nations, and ensuring future peace, justice, prosperity, political stability, and general welfare. In such pronouncements, usually drafted by Czartoryski himself, Alexander echoed many of the ideals of the Polish prince. With more or less sincerity, these ideas often reappeared in the pronouncements of foreign statesmen and in vague form found their way into many of the treaties and official declarations of the period, but they did little to strengthen the coalition. High ideals ran through the negotiations, but power and traditional prejudices and patterns proved to be greater molders of political practice. Czartoryski was no more the statesman than Alexander, when it came to bridging the gap between them. He was left to lament in his memoirs that most of his cherished ideals remained sterile in the diplomatic developments of the day.

With the return of the emperor and his entourage to Russia in early 1806 following the disasters in the West, the relationship between Alexander and Czartoryski drastically altered. In his traumatic personal reaction to Austerlitz, the emperor wanted neither to assume the responsibility for the disaster himself nor to admit that Czartoryski's policy might have been better. In effect, Alexander chose to make a complete break with his former advisers. Czartoryski became the scapegoat for the ill-fated military venture on the continent. Yet it was half a year before Alexander was ready to implement the change in staff formally; Czartoryski stayed in the foreign office until June, only to make recommendations which were rarely considered.

In the early months of 1806 Czartoryski continued to set forth his views on the active diplomatic system he believed Russia must follow. Above all, he argued, "Russia must naturally try to conserve and extend her influence on the Continent," being "now the only power who can counterbalance France." [71] Following the defeat at Austerlitz, he considered it particularly important for Russia to continue to support Austria and to do everything possi-

---

[71] Czartoryski, "Mémoire sur les rapports de la Russie et l'Angleterre," Feb. 1806, CA 5230/IV (TsGADA, 1278/1/41); see also Czartoryski to S. R. Vorontsov, Sept. 6, 1806, *AKV*, XV, 414–419.

ble to prevent an Austro-French alliance. Blind friendship with Prussia should be avoided, he counseled. Russia should endeavor to prevent Napoleon from making further inroads in northern and eastern Europe, even if it should mean war with Prussia.[72] Pressure should be placed on the Ottoman Empire to take strong defensive measures against French advances; if the Porte did not stand firm against France, Czartoryski advised, Russia should be prepared for action in that area. Russian troops in Corfu should be ready to act; reinforcements should be sent to the Adriatic, and Russia should give further support to the King of Naples. To the north, Russia should stand firmly behind the King of Sweden and give reassurance to Denmark. Close alliance with England should be maintained, as England remained the only other power capable of standing up to Bonaparte. Most important, Czartoryski believed, Russia should prepare and remain prepared for action befitting her position and dignity. He reminded Alexander of the words of Peter the Great: "We have nothing but our honor; to renounce it is to cease to be a monarch."[73] When the time came for war, Czartoryski suggested two possible theaters of action — northern Europe and the Ottoman Empire. The northern Europe plan involved gaining full support from the Poles and from Prussia, while the southeastern approach involved inciting rebellion and gaining the support of the Greeks and southern Slavs.

Completely discouraged by the failure of the Third Coalition, Alexander resolved on the contrary "to remain absolutely passive and not to budge in any way until the time when we are attacked on our own soil." As Czartoryski lamented, the emperor was already professing the policy that was to dominate after the Treaty of Tilsit was signed in 1807. "The tendency of the emperor Alex-

[72] Czartoryski, "Mémoire sur les rapports de la Russie et l'Autriche," Feb. 12, 1806, CA 5230/IV (TsGADA 1278/1/41); "Mémoire sur les rapports de la Russie et la Prusse," Jan. 17, 1806, Czartoryski, *Mémoires,* II, 66–82.
[73] Czartoryski, "Mémoire sur les rapports de la Russie et l'Angleterre," Feb. 1806, CA 5230/IV (TsGADA 1278/1/41); "Mémoire sur la situation actuelle de la Russie," March 1806, Czartoryski, *Mémoires,* II, 83–95. See also, for example, Czartoryski to Italinskii, Jan. 15, 1806, *VPR,* III, 24–25, and Jan. 30, 1806, *VPR,* III, 35–37, and Czartoryski to Stroganov, May 25, 1806, *VPR,* III, 168–173.

ander to remain an idle spectator to European events cannot be hidden," reported the Austrian ambassador. Czartoryski was disgusted. In his view there were two alternatives: "Either we must act with dispatch and vigor in conjunction with England, or we must make peace," he stated in May. The first alternative was decidedly better, he believed, but either one was better than "the impossible intermediate state" of doing nothing.[74]

Realizing that there was no chance for his active program, Czartoryski began to press the alternative. "Once it was clear that there was no hope in forcing our court out of the passive and vanquished attitude which it has taken, peace with Bonaparte — such as it is — becomes a precious thing for Russia and for Europe at this moment." [75] The peace that Czartoryski advocated, however, had many strings attached. Even if a satisfactory peace treaty could be effected in conjunction with England, he doubted that it would prove lasting. It would be disastrous for Russia merely to wait to be attacked on all sides — "Any policy founded on the premise that war can be avoided is defective," he insisted.[76]

Czartoryski agreed with the emperor on the advisability of sending Oubril as a Russian plenipotentiary to Paris to negotiate peace, but he was careful to draw up his instructions so the terms of that peace would be firm.[77] Yet, as in other important diplomatic affairs at the time, Czartoryski's participation in this mission was marginal. He was not informed of the secret instructions that Oubril received orally from the emperor, which led Oubril to assume that Alexander was much more eager for peace than his minister. Czartoryski's "warlike plans . . . were strongly

[74] Czartoryski to Stroganov, May 25, 1806, *Stroganov*, II, 381–382; (a second, more official letter of that date, describing this policy is in *VPR*, III, 168–173). Merveldt to Stadion, June 28, 1806, HHS/Russ. II, 110.

[75] Czartoryski to Stroganov, May 25, 1806, *Stroganov*, II, 382; he had earlier suggested this possibility to S. R. Vorontsov, Feb. 18, 1806, *AKV*, XV, 364.

[76] Czartoryski, "Mémoire sur les déterminations à prendre d'après les dernières ouvertures de l'Angleterre," May 1806, CA 5228/IV, fols. 210–211 (TsGADA, 1278/1/41).

[77] Czartoryski to P. J. Oubril, May 12, 1806, *VPR*, III, 134–137; the treaty is in *VPR*, III, 226–231. See also the explanation in *VPR*, III, 672–673, and other materials on the mission in *Stroganov*, III, 45–143, and *SIRIO*, LXXXII, 354–472.

contrasted to the peaceable dispositions" of the emperor, the British ambassador later explained, going on to suggest that when Oubril heard of Czartoryski's dismissal, he was induced "to sign any conditions which he thought might ensure Peace, and thus prove agreeable to the private wishes of the Emperor." Czartoryski was "surprised and indignant" at the Oubril treaty and "would never have thought it possible for him to sign it." But he was no longer in office in July when Oubril returned with the treaty — which was never ratified — making extensive concessions to Bonaparte contrary to the terms of Czartoryski's instructions.[78]

Throughout the spring months, Czartoryski was disheartened to find his "opinons completely discordant with those of the emperor on cardinal issues," and even more so by the personal antagonism which accompanied that divergence. "My suggestions were never considered; all my proposals remained ineffectual," he lamented later to Simon Vorontsov; "the events followed their course, awaiting and presaging the most unfortunate results." [79] It was apparent to most observers that "the emperor did nothing that [Czartoryski] proposed and often acted in the opposite way." Czartoryski was consulted less and less on important decisions; and personal relations between the emperor and him became notably strained. "I have had many very lively and perhaps unduly bitter discussions with the emperor," he wrote a friend in May; with "each dispatch, any news from abroad, each decision to be made, they got worse. Often it seemed that the emperor was annoyed, and that he was discontented with an instrument that did not fulfill its duties by adhering to the opinions of the master." [80]

---

[78] Stuart to Fox, Aug. 20, 1806, PRO/FO 65/63; Czartoryski to S. R. Vorontsov, Sept. 6, 1806, *AKV*, XV, 414, and to Stroganov, July 26, 1806, *Stroganov*, II, 389–390.

[79] Czartoryski to S. R. Vorontsov, Feb. 18, 1806, *AKV*, XV, 363; Czartoryski to Stroganov, Feb. 18, 1806, *Stroganov*, II, 357; Czartoryski to S. R. Vorontsov, Sept. 6, 1806, *AKV*, XV, 411.

[80] Stedingk to Gustav IV, July 11, 1806, Stedingk, *Mémoires*, II, 183–184; Merveldt to Colloredo, April 19, 1806, HHS/Russ. II, 110; Czartoryski to Stroganov, May 25, 1806, *Stroganov*, II, 384.

Czartoryski was not a man to be the blind instrument of anyone's will, particularly when that will was opposed to his own
convictions. For all his admiration of Alexander and his hope to
advance the Polish cause, his position became intolerable. "Your
Imperial Majesty has too much goodness," he wrote, "to wish to
impose on me any longer the hard obligation — I dare say the
martyrdom — of participating in a state of affairs and executing
measures that I believe to be directly opposed to the good of the
Empire and of yourself." [81]

Czartoryski was not alone in his reaction. The emperor's
"young friends" all had come to feel that Alexander had completely changed toward them. They were not consulted, and their
opinions were not respected. As Novosiltsev wrote Stroganov,
"It is certain that [Alexander] believes me to be entirely sold out
to the English and that he wants to separate me from Prince
Adam by replacing him with one who will be a machine without replies." Their reactions were equally bitter. "What kind of
future is there for those who might form his ministry?" Stroganov rhetorically asked: "In the mind of the emperor they would
be destined to be only blind instruments of his will." [82]

Things would have been easier had Alexander dismissed Czartoryski right away; but such was not the emperor's way. Czartoryski began requesting his dismissal early in the winter. Alexander only hesitated and refused his request. The prince became
more distressed about his situation. His entreaties to the emperor
became stronger; his criticism, more bitter and outspoken. In a
letter in March, for example, Czartoryski posed the question:
"What advantage would you have, Sire, to retain a minister
whose advice Your Majesty does not like, in whom you do not
have confidence, and who, on his part, is always recalcitrant, opposed to almost all your wishes, who feels discouraged and lacks
the zeal and ability to comprehend and to execute orders con-

---

[81] Czartoryski to Alexander, March 22, 1806, Czartoryski, *Mémoires*, II, 99.
[82] Novosiltsev to Stroganov, May 17, 1806, CA 5462/IV; Stroganov to his
wife, Feb. 18, 1806, *Stroganov*, III, 200. See also Novosiltsev to Stroganov,
March 29, 1806, *Stroganov*, III, 171; Novosiltsev to Stroganov, Aug. 25, 1806,
Stroganov Papers, TsGADA, 1278/1/64; Kochubei to S. R. Vorontsov, Feb. 12,
1806, *AKV*, XIV, 192.

trary to his conviction, even if his character premitted him such a role?" Alexander nonetheless remained ambivalent; he was exasperated with the minister, but wanted him at his side. Czartoryski continued working in the ministry "in a completely passive role." Finally in May, "during several heated controversies," Alexander agreed to accept his offer to resign. "At heart, I believe that he is tired of me," the prince sadly concluded.[83] But it was not until the end of June that Andrei Budberg was appointed minister for foreign affairs — ironically, to carry out many of Czartoryski's policies.

Czartoryski had been one of the closest friends and most important diplomatic advisers to the emperor since the early months of his reign. Personally and intellectually close to Alexander, he assumed a more significant role and demonstrated greater diplomatic abilities than any of Alexander's other foreign ministers. The view that Russia was the motive force behind the Third Coalition suggests the potential importance of Czartoryski's ministry; but the defeat of that coalition before the diplomacy and the armies of Napoleon hardly marks Czartoryski's diplomatic career as a success. Czartoryski worked against difficult, if not impossible, odds. It would have taken much closer agreement and coordination among the powers to overcome the diplomatic and military maneuvers of the French emperor. It would have taken more than a master statesman to reconcile the divergent interests of the European powers and bring about decisive action. And in Russia itself it would have taken a stronger minister than Alexander would have tolerated to overcome the emperor's lack of resolution.

Had Czartoryski succeeded in organizing a strong coalition, Europe might have been saved from the next ten years of turmoil. But Europe was not ready to rid itself of Napoleon in 1805 — if indeed it could have done this — and Alexander was not ready to insist on a Russian initiative to that end. Through his failure in implementing a strong coalition against Napoleon, Czartoryski

[83] Czartoryski to Alexander, March 22, 1806, Czartoryski, *Mémoires*, II, 99–100; Czartoryski to Stroganov, May 25, 1806, *Stroganov*, II, 384.

learned the limits of initiative possible in Alexander's Russia even for a minister as trusted as himself. In the diplomatic preparations for war and for peace Alexander relied heavily on the ideas, advice, and activities of his "acting" foreign minister. The emperor turned to Czartoryski and gave him an active part in proceedings when his friend's ideas seemed to correspond to his own. In disagreement, crisis, and defeat, however, Alexander personally supervised affairs, turned to alternate advisers, or let things drift in order to avoid decisive action. Even Czartoryski, with all the respect and friendship which Alexander held for him, with all his own awareness of Alexander's character, could not overcome the difficulties of dealing with a man who at some times was torn with indecision and at others was filled with such obstinate resolve that no advice or reason could change his mind.

The whole episode of the Third Coalition revealed a basic split between Alexander and his minister, as it revealed some of the emperor's basic tendencies in this period. Alexander was eager for grandiose schemes and wanted to endorse a minister who was equally committed to such projects for Europe, but he was hesitant to take decisive action. Czartoryski was more ready for action, but less able than he should have been to deal with the practical problems of forming a coalition and to relate his grand schemes to the political passions and demands of the nations with which he was dealing. Whereas Czartoryski looked at the coalition as a clear preparation for war, a necessary prelude to the reconstruction of Europe, Alexander was less certain about the inevitability of armed conflict and continued to hope that the coalition might force Bonaparte to the conference table.

Throughout the negotiations for the coalition, Alexander revealed his basic tendency to follow two rival policies simultaneously. He was hesitant to close the door either to war or to peace. He had Czartoryski pursuing the active policy of coalition and war, but, despite his great confidence in his minister, the emperor made certain that the alternate policy was not ruled out. On another level and occasionally through other channels, he was simultaneously pursuing a more passive policy. Czartoryski was caught in the middle; his policy was never fully enacted, yet he was pushed into the background when his incomplete coalition failed. His fate too well illustrates the difficulty of holding office under Alexander I.

Czartoryski's Polish patriotism raised conflicts for him as Russian foreign minister, and his eighteenth-century ideals often conflicted with the realities of nineteenth-century diplomacy. Yet many of his foreign policies, like his commitment to reform, outlasted his term of office and continued to exert an influence on the emperor's outlook. In retrospect, Czartoryski's foreign policy proved to be more in Russia's national interest than in the long-run interests of his tragic homeland. More through his zeal on behalf of Alexander's Russia than through any neglect of the Polish cause, his deepest hopes for Poland, like his cherished ideals of humanitarian reform, were too easily subverted through the indecision and uncertainties of the emperor he idolized. His plans for northern and southern theaters of war against Napoleon became a reality soon after he left office; but his hopes for a grand coalition against Napoleon and the subsequent stabilization of the continent had to await 1812. And then his ideals were easily subverted by great-power politics. Czartoryski, like Alexander, had idealistically hoped that a great role for Russia could be meshed with a respect for popular aspirations, national traditions, and international justice. Realization of this premise however, demanded a deeper penetration of Enlightenment precepts in Russia than had been the case, and it demanded more perseverance on behalf of those ideals than Alexander I was willing or able to put forth.

Czartoryski's role did not end with his departure from the foreign ministry in 1806. Correspondence between him and the emperor continued, and the friendship was renewed from time to time. Czartoryski retained his important position in the educational affairs of the Polish provinces; and his advice on more general matters was considered on several occasions, particularly in regard to Poland. Most notably, at the Congress of Vienna, when Alexander was most deeply preoccupied with the Polish question, Czartoryski again took his place at the emperor's side. In 1806, however, Alexander turned to a much less capable man for the conduct of foreign affairs — a man who was more willing than Czartoryski to subordinate himself to the imperial will, but who was impelled to resurrect Czartoryski's plans for the stabilization of the continent.

## Chapter 5

# BUDBERG AND RUMIANTSEV: A SPOKESMAN FOR WAR AND A SPOKESMAN FOR PEACE

The alternatives of war or peace with Napoleonic Europe remained at the core of Russian foreign policy for the next six years. Russia's failure at both during Czartoryski's ministry resulted more from Alexander's own passivity and vacillation than from his minister's diplomatic efforts. Alexander's underlying policy of trying to leave the door open for either alternative generated oscillation between them and the seemingly contradictory strands of Russian foreign relations during the entire period. As oscillation between war and peace and shifts in alliances brought changes in foreign ministers, the central Russian dilemma between involvement or noninvolvement on the continent continued, linked as it was in these years with domestic crises of the attempts and failures of Alexander's reform efforts. Czartoryski's term was over, but the men who succeeded him shared his problems, and in their weaker and less creative ways they followed his policies.

Recognizing Russia as "the only power who can counterbalance France," Czartoryski had clearly identified the alternate paths open to Russian foreign policy — either renewed war to the south and west with a strengthened coalition or an honorable peace. He rightly feared that a policy of peace could only bring a temporary settlement, given Napoleon's designs. But what Czartoryski was loath to recognize — although the fate of his own policies proved it — was that Alexander was not prepared to decide conclusively between these alternatives. Even as he had before, Alexander continued to pursue both policies simultaneously. If at a particular juncture he might officially commit Russia to one course, he did his best to keep channels open so that the alternate course could be easily adopted. The net result was a predominantly passive foreign policy which developed in response to external conditions and which, to the extent that it was preconceived, remained flexible in its response to the challenge of Napoleon.

That challenge in 1806 increasingly demanded renewed war. The treaty which Oubril brought from Paris in the summer of 1806 proved unacceptable for Russia; Napoleon organized the Confederation of the Rhine, dissolved the Holy Roman Empire, garrisoned French troops through large portions of Germany, and, by forcing Prussia to close her ports to British commerce, stifled Prussian commerce and brought a declaration of war from England. These developments, accompanied by other threatening acts against Prussia, made King Frederick William more determined to take to the field against Napoleon. Memories of the military glory of Frederick II did not help the divided, poorly organized, and ill-equipped Prussian army to meet the French onslaught, however. Advancing Prussian troops were first defeated at Saalfeld; the main armies were completely routed in the battles of Jena and Auerstadt; and Napoleon occupied Berlin in the last week of October, before Russian troops could even be dispatched for assistance. Alexander sent a Russian army which did not have its first encounter until the end of November; he wanted to do all he could to keep Prussia from total annihilation and to prevent Napoleon from penetrating further into Poland, but his efforts were futile. Czartoryski's two-front war had arrived without Russian planning, as French pressures on the Ottoman Empire which seemed to threaten the primacy of Russian influence in the eastern Mediterranean, brought renewed war between Russia and Turkey at the end of 1806.

When Alexander first approached Andrei Gotthard Budberg about an appointment to the foreign ministry in April 1806, he was not seeking out a man of any particular political persuasion. In fact, the emperor had not decided on a definite course of action for Russia abroad, except in the sense that he was ignoring

Czartoryski's advice and had sent Oubril to negotiate a treaty of peace with Napoleon. The emperor may have assumed that Budberg would be less antagonistic to Prussia than Czartoryski had been and in favor of continuing war in the West, but there is no evidence of any diplomatic rationale in the appointment. Budberg had been completely uninvolved in diplomacy in Alexander's reign, had never developed any principles about Russian foreign policy, and apparently had never expressed any opinions which might have led the emperor to respect his views. Even Budberg's private correspondence with Alexander at the time of the appointment is devoid of political content. There seems to be no better explanation for the appointment than the emperor's desire for a clean break with his former advisers of the Secret Committee, for a fresh start with a man unassociated with early domestic difficulties and recent foreign failures, who had no predetermined policies for Russia.

Budberg had been one of Alexander's tutors at his grandmother's court; while the young emperor undoubtedly had pleasant memories "of friendship and my appreciation for all your help and for the beneficial instruction during my childhood," he had had virtually no contact with Budberg since his early years.[1] Born near Riga in 1750, Budberg had risen in military service to the rank of general. His diplomatic experience had been limited to several minor missions to Sweden during Catherine's reign and a brief term as Russian ambassador to Sweden under Paul, which ended with his recall at the request of the Swedish court. When Alexander had tried to appoint him military governor of St. Petersburg in 1801, he had declined on the grounds of poor health. Although he had been soliciting a diplomatic assignment, he gave the same excuse when Alexander first approached him about the foreign ministry in the spring of 1806. The emperor, not to be dissuaded, suggested a two-month health cure: "For the post of foreign minister, especially at the present moment, I need a man

[1] Alexander to Budberg, March 9, 1794, Budberg Papers, TsGAOR, 860/1/7; a similar expression occurs in Alexander's letters of Jan. 8, 1794 (*ibid.*) and May 18, 1794 (GBL, M 8302/3). The private correspondence between Alexander and Budberg about the appointment is in the same TsGAOR packet.

on whose integrity, sentiments, and talents I can count entirely,"
the emperor wrote the Livonian general. "I may say that you are
the only man in whom I find united the necessary qualities." [2]

The "pitiful state" of Budberg's health — which made it impossible for him to work for any length of time — was perhaps
the least of his handicaps. Budberg wrote Alexander that it was
"not so much health that makes me hesitate. . . but the importance of the position. . . and the scant capacity with which I believe I would fulfill it." His self-appraisal was sound. As a "Baltic
baron," Budberg, like Czartoryski, immediately aroused opposition from circles who wanted a native Russian as foreign minister, but, unlike the Polish prince, he also was opposed by persons
who doubted his competence. "This general has everything
against him with which the prince was blamed," reported the
Austrian minister, "without having the same talents, the same independence, or the same birth." The diplomatic corps appreciated his weekly dinners but found him to have "only a very
superficial knowledge of affairs." [3] "He listens to us with extreme
politeness and replies to the least of our notes with an exactitude
which is infinitely agreeable to us," wrote Joseph de Maistre, the
Sardinian minister, but "as to character, that is something else."
His subordinates often considered him "vastly ignorant of well-
known occurrences"; they often had to correct his "stupid mistakes" and "embarrassing oversights" in an attempt to save appearances. He proved difficult to work with partly because he
recognized his own failings. "He has a passion for his place
which makes him defiant of all those who know more about it
than he does," one observer noted. There was general agreement

---

[2] "Imperator Aleksandr Pavlovich i ego dvor v 1804 g.," ed. F. F. Schiemann,
*Russkaia starina*, XXIX (Dec. 1880), 821–822. Alexander to Budberg, April 25
[1806], TsGAOR, 860/1/7. His desire for a diplomatic assignment is revealed
by P. Oubril to Czartoryski, June 12, 1806, CA 5463/IV, fols. 55–58; the report
of Merveldt to Stadion of June 28, 1806 (HHS/Russ. II, 110), suggested that it
was because he wanted to get a better pension.
[3] Budberg to Alexander, April 30, 1806, draft, Budberg Papers, TsGAOR,
860/1/7. Merveldt to Stadion, June 28, 1806, HSS/Russ. II, 110. Stedingk to
Gustav IV, July 11, 1806, Stedingk, *Mémoires*, II, 188–189. In the winter of
1807, for example, his health was so bad that he was unavailable for as much
as six weeks at a time (See Merveldt to Stadion, March 17, 1807, HHS/Russ. II,
111, and N. M. Longinov to S. R. Vorontsov, March 30, 1807, *AKV*, XXIII, 26).

with Nesselrode's opinion that "he was a gallant man, but ailing, with a mediocre mind, and was in no way meant for the high position he occupied." [4]

Alexander considered Budberg a friend, but there were neither the ideological affinities nor the closeness that had united Czartoryski with the emperor. Alexander himself soon became aware of Budberg's failings and, according to one report, even tried to get Budberg to consult Czartoryski in his work, but the prince, on principle, declined. Budberg presented a new face on the scene and at the outset was heeded more than Czartoryski had been during his last months in office. Budberg demanded much less in the way of systematic policy than Czartoryski, which suited Alexander's desire to let things drift. The emperor found himself "more free to act from day to day, without having to follow . . . a set plan . . . which could often require vigorous actions." Perhaps, as some suggested, "It was his mediocrity which supported him" at a time when Alexander wanted to assume the direction of foreign affairs himself. [5]

Budberg did not press the emperor so much, but ironically the foreign policies he adopted were in effect those of Czartoryski and basically called for vigorous action against Napoleon. Without the moral or humanitarian concerns of Czartoryski, Budberg more blatantly advocated a power-oriented, aggrandizing policy for Russia. Basically a military man, he was more inclined to emphasize military than diplomatic solutions. Future plans for Europe had none of the attraction of troop movements against Napoleon. Given continental developments, Russia's commitment to Prussia, and its interest in the Ottoman Empire, there was little

[4] Maistre to Rossi, March 1807, in Maistre, *Mémoires*, p. 268. Mikhail Semenovich Vorontsov to S. R. Vorontsov, Oct. 27, 1806, *AKV*, XXII, 362; P. A. Nikolai to S. R. Vorontsov, Jan. 18 and 22, 1807, *AKV*, XXII, 369–370, 372. Chichagov, *Mémoires*, pp. 66–67. Nesselrode, "Autobiographie," *LPN*, II, 53. "Imperator Aleksandr Pavlovich i ego dvor v 1804 g.," ed. F. F. Schiemann, *Russkaia starina*, XXIX (Dec. 1880), 822. "Even the suggestion of his nomination," wrote Novosiltsev bitterly, "makes some shrug their shoulders and others laugh" (to Stroganov, March 29, 1806, *Stroganov*, III, 172). See also S. R. Vorontsov to Stroganov, Aug. 4, 1806, *ibid.*, pp. 149–150.

[5] Merveldt to Stadion, June 28, 1806, HHS/Russ. II, 110. Stedingk to Gustav IV, June 8, 1807, Stedingk, *Mémoires*, II, 309. See also Merveldt to Stadion, March 23, 1807, HHS/Russ. III, 1.

choice; yet the two major military encounters during Budberg's ministry followed Czartoryski's blueprint for creating two theaters of operation to counter Napoleon; the Russo-Turkish war started in the fall of 1806, while the spring of 1807 saw renewed hostilities in the north in conjunction with Prussia.

The circumstances surrounding the opening of the Russo-Turkish war suggest the continued appeal of many aspects of Czartoryski's Eastern policy. Budberg was as devoted as any of Alexander's foreign ministers to the primacy of Russian influence in the Ottoman Empire, although he never expressed himself in terms of Czartoryski's nationalistic concerns for the emancipation of Slavs and Greeks from the Ottoman yoke, nor gave much concrete thought to the economic importance of the area. A crass expansionist concern for "Russian glory" in the tradition of Catherine the Great and a more immediate concern for the defense of Russian provinces against Napoleon were his predominant motives. Alexander had been hesitant about involving Russia in continental wars in the West; but the speed with which he was prepared to send troops in response to threats to the Russian position in the eastern Mediterranean suggests the potential explosiveness of the Eastern Question in the early nineteenth century and further suggests his support for the policies Budberg pursued.

Given the high degree of Russian commitment to the area, the Russian court had reason for alarm at the increasing French pressure in the eastern Mediterranean following the occupation of the Dalmatian coast. The situation reached a crisis in the summer of 1806 when, largely in response to French demands, the Turks closed the Straits to Russian warships and deposed the Russian-approved hospodars from the provinces of Moldavia and Wallachia. Russia presented a series of demands, mostly involving the satisfaction of existing treaties, but aimed at strengthening the Turkish defense against Napoleon. When no satisfaction had been received from Constantinople by the end of October, with Budberg's urging Alexander gave the order for Russian troops to enter the Danubian principalities.[6] In the meantime, the

---

[6] Budberg justified the initial invasion in his "Note circulaire communiqué

Turks agreed to reinstate the hospodars in accord with previous treaty stipulations. But Budberg argued that this action was not enough to justify calling off the invasion, since other Russian demands had not been met and since the Turks appeared more responsive to French demands than to their treaty agreements with Russia.[7]

Budberg justified the war with Turkey on the grounds of forcing the Porte to oppose the French advances, but his underlying motive was the assurance of continued Russian influence, if not advances, in the region. "The preponderance of Russian influence [in the Ottoman Empire]," he explained to the emperor late in 1806, "has become an absolute necessity for Russian glory as well as Russian security." The British ambassador may have reflected his country's fears of Russia's Eastern policy, but there was a modicum of truth in his report that Budberg's policy contained "arrière-pensées not less extensive than the most gigantic plan of Catherine II." [8]

To blame Budberg for initiating the Russo-Turkish war in 1806 suggests a greater degree of influence than he actually possessed and fails to account for the more underlying causes of the conflict.[9] Nevertheless, Budberg's insistence on the occupation of Moldavia and Wallachia, even after the Turks had met some

---

au corps diplomatique residant à la cour de St.-Pétersbourg, à l'occasion de l'entrée des troupes russes en Moldavie et en Valachie, datée du 23 octobre [Nov. 3], 1806," *SIRIO*, LXXXIX 127–131.

[7] It would appear that the Russian ambassador, A. Ia. Italinskii, thought the crisis could be resolved without further war; Budberg explained his reasons for continuing the Russian occupation in two dispatches of Nov. 27, 1806 (*VPR*, III, 381–390). Earlier in August the Russian demands were outlined in a note dated August 28, 1806, from Italinskii to the Turkish government (*VPR*, III, 273–278); a further explanation of the demands were presented by Italinskii on September 22 (*VPR*, III, 322–325). See also "Doklad Budberga," late 1806, *SIRIO*, LXXXII 491–494.

[8] "Doklad Budberga," late 1806, *SIRIO*, LXXXII, 490. Stuart to Howich, No. 9, Jan. 17, 1807, PRO/FO 65/67.

[9] For a sample of contemporary attacks blaming Budberg for the war, see Chichagov, *Mémoires*, p. 67, and Langeron to Razumovskii, July 6, 1811, *Razoumowski*, II, Part 4, 57. Boris Nol'de agrees with this contemporary view, in opposition to most other interpretations of the war's outbreak, in his chapter on the annexation of Bessarabia, *La formation de l'empire russe. Études, notes et documents* (2 vols.; Paris, 1953, "Collection historique de l'Institut d'Etudes Slaves," No. 15), II, 259–265; but this can hardly be considered a complete explanation.

of the Russian demands, had much to do with the Turkish declaration of war and the further pursuance of hostilities. Not content
with initial Russian advances or Turkish overtures for peace, he
urged the continuation of the war and especially the occupation
of Wallachia and Moldavia. But, however strongly Budberg
argued for this long-drawn-out war, he should not bear the full
responsibility. Czartoryski and others had been pushing for a
Russian advance in the Balkans for some time, and there is no
evidence that the emperor was opposed to the occupation of the
provinces. The French advances in the eastern Mediterranean,
especially the heavy troop build-up in Dalmatia, Turkish displeasure with the Russian annexation of Georgia, the incapacity of
the Ottoman Empire to sustain itself against Napoleon, and the
Porte's consequent willingness to listen to French entreaties and
to evade Russian demands, all had created a potential for conflict.

In his policies toward the West, Budberg similarly "changed
nothing in the system of Prince Adam"; even before the emperor
was ready to move in the fall of 1806, he was "zealous for vigorous measures." [10] The Prussian minister recognized that Budberg
had "an outlook which would suit us better than that of his
predecessor." However, despite his alleged German sympathies,
Budberg was appalled by Prussia's passivity and argued for
strong action against Prussia if necessary, including, in the vein
of Czartoryski's 1805 plan, the occupation of Prussian Poland.
The British representative noted that Budberg was anxious to
convince him that had he "been in office two years ago he would
have sent an army of 50,000 Russians to drive the French out of
Italy." [11]

Adopting the anti-Napoleonic plans of his predecessor, Budberg faced the same vacillation on the part of the emperor. He "is
wound up to a Pitch of Fury against Bonaparte," remarked the
British ambassador, "which His Imperial Majesty's gentle Dispo-

---

[10] Rogerson to S. R. Vorontsov, Oct. 2, 1806, *AKV*, XXX, 228–229. Merveldt to Stadion, Sept. 2, 1806, HHS/Russ. II, 111.

[11] Goltz to Hardenberg, July 27, 1806, Hardenberg, *Denkwürdigkeiten*, III,
95. Leveson-Gower to Fox, No. 20, July 17, 1806, PRO/FO 65/62.

sition in vain endeavours to curb." [12] Although it is hard to determine how much Alexander would have been willing to concede to obtain peace with France in 1806, he was certainly prepared to go much further than was his minister, as was evidenced by their divergent reactions to the Oubril treaty in the summer of 1806. The secret imperial instructions with which Oubril had been sent to negotiate in Paris indicated a strong desire for peace. When Oubril returned to St. Petersburg in July with a treaty making extensive concessions to Bonaparte, Budberg was horrified; he blamed Czartoryski for sending Oubril in the first place and declared his own repugnance at any peace with the French. Alexander, although he ultimately refused to sign the treaty, initially welcomed Oubril, hesitated to take punitive measures against him, and indicated a willingness to pursue further negotiations.[13] Budberg had no misgivings about rejecting the agreement. Later in the fall, in opposing some British proposals for peace with France, he declared that "he was not the minister to conduct such a negotiation." [14]

Budberg's stand against Napoleon and his support for new military efforts largely refute the charge of the Swedish ambassador that he was "one of those . . . ministers and courtiers . . . who await an order to think." Yet he pushed his convictions with sufficient moderation that he usually appeared to others to be "willing to abandon himself entirely to the emperor's point of view." [15] Many people eager for Budberg to pursue his policies

[12] Stuart to Leveson-Gower, in Lord Granville Leveson-Gower, *Private Correspondence, 1781–1821*, ed. Castalia Countess Granville (2 vols.; London, n.d.), II, 228.

[13] For the British ambassador's interpretation of Budberg's reaction, see Stuart to Fox, Aug. 20, 1806, PRO/FO 65/63. Budberg's official stand was expressed in his letter to Stuart enclosed with this dispatch. A few reports suggested that Alexander secretly wanted to sign the treaty although it made concessions to Napoleon, especially in the Adriatic, and that when the State Council rejected ratification, he reluctantly acquiesced and banished Oubril. That he even summoned a formal council to deal with the issue indicated to some diplomats that he preferred not to refuse the treaty himself; see Bray, "Mémoire particulier et secret sur la Russie," Dec. 1807, AE/MD: Russie, 32.

[14] Stuart to Spencer, No. 35, Oct. 11, 1806, PRO/FO 65/64.

[15] Stedingk to Gustav IV, Aug. 9, 1806, Stedingk, *Mémoires*, II, 197. Czartoryski to Stroganov, Aug. 21, 1806, *Stroganov*, II, 395.

were critical of his conduct; but, explained the British ambassador, "whatever may be the result, by submitting his own private opinions to the impulse of his Sovereign, he has chosen the surest method to preserve his situation." Budberg himself once claimed in a conference that he was "only the channel through which His Majesty chose to intimate His decided intentions." [16]

During the winter of 1807 there were rumors that he had lost favor, and, especially when Budberg suffered a prolonged illness, there were many intrigues on behalf of other candidates for his office, including Czartoryski. Yet the rumors had little foundation. "It is remarkable that the possibility of a change in favor of Prince Czartoryski is by no means increased, since the system which he has long recommended to the attention of His Imperial Majesty has been in part adopted." Even those who wanted Czartoryski's return had to conclude that "Budberg is well anchored." [17]

Although Budberg's anchorage was not that of a major policy adviser to the emperor, his urgings for the renewal of the war made him a most appropriate spokesman once Alexander decided to pursue that policy. Alexander had hoped to avoid another encounter with Napoleon, but as the Prussian armies proved so helpless against the French advance that even Poland was menaced, the emperor hastened to use his armies. While Budberg was personally enthusiastic about the renewed hostilities in the fall of 1806, his health prevented his departure for the battlefront in Alexander's immediate suite. Joining the emperor later to handle the business of the diplomatic chancellery during the campaign, he remained adamantly opposed to negotiated settlements, even in the face of military reverses. The French captured Danzig in May 1807 and continued their victorious march eastward in June. A few days before the battle of Friedland many of

---

[16] Stuart to Howich, No. 10, Jan. 17, 1807, PRO/FO 65/67. Stuart to Spencer, No. 35, Oct. 11, 1806, PRO/FO 65/64.

[17] Stuart to Howich, No. 10, Jan. 17, 1807, PRO/FO 65/67. Merveldt, the Austrian ambassador, noted (to Stadion, March 22, 1807, HHS/Russ. III, 1) that Czartoryski had refused to return but was occasionally consulted by the emperor. Rogerson to S. R. Vorontsov, May 22, 1807, *AKV*, XXX, 239.

Alexander's key advisers, themselves urging peace, claimed "that Budberg is the only one to persist in the opinion of continuing the war." Budberg held firm in stating "that our army is not yet beaten, that besides we have a large army in reserve, that we can rest on the faithful support of our Polish provinces, and that the emperor can count on the nation." The others could not persuade him to accept their arguments in favor of negotiation.[18]

Budberg's resolve was respected because Alexander was himself determined not to bow to Napoleon without further struggle and was pleased that Budberg reinforced his decision. The war continued, but the Russian forces without allied support were no match for Napoleon's armies. Horrified by the severe Russian defeat at Friedland on June 14, Budberg still took a dim view of negotiations with the French, but Alexander, deeply discouraged by the military catastrophe, decided that peace was in Russia's best interests. "Here, General, is the fatal news that I have just received," Alexander wrote his minister. "It is useless to dwell on the arguments to be made. You can conceive all the difficulty of my position. The enclosed copies will instruct you regarding the decisions which I believed necessary to make." Budberg, however, had no part in those decisions and had little to say about the instructions for Dmitrii Lobanov-Rostovskii, who was appointed to arrange the armistice with Napoleon. He was forced to "recoil from that tenacity in favor of the continuation of the war" that political opponents "regretted so much in him." [19]

When it came to the negotiations and then to a peace treaty with France in 1807, Budberg's opposition to Napoleon cost him his position. Although he was willing to subordinate his personal

---

[18] Reported by Kurakin to Maria Feodorovna, Tilsit, June 15, 1807, "Pis'ma s dorogi ot kniazia A. B. Kurakina k gosudaryne imperatritse Marii Feodorovne, 1807g," *Russkii arkhiv*, VI (1868 No. 1), 76; see also Martens, *Recueil*, VI, 419.

[19] Alexander to Budberg, June 4 [1807], Budberg Papers, TsGAOR, 860/1/7. Kurakin to Maria Feodorovna, June 22, 1807, *Russkii arkhiv*, VI (1868, No. 2), 186–187. For the differences between emperor and minister in editing the instructions for Lobanov-Rostovskii, see Sergei Tatishchev's analysis of various drafts in *Alexandre Ier et Napoléon d'après leur correspondance inédite, 1801–1812* (Paris, 1891), pp. 140–149. An additional text of the instructions found recently in Budberg's private papers in TsGAOR is printed and discussed in *VPR*, III, 754–760.

opinions in serving as Alexander's minister, his views were too well known to the French for him to officiate as Russian plenipotentiary for the negotiations. Budberg, reportedly on Napoleon's request, left Tilsit, then, under the pretext of illness and did not sign the final treaty.[20] Alexander Kurakin, a strong partisan of negotiation and peace with Napoleon, was summoned as chief plenipotentiary despite his current confinement to bed. Kurakin related, however, that he had "no responsibility" for the treaty, "because all the articles of which it is comprised were formulated, ordered, reviewed, and approved after their editing by His Majesty the emperor himself." [21]

Soon after the Tilsit interviews, Budberg submitted his resignation, but Alexander refused to grant him leave at that time. "You want to abandon me in the present moment when I most count on your aid," the emperor replied. "You seem to have completely lost sight of the trouble, I can even say the difficulty, which I would have to replace you. I should also add that your retirement could have consequences which would be prejudicial to the matters recently arranged." [22] Budberg's role in major diplomatic affairs had been cut short, but Alexander felt that the time was not ripe for a change in the foreign office. Budberg remained during the summer and was forced to absorb the criticism of the Tilsit treaty and to represent the new Russian policy.

With the violent wave of opposition to the Treaty of Tilsit on the part of the Russian gentry, Budberg was accused of having compromised Russian interests by allowing its ratification. "He is much more attached to his place than to the honor of his sovereign," wrote Simon Vorontsov from London. "Only a former Swedish subject could ratify such a treaty on the anniversary of Poltava," he chided.[23] Budberg, however, had nothing to say about its adoption and remained opposed to the terms of the treaty, particularly the provision for halting trade with England.

[20] Hardenberg, *Denkwürdigkeiten*, III, 488.

[21] Kurakin to Maria Feodorovna, July 2 and July 10, 1807, *Russkii arkhiv*, VI (1868, No. 2), pp. 208–212, 215.

[22] Alexander to Budberg, July 22, 1807, Budberg Papers, TsGAOR, 806/1/7.

[23] S. R. to M. S. Vorontsov, Aug. 12, 1807, *AKV*, XVII, 167–168.

Nevertheless, he represented the treaty so convincingly to foreign diplomats as having been necessary and beneficial for Russia that even the French envoy could report, "He has completely come around to our way of thinking since Tilsit." [24]

Budberg's personal views were diametrically opposed to official Russian policy, but he was not in any position to decide what that foreign policy should be. "It seems that the emperor exclusively directs this part himself," wrote Kochubei, "and that General Budberg has little influence on the actions of our government." In this period of crisis as in most others, Alexander personally became the sole diplomatic decision-maker. At Tilsit diplomatic arrangements grew out of the personal relations of tsar and emperor, justifying Napoleon's oft-quoted remark, "I will be your secretary, Sire, and you will be mine." [25] The foreign minister was similarly ignored in St. Petersburg while Alexander was conducting the most important aspects of diplomacy with Napoleon's personal representative, General Savary, especially since neither Napoleon nor his envoy had much respect for Budberg. One of his assistants in the ministry reported that during "the past months, Budberg has not written a single line and has left the emperor himself to arrange the important affairs." Budberg's health provided the pretext for an extended leave at the beginning of September, followed by full retirement in February. General Savary expressed the feelings of many when he reported to Napoleon, "It is no great loss." [26]

At the end of the summer, Budberg amazed several foreign

---

[24] Savary to Talleyrand, Aug. 23, 1807, *SIRIO*, LXXXIII, 34; cf. Lesseps to Talleyrand, Aug. 19, 1807, *SIRIO*, LXXXVIII, 95–113. For his explanations to other diplomats, see, for example, Budberg to Leveson-Gower, June 30, 1807, with Leveson-Gower to Canning, July 2, 1807, PRO/FO 65/69; Leveson-Gower to Canning, Aug. 16, 1807, PRO/FO 65/70; and Merveldt to Stadion, Sept. 5, 1807, HHS/Russ. III, 3.

[25] Kochubei to Richelieu, Aug. 22, 1807, *SIRIO*, LIV, 262. Hardenberg, *Denkwürdigkeiten*, III, 470; Hardenberg to Jacobi-Kloest, July 12, 1807, *ibid.*, V, 540.

[26] P. A. Nikolai to S. R. Vorontsov, Oct. 6, 1807, *AKV*, XXII, 389; Merveldt to Stadion, Sept. 15, 1807, HHS/Russ. III, 3. Savary to Talleyrand, Sept. 9, 1807, *SIRIO*, LXXXIII, 66. Budberg claimed that it was his illness since Tilsit that had kept him from taking care of business (Lesseps to Talleyrand, Aug. 19, 1807, *SIRIO*, LXXXVIII, 103); the official notifications of his leave all gave the reason of health.

diplomats when he admitted "in private conversation" that he had strong reservations about the Tilsit settlement and, in fact, about the general policy of Russia vis-à-vis Napoleon. Opposed to the treaty's secret articles against England, Budberg wanted to exonerate himself personally, but he was not merely acting in a personal capacity. "He expressed the conviction," the British ambassador reported, "that any peace with France . . . must be considered as a momentary respite and by no means as affording any prospect of permanent tranquillity. Neither the French Government, nor the French People are ripe for peace; they retain too much of their revolutionary restlessness." The departing minister's private attitude and willingness to speak out also revealed Alexander's hesitations about the French alliance. Although counter to the official Russian policy, Budberg's words reflected — and helped lay the foundations for — what was to continue as Alexander's unofficial policy. "We must employ this moment of repose in preparing the means of resistance against another attack," said Budberg, foreshadowing the secret Russian diplomatic maneuverings which were to continue until war came in 1812.[27]

In dismissing Budberg, the emperor was not dismissing a minister entirely opposed to his own personal views, for Alexander was not so "completely overwhelmed" or seduced by Napoleon as many contemporary critics and subsequent historians have suggested. Rather, his attitude reflected his characteristic ambivalence. Certainly Alexander was deeply impressed by the French emperor, especially by his military prowess and his reform projects. He found in many of Napoleon's promises the expression of his own inward hopes for peace. He was quite sincere when he assured Napoleon's ambassador that the alliance "better

---

[27] Leveson-Gower to Canning, No. 19, Sept. 2, 1807, PRO/FO 65/70. Puzzled by this attitude and uncertain about its cause or significance, the British ambassador apparently did not send all these more confidential details in his official dispatch; the copy in the Foreign Office files is a draft with most of these quoted portions lined out. Budberg also expressed the same views in a final conversation with the Austrian representative (Merveldt to Stadion, Sept. 15, 1807, HHS/Russ. III, 3).

than any other political combination . . . could maintain the peace of Europe." [28]

On the other hand, the Napoleonic conquests and the principles underlying Napoleon's aggressive system were anathema to Alexander. He had been eager to continue the war to rid Europe of this "tyrant," to restore a political equilibrium and lasting peace; in the spring of 1807 he had only a deaf ear for the entreaties of those advisers pressing for mediation. While Alexander's own hesitations in facing the military crisis gave full scope to forces of intrigue, Napoleon's armies played the most important role. Friedland was as traumatic a catastrophe for Alexander as Austerlitz had been in 1805; following this second major defeat, without the support of his allies, with exhausted armies and poor lines of supply, and with his trusted advisers urging the hopelessness of war, Alexander felt that he had little choice. "There are circumstances when one must think in preference of one's own survival and follow no other rule than that of the good of state," he remarked.[29] In the course of what Alexander described as "the most thorny negotiations which have cost us so much pain," he was naturally impressed by Napoleon's personal flattery and the terms he proposed for Russia. But it was more the demands of his official policy than his own undivided conviction which could lead him to assure the French ambassador in 1808 that "nothing can change me" or that "I am attached to [Napoleon] as well as his system *for life* and that I will attach

[28] Caulaincourt to Napoleon, May 6, 1811, Tatishchev, *Alexandre Ier et Napoléon*, p. 563.

[29] Kurakin to Maria Feodorovna, June 22, 1807, *Russkii arkhiv*, VI (1868, No. 2), 177–178. Hardenberg said that Russia's defeat came because Alexander's "extreme weakness prevented him from taking a decisive stand" against "the abominable intrigues . . . which had begun to paralyse the army and facilitate Napoleon's success" (Hardenberg to Stein, July 10, 1807, and to Jacobi, July 12, 1807, in Hardenberg, *Denkwürdigkeiten*, V, 533, 536–543). Alexander's remark lends credence to the report that Grand Duke Constantine, in affirming the opposition of the army to continued war, "had recalled to Alexander his father's fate" (Schladen to Hardenberg, June 21 and 23, 1807, *ibid.*, p. 522–526). But whatever the importance of Constantine's influence and the force of intrigues (see also Merveldt to Stadion, Aug. 2, 1807, HHS/Russ. III, 3, and Bray, "Mémoire secret sur la Russie," AE/MD: France, 32), it seems most unlikely that defeat could be attributed principally to this cause.

this country to it." [30] For within months of such a statement he
explained to his mother at the time of his personal conference
with Napoleon at Erfurt in 1808 that "Our interest obliged me"
to conclude the alliance with Napoleon. "We will see his fall with
calmness, if such is the will of God . . . ; the wisest policy is to
await the right moment to take measures." A second interview
with Napoleon was necessary in 1808 because, he hoped, "it
would save Austria and conserve its strength for the true moment
when it can use it for the general good. This moment may be
near, but it has not sounded; to accelerate it would be to ruin everything, to lose everything." [31]

Despite his official policy of devotion and submission to
France and his warm reception of Napoleon's envoys in St. Pe-
tersburg, the emperor was well aware of the difficulties of the
French alliance. In face of violent public opposition against the
Tilsit treaty and economic problems engendered by Russia's adherence to the Continental Blockade, which prohibited trade with
England, Alexander persisted in his outward support of Napoleon. "I am content to say that it would be criminal on my part if
I were to stop pursuing the policy which I feel useful for the interests of the empire on account of what the public says," he assured his mother. He readily saw that Napoleon was not adhering
to the treaty provisions and realized that sooner or later, further
war was likely, if not inevitable. But even if the alliance could
not avert war, at least it would give Russia more time to prepare.
Friendship with France must be promoted, he argued, so that
Russia would "be able to breathe freely for a while and, during
this precious time, augment our means and our forces. . . It is
only in the most profound silence that we must work, and not in
publicizing our armaments or our preparations, nor in declaring
loudly against the one whom we are defying." [32] While he was

[30] Alexander to Kurakin, July 10, 1807, quoted in Kurakin to Maria Feodorovna, Aug. 25, 1807, *Russkii arkhiv*, VII (1869, No. 3), 405. Caulaincourt to
Napoleon, April 11, 1808, *DSFR*, II, 64.

[31] Alexander to Maria Feodorovna, Sept. 6, 1808, "Nakanune Erfurtskogo
svidaniia 1808 goda," ed. N. K. Schilder, *Russkaia starina*, XCVIII (April
1899), 21–23.

[32] Alexander to Maria Feodorovna, Sept. 1808 and Sept. 6, 1808, *Russkaia*

openly chanting Napoleon's praises, Alexander secretly was preparing diplomatically and militarily for a further struggle, which
seemed more and more imminent.

The delicate nature of this policy and the emperor's own vacillation toward war and peace dictated Alexander's methods of
conducting diplomacy and the role of his foreign minister between 1807 and 1812. The official foreign minister, Nikolai Petrovich Rumiantsev, fulfilled the most important and delicate role
of serving as spokesman for the official policy of alliance with
France. At the same time and behind the back of the foreign
minister, the emperor worked through a variety of individuals to
keep open his lines of information and pursue his diplomatic and
military preparations for renewed combat. Thus Alexander himself carefully controlled the different and often contradictory
strands of Russian foreign relations.

For all his willingness to be "the channel" for Alexander's "decided intentions," Budberg was not an appropriate agent for the
official policy of peace and alliance with Bonaparte, even if his
health had been good. Alexander, eager to please his new ally
and demonstrate good faith in the engagements, most appropriately appointed a man infinitely agreeable to Bonaparte, the then
minister of commerce Count Nikolai Petrovich Rumiantsev. Few
men endorsed the French alliance as completely or as sincerely as
Rumiantsev did in the first years of its establishment. "The emperor and his minister, the Count Rumiantsev, are the only true
friends of France in Russia," remarked Napoleon's envoy in December 1807.[33] Throughout the early years of Alexander's reign,
he had advocated mediation with Napoleon. Following the assassination of the Duke d'Enghien in 1804, Rumiantsev's was the
strongest voice in council against breaking diplomatic relations

---

starina, XCVIII (April 1899), 23, 20. Alexander's early sense of the difficulties
of the alliance was noted by the Austrian diplomat Merveldt to Stadion (Sept. 15,
1807, HHS/Russ. III, 3), and was apparent in his instructions for his envoy to
France, P. A. Tolstoi, (Sept. 26, 1807, SIRIO, LXXXIX, 97–113).

[33] Savary to Champagny, Dec. 6, 1807, SIRIO, LXXXVIII, 327. For Rumiantsev's early opposition to Czartoryski's policy of a strong stand against France,
see Czartoryski, Mémoires, I, 382, and "Journal du Colonel Baron Stutterheim,"
diary entry for Nov. 23, 1804, HHS/Russ. II, 138.

with France. He consistently opposed the formation of the Third
Coalition and preparations for further war with Napoleon. He
urged an immediate arrangement with Napoleon after Austerlitz
and continued to support plans for making peace with France before Tilsit. It was thus not surprising that he would be chosen to
deal with Napoleon during the new peace. No man in the empire
was better suited for the important role of carrying out the policy
of alliance with France; and no man, aside from the emperor
himself, contributed more to the effective implementation of that
official policy.

Count Rumiantsev came from one of the wealthiest and most
prominent families of Russia. According to one estimate, his estates held approximately thirty thousand serfs. Born in 1765, son
of Catherine's eminent field marshal, Peter Aleksandrovich Rumiantsev, he was educated at court, traveled widely abroad, and
briefly attended the University of Leiden. Although he had initially been inscribed for military service and had started his career at court, he was launched into diplomacy by his appointment as minister to the German Diet in 1779. Along with several
court positions under Paul, Rumiantsev was Procurator General,
a member of the Council of State, and an important leader in
finance. During the first years of Alexander's reign he was prominent in transportation and commercial affairs for the government,
being appointed minister of commerce in 1802. He combined
the posts of foreign affairs and commerce after his replacement
of Budberg in September 1807.[34] In September 1809 after the
treaty of peace with Sweden and the annexation of Finland, he
also assumed the title of State Chancellor.

Contemporaries found Rumiantsev to have "the manners of a
courtier," and to be "well educated," with a "sweet smile aimed
to please." Completely at home in diplomatic circles, Rumiantsev
was a cultured, cultivated "man of the world," reflecting the general traditions of Catherine's court. There was a "trait of duplicity" in his "thorough grounding in diplomatic jargon," for,

---

[34] His appointment as foreign minister was official as of Feb. 24, 1808, although he assumed the office the previous autumn.

as one diplomat put it, "this minister, who . . . with the most fortunate choice of expressions knows how to say the most obliging things . . . has a peculiar talent for passing without opinion from one subject to another and thus eluding an adversary whose arguments are of sufficient strength not to be victoriously combatted." [35] Such tendencies no doubt masked some of the insecurity Rumiantsev must have felt in office, for his strengths were clearly in "the exterior manner" or "the forms" rather than the "essential qualities which the position requires." He had "an outstanding preparation for a statesman," but lacked the strength of character and intellect to be one. By 1812 his persistence in the policy of alliance with France aroused such general public disgust that some of the contemporary criticism of him reflected political antagonism. Although "assuredly neither a traitor nor an ass," as many had accused, his lack of statesmanlike qualities is well substantiated.[36]

However, Alexander, at the time eager to direct foreign relations closely himself, did not need a minister of strong character or outstanding ability. He needed a prominent man of wide respect to lend stature and dignity to the alliance with Napoleon, to support and implement the new French-oriented policy which aroused such strong opposition in gentry and court circles. This Rumiantsev was able to do with great effectiveness. The emperor had confidence in Rumiantsev, but there were none of the close personal bonds which had united the emperor with some of his earlier officials. Most significantly, Alexander appreciated Rumiantsev's willingness "to utilize his own small talents in formulating or substantiating the imperial will." Alexander had been satisfied with his handling of the Ministry of Commerce and was not willing to follow Napoleon's suggestion of sending Rumiantsev as

[35] Ludwig von Lebzeltern, "Souvenirs," 1812, Lebzeltern Papers; Stein, diary entry for June 14, 1812, *Briefe*, III, 755; Madame Anne Louise Germaine de Staël, *Dix années d'exil* (Paris, 1904), p. 326. St. Julien to Metternich, Nov. 28, 1809, HHS/Russ. III, 9.

[36] Binder to Stadion, Aug. 28, 1808, HHS/Russ. III, 7; Stedingk to Gustav IV, Sept. 18, 1807, Stedingk, *Mémoires*, II, 339; Stein, diary entry for June 14, 1812, Stein, *Briefe*, III, 755. S. R. to A. R. Vorontsov, Dec. 24, 1802, *AKV*, X, 183–184. Lebzeltern to Metternich, June 19, 1812, HHS/Russ. III, 12.

ambassador to Paris. "I found him so weakened and so sickly that I fear that in Paris he could never follow the emperor like a young man," Alexander explained to Napoleon's envoy; "and besides, he is charged with a position which he conducts very well here and for which it would be difficult for me to replace him." [37]

Rumiantsev had long wanted to be foreign minister and had been "assuring people that it is the only position for which he was made." Once in office he was extremely eager to stay there, which made him all the more careful to please the emperor. His policy, too, became tied to his position. Even by 1807 the Austrian ambassador recognized that, although Rumiantsev's "attachment for France is entire and without limits," it was still "reinforced by his desire to remain at the head of the department of foreign affairs." That correlation became more evident as the years went by, because he no doubt did recognize that his position depended on that policy. As the French ambassador aptly remarked in 1811, "He is personally interested in the maintenance of the system; if things change, he is ruined." [38] Whatever the accusations of Rumiantsev's critics at the time, Rumiantsev supported the French alliance, not as a Western-oriented Francophile who blithely sanctioned the aggressive conquests of Napoleon, but rather as a patriotic Russian who believed the alliance to be in the best interests of his native country. For Rumiantsev, these "best interests" embraced cultural and economic as well as political considerations.

Rumiantsev's national consciousness was one of the most significant elements in his general cultural outlook. By the end of the eighteenth century his "remarkable learning in the history of his fatherland" and his interest in early Slavic studies were already apparent.[39] His collection of books and manuscripts relat-

[37] Castelchikal to S. R. Vorontsov, Sept. 26, 1808, *AKV*, XXVII, 383. Reported by Savary to Napoleon, Aug. 6, 1807, *SIRIO*, LXXXIII, 4. See also Caulaincourt to Napoleon, April 11, 1808, *DSRF*, II, 63–64.

[38] Merveldt to Stadion, June 28, 1806, HHS/Russ. II, 110, and Dec. 19, 1807, HHS/Russ. III, 3; report of Lauriston, May 29, 1811, *DSRF*, VI, Part 2, 19; Stedingk to Gustav IV, Sept. 18, 1807, Stedingk, *Mémoires*, II, 339.

[39] Report of Stadion, Feb. 15, 1791, quoted by A. A. Kochubinskii, *Nachalnye gody russkogo slavianovedeniia. Admiral Shishkov i kantsler gr. Rumiantsev* (Odessa, 1887–1888), p. 63.

ing to the history and culture of Russia and the Slavic world were
to make him one of the earliest and most renowned Slavic bib-
liophiles. Through the aid of a network of friends, literary figures,
and agents throughout the continent, in the course of his life he
gathered one of the most important libraries in Russia, later established as the Rumiantsev Museum, which in turn formed the
base for the present-day Lenin Library in Moscow. While still active in the ministry of foreign affairs, Rumiantsev also started
many of the activities as a great patron of letters and scholarship
which made him such an important figure in Russian cultural history. He did much to encourage scholarship in Slavic studies, especially through the Moscow Society of History and Antiquities
and through his patronage of one of the first Russian documentary publications. Rumiantsev often spoke of "the predilection,
I might say almost the passion, which I nourish for all that relates
to our national antiquities." [40]

Rumiantsev's extensive cultural preoccupations and his policies as Russian foreign minister coincided in his political ambitions for Russia in the Balkans. Whereas his enthusiastic patronage of cultural projects in the Slavic world is usually associated
with early strains of Russian nationalism and interest in the aspirations of awakening Slavic nations, Rumiantsev himself had no
developed theories which he sought to apply in the political
realm. His regional interests were nonetheless reflected in his
view that Russia's political activities should be oriented to the
East more than to the West. His strong sympathies with the
Slavic peoples under the oppression of Turkish rule and his desires to see them under the protection of the Russian Empire foreshadowed the sentiments of later Panslavists. His political aims
for Russia in the East, however, stemmed more directly from such
eighteenth-century ambitions as were manifested in the Greek

---

[40] Rumiantsev to Bludov, Feb. 13, 1813, Rumiantsev Papers, GBL, 255/5/29.
The Moscow Society of History and Antiquities was established in 1804 and
headed by Kh. A. Chebotarev. The first volume of the Rumiantsev-sponsored
treaty series, *Sobraniia gosudarstvennykh gramot i dogovorov*, was published
in 1813 under the direction of the chief of the Moscow archives, N. N. Bantysh-
Kamenskii; on this series alone Rumiantsev reportedly spent more than 66,000
rubles.

project of Catherine the Great and her partitions of Poland (both of which he approved) than from the aggressive Panslavism of the later nineteenth century. Although Talleyrand never recognized Rumiantsev's real Slavic sentiments, his appraisal well suggested the eighteenth-century aspects of Rumiantsev's attitude when he explained: "Rumiantsev saw in the destruction of the Ottoman Empire a family trophy"; wanting "to consummate the great work begun by his father," he "attached the glory of his name to the acquisition of Constantinople." [41]

Rumiantsev's desire that Russia avoid political entanglements in Europe, like his support for the 1807 alliance, was based on his prime concern for Russia's mission in the East. He believed that inevitably the Turks would be chased out of Europe, which would only lead to Russia's benefit. Since Turkey was, in his words, "an empire ready to die without making a will," it followed that "those entitled to an inheritance would be obliged to present themselves with their claims." As a first step before trying to make peace in the current war with Turkey, Russia had to show force by crossing the Danube and claiming the two adjoining provinces of Wallachia and Moldavia.[42] What appealed to Rumiantsev most about the Tilsit settlement was Napoleon's apparent willingness to allow Russia a free hand in the eastern sphere. The idea of "a division of the world" held tremendous allure for Rumiantsev. He felt completely at home in the discussions focusing on such a plan with Napoleon's ambassador, Caulaincourt, in the winter of 1808. He recognized the possibility that Constantinople might have to remain under "an invalid power such as Turkey," but otherwise, he claimed, "this city, from its position and from ours and from all the interest of our commerce, should revert to us along with a large adjoining territory . . . including the Bosporus and the Dardanelles." Willing to abandon other areas to France, he became most dis-

---

[41] Talleyrand, *Mémoires*, I, 397. Rumiantsev's approval of Catherine's Polish partitions was noted by Caulaincourt to Champagny, Oct. 3, 1809, *DSRF*, IV, 112. See also Albert Vandal, *Napoléon et Alexandre Ier. L'alliance russe sous le premier empire*, 2nd ed. (Paris, 1893), II, 546–548.

[42] Rumiantsev to Alexander, Paris, Dec. 27, 1808, and Jan. 8, 1809, *VPR*, IV, 439, 456–457.

tressed when it appeared that Napoleon was not willing to relinquish control of the Straits to Russia. "You dispose of territories at your will. . ." he complained to Caulaincourt; but "we never get what we ask for. . . . You must be fair," he continued; "what we have done for you is apparent to everyone, but what have you done for us?"[43] Alexander was willing to condone these discussions not out of commitment to such schemes, but only because he deemed them necessary to prolong the tenuous peace with Napoleon.

Undoubtedly, Rumiantsev was much more ambitious territorially for Russia than Alexander I. With regard to the Swedish war in 1808, Rumiantsev complained about the lack of prospective gains for Russia: "only spilt blood without advantage for the country." Advantage to him meant territorial aggrandizement, but he confided to the French ambassador that the emperor was "often discontented with me because I do not think the same [as he does about the situation]." Rumiantsev was eagerly pressing for the incorporation of the duchy of Finland into Russia; but only after much hesitation did the emperor sign the proclamation of war against Sweden in the spring of 1808 and agree to annexation of Finland in 1809.[44] The French ambassador, Caulaincourt, noted that Rumiantsev "is always politically ambitious in outlook — he wants to enlarge the empire." By contrast, Alexander, the ambassador believed, "personally had no desire for the aggrandizement" of Russia, but in order to make the French alliance "seem more legitimate in the eyes of his people — that is, the leaders and the army — it was necessary to demonstrate that there were advantageous results." In contrast to Rumiantsev, recalled Talleyrand, Alexander was much "less directed by political views than by philosophical maxims." "Pushing the Turks back into Asia," in Alexander's words, was "a noble action

[43] Report of Caulaincourt, March 2, 1808, *DSRF*, I, 199–200; Caulaincourt to Champagny, Feb. 25, 1808, *SIRIO*, LXXXVIII, 507. Rumiantsev's plans for Turkey were set forth in his memorandum, "Vues générales sur la Turquie," 1808, quoted by Martens, *Recueil*, XIV, 45–54, which was apparently the same document printed by Tatishchev, *Alexandre Ier et Napoléon*, pp. 365–370.

[44] Caulaincourt to Champagny, Jan. 13, 1808, *SIRIO*, LXXXVIII, 416. Merveldt to Stadion, April 6, 1808, HHS/Russ. III, 5.

which would enfranchise these fine countries." The Russian emperor, somewhat uneasy about political bargaining with Napoleon, reportedly explained that such plans served the purpose of "giving the projects we have conceived at Tilsit a liberal shade which the acts of enlightened sovereigns must have." [45]

With the war of 1812, Rumiantsev's expansionist tendencies took a more blatantly nationalist hue, showing more influence of his Slavic concerns on his political attitudes. The Napoleonic advances which aroused popular patriotism throughout Europe and left nationalistic sentiments in their wake had a similar effect on the chancellor. When the French emperor marched his armies into Russia, Rumiantsev's political utterances, in marked contrast to his earlier statements, assumed a more self-consciously Slavic cast. He viewed the Napoleonic invasion as "a war to enslave the Slavic nations." He spoke of Alexander as "the sovereign of this great nation of Slavs of which all the other tribes are only the sources," who should send "aid quickly to those same tribes which he regards and cherishes as his children" in order to prevent "those people, who are so brave and famous in history . . . [from falling] victim to the foreigner." [46] Alexander was quite prepared to utilize the nationalist sentiments in line with Czartoryski's early plan for a diversion against Napoleon in the Balkans. "Care must be taken," the emperor said, "to use the spirit of the Greeks and of all the peoples who suffer under the Ottoman yoke and who are attached to us by the conformity of their religion as well as their ancient lineage." But his views differed from his minister's in that he was principally concerned "to use all possible means to exalt the Slavic populations in order to lead them to our ends" against Napoleon, while Rumiantsev's expressions contained the seeds of more outright support for Slavic nationalism and for Russian expansion in the Balkans. [47]

---

[45] Caulaincourt to Champagny, Dec. 29, 1807, *SIRIO*, LXXXVIII, 389. Talleyrand, *Mémoires*, I, 398.

[46] Rumiantsev to Alexander, July 17, 1812, *VPR*, VI, 487.

[47] Conversation with Alexander recorded in Chichagov, *Mémoires*, p. 55. Chichagov had proposed an appeal to Balkan nationalism to Alexander; with the emperor's approval it was included in his written instructions (Alexander to Chichagov, April 19, 1812, quoted in Chichagov, *Mémoires*, p. 60). See also

By 1812, however, Rumiantsev no longer had any real influence on Russian political developments.

Rumiantsev's economic concerns for Russia paralleled his cultural or nationalistic sentiments as a basis for his preoccupation with Russia's mission in the East, and also influenced his reaction to the Napoleonic alliance. Rumiantsev, as minister of commerce from 1802 to 1809 and in other personal and official roles, stands out as one of the pioneer spokesmen for Russian economic development in the early nineteenth century. Substantial personal financial investment went hand in hand with his support of state initiative in a variety of projects aimed at economic modernization and commercial development. He was particularly eager to increase canals and communication facilities and as superintendent of waterways initiated one of the most important canal extension projects. He stressed the need for improvement of agriculture and agricultural industries; he personally imported new strains of grain and other plants into Russia and on both individual and official levels was deeply involved in the beet sugar and textile industries. His projects for extending Russian trade were at the heart of many of his diplomatic activities. Both in terms of personal finance and official political support, he was one of the principal sponsors of the Krusenstern mission which set out to initiate trading contacts with Japan in 1804 and 1805, viewing this as a starting point for developing commercial ties with Asia. Similarly, he gave financial and political support to the Russian-American Company, which was engaged in trade in Alaska and the Bering Sea and which successfully established a trading colony at Fort Ross, California, in 1812.[48] He encouraged closer diplomatic ties with the United States and with Latin America in the hope of facilitating trade, while his support of American com-

---

Alexander to Chichagov, May 2, 1812, *SIRIO*, VI, 67–73, and Rumiantsev to Chichagov, May 26, 1812, Chichagov Papers, GBL, 333/25.

[48] One of his many agricultural projects is discussed in his correspondence with Borel (1812–1814), Rumiantsev Papers, GBL, 255/6/61. Among many statements about the Russian-American Company are his report to Alexander, Oct. 13, 1805, Rumiantsev Papers, GBL, 255/5/26 and his draft letter to Alexander, Dec. 3, 1813, Rumiantsev Papers, GBL, 255/5/25; his financial support is well substantiated.

mercial interests led him to press Alexander to mediate in the Anglo-American War of 1812.[49]

Behind many of these projects was the aim for Russia to become an important commercial power and a real center of commerce for the Eurasian continent — not unlike Kiev in the Middle Ages — functioning as a commercial bridge between western Europe and Asia. Like many forward-looking Russians of his day who were resentful of British maritime dominance, Rumiantsev was very eager to overcome the preponderant British economic influence in Russia and to cut Russia's commercial dependence on England, whose fleet was the major carrier for Russian foreign trade. Rumiantsev had been as suspicious of the British interests in the Near East as the British were of Russian ambitions; his hopes for the consolidation of Russian control in the Black Sea area thus directly involved his desire to exclude British influence. In much the same terms as Czartoryski used, Russia's expansion in the Balkans for him had a most important economic dimension, which was an integral part of Rumiantsev's plans for Russian commercial development.

Unlike Czartoryski, Rumiantsev's interest in establishing a commercial balance with other nations and reducing the commercial dependence on England, carried no political illusions about the superiority of British political institutions or the desirability of Britain as a close ally against Napoleon. Politically and economically, he had "no very favorable sentiments toward Great Britain." While Rumiantsev's expansionism had led directly to his support of the alliance with France, his economic ambitions for his country could easily — at least on a general level — coincide with the treaty provision calling for the closing of Russian ports to British trade. Such a move could only help to destroy "the despotism which [England] exercises on the seas,"

---

[49] During his ministry the American mission was raised to ministerial rank. His interests in American commerce were recorded frequently by John Quincy Adams (e.g., *Memoirs*, June 4, 1811, and Feb. 4, 1812, II, 271, 335–337). As an example of his support for commercial relations with Latin America, see "Zapiska ministra inostrannykh del N. P. Rumiantseva Gosudarstvennomu sovetu," March 3, 1811, *VPR*, VI, 83–84. See also "Zapiska ob otkrytii torgovykh snoshenii s rishpanskimi koloniiami," Sept. 28, 1811, *VPR*, VI, 171–172.

encourage Russian economic independence from England, and promote the development of commercial relations with other powers.[50] This policy aroused much antagonism toward Rumiantsev among those who favored Britain or who depended on English goods and services. "As his system of Policy is anti-Britannic," reported John Quincy Adams in 1810, "he is most notoriously hated by all the British party in this country."[51] He further alienated British sympathizers by his encouragement of American interests in the War of 1812.

While Rumiantsev supported the Tilsit agreements and even was sympathetic in theory to the trade break with Britain, he was responsive enough to commercial realities to realize that complete and immediate adherence to Napoleon's Continental Blockade against England would have been disastrous for Russian commerce. France was simply not prepared economically to replace British commercial functions, nor were business patterns well enough established with other powers to overcome the economic dislocations involved. Rumiantsev accordingly showed his discontent with various economic difficulties of the French alliance and even openly voiced his opposition to "Napoleon's erroneous ideas of commerce." He explained his view to John Quincy Adams: "Commerce is the concern of us all," he stated. It "is the very chain of human association; it is the foundation of all the useful and pacific intercourse between nations; it is a primary necessity to all classes of People. The Emperor Napoleon will never see it in this light, and so his commercial regulations and promises will never be systematic or consistent — you can place little dependence upon them."[52]

---

[50] Leveson-Gower to Canning, Sept. 9, 1807, PRO/FO 65/70; Rumiantsev to Kurakin, Dec. 6, 1810, *VPR*, V, 624.

[51] J. Q. Adams to William Eustis, Feb. 28, 1810, Adams, *Writings*, III, 404. See also Czartoryski, *Mémoires*, I, 382, and Merveldt to Stadion, Sept. 15, 1807, HHS/Russ. III, 3, Stein (diary entry for June 14, 1812, *Briefe*, III, 755–756) recorded an anecdote suggesting that Rumiantsev's Anglophobia stemmed from an episode when he competed for a woman with Whitworth, an earlier British ambassador; Rumiantsev believed that the British ambassador had won the woman by cheating him.

[52] Adams, *Memoirs*, Nov. 15, 1809, II, 66; Jan. 3, 1811, II, 211, and Feb. 4, 1812, II, 336. The French ambassador sensed Rumiantsev's discontent with

Recent Soviet research has shown that the period of the Continental Blockade was not as economically disastrous for Russia as had previously been believed. Indeed, despite some severe economic dislocations and difficulties, especially in 1808, the total trade picture after 1808 showed no less improvement than had been usual before 1807. Rumiantsev, accordingly, had some basic economic justification for his support of the Napoleonic alliance. When Russia sought to introduce tariff revisions in 1810 and 1811 which were to prove unfavorable to French trade and were counter to Napoleon's plans, Rumiantsev, at least officially, opposed them in the Council of State. There may well have been some political motives in such an official stand, but only after Alexander had irrevocably decided on the new policy did Rumiantsev withdraw his protest.[53] Whatever his awareness of the economic disadvantages of specific French policies, Rumiantsev sought not to antagonize Napoleon in ways which might destroy the alliance, which after 1810 grew increasingly shaky. He fully believed that Russia had more to gain than to lose from continuing the alliance and that further war would be economically much more disastrous for Russia.

Cultural, political, and economic considerations were thus all involved in Rumiantsev's support of the alliance. The fact that he had so many reasons to support the peace with Napoleon which were all so intricately related to his ambitions for Russia had much to do with his obvious conviction in implementing this policy. And his sincerity, in turn, had much to do with the effectiveness with which Alexander could pursue it officially.

Those in good positions to judge Rumiantsev at the time

---

the economic arrangements in the winter of 1808 (Caulaincourt to Champagny, Feb. 25, 1808, *SIRIO*, LXXXVIII, 519).

[53] V. G. Sirotkin (*Duel' dvukh diplomatii, Rossiia i Frantsiia v 1801–1812 gg.* [Moscow, 1966], pp. 134–162) cites and briefly analyzes much of the recent research on Russian trade during the Continental Blockade. But further analysis remains to be done on Rumiantsev's economic views and recommendations during this period. See his report for the year 1809 presented to the senate Oct. 29, 1810, in *VPR*, V, 558–566. J. Q. Adams to R. Smith, Jan. 27, 1811, Adams, *Writings*, IV, 3–5; Adams, *Memoirs*, Feb. 4, 1812, II, 336. See Rumiantsev's justification of the new tariff to the Russian ambassador in France (Rumiantsev to Kurakin, Jan. 18, 1811, *VPR*, VI, 14–15).

"doubted not that he took this alliance to be quite sincere." His reservations were minor, for he shared none of Alexander's major misgivings. The French had every reason to be satisfied with his reactions: "Count Rumiantsev . . . is reputed for his uprightness, very attached to his country, and strong in the intimate conviction that it is the best interest to remain united with France." So read a police report to Napoleon in the winter of 1807/1808.[54] Russian envoys who tried to convince Rumiantsev that he was seeing "everything in rosy colors" had no success. "Dispatches which were not always very favorable to the French alliance," recalled Nesselrode, then serving as secretary in Paris, "were displeasing to Rumiantsev, the devilish soul of Napoleon."[55] Following the meetings at Erfurt in 1809, Rumiantsev visited Paris, where Napoleon did his best to allay any doubts the chancellor may have had about the alliance; Metternich thought that Rumiantsev "was caught in the nets which Napoleon spread for him." Rumiantsev boasted that he persuaded Alexander to agree to the proclamation of Napoleon's brother as King of Spain, and he called the French take-over of Spain "the foundation of peace for the continent of Europe." Once Rumiantsev was back in St. Petersburg, Caulaincourt could report, "He returned more attached than ever to the system of alliance between Russia and France." As late as August 1811, John Quincy Adams could still rightly claim that Rumiantsev "is the man of the Russian dominions most deeply pledged and most strongly attached to the French alliance."[56] The apoplectic stroke which Rumiantsev suffered at the beginning of the war of

[54] Metternich, "Autobiographie," *Mémoires*, I, 61 (see also extracts of Metternich's reports to Stadion, Jan. 11 to Feb. 17, 1809, *ibid.*, II, 257–274). Police report quoted by René Bittard des Portes, "Les préliminaires de l'entrevue d'Erfurt, 1808," *Revue d'histoire diplomatique*, IV (Jan. 1890), 109–110.

[55] P. A. Tolstoi to Rumiantsev, Jan. 26, 1808, *SIRIO*, LXXXIX, 390. Nesselrode, "Autobiographie," *LPN*, II, 64. See also, Merveldt to Stadion, Dec. 19, 1807, HHS/Russ. III, 3.

[56] Metternich, "Autobiographie," *Mémoires*, I, 61; Metternich to Stadion, Jan. 11, 1809, Metternich, *Mémoires*, II, 259. Caulaincourt to Champagny, March 22, 1809, *DSRF*, III, 170. Adams to Monroe, Aug. 9, 1811, Adams, *Writings*, IV, 170–174.

1812 was symbolic of the severe shock he felt when Napoloen invaded Russia.

The sincerity with which Rumiantsev supported the French alliance made him a perfect spokesman for Alexander's official policy, but his importance as Russian foreign minister was not predicated on his filling a major decision-making role. In St. Petersburg or at Erfurt, as at Tilsit, Alexander continued to handle important diplomatic affairs himself, dealing directly with Napoleon or his representative. Normal diplomatic channels were frequently avoided. "Your letter makes me believe that you are no more instructed than I about the private correspondence between the two emperors," complained the Russian envoy in Paris to Rumiantsev. The French ambassador dined frequently at court and had easy access to Alexander; as one of his diplomatic colleagues noted, "The Duke de Vicene has during the whole of his embassy here been treated by the Emperor Alexander with a degree of favor and until lately of confidence, which he never showed to any other ambassador." [57] More often than not, Rumiantsev remained poorly informed about the emperor's personal conferences, and papers stayed on the emperor's desk for months at a time without Rumiantsev's knowing their contents. The American minister aptly noted, "Count Romanzoff [sic] transacts business personally with the Emperor of which the Council knows nothing, the French ambassador transacts business personally with the Emperor, of which neither the Council nor Count Romanzoff himself is informed." [58]

Although Alexander depended on Rumiantsev as his spokesman for the French alliance, the emperor never really had a high opinion of his talents and gave him little room for initiative or responsibility. The emperor might assure his minister, "Our friendship dates from a long time ago, and I have more and more occasion to convince myself of the sincerity of your attachment for

[57] Tolstoi to Rumiantsev May 8, 1808, *SIRIO*, LXXXIX, 526–527. Adams to R. Smith, March 25, 1811, Adams, *Writings*, IV, 37. The unprecedented imperial reception of the French envoys in contrast to their ostracism from Russian society is noted in their reports and memoirs.

[58] Adams, *Memoirs*, Aug. 9, 1810, II, 148–149.

me"; and he might often ask his minister's opinions and welcome
his comments or express satisfaction with the correspondence he
drafted. But such compliments failed to compensate Rumiantsev
for the type of statement Alexander reportedly made behind his
back, claiming that "he was his own minister for foreign affairs
and that Rumiantsev was only for menial tasks." An Austrian
diplomat reported at one point that Rumiantsev did not even
have "permission to issue a passport without the orders of his
master." [59] While such a statement was undoubtedly exaggerated
and reflected the frustrations of the cumbersome Russian bureaucracy, its tenor does indicate the often demeaning subordination under which Rumiantsev was forced to operate.

If Rumiantsev did not always have a responsible role in relations with France, there was political method in his exclusion
from the negotiations against France. As the drift toward war between France and Russia became more apparent, Alexander was
trying to establish lines of cooperation with other powers, usually through a variety of special secret channels, while Rumiantsev,
through the regular diplomatic channels, continued as spokesman for the official policy. Rumiantsev, even though he disapproved, was often required to take part in such anti-French negotiations as the project for a convention with Prussia which "the
doubtful intentions of Napoleon" might make necessary.[60] In
such cases he usually tried to make clear that such overtures
came from Alexander himself. "I have just written you by his order, and I should say, from his dictation," he explained to Lieven. Rumiantsev, with his strong support of the French alliance — "stemming as much from [his] personal conviction as our
[Russia's] political interest" — "inspired little confidence"
among those who were pressing the emperor to take measures

[59] Alexander to Rumiantsev, note received Nov. 20, 1809, Gosarkhiv V,
TsGADA, 5/209; see also the notes received Nov. 7, 1810, and July 16, 1811.
St. Julien to Metternich, April 25, 1811, HHS/Russ. III, 11. Merveldt to Stadion,
April 6, 1808, HHS/Russ. III, 5.
[60] Rumiantsev to Lieven, Oct. 7, 1811, *VPR*, VI, 177–178. This letter enclosed
Alexander's draft of a project of alliance; further consultations about Prussian
projects were evident in Alexander to Rumiantsev, penciled note received
Nov. 10, 1811, Gosarkhiv V, TsGADA, 5/209.

against Napoleon. Therefore diplomats usually avoided him when dealing with such projects.[61]

Rumiantsev had a scant role, for example, in the secret negotiations with Austria, which were mostly conducted through Alexander's friend and court associate R. A. Koshelev, who strongly opposed Rumiantsev both personally and politically. Starting in 1809, Koshelev dealt directly with the special Austrian envoy St. Julien and arranged meetings for him with the emperor, which Rumiantsev was unable to prevent, much to his distress. As St. Julien reported, the emperor instructed him to talk about things with Rumiantsev only in vague or general terms and discuss the details and important issues with Alexander himself, either directly or through Koshelev.[62] Stackelberg, the Russian minister in Vienna after 1810, had also been instructed by secret order of the emperor — sent by courier from the war department to avoid the suspicion of Rumiantsev — to communicate directly with him on all important affairs through Koshelev." Koshelev served as an important intermediary for the emperor in similar relations with Spanish, British, and Neapolitan agents, especially in 1810 and 1811; by the beginning of 1812, however, his favor had waned, and other individuals took over this function.[63]

There were special agents in Vienna who reported through a

[61] Rumiantsev to Lieven, confidential, Feb. 20, 1811, *VPR*, VI, 71–72. Lieven to Rumiantsev, March 29, 1811, *VPR*, VI, 93. St. Julien to Metternich, Feb. 22, 1811, HHS/Russ. III, 11.

[62] St. Julien to Metternich, No. 2, Dec. 12, 1809, HHS/Russ. III, 9; St. Julien to Metternich, Feb. 15 and 22, 1811, HHS/Russ. III, 11. Koshelev in 1806 had recommended a strong defensive alliance against Napoleon. His later memoranda — for example, one dated April 19, 1811 (NM, *Alexandre*, II, 27–31) — also pressed for a stronger stand against Napoleon than was official policy; Koshelev's opinions on this were described by St. Julien to Metternich (April 26 and Sept. 28, 1811, HHS/Russ. III, 11).

[63] St. Julien to Metternich, April 26, 1811, HHS/Russ. III, 11. Martens, *Recueil*, III, 78–81, mentioned secret instructions in Alexander's hand of Feb. 25, 1811, but doubted Stackelberg received them; apparently he did, however, as Grand Duke Nicholas Mikhailovich printed copies of his letters to Koshelev (March 30–Oct. 6, 1811), in *Alexandre*, II, 79–102. Koshelev's letters to Alexander and the reports from other agents are in NM, *Alexandre*, II, 13–78 and 118–137; references to many of the British reports are in the collections in PRO/FO 65/76 and 78. Alexander's displeasure with Koshelev was expressed in his letter to Koshelev of Oct. 11, 1811, NM, *Alexandre*, II, 4; see also St. Julien to Metternich, Jan. 27, 1812, HHS/Russ. III, 12.

variety of channels. For example, Count Andrei Kirillovich Razumovskii remained in Vienna unofficially after the Francophile Kurakin replaced him as Russian ambassador in 1807 and continued as an agitator against Napoleon; Mallia, an Italian resident in Vienna who served Russia earlier in an intelligence capacity, continued as an occasional informer. The Corsican adventurer-diplomat Pozzo di Borgo, who had been in the Russian service since 1804, was also in Vienna during most of these years, but because his outspoken vendetta against Napoleon resulted in his being completely under surveillance by the French, he was usually not in direct communication with the Russian court. Russia officially denied that he was in Russian service after 1809 when Napoleon had demanded his dismissal. But when he embarked on a secret mission to Turkey in 1810 and 1811 under the aegis of the British mission, Russian officials nevertheless kept in touch with him secretly and sought his support; his contribution to Russia during this period, however, was barely marginal. A much better channel for Russian-Austrian relations was established when the young Austrian diplomat Lebzeltern arrived as Metternich's special envoy in St. Petersburg in early 1811 to establish direct contact with Alexander; bypassing both Rumiantsev and Koshelev, he even accompanied the emperor secretly to the imperial headquarters in Vilna during the last weeks of May 1812.[64]

Throughout his active period in the foreign ministry from 1807 to 1812, Rumiantsev was overshadowed in the emperor's confidence, and consequently in his political role, by the reforming bureaucrat, Michael Speranskii, who served in fact, if not in name, as the emperor's prime minister. Speranskii's comprehen-

[64] See *Razoumowski*, II, Part 3, 16–22. Regarding Pozzo di Borgo, see, for example, Alexander to Shuvalov, 1810, Gosarkhiv V, TsGADA, 5/211; Caulaincourt to Champagny, June 8, 1808, *DSRF*, II, 181; Rumiantsev to Shuvalov, Aug. 25 and Sept. 28, 1810, *VPR*, V, 493–494, 534–535. Lebzeltern's account of his mission is in his journal, "Souvenirs," MSS in Lebzeltern Papers, and in the fragmentary reports to Metternich among his private papers and in HHS/Russ. III, 11–12. Alexander's reaction to the mission is in part expressed in a letter to Chichagov soon after Lebzeltern's departure (June 19, 1812, in Goriainov, *1812*, Part II, 57–60).

sive constitutional project and his efforts toward restructuring the
Russian government and legal system had as their goal a strong
constitutional monarchy with a national legislative assembly, lo-
cal self-government, an improved bureaucracy and financial administration, and a firmly established legal basis for government
and society. His activities gave a progressive aura to the period
and stand out among the most impressive hopes for reform in
Russia, but they shared the fate of other similar projects during
Alexander's reign. Few of Speranskii's plans were translated into
practice before Speranskii himself was dismissed abruptly under
still-hazy circumstances in March 1812. Although he enjoyed
full imperial confidence while in office, Speranskii's plans were
victims of the emperor's fears and his hesitation to translate projects into action, which were increased by the lack of social support for these reforms and by the ominous foreign situation.

Rumiantsev shared none of Speranskii's concern for major
governmental and legal reform. Further, he had scant personal
respect for Speranskii, not so much because Speranskii was the
highly intelligent son of a minor clergyman, but because, satisfied
with the emperor's personal support and friendship, Speranskii
kept himself aloof from the inner circles of court and society.
Furthermore, Speranskii's marriage to an English girl had
strengthened his ties to English interests who were vocally opposed to the French alliance. Rumiantsev became quite sympathetic to the intrigues at court which eventually succeeded in
bringing about Speranskii's fall.

What appeared to Rumiantsev as an even greater threat to his
position, was that Speranskii, in addition to his work for domestic reform, had also assumed some responsibility for foreign affairs. Most particularly, Speranskii had an increasingly important
role in implementing the emperor's unofficial, secret policy of
preparation for war against Napoleon, and he often made general
recommendations to the emperor on diplomatic affairs.[65] On the

---

[65] See Speranskii's memoranda on foreign affairs: "Zapiska M. M. Speranskogo
o veroiatnostiakh voiny s Frantsieiu posle Til'zitskogo mira," ed. N. Dubrovin,
*Russkaia starina*, CI (Jan. 1900), 57–65, and "Dve zapiski M. M. Speranskogo
po politicheskim delam," *Russkaia starina*, CIV (Nov. 1900), 429–440, and
"O delakh shvedskikh," April 1809, *VPR*, V, 8–10.

whole, Rumiantsev was poorly informed about the secret channels of communication with France, although he did receive
some intelligence reports about French military preparations
from Alexander's aide-de-camp, A. I. Chernyshev, who, while
serving as a courier for the tsar's personal letters to Napoleon,
also organized an effective intelligence network in Paris.[66] Speranskii accompanied the emperor to the conference with Napoleon at Erfurt in 1808 and thereafter handled many of the subversive Russian contacts with the French minister, Talleyrand.
Speranskii also dealt with some of the secret communications
with the Austrian court. When Count Nesselrode was sent on a
secret mission to France in 1810 and 1811 — ostensibly to arrange a loan and serve as secretary in the Russian embassy in
Paris — Speranskii was his intermediary for reports to the emperor. Nesselrode reported to Speranskii his recommendations
and the results of his secret conversations with "Uncle Henry"
(the code name for Talleyrand) in a correspondence carried on
for eight months "without the suspicions of Kurakin or
Rumiantsev." [67]

Rumiantsev became increasingly jealous of others who were
working directly with the emperor in foreign affairs, realizing
that they were often involved in intrigues to have him removed
from office and to reverse official Russian policy toward France.
His jealousy and his opposition to making further preparations
for war with France caused him to oppose sending Nesselrode
back to Paris on another special mission. Although the French
ambassador may not have known all the details of the mission,
his appraisal of Rumiantsev's reaction was pertinent when he

[66] Many of these reports both to Alexander and to Rumiantsev are published
in *Bumagi A. I. Chernysheva za tsarstvovanie Imperatora Aleksandra I, 1809–
1825 gg.*, *SIRIO*, CXXXI; see also, Savary, *Mémoires*, V, 124–133, 144–145, 201,
204–217.

[67] Nesselrode, "Autobiographie," *LPN*, II, 66–71. Talleyrand had met Speranskii at Erfurt and recommended him as an intermediary in a letter to Alexander
(Feb. 10, 1809, printed as a note in Evgenii Viktorovich Tarle, *Taleiran*, in *Sochi-
neniia* [12 vols.; Moscow, 1957–1961], XI, 849); many of Nesselrode's letters
to Speranskii regarding contacts with Talleyrand were printed in *LPN*, III,
225–387. Speranskii's secretary, Gervais, spoke of Speranskii's communications
with France through Nesselrode and with Austria through Mallia (Gervais to
Alexander, April 7, 1812, Schilder, *Aleksandr*, III, 494).

suggested that Rumiantsev "would prefer to conduct business at a distance rather than see the discussion escape him." [68]

Rumiantsev may have had "the self-esteem to believe that he alone can conclude matters satisfactorily," but clearly he was only one of many individuals with whom Alexander was working in his diplomatic maneuvers. [69] Different advisers claimed Alexander's confidence, because he encouraged them all to believe they possessed it, but in fact "the emperor did not place his entire confidence in anyone." Alexander had a way of informing "many individuals partially of things that occupy him the most while he is talking to them. . . . The result of these streams of confidence is that no one knows about matters in their entirety." [70] Sometimes with determination and political foresight, sometimes because of vacillation and uncertainty, Alexander did support differing opinions, but only in his own mind were the conflicts to be resolved — or left unresolved.

To say that Alexander did not have full confidence in Rumiantsev or that Rumiantsev "did not know the sovereign's soul or private opinions" [71] is not to suggest that Rumiantsev did not have an extremely important role in the conduct of Russian diplomacy during his tenure. Even while he was not a key decision-maker, his support of the official policy made him a valuable assistant for Alexander during the French alliance, which was maintained through his sincere devotion to it and Napoleon's confidence in him. Privately, Napoleon taxed Rumiantsev "with a lack of judgment and character, and with sacrificing everything to his own fancies," but, recognizing Rumiantsev's naïve reliance on his assurances that he would never invade Russia, Napoleon valued Rumiantsev highly as foreign minister. "By his talents and his consummate prudence," Napoleon wrote Alexander following

---

[68] St. Julien to Metternich, April 26 and Sept. 1, 1811, HHS/Russ. III, 11; Lebzeltern to Metternich, Jan. 14, 1812, HHS/Russ. III, 12. Report of Lauriston, Dec. 14, 1811, *DSRF*, VI, Part 2, 168.

[69] Report of Lauriston, Jan. 2, 1812, *DSRF*, VI, Part 2, 174.

[70] Lebzeltern to Metternich, June 18, 1812, HHS/Russ. III, 12. See also St. Julien to Metternich, Sept. 1, 1811, HHS/Russ. III, 11.

[71] N. I. Grech, "Vospominaniia starika," in *Zapiski o moei zhizni* (Moscow, 1930), p. 338.

Rumiantsev's visit to Paris, "no one is more suited to realize what we have conceived for the good of the world." [72] And Alexander could assure the French ambassador, "I am very content with Rumiantsev, and doubly so because he has been appreciated by the emperor Napoleon." [73] The Russian public scorned the man whom they considered "bought by the ribbon of the Legion of Dishonor," but Alexander could not easily have found anyone else to support his official policy as enthusiastically as Rumiantsev, who even in October of 1811 could sincerely call the alliance "one of the most beautiful creations of the genius of Napoleon." [74] As Budberg had served as spokesman for the earlier war against Napoleon, so Rumiantsev served Alexander as a perfect figurehead for the policy of peace.

Soon after arriving in St. Petersburg, Caulaincourt summarized Rumiantsev's position: "The experience of the minister, the confidence which has surrounded him for a long time — perhaps more than his talents — , the memories of Catherine attached to his name and to his opinion which is the compensation necessary for the country after its defeats, all this serves the emperor in his chosen policy." The dignity which Rumiantsev's background brought to his office did not prove much of a bulwark against the violent public "ridicule" with which he was treated.[75] Yet by the very distrust and scorn which he aroused by his support of France, Rumiantsev further served the Russian emperor as a scapegoat for the public hatred of the Napoleonic alliance. In all these ways, even though he did not directly make important decisions, Rumiantsev filled a crucial role in the period before the 1812 war.

[72] Napoleon was quoted by Metternich to Francis, April 4, 1810, Metternich, *Mémoires*, II, 329. Napoleon to Alexander, Feb. 14, 1809, *Correspondance de Napoléon I* (32 vols.; Paris, 1858–1869), XVIII, 311 (No. 14778).

[73] Alexander was quoted by Caulaincourt to Napoleon, March 17, 1809, *DSRF*, III, 156. See also Alexander to Napoleon, March 25, 1809, in Tatishchev, *Alexandre Ier et Napoléon*, pp. 470–471; Report of Lauriston, June 25, 1811, *DSRF*, VI, Part 2, 37, and Caulaincourt to Champagny, Sept. 16, 1809, *DSRF*, IV, 88.

[74] Langeron to Razumovskii, July 6, 1811, *Razoumowski*, II, Part 4, 58. Report of Lauriston, Oct. 7, 1811, *DSRF*, VI, Part ii, 119.

[75] Report of Caulaincourt, Dec. 31, 1807, *DSRF*, I, 33; Caulaincourt to Champagny, Sept. 16, 1809, *DSRF*, IV, 88.

The very fact that Rumiantsev had served so well "as a patient tool for . . . the system of submission to France" made it more difficult for Alexander to dismiss the chancellor when war came. Alexander stood firm in the face of the violent public outcry against the man they blamed for having "brought the enemy to the gate of Moscow" and evidenced continuing regard for the chancellor, especially after Rumiantsev's apoplectic stroke en route to Vilna. Rumiantsev was extremely eager to continue in Alexander's service, despite the partial paralysis with which he arrived at imperial headquarters.[76] Without dismissing him, Alexander assigned him a diminishing role in the conduct of diplomacy, less in retaliation for his earlier policies than because of the growing divergence between emperor and minister produced by the outbreak of war.

In the early months of 1812, Alexander realized that war was imminent. Despite his misgivings about war, the uncertainties about alliances, and the continuing vacillations which characterized his activities, he was nevertheless still trying to continue his simultaneous policies of war and peace. Yet, unlike Rumiantsev, he had few illusions about the chances for further accommodation with Napoleon or for avoiding the impending invasion of Russia. By early 1812 Rumiantsev, too, was talking more openly of the coming war with France and, following Alexander's desires as well as his own, he wanted to postpone it as long as possible. Rumiantsev's underlying commitment, however, was well identified by Napoleon when he remarked to an aide, "Up until the last day, Rumiantsev did not want to believe in war. He had persuaded Alexander that our movements were only men-

[76] Diary entry for June 14, 1812, Stein, *Briefe*, III, 755. Wilson to Cathcart, Aug. 27, 1812, in Robert Thomas Wilson, *Private Diary of Travels, Personal Services, and Public Events, During Mission and Employment with the European Armies in the Campaigns of 1812, 1813, 1814*, ed. Herbert R. Wilson (12 vols.; London, 1861), I, 389. Rumiantsev confided to Chichagov (July 19, 1812, Chichagov Papers, GBL, 333/24) that, contrary to reports that he had almost succumbed to apoplexy, he could still get around. Lebzeltern described Rumiantsev's condition when he arrived at Vilna and noted his extensive paralysis (to Metternich, No. 118, June 18, 1812, HHS/Russ. III, 12); see also Nesselrode to Countess Gur'ev, May 9, 1812, *LPN*, IV, 22–23.

aces and that I had too much interest in conserving the Russian alliance to have decided on war." [77]

Even after Napoleon crossed the Neman, Rumiantsev initially favored accommodation. On the twenty-fifth of June, while Napoleon's armies were progressing into Russia, Rumiantsev wrote Alexander urging further negotiation to prevent war: "Would you find, Sire, some inconvenience in writing to the emperor Napoleon yourself, that you are too covetous of blood, not only of your own subjects, but of all peoples, to expose it to being spilt by a misunderstanding?" Napoleon was right in thinking that Rumiantsev had not taken the threat of war seriously. "Today he sees that it is serious and that his army is broken," Napoleon remarked early in the Russian invasion. "He is now afraid and wants to make an arrangement, but it is in Moscow that I will sign the peace." [78] Alexander however, refused to make peace once the Grand Army was on Russian soil.

Differences emerged, too, over the conclusion of the Russo-Turkish war. Alexander was in such haste to make immediate peace with the Turks, in order to concentrate on the war with Napoleon, that he was ready to settle for the Russian annexation of Bessarabia and the abandonment of Russian claims on the Danubian provinces of Moldavia and Wallachia, which Rumiantsev had so strongly pushed. Rumiantsev tried to mask his disagreement in official correspondence, but he confided his opposition to the terms of the Treaty of Bucharest and the abandonment of the principalities in a personal letter to Admiral Chichagov, the Russian plenipotentiary: "What rights will we have in arousing the Slavic peoples to join us [in opposing Napoleon] when they will have under their eyes such a striking and complete example of the weakness with which we will abandon and betray those whose hopes rested on us and who were devoted to

[77] Lebzeltern to Metternich, No. 94, Feb. 10, 1812, HHS/Russ. III, 12. Napoleon's remark was quoted by Armand A. L. Caulaincourt, *Mémoires du général de Caulaincourt, duc de Vicence, grand écuyer de l'empereur*, ed. Jean Hanoteau (3 vols.; Paris, 1933), I, 354–355; see also II, 275–276.

[78] Rumiantsev to Alexander, June 25, 1812, *VPR*, VI, 441. Napoleon quoted by Caulaincourt, *Mémoires du général de Caulaincourt, duc de Vicence*, I, 354–355.

our empire? I confess that in my view, these preliminary articles will for a long time ruin our credit in the Orient among the Greek and Slavic peoples who are today placed under Mohammedan domination." In a letter to the emperor he recommended changing the terms of several articles, expressing the belief that Alexander "would find many difficulties for his empire in the total execution of this treaty," but Alexander was not prepared to listen.[79]

Rumiantsev also disagreed basically with Alexander about the conduct of the war. He was not enthusiastic about continuing the war beyond the western frontiers when Napoleon's armies were in retreat; because he believed that Russian interests lay in the East, he considered any extensive involvement in the West to be contrary to national interest. However, wanting to preserve his place and accompany the emperor, once he realized Alexander had resolved on the western war he endorsed Alexander's actions and even expressed enthusiasm for the emperor's "mission": "Heaven has chosen you to accomplish its decrees, opening its career to you in presenting you already to save Europe." [80] But such statements still masked a basic skepticism about the Fourth Coalition, for Rumiantsev was particularly hesitant to coordinate efforts with Austria and England, both of which he believed were too suspicious of Russian moves in the Near East. Such policy splits were especially apparent in June 1812 to the Austrian envoy, who noted that Alexander, regretting the lack of closer coordination which had been urged by Austria earlier, "inwardly reproached the chancellor for having suggested to him the less fortunate attitude which he finally adopted." [81]

[79] Rumiantsev to Chichagov, May 26, 1812, Chichagov Papers, GBL, 333/25; he assured Chichagov, "In conclusion, I repeat to you, Admiral, it is not the chancellor who speaks to you thus; as chancellor, I have signed the dispatches approved by His Majesty which accompany this letter and all is restrained to those." Rumiantsev to Alexander, July 5, 1812, *VPR*, VI, 452–453.

[80] Rumiantsev to Alexander, Jan. 11, 1812, *VPR*, VI, 675; see also Cathcart to Castlereagh, No. 9, Aug. 30, 1812, PRO/FO 65/79, and No. 7, Jan. 29, 1813, PRO/FO 65/85.

[81] Rumiantsev to Alexander, July 17, 1812, *VPR*, VI, 487. Lebzeltern to Metternich, No. 118, June 18, 1812, HHS/Russ. III, 12; see also Lebzeltern's MS journal, "Souvenirs" and a draft of this long report from Vilna in the Lebzeltern Papers.

Differences in policy produced occasional heated disputes, revealing definite personal antagonisms between Alexander and his
chancellor. In mid-May, for example, Rumiantsev's failure to
carry out the emperor's intentions strictly brought a severe repri-
mand. "What is more simple than that we might be of a different
opinion?" Alexander inquired in a penciled note. "If I have reasons for holding mine, what means will I have for seeing it put in
execution if my ministers refuse to sign replies as I deem it necessary to make them? . . . In my position, do I not have the right
to indicate what response I want my minister to make? . . .
Your signature is thus not under the command of a foreign
power; . . . when I need to reply to a minister of a foreign court,
my chancellor must place his signature on it." [82] The episode was
not easily forgotten, despite the emperor's later attempts to
soothe Rumiantsev's feelings.

Alexander may have sincerely wanted to appease Rumiantsev
as he wrote him in apology, "Never could your services be anything but of the greatest utility to me, because no one possesses
more of my confidence and esteem than you," but the emperor's
kind words proved empty. "Rumiantsev is still ill," reported a
British envoy at the end of May, "and at the present time, he is
very low in the mind of his master." [83] Rumiantsev found himself
excluded from Alexander's immediate entourage on many occasions; he was poorly informed about proceedings and assumed a
less important role in negotiations. "There is neither advantage
nor satisfaction for me in drawing myself away from the person
of Your Majesty," he pleaded.[84] His entreaties, however, were to
no avail; Alexander was already using more sympathetic advisers
in conducting the diplomatic affairs of the war. For example, Alexander was dealing with Stackelberg, the Russian ambassador in

[82] Alexander to Rumiantsev, May 19, 1812, Goriainov, *1812*, Part 2, pp. 7–8;
an undated copy of this letter was printed in *Russkii arkhiv*, VII (1869, No. 4),
609–614.

[83] Alexander to Rumiantsev, received May 22, 1812, Goriainov, *1812*, Part 2,
p. 8. Cathcart, May 30, 1812, fragments from private letters, Cathcart Papers
C-48.

[84] Rumiantsev to Alexander, July 5, 1812, *VPR*, VI, 452–454; he earlier expressed regret at not being in the immediate suite of the emperor (Rumiantsev
to Alexander, June 25, 1812, *VPR*, VI, 441).

Vienna, with Kochubei as the intermediary. Rumiantsev, distressed that important matters were evading him, ordered Stackelberg to report directly to him, because, he told the ambassador, "Kochubei has no part in foreign affairs." Stackelberg, however, received other instructions from the emperor. By November, he, like Russian ambassadors elsewhere, found that their most important communications were being handled by Nesselrode at the imperial headquarters, although they still received dispatches and handled routine matters through Rumiantsev.[85] The emperor was through working directly with Rumiantsev on all but insignificant details and had little need for the minister whose policies diverged so basically from his own.

When Alexander left St. Petersburg to join the army in December 1812, he left the secret order that in a few days Count Karl Robert Nesselrode was to follow him to serve as secretary in the important diplomatic negotiations which were to be handled from the imperial headquarters. Alexander also asked the British envoy, Lord Cathcart, to delay his departure; as Cathcart explained, Alexander confided "to me that he had used his leaving me as an argument to satisfy M. Romanzow [sic] that he could not take him and to get rid of all the advisers who are most cautious of vigorous measures by assuring them, from the description of his attendants, that His Majesty's journey is a tour of inspection."[86] Apparently Alexander wanted to save Rumiantsev from the disgrace of outright dismissal. Apparently, too, he was not ready to appoint a new foreign minister. Rumiantsev was told that he would not be needed on this "tour of inspection" because no diplomatic affairs would be handled. When Alexander remained with the army, Rumiantsev was led to expect that he would be invited to join the emperor and would be kept up to

[85] Rumiantsev to Stackelberg, June 14, 1812, *VPR*, VI, 466; see also for example, Stackelberg to Kochubei, No. 2, June 25, 1812, *VPR*, VI, 444–449; Lebzeltern, draft of dispatch to Metternich, Nov. 16, 1812, Lebzeltern Papers. To cite another example, copies of several sets of dispatches from both Nesselrode and Rumiantsev to Italinskii from AVPR are in the Schilder Papers, GPB, 859/8/2, 859/8/4.

[86] Cathcart to Castlereagh, No. 58, Dec. 14, 1812, PRO/FO 65/80; this instruction was confirmed by Longinov to S. R. Vorontsov, Dec. 22, 1812, *AKV*, XXIII, 213.

date and consulted about important matters. When he realized that such would not be the case, Rumiantsev requested dismissal. The emperor continually refused. He gave Rumiantsev's health as a reason for not taking him along or else explained, "I can guarantee you that . . . it is my intimate conviction that diplomats and negotiators have almost nothing to do in the present time, that the sword alone must decide the issue of events." [87]

Rumiantsev retained the titles of Chancellor and Foreign Minister, but, in the words of one contemporary, "he has become merely the depository or guardian of archives for acts in which he has in no way participated." [88] Alexander may have thought he was placating Rumiantsev by not retiring him, but to remain in office uninformed of diplomatic developments was a much greater disgrace for the elderly minister. "To be Chancellor of the Empire for the sake of signing passports, and giving orders about lawsuits, is not worthwhile," Rumiantsev complained. Finally, on his own initiative in February 1814 Rumiantsev advised the diplomatic corps in St. Petersburg that "due to the ill health of the Chancellor" they should refer their business to the chief clerk in the chancellery, Count Weydemeyer. [89] Official retirement did not come until August.

Rumiantsev had served Alexander's purpose as spokesman for the alliance with Napoleon from 1807 to 1812, but a major shift of policy required a new foreign minister. The pendulum had swung back from peace to war, from the domestic reform of the Speranskii era to foreign involvement and the Fourth Coalition. While Rumiantsev had been handling the minor affairs of the chancellery in St. Petersburg, Karl Robert Nesselrode at the emperor's side had taken over the functions of foreign minister of the Russian Empire.

---

[87] Alexander to Rumiantsev, July 24, 1813, Schilder, *Aleksandr*, III, 514.

[88] Longinov to S. R. Vorontsov, Aug. 22, 1813, *AKV*, XXIII, 270.

[89] Rumiantsev quoted by Adams, *Memoirs*, Feb. 1, 1814, II, 571. Circular included with Walpole to Castlereagh, No. 20, March 8, 1814, PRO/FO 65/94; Adams, *Memoirs*, Feb. 23, 1812, II, 579. Rumiantsev wrote the emperor again without reply in April, complimenting him in glowing terms on the success of the campaigns, once more requesting leave, and pleading with the emperor for his liberty (Rumiantsev to Alexander, April 14, 1814, draft, Rumiantsev Papers GBL, 255/5/25).

# Chapter 6

# NESSELRODE AND THE CONGRESS OF VIENNA: SPOKESMEN FOR RESTORATION

Alexander's vacillation between war and peace disappeared when the Grand Army invaded Russia. The immediate menace to Russian soil brought a strong patriotic commitment to war; there was to be no compromising with the man who led that army into Russia after all the trying years of alliance. Both Alexander and Napoleon had long been preparing for war as they had talked peace and eternal friendship between 1807 and 1812, but Napoleon's invasion still came as a rude shock. First, Russia had to be defended and the tyrannical invader driven out. Then a unified general alliance had to be created for the annihilation of the French aggressor. Alexander's profound psychological reaction, apparent in the religious "conversion" which he supposedly experienced in 1812, gave a new sense of mission and resolve to his policies and actions. He was ready to take upon himself the burdens of the empire, to direct efforts in defense of the fatherland, and to devote himself completely to a prolonged struggle to rid Europe of Napoleon and establish a lasting peace.

Gone was the early vacillation between withdrawal and active involvement on the continent. With the Napoleonic invasion Alexander became fully committed to what he viewed as not only his own, but Russia's historical mission as leader of European defense against Bonaparte's despotic designs for continental hegemony. His personal or national mission was undistinguished in his own mind from his mission on behalf of Europe. It was his total lack of concern for a distinctive Russian national interest in this period which so completely committed Russia to its most impressively cosmopolitan, continentally oriented foreign policy and to its greatest and most significant role in continental affairs. Thus Alexander, at tremendous cost to his country — and with little more than prestige to gain — turned his undivided attention to the West. The impressive potentialities of the Speranskii-led reform efforts, which had already met frustration before Napoleon's invasion, were all but forgotten as Alexander decided to bring together a general coalition against Napoleon. His diplomatic efforts were successful. The Fourth Coalition owed much of its spirit and its success to the undivided enthusiasm of the emperor who led the allies across the continent to France, and who then, as if in childish revenge, would settle for nothing less than his own triumphal entry into Paris.

Russia had its great moment of continental glory, and Alexander had the eulogies of world opinion. But the emperor obviously lacked the strength of character and the abilities befitting a continental statesman. He proved unable to turn military success into political achievement, incapable of using his position of power and prestige for enlightened goals rather than despotic demands. Earlier plans for continental reconstruction were revived with the defeat of Napoleon, but the extremes of religious mysticism in which the emperor indulged himself during the period gave them a pietistic but entirely unrealistic cast; the personal insecurity and political inexperience which characterized his conduct contributed more to the spirit of a futile Holy Alliance than to the constructive plans for European reconstruction proposed by his Western colleagues. Alexander's constitutional concerns, so deeply frustrated in his own country, did have some impact on the settlements in Switzerland, France, and Poland, but his constructive efforts in these directions were overshadowed by his whimsical, despotic insistence on his own assumption of the Polish crown. His general lack of concern for the national aspirations of smaller states meant inadequate consideration for such questions at the Congress of Vienna, to the bitter disappointment of those foreign advisers who looked to him as the great benefactor of their own patriotic interests. The tremendous cost of the wars of liberation and the glaring neglect of internal problems in favor of European involvement and foreign glory failed to pay off for Russia and set the pattern for the escapist foreign policies which proved so disastrous in the later nineteenth century.

The somewhat changed character and orientation of Russian foreign policy between 1812 and 1815 had its parallel in certain changes in the conduct of Russian diplomacy. "Whether because he enjoys the satisfaction of working along lines conforming more to his own likes and sentiments, whether because of the fortunate absence of the chancellor [Rumiantsev], whose systematic procedure was always causing delays and incumbrances, or whether from other motives, the emperor has very fortunately completely changed his manner of conducting business," reported an Austrian diplomat. "He works alone; he gives a strong and uniform impulse to everything; he has found a great deal of confidence in himself." [1] Two major changes resulted. Alexander's active supervision of all aspects of business left little place for ministerial reponsibility during this period. In fact, none of the men through whom he conducted Russian diplomacy then was given Rumiantsev's titles of Foreign Minister or State Chancellor. Nesselrode, the effective minister rose to the rank of State Secretary for Foreign Affairs in 1814, and this very designation suggests his relatively subordinate role. Second, as Castlereagh remarked in November of 1814, "It is unfortunately [Alexander's] habit to be his own minister, and to select as the instrument of his immediate purpose the person who may happen to fall in most with his views." [2] The tendency noted during the French alliance became more prominent by the time of the Congress of Vienna, when Alexander conducted diplomatic affairs through a variety of individuals who represented particular causes or who supported particular policies which coincided with his own. The conduct of diplomacy during this period thus involved not only the designated foreign secretary, but also the prominent advisers who formed the inner circle of Alexander's diplomatic entourage.

When Alexander gave orders for the young Count Karl Robert

---

[1] Lebzeltern to Metternich, March 30, 1813, HHS/Russ. III, 15.
[2] Castlereagh to Liverpool, Nov. 5, 1814, *British Diplomacy*, p. 222.

Nesselrode to join him at imperial headquarters in 1812, he little realized that he was singling out the man who would serve as Russian foreign minister for the next half-century. Nesselrode's singularly long term of office might suggest that he was a major figure in diplomatic affairs, yet he is almost forgotten beside such contemporaries as Talleyrand, Castlereagh, and Metternich. In large part, Nesselrode was eclipsed by his sovereigns, as Alexander and later his brother, Nicholas I, gave the impress of their own personalities and ideologies to the diplomacy of their reigns. Moreover, Nesselrode himself had neither the intellect, the stature, nor the character to recommend him as a great statesman, nor the personality and ideological interests to make for close friendship with Alexander. He did have all the qualifications for a successful diplomatic secretary who agreed with the emperor's prevailing policies at the time of his appointment.

A foreigner in the Russian service in name, background, and outlook, Nesselrode first came to Russia in 1796 at the age of sixteen with a commission as midshipman in the Baltic fleet. His father, a minor Westphalian nobleman, had entered the Russian diplomatic corps but never lived in Russia. Born in Lisbon, Nesselrode attended a gymnasium in Berlin while his father was Russian minister there. Under Paul he was assigned to the horse guards and appointed imperial aide-de-camp; promoted to the rank of colonel in 1799, he was made chamberlain in 1800. Starting his diplomatic career soon after Alexander assumed the throne, Nesselrode served successively as secretary in the Russian legations in Berlin, The Hague, and Paris and had several assignments of a diplomatic nature with the army. "A spectator in the most absolute retreat" at Tilsit in 1807, he did have the job "of copying the treaty after all the conditions had been established." [3] His most important assignment before 1812 was the maintenance of secret relations between Alexander and Tal-

---

[3] To his father, July 19, 1807, *LPN*, III, 184; "Autobiographie," *ibid.*, II, 63. Sergei Tatishchev (*Alexandre Ier et Napoléon d'après leur correspondance inédite, 1801–1812* [Paris, 1891], pp. 615–616) confirms the fact that the treaty documents were copied by Nesselrode.

leyrand through his correspondence with Speranskii in 1810 and early 1811.

During his stay in Paris, Nesselrode won Napoleon's recommendation as "the only man of considerable talent" in the Russian embassy, but few of his contemporaries gave him credit for more than mediocrity. Lacking brilliance, he was nonetheless a very competent bureaucrat — "honest, loyal, hardworking, and willing to oblige." Of short and unimpressive physique, Nesselrode reminded one of "a former academician of the second order." "He is an unimposing man without pretention or ostentation — a man of simple and restrained tastes," noted Gentz, who admired him as "a man of upright character, of good judgment, born for work and solid things," but felt, like most of Nesselrode's associates, that "he will never have a brilliant existence nor an evident ascendency over the emperor." [4]

When Metternich said of Nesselrode, "if he were a fish, he would be carried away with the current," he was identifying one of Nesselrode's most distinguishing characteristics as foreign minister. "I abstain from all personal reflection," Nesselrode wrote once to a colleague. "His Majesty is acquainted with me well enough to know that the first aim of my actions is the good of his service and that if he does not agree with my opinions, I am not in a position to say anything." Nesselrode's words were prophetic of his role throughout Alexander's reign, a position well supported by his own personality. As years went by, Nesselrode showed slightly more initiative, for his long career allowed him to "supplement by experience what he lacks by more heightened talents." Greater familiarity with diplomacy and the diplomats of his day led him to take stronger stands on certain issues. But even when his recommendations were not followed, with his "spirit of ready obedience" he was always "disposed to second the supreme

[4] Napoleon's remark in 1811 was recorded by the Swiss diplomat, Jean-Gabriel Eynard, *Au Congrès de Vienne. Journal de Jean-Gabriel Eynard*, ed. Édouard Chapuisat (Geneva, 1914), p. 133; see also A. I. Chernyshev to M. B. Barclay de Tolli, Sept. 1811, *SIRIO*, CXXI, 176. Stein to his wife, Feb. 19, 1813, *Briefe*, IV, 43. Maistre, letter of Aug. 27, 1814, *Correspondance*, II, 2–3. Gentz to Karadja, Sept. 16, 1814, Gentz, *Dépêches*, I, 96–97.

will." [5] Nesselrode could thus be a willing servant of three emperors as different in personality and political attitudes as Paul, Alexander, and Nicholas.

Whereas Rumiantsev's intellectual and political outlook led directly to his support of the Napoleonic alliance, Nesselrode's led naturally to war with Napoleon and concern for a conservative European settlement. Like many of the foreigners of Western background in the Russian service, he was strongly committed to an active role for Russia in European politics. He inherited and retained his father's attachment to the *ancien régime* and the principles upon which it rested. "Like you, my dear son, I cannot think without horror and without fear," his father wrote in 1805, "of the general development of European affairs in a moment of general crisis such as perhaps has never existed since the creation of the world." With many aristocrats of similar background, Nesselrode shared a strong opposition to the French Revolution and vigorous enmity to Napoleon, who personified the revolutionary threat to their positions and to the traditional political organization which supported their privilege. Having witnessed Napoleon's inroads in the Low Countries as embassy secretary in The Hague, Nesselrode's greatest fear was "the return of the Reign of Terror, of the *Comité du Salut Publique*," and his strongest wish was that "a considerable fortune could shelter men from this pillaging spirit which has characterized the revolutionaries." He looked forward to a "resurrection of the political equilibrium without which, whatever happens, the dignity of sovereigns, the independence of countries, the prosperity of peoples will only be sad memories." [6] With great hope he looked to Russia as the best potential leader for such a restoration and as the only power capable of assuring Napoleon's demise.

Nesselrode believed that the European political arrangement

---

[5] Metternich, Jan. 4, 1821, *Mémoires*, III, 447. Nesselrode to Lieven [1813?], Lieven Papers, BM/Add. MSS. 47251. Pasquier, *Histoire*, V, 24; see also Countess Edling, *Mémoires*, pp. 87–89. Jean Bapiste Capefigue, "Nesselrode," *Les diplomats européens* (4 vols.; Paris, 1843–1847), I, 329.

[6] William to Karl Nesselrode, May 5, 1805, *LPN*, III, 29. Karl to William Nesselrode, March 27, Feb. 17, 1804, *LPN*, II, 298, 276. Nesselrode, memorandum to the emperor, Oct. 1811, *LPN*, III, 429.

should be restored to its traditional form to ensure a strong bulwark against revolutionary inroads. A strong supporter of the principle of the legitimacy of established thrones, he had no sympathy with popular aspirations, "liberal ideas," or any of Alexander's constitutional projects. He admired the British constitution at a distance, but believed that "to wish to borrow foreign forms for a constitution for any people is to substitute the ascendency of accident or will for an extensive series of developments, often from time immemorial; it is to force on people the imitation of the effects of such developments. Such a plan might provide only the letter of a constitution, but never its spirit." Although Nesselrode urged the restoration of "the independence of peoples" who had been subject to Napoleon, national aspirations were completely foreign to his way of thought. Austrian power was to be reestablished in Italy, as Russian power should be maintained in Poland. The reestablishment of an independent Poland could never be considered as an end in itself, because Poland was "a superficial and restless nation," in his view. "If the partition of this country was in principle an illegal measure contrary to public law and the maintenance of the equilibrium, at least it had the fortunate result of diminishing the germs of discussion and troubles in Europe." [7]

Nesselrode's conservatism stemmed from his character and background and was further nourished by his early associations. While serving at his first diplomatic post, in Berlin, he came to know the diplomat Friedrich von Gentz, thereafter a lifelong friend. Nesselrode considered him "the most courageous and most enlightened defender of right principles," despite his qualms about Gentz's personal moral character, which he felt was "quite as light as his writings are profound." He was particularly impressed with Gentz's essay "On the State of Europe Before and After the French Revolution," calling it "a masterpiece which can only pass to posterity and be placed beside the works of Montesquieu,

---

[7] Nesselrode to Grand Duke Nicholas Pavlovich, Memorandum on the occasion of Nicholas I's trip to England, Sept. 10, 1816, Schilder, *Imperator Nikolai Pervyi, ego zhizn i tsarstvovanie* (St. Petersburg, 1903), I, 590. Nesselrode to Alexander, Memorandum on the Polish problem, 1812, *LPN*, IV, 315–316.

Blackstone, and Burke." Nesselrode remained in correspondence with Gentz; as a disciple, he felt "by each letter I acquire new and flattering proofs that our ideas on the general development of affairs agree perfectly." Gentz considered Nesselrode clearly "above his place" as Russian foreign minister, "too weak for the pounds that weigh on him," yet he always thought of him as a close friend. "When I think that I have spent the most interesting periods of my life with this man, what attachment he has inspired in me . . . when I recall with what friendship he has constantly treated me, and how many real services he has rendered me, I would be ashamed to direct the least sentiment of bitterness against him." Although in the early 1820's some political issues divided them, Gentz could still say, "Despite the things I have against him, I like and will always like him to the bottom of my heart." [8]

Gentz was but one of several important conservative leaders with whom Nesselrode was associated in Berlin. He followed a course of law under Friedrich Ancillon, a cousin of Gentz and a conservative historian, who in 1831 became Prussian foreign minister. He knew Austria's ambassador, Philipp von Stadion, a violent adversary of Napoleon who became foreign minister in 1806 and was later one of Nesselrode's colleagues at the Congress of Vienna. Following the Tilsit settlement Nesselrode came to know Metternich in Paris and retained a very high regard for the Austrian statesman. Metternich, never impressed with Nesselrode's ability or strength of character, was one of his strongest supporters during Alexander's reign. "[Metternich] is charmed by you," Gentz told Nesselrode, "by your way of looking at things, by your manner of handling affairs, by the rectitude of your judgment, your wisdom, your spirit of justice, etc., etc." [9] Nesselrode was often accused of "having sold out to the Austrians," and the charge was not without foundation. His political

[8] Nesselrode, "Autobiographie," *LPN*, II, 33–35. Karl to William Nesselrode, Nov. 12 and 15, 1801, *LPN*, II, 150, 153–154. Nesselrode to Gentz, March 26, 1813, *LPN*, V, 59. Gentz to Lebzeltern, Aug. 18, 1826, and Aug. 7, 1825, Lebzeltern Papers. See also Nesselrode to Gentz, Feb. 19, 1822, HHS/Russ. III, 55a.
[9] Gentz to Nesselrode, June 13, 1813, *LPN*, V, 104–105.

outlook, like his personal sympathies, placed him closely in line with the policies of the Austrian court. Metternich fully recognized this, and, like Napoleon with Rumiantsev, he was always eager to have Nesselrode kept in his high position in Russian diplomacy.

A cosmopolitan German in the Russian service, Nesselrode never developed intellectual ties with Russian thought and culture. He had scant knowledge of the Russian language and even at the end of his career was unable to write it with any command. He was especially out of sympathy with the Orthodox element in Russian conservative thinking and had little more association with the Roman Catholic basis of the European Restoration: "My mother was Protestant, my father, Catholic. . . I was baptized and became Anglican for the rest of my days," he explained in his autobiography.[10] In fact, religion was a formality which had little significance for him; he had no interest in Bible Societies, or in any of the pietistic currents whch excited Alexander during that period. Ironically in light of his later role, Nesselrode complained about the retirement of Alexander Vorontsov in 1803 and the impending appointment of Czartoryski as foreign minister: "I doubt that it is very good for us, particularly because his successor does not have . . . enough true attachment to the interests of Russia to repulse all foreign influence." He spoke of the role to which Russia was "destined by the extent of her territory, her geographical position, her military force, and her production, which give her the precious advantage of needing no one and the power to wait peacefully for others to come to her."[11] Yet, in contrast to Rumiantsev, Nesselrode had little interest in Russian expansion and, despite identification with the country of his adoption, he showed few real nationalistic sympathies for Russia.

Nesselrode's ties with Russia were significantly augmented by marriage. In 1811 he was betrothed to a young Russian woman

---

[10] Nesselrode, "Autobiographie," *LPN*, II, 17. Nesselrode's mother, reportedly partially Jewish, died when he was very young.

[11] Karl to William Nesselrode, Jan. 20, 1803, *LPN*, II, 206–207.

of great wealth and high social position, Maria Dmitrievna, the daughter of the finance minister Count D. A. Gur'ev. His bride provided him with an invaluable link with the country of his adoption and with the most influential elements in Russian society. She also brought him closer to Russian conservative opinion, particularly her own exaggerated monarchical sentiments. During her visit to Paris in 1819, she wrote him, "All that I have seen and heard disgusts me to the highest degree with the word liberty, and if I were the emperor of Russia, I would not want to renounce the title or the surname of despot." She blithely echoed reactionary sentiments: "All the well-thinking people here say that the emperor would be foolish to change the least thing in the administration of his country with regard for liberty. If only he could think the same way! What evil this simple word liberty will produce! Far from attaining it, they acquire and will acquire only heavy chains." [12]

Many of Nesselrode's more conservative ideas diverged sharply from Alexander's general political values, and the spiritual gap between the two men accentuated the difference. But in 1812 basic ideological differences were less important than the immediate goals which united them: the destruction of Napoleon by a strong coalition and active Russian involvement in the establishment of an enduring European peace. Nesselrode was a most appropriate spokesman for the changed orientation of Russian foreign policy at the start of the 1812 war.

During the French alliance, Nesselrode had been involved in the anti-Napoleonic strains of Russian diplomatic relations. As secretary to the ambassador, Count P. A. Tolstoi, in Paris in 1807 and 1808, he had edited dispatches warning Rumiantsev and the Russian court against taking Napoleon at his word. Later, under the guise of negotiating a loan, he was sent back to Paris to contact Talleyrand and serve as intermediary for his communication with the tsar. His work won him the recommendations of several close imperial advisers, including Speranskii and Chernyshev, and put him in immediate touch with Al-

---

[12] Maria to Karl Nesselrode, May 3 and 4, 1819, *LPN*, VI, 71, 74–75.

exander.[13] Even before war broke out, the emperor had singled out Nesselrode for appointment as state secretary attached to the foreign ministry. In the event of war, he explained, "I plan to place myself at the head of the armies. I will need to have with me a young man, capable of following me everywhere on horseback, to be in charge of my diplomatic correspondence. . . . I have cast my eyes on you and I hope that you will fulfill such a position of confidence with faithfulness and discretion." [14]

Nesselrode presented a new face on the scene for Alexander in 1812. A few years younger than the emperor, Nesselrode had had no youthful contacts with Alexander; neither had he been associated with the sovereign's "young friends" nor the discouraging failures of the early part of the reign. His youth, inexperience, diligence, and competent mediocrity made him definitely a subordinate, and he nurtured no pet projects which would challenge Alexander's own conduct of affairs. Even before the rupture with France, Nesselrode had been called upon by the emperor to draw up dispatches "when Rumiantsev was opposed to his views"; in May he "emerged victorious from a rather violent crisis with Rumiantsev." [15] Alexander was ready to turn to a more willing subordinate who was closely allied with his current goals.

When Napoleon crossed the Neman in the spring of 1812, Nesselrode was ready for war. Never having entertained illusions about a lasting arrangement with France, he had considered war inevitable all along. In March he had suggested that the increase of French preparations "would render all arrangements . . . if not impossible, at least infinitely difficult," but was willing to attempt negotiation, both to provide a legal basis for the war, and,

[13] Nesselrode, "Autobiographie," LPN, II, 63–64, 69–71, 75–77; Nesselrode to Speranskii, 1810–1811, LPN, III, 225–387; Talleyrand, Mémoires, I, 321; Edling, Mémoires, pp. 87–89. Nesselrode was constantly requesting more money to pay off "Cousin Henry," as the French minister was called in his reports.

[14] Nesselrode, "Autobiographie," LPN, II, 74–75. According to this account, Alexander explained that "the Chancellor, Count Rumiantsev, is old and ill and would not be able to fulfill this task."

[15] Nesselrode, "Autobiographie," LPN, II, 75; Karl to Maria Nesselrode, May 25, 1812, LPN, IV, 32. According to Lebzeltern (to Metternich April 3, 1812, HHS/Russ. III, 12), by March 1812 Nesselrode had been given many important assignments.

most important, to ensure better Russian military preparations and diplomatic alliances, especially with Austria.[16] By the time the Grand Army had reached Russian soil, Nesselrode wanted none of Rumiantsev's last-minute settlements and was in full agreement with the emperor's willingness to make an immediate settlement with Turkey. At least since 1811 he had been arguing "how much the war with Turkey and the project to aggrandize ourselves at her expense was against our true interest." [17]

Once Napoleon was on retreat, Nesselrode's eagerness to pursue him across Europe coincided with the emperor's and countered Rumiantsev's hesitations about both further war and negotiations with Austria and Prussia. Nesselrode's memorandum to the emperor at the end of 1812 recommending the continuation of the war, close alliance with Austria and Prussia, and the procurement of British subsidies may not have influenced Alexander's decided policies, but they gave reinforcement to the emperor's intentions. Because the memorandum outlined the specific steps which were ultimately followed in establishing the alliance, it also assured its writer of a key position in those negotiations. When Nesselrode joined the emperor at the front in December, his position as the effective foreign minister was assured: "From this moment, dates my active participation in all the great affairs which give luster to his reign." [18]

The complicated negotiations bringing Austria into the coalition were Nesselrode's most significant specific assignment during this period. With his long-established friendship with Austrian leaders and his sympathy for their policies, he was a natural

[16] Nesselrode to Alexander, March 19, 1812, *LPN*, IV, 5–10. The recommendations of an earlier memorandum, dated October 1811 (*LPN*, III, 417–431), were essentially the same.

[17] Nesselrode to Speranskii, Feb. 16, 1811, *LPN*, III, 318; see also Nesselrode to Speranskii, Feb. 21, 1811, *VPR*, VI, 75–77.

[18] Nesselrode, "Autobiographie," *LPN*, II, 90. An abridgment of the late 1812 memorandum was published in F. I. Brunov, "Aperçu des transactions politiques du cabinet de Russie," *SIRIO*, XXXI, 298–301; the summary analysis by Martens (*Recueil*, III, 92–96) is misleading in suggesting that Nesselrode did influence the emperor in his decision to continue the war, more than evidence would support. Alexander's early resolution to pursue the war beyond Russian frontiers was evident to the British envoy Lord Cathcart in August 1812 (Cathcart to Castlereagh, No. 10, Aug. 30, 1812, PRO/FO 65/79).

choice for such a role, particularly since he had long been urging close ties with Austria and had tried to disrupt Austria's alliance with France early in 1812. His ties with Gentz proved especially useful, since Gentz was much more eager than Metternich in the early months of 1813 to join Prussia and Russia and continue the war.[19] Nesselrode had the further advantage of family friendship and early diplomatic association with Stackelberg, another spokesman for this policy, who was currently Alexander's representative in Vienna. The emperor himself often dealt personally with the Austrian envoys Lebzeltern and Stadion, and other Russian diplomats handled some aspects of the negotiations. When difficulties remained, however, it was Nesselrode who was sent to deal personally with Emperor Francis in March and again late in the spring. "He has my complete confidence and Your Majesty can grant him your own," Alexander wrote in a letter of introduction. "Count Metternich has known his trustworthiness and his principles for a long time; I did not think it possible to make a better choice." Metternich, however, was holding out for negotiations with Napoleon at the Congress of Prague after allied defeats in the spring; as it turned out, the failure of these illusory peace efforts at Prague were more significant than Nesselrode's efforts in joining Austria to the allied cause by the Treaty of Toeplitz, signed September 9, 1813.[20]

Nesselrode's position as Russian plenipotentiary gave little more room for independence or initiative in these negotiations, than it did in the procurement of British subsidies or in drawing Prussia to the allied cause. Unlike the formation of the Third Coalition, when Czartoryski supplied much of the incentive and coordinated many of the proceedings while the emperor was vacillating and unsure of his aims, in 1812 and 1813 Alexander

[19] Nesselrode's early policy toward Austria was apparent in his memorandum of March 19, 1812, *LPN*, IV, 5–10. A main reason for his policy of nonaggrandizement at the expense of Turkey was his desire to promote Austrian friendship (Nesselrode to Speranskii, Feb. 16, 1811, *LPN*, III, 318). Gentz's willingness to help Nesselrode in this appears in his letters to Nesselrode, *LPN*, V.

[20] Alexander to Francis, March 30, 1813, HHS/Russ. III, 46. Nesselrode's career can be best followed in the reports of Lebzeltern and Stadion from Alexander's headquarters in HHS/Russ. III, 14–16.

provided his own incentive and direction and coordinated the war effort. "I am called when I am needed," Nesselrode wrote his wife soon after joining the emperor in 1812, "and otherwise I do not put myself forward to multiply the occasions. I am completely passive." Nesselrode characteristically made no attempt to assume a larger role. The British envoy was right in his opinion that "the Emperor Alexander is his own minister." Lord Cathcart explained, "His regular ministers are in St. Petersburg, and the few confidential servants he employs here cannot assume the authority of ministers without special instructions in the cases which present themselves." [21]

A willing secretary was nonetheless indispensable to Alexander. There were many letters and diplomatic instruments to be edited; there were many foreign diplomats to be received and dealt with. While the more purely military aspects of the campaigns were handled by the emperor's aides-de-camp and army leaders, business of a more diplomatic character fell to Nesselrode, whom many called "the most sincere and the most devoted of Alexander's interpreters." To the extent that there was a minister at all, it was clear to observers that "Nesselrode, with the title of Secretary of State, is today the true minister for foreign affairs of Emperor Alexander." [22]

Initially, Nesselrode's recommendations and his personal aims coincided completely with the policies and goals of Alexander in the conduct of the war. Once the Austrian alliance was concluded and the allies were sweeping the continent, however, a sharp divergence developed on the most crucial issues. Fundamentally, while the allies pressed for "a more accommodated peace," Alexander "would hear of no communication with France" until the complete defeat of his rival. Nesselrode, believing that negotiation was becoming more possible as the campaign progressed, argued for the more conciliatory policy of Metternich, but Alexander's view won out in 1813. Subsequently, Nes-

[21] Karl to Maria Nesselrode, June 1, 1812, *LPN*, IV, 43. Cathcart to Castlereagh, Nov. 28, 1813, *British Diplomacy*, p. 43.
[22] Capefigue, "Nesselrode," *Les diplomats européens*, I, 332. Gentz to Karadja, July 15, 1813, Gentz, *Dépêches*, I, 31.

selrode was satisfied when France had been pushed to her "natural frontiers," which he had long considered the legitimate goal of the war. Alexander, on the other hand, wanted to cross the Rhine; even when Napoleon would have agreed to allied terms in the early months of 1814, Alexander was not satisfied. "There are some men who want to push as far as Paris," Nesselrode complained to his wife. "I only want to push as far as negotiations. . . . The moment has come when peace can be well, surely, and gloriously attained. There is my profession of faith. I have presented it in writing, but it has not had the good fortune at all to please." [23] Despite the beneficent phrases about freeing the French people from their tyrant, there was something of the spirit of revenge in Alexander's desire for a triumphal entry into the French capital. Nesselrode continued to press for peace: "The powers have perfectly fulfilled their duty toward themselves and toward Europe, if they obtain peace with the conditions which have been put forward. Drawing the war out any further certainly could not suit anyone, and to have arrived where we are is truly all that can be expected of the coalition." Nesselrode's arguments were to no avail. Alexander followed his own plan, while allied statesmen, "fearing to set themselves at variance with Alexander, observed a type of neutrality." [24]

Nesselrode further disagreed with Alexander once Napoleon had capitulated. The emperor lacked confidence in the Bourbon aspirant and doubted that there was popular support for the restoration of the French royal line. Nesselrode had none of Alexander's faith in the ability or the rights of the French people to choose their new government. Alexander's projects of calling a national assembly or his insistence on constitutional safeguards for France had no support from his would-be foreign minister,

[23] Charles William Vane, *Narrative of the War in Germany and France in 1813 and 1814* (Philadelphia, 1831), p. 179, and *passim*. Stadion to Metternich, June 11, 1813, HHS/Russ., III, 16. Nesselrode to Gentz, March 26, 1813, *LPN*, V, 59. Karl to Maria Nesselrode, Jan. 16, 1814, *LPN*, V, 152.

[24] Nesselrode to Lieven, March 11, 1814, Lieven Papers, BM/Add. MSS. 47251. Gentz to Karadja, March 8, 1814, Gentz, *Dépêches*, I, 61. See also, for example, Münster to the Prince Regent of England, Jan. 30, Feb. 12, 1814, in Fournier, *Châtillon*, pp. 295–298.

whose main aim was the restoration of the "legitimate" authority. Nesselrode, nonetheless, did not put himself forward strongly in support of the Bourbon cause. "The Russian project [for a change of government in France] in its laconic and dictatorial style seemed to me as if it had been written with the sword of a Cossack," wrote Gentz in distress. "And I felt very sorry for poor Nesselrode, who could not very well have been anything but a subservient instrument." [25] Even when Alexander finally supported the restoration of the Bourbons, Nesselrode had virtually nothing to do with his decision, although his position was slightly stronger for having supported the policy established.

Alexander was less concerned with differences in policy between himself and his ministers during these years than in other periods of his reign, in part because he was more effectively conducting the affairs of diplomacy himself. Even more important, Nesselrode's disagreements with imperial policy had little bearing on the effectiveness with which he fulfilled his office. Nesselrode may have regretted that a recommendation which he presented to Alexander "has not had the good fortune at all to please," but, as he explained to his wife, "As that is not my aim, and as I have no other than to do my duty and be useful, that does not make any difference to me." [26] Throughout the final stages of the Napoleonic campaigns, Nesselrode remained as Alexander's chief diplomatic assistant. He was sent to the council at Châtillon during February and was the Russian plenipotentiary for the signing of the treaties of Chaumont in March 1814. In the final acts of capitulation at the end of March, Nesselrode symbolically received the deputies from the City of Paris and presented them to the emperor. He was sent into Paris ahead of Alexander to meet with Talleyrand and prepare the way for the final negotiations, himself serving as the Russian plenipotentiary in preparing the first Treaty of Paris.

The conscientious efforts of the self-effacing man most people considered "merely the Emperor's secretary" were rewarded dur-

[25] Gentz to Metternich, March 21, 1814, Gentz, *Briefe*, III, Part 1, 280.
[26] Karl to Maria Nesselrode, Jan. 14, 1814, *LPN*, V, 152; Nesselrode was here commenting on his recommendation not to advance to Paris.

ing Alexander's brief visit to St. Petersburg in the summer of
1814. After Rumiantsev's formal retirement in August, Nesselrode was named director of the foreign ministry, to advance
"one of the most rapid careers ever made in Russia without
being what is called a 'favorite.'"[27] Most observers, surprised by
the appointment, viewed it as temporary, but its significance soon
became clear. "The tsar, in naming Nesselrode . . . was dis-
closing that he himself would control this department," remarked
an imperial aide-de-camp. Diplomats soon realized that the situation was not changed with Nesselrode's appointment and that, as
in recent years, "It is the emperor with whom it is necessary to
deal." Nesselrode's appointment — although he was not given
the official rank of minister — was followed by his appointment
as chief Russian plenipotentiary for the Congress of Vienna.
While observers could rightly claim that in regard to important
things "it is the emperor himself who does all," Nesselrode's position linked Alexander to the foreign representatives with whom
he dealt.[28]

Although Nesselrode's strength lay in his willingness to implement Alexander's views, he occasionally spoke out, even to his
own detriment. The issue which most significantly divided the allies also most significantly divided him from the emperor. Perhaps he did not realize that the fate of Poland was the most important question at the congress for Alexander, or perhaps he
was intelligently trying merely to preserve allied unity, but he
soon found that in opposing his sovereign's views on this, he was
treading on sacred ground. Alexander had a deep emotional
commitment to the restoration of Poland as a constitutional kingdom under Russia from which he was not willing to budge even
if it meant war. In 1812 Nesselrode had already declared to the
emperor that the restoration of Poland was "entirely opposed to

---

[27] Walpole to Castlereagh, Aug. 9, 1814, Castlereagh, *Correspondence*, X, 83.
Gentz to Karadja, Sept. 16, 1814, *Dépêches*, I, 95–97.
[28] A. I. Mikhailovskii-Danilevskii, "Predstaviteli Rossii na Venskom Kongresse
v 1815 godu," *Russkaia starina*, XCVIII (June 1899), 645. Maistre, letter of
Aug. 27, 1814, *Correspondance*, II, 2–3. Police report to Hager, quoting Golovkin, the Russian envoy to Stuttgart, Nov. 19, 1814, Weil, *Congrès*, I, 561;
Talleyrand, *Mémoires*, II, 276.

the interest of Russia." He believed that Poland was unfit for liberties, that its population was by no means worthy of or entitled to any special consideration. The restoration of Poland, he argued, would mean the loss of some valuable provinces for Russia; the extension of Polish privileges would arouse the resentment of the Russian nation; and the Polish question would be a source of bitter conflict between Russia and Austria.[29]

Many of Nesselrode's misgivings about the effects of a Russian restoration of Poland were borne out at the Congress of Vienna, but he was certainly not the person to effect any change in what he termed his sovereign's "unfortunate ideas" on "this fatal Polish question." [30] Nesselrode's convictions about Poland resembled those of the vast majority of the diplomats in Vienna, all the emperor's advisers (except Czartoryski), and the vocal segments of the public both in Russia and Poland. Alexander's mind was made up, however, and nothing could change his commitment to his constitutional kingdom of Poland. He had won the support of the Prussian king by promising to honor Prussia's claim to Saxony, but the staunch opposition of England and Austria brought the congress to the point of war over the issue. Nesselrode's official declarations clearly showed that, even when he disagreed with Alexander, he was willing to subordinate his own opinion and work for his sovereign's goals.[31] Alexander, however, required much greater conviction from his advisers and quickly lost regard for Nesselrode, who continued to argue against the imperial decision. The net result of Nesselrode's efforts to modify the emperor's stand on Poland and to avoid a major conflict among the allies was the loss of imperial favor.

What weakened Nesselrode's position even more was that his opposition on the Polish issue, like his opposition to some of Alexander's own aims, revealed a basic ideological divergence be-

[29] Memorandum to Alexander on the Polish question, 1812, *LPN*, IV, 313–320.

[30] Nesselrode to Pozzo di Borgo, July 2, 1814, personal, Pozzo, *Correspondance*, I, 30.

[31] Castlereagh to Liverpool, Sept. 24, 1814, *British Diplomacy*, pp. 193–195; cf. Martens, *Recueil*, III, 211–219.

tween him and the emperor. And, politically more damaging at the moment, it reflected his associations with Austrian leaders, bringing complaints that Nesselrode "merely follows the dictates of Metternich" or that he was "in Metternich's pocket." [32] His extensive alignment with Austrian policies had severe repercussions on his position in Vienna, particularly at a time when Russia and Austria were almost at war over the Polish question and when Alexander, amidst his violent personal disputes with Metternich, was reportedly prepared for a duel with the Austrian chancellor. [33]

Many had noted Nesselrode's loss of favor by November, and he even had admitted that he had not recently seen the emperor for a week at a time; by the end of December many of the important negotiations were proceeding without Nesselrode. While Count Andrei Kirillovich Razumovskii was officially communicating the emperor's propositions regarding Poland and Capodistrias and others were dealing directly with Alexander on many matters, Nesselrode found he had no voice in affairs. Diplomats were often advised to avoid him, because, as the Danish representative reported, "He dares not speak to the emperor, who, in turn, does not permit him to speak to him for two weeks at a time." Nesselrode's attachment to Austrian interests was the usual explanation for such exclusion. "He had to fall," noted Stein, "because . . . he was led by a foreign minister who was hated by the tsar. . . . He adopted Metternich's ideas of peace with France, acted entirely according to Metternich's views about Swiss affairs, disapproved of the Saxon plan, and finally was directly opposed to the Polish plan. . . . He had to fall the mo-

---

[32] For example, Münster to Prince Regent of England, Feb. 12, 1814, in Fournier, *Châtillon*, pp. 297–298; Czartoryski to Novosiltsev, March 14, 1814, *SIRIO*, IX, 436; Maistre, letters of Aug. 27 and Oct. 8, 1814, *Correspondance*, II, 2–3, 25, 27.

[33] The British diplomat Wellesley suggested that Alexander's quarrel with Metternich would have come to a duel had the Emperor Francis not interceded; apparently for several months in Vienna Alexander would not speak to Metternich, until it was Metternich who actually informed him about Napoleon's escape from Elba (diary entry, 1822, *The Diary and Correspondence of Henry Wellesley, First Lord Cowley (1790–1846)*, ed. F. A. Wellesley [London, n.d.], pp. 97–98).

ment he tried to be something more than the tool of his master, as soon as he achieved a sort of self-sufficiency." [34]

Nesselrode's "fall" was not final, however; his disfavor, while real, was temporary. By March he was again being consulted on important matters, and as soon as Alexander felt more favorably toward Metternich after Napoleon's escape from Elba, Nesselrode was restored to the good graces of his sovereign.[35] Political bargaining had resolved the major problems at the Congress of Vienna. Disputes between the allies were suppressed with the call for renewed military action leading up to the Battle of Waterloo. After the final defeat of Napoleon, Nesselrode returned to St. Petersburg as the director of the Ministry for Foreign Affairs.

If Nesselrode's importance was sometimes limited by the divergence of his opinions from those of the emperor and by his personal associations with Gentz and Metternich, it was even more limited by the extent to which "the presence and personal activity" of the emperor naturally "places the minister in the subordinate role of an ambassador." [36] Clearly Alexander retained the spotlight, as the most important affairs of the congress were usually discussed and resolved at informal meetings or at the many social events in and around Vienna. Nesselrode could only serve as Alexander's spokesman in the official conferences or in relatively minor interviews. During the campaigns, as in Vienna, Alexander often preferred to meet important foreign ministers

[34] Niels Rozenkrantz, diary entry for March 11, 1815, *Journal du congrès de Vienne 1814–1815*, ed. George Norregàrd (Copenhagen, 1953), pp. 170–171; Stein, "Tagebuchaufzeichnungen," Nov. 18–23, Dec. 1814, *Briefe*, V, 336, 349–350. Stein's interpretation coincides with many other accounts, e.g., Gentz to Karadja, Jan. 1, 1816, Gentz, *Dépêches*, I, 202–203; anonymous to Stein, Jan. 15, 1815, Weil, *Congrès*, II, 134; Freddi to Hager, Feb. 6, 1815, *ibid.*, II, 152–153; and Münster to Prince Regent, Dec. 29, 1814, *Political Sketches of the State of Europe from 1814–1867, containing Count Ernst Münster's Despatches to the Prince Regent from the Congress of Vienna*, ed. George Herbert, Count Münster, tr. Countess Münster (Edinburgh, 1868), p. 219.

[35] Stein, diary entries for early March, *Briefe*, V, 368–373; Gentz to Karadja, June 26, 1815, Gentz, *Dépêches*, I, 160–161. Stein confirmed in his diary (March 14, 1815, *Briefe*, V, 374–375) that with the renewed struggle against Napoleon Alexander reconciled with Metternich and even promised the Emperor Francis not to mention his aversion for him.

[36] Karl von Nostitz, *Leben und Briefwechsel* (Dresden and Leipzig, 1848), p. 133.

personally before they had talked to any of his subordinates. As with Lord Cathcart, the British military envoy and later the ambassador to Russia, the emperor retained some foreign representatives in his immediate entourage throughout the campaigns, handling business with him directly. "The emperor and my father are on the best of terms," wrote Cathcart's son, who was serving his father as aide-de-camp. "The former never fails to mark his approbation and attachment." During the winter of 1814, Lord Castlereagh could report that Alexander "now encourgages me to come to him without form. I see him almost every day, and he receives me with great kindness, and converses with me freely on all subjects." [37] Metternich recalled the same type of relationship with Alexander in 1813 and 1814.

Nesselrode's disagreements with Alexander were minimized and his own role was further limited by the emperor's practice of consulting a variety of individuals who performed specific functions, spoke for particular policies, or advised the emperor on limited problems. One such figure was the well known Prussian reformer Baron Friedrich Karl von Stein, who went to Russia in the spring of 1812 and remained in Alexander's entourage through the Congress of Vienna. Stein was a hearty spokesman for enlightened reform and was deeply committed to the cause of German unification. Rather than enter the Russian service with a regular rank, he "preferred to conserve his liberty to act for German interests in the most useful manner." But Alexander greeted him not as a spokesman for the German cause, but as "one of the most brilliant" among "the friends of virtue and of all beings animated by the sentiments of independence and love of humanity" and as a statesman "who could nourish no other sentiment than that of contributing to the success of the efforts which will be

[37] George to Charles Cathcart, Jan. 28, 1814, Cathcart Papers 21/51. See also Cathcart to Castlereagh, Nov. 28, 1813, *British Diplomacy*, pp. 43–44, and Lebzeltern to Metternich, May 8, 1813, HHS/Russ. III, 15; Maistre (May 1, 1813, *Correspondance*, I, 324–325) considered Cathcart "very mediocre" and doubted that he could have any influence. Castlereagh to Liverpool, March 5, 1814, *British Diplomacy*, p. 164; see also Cathcart to Castlereagh, Jan. 8 and Jan. 16, 1814, Castlereagh, *Correspondence*, IX, 149, 170.

made in the North to triumph over the invasion of Napoleonic despotism." [38]

During the summer and fall of 1812, Stein was active in the emperor's "German committee," formed to deal with such problems as the organization of an underground resistance to Napoleon in Germany, the encouragement of German troops to join the Russian service, and the formation of a German legion which would help fight against the French. Stein has sometimes been given credit for influencing the emperor to continue the war into Europe in 1812, but, as with Nesselrode's support for this policy, his recommendations appear to have come after Alexander's decision. The emperor responded to Stein's conviction that the war to overthrow Napoleon would "bring the deliverance of the human race from the most absurd and the most enslaving tyrannies," but, for all Stein's enthusiasm, there was little practical result from his activities.[39] Nor was there much outcome from his attempts to arouse Alexander's support for German nationalist sentiments which might lead to unification under a new constitution; Alexander was interested only in the possible use of such sentiments in the struggle against Napoleon.

Once the war was under way beyond Russian frontiers, Stein served Alexander as an adviser on German affairs. He particularly wanted Prussia to join the Russian cause and, at Alexander's request, wrote urging Frederick William to prevent "the blood of his people from flowing for the enemy of humanity" and exhorting him "to reunite under the victorious banners of Emperor Alexander, which are those of honor and the independence of nations." [40] Although his actual part in bringing about the adherence of Prussia to the allied cause was minor, Stein did make important contributions to the military government of Germany, to the formation of a German legion, and later to the organization of occupied France.

---

[38] Stein, journal to his wife, Sept. 8, 1812, *Briefe*, III, 720. Alexander to Stein, April 8, 1812, Stein, *Briefe*, III, 627.

[39] Stein to Princess Louise Radziwill Aug. 12, 1813, Stein, *Briefe*, IV, 230. Stein's memorandum of Nov. 17, 1812 (*Briefe*, III, 805–811), enthusiastically set forth plans for the continuing war in Germany.

[40] Stein to Frederick William, Dec. 28, 1812, Stein, *Briefe*, III, 842.

Stein's influence diminished somewhat after Austria joined the allies, since his position in the Russian service was strongly opposed by Metternich. As a champion of German unity, favoring "the restraint on the arbitrary authority of all these miserable despots who vex Germany," Stein was quite opposed to Metternich's projects. His enlightened outlook and advocacy of constitutions contrasted with the views of the Austrian chancellor and hence with those of Nesselrode on many issues. Conversely, most of his policies gave strong support to the emperor's, especially his encouragement of the war and the march to Paris. He did, however, oppose Alexander's idea of giving the French people a chance to choose their new government. An advocate of the restoration of legitimate thrones and very critical of the abilities of the French, Stein argued that the "legitimate" Bourbon successor to Louis XVI would accept Alexander's advice and "adopt all the fundamental, liberal ideas on which Your Majesty wishes to see the social organization of France based." He was glad when Alexander finally agreed to support the Bourbons, believing theirs to be "the cause of right and honor." [41]

Although Alexander was disappointed with Stein for "siding with his enemies" in opposing the establishment of a Russian kingdom of Poland, the emperor retained him as one of his chief advisers at the Congress of Vienna and considered him his chief consultant for German affairs. Stein argued well for his main cause — a liberalized federal structure for Germany; Alexander listened, often with tacit approval, but Stein's proposals were overlooked in the congress proceedings. Alexander was too worried that he might lose the support of the Prussian monarch for his Polish project or further antagonize Metternich if he pushed the issue of reform in Germany. For the most part, Stein remained in the background, consulted from time to time and sometimes given important assignments. His disappointment grew to bitterness as it became clear that no real steps would be

---

[41] Stein to his wife, March 14, 1814, Stein, *Briefe*, IV, 640; Hardenberg, "Tagebuch," Jan. 27, 1814, in Fournier, *Châtillon*, p. 361. Stein to Alexander, Feb. 10, 1814, Stein, *Briefe*, IV, 515–517. Stein to D. Alopeus, March 29, 1814, Stein, *Briefe*, IV, 675.

taken toward an enlightened and unified Germany. "We just hope that God will find us a way out of the abyss into which we are about to be thrown by the frivolity or foolishness of some and the false ideas of others," he wrote. "I had influence without authority," he lamented, "influence on very imperfect human beings. . . The frivolity of all was the reason that no great, noble, and salutary idea . . . could be brought into being." [42]

Another important member of Alexander's entourage from 1812 to 1815, Jean Protadius Anstedt, shared many of Stein's views. Of Alsacian origin, Anstedt had entered the Russian service at the beginning of the French Revolution and had served in several minor posts in the foreign ministry and the Russian diplomatic service abroad. Gentz recognized him as "a man of much brilliance and talent," but, while he credited him with a strong aversion to Napoleon, he had little sympathy with his character and outlook. "One of the most evil and most dangerous men," Gentz called him at one point, "and one of the most bitter enemies of Austria." [43] Gentz was particularly apprehensive of Anstedt's intrigues to bring about Nesselrode's fall.

An avid opponent of any agreement with Napoleon, Anstedt was sent as Alexander's representative to the Congress of Prague in the summer of 1813, where by his very presence he served as a spokesman for Alexander's opposition to an accommodation with Bonaparte. In the late spring of 1814, Anstedt went on a secret mission to Poland to determine probable public reaction to Russian rule. His report demonstrating the hostility of the Poles toward Alexander's intentions angered his sovereign, and he was given an indefinite leave. [44] Although his opposition to Alexander's Polish policy thus cost Anstedt his favor for several months

---

[42] Stein spoke clearly against Alexander's Polish project verbally and in a series of memoranda: Stein, diary entry for Nov. 5, 1814, *Briefe*, V, 333; memorandum to the Russian cabinet, Oct. 6, 1814, *Briefe*, V, 158–159. Stein to his wife, Nov. 16, 1814, *Briefe*, V, 197; diary entry for end of March 1815, *Briefe*, V, 369.

[43] Gentz to Karadja, July 15, 1813, Gentz, *Dépêches*, I, 32. Gentz to Metternich, June 24, 1813, Gentz, *Briefe*, II, Part 1, 112–113; see also anon. report of Oct. 1, 1814, Weil, *Congrès*, I, 181–182.

[44] Anon. report to Hager, Sept. 25, 1814, Weil, *Congrès*, I, 108–109.

in the summer of 1814, he was summoned to Vienna as one of the emperor's chief advisers for the congress. Not one to keep his opinions to himself, he continued speaking against the Polish project. When he realized that Alexander was intractable on this issue, he requested leave, but to no effect. Eager to move Alexander toward the support of liberal ideas and very opposed to Austrian policies which he believed Nesselrode was promoting, he assumed a more important position during the eclipse of Nesselrode which followed Alexander's disputes with Metternich.[45] Anstedt's importance was short-lived, however; his influence was even less than Stein's. He remained in the Russian service until his death in 1835 as Russian minister to the German diet in Frankfurt, where he was a continual source of distress to Metternich.

The distinguished Count Andrei Kirillovich Razumovskii was brought in to serve in an important capacity at a point when his political outlook was especially appropriate. His prestigious background was useful to the emperor throughout the Congress of Vienna. The elderly count had served for many years before 1807 as Russian ambassador to Austria, where he had gained great wealth and prestige in Vienna. Following French inroads into Austria, Razumovskii gained a reputation as "one of the most intractable, uncompromising enemies of Napoleon," and his salon was a center of resistance to the French emperor.[46] His efforts to win the Austrian government to the Russian side in 1813 won him favor; Alexander's regard for him increased because, like Stein and Anstedt, he was one of the few to urge Alexander against peaceful accommodations with Napoleon. Alexander, recognizing his "zeal, talents, and experience which," as he wrote to Razumovskii, "acquired for you the true title of my confi-

[45] Reports to Hager, Sept. 28 and 30, Oct. 1 and 11, 1814, Weil, *Congrès*, I, 152–154, 180, 181, 265. His request for leave is confirmed by two different reports to Hager dated Nov. 12, 1814, *ibid.*, pp. 510–514.

[46] Gentz to Karadja, March 8, 1814, Gentz, *Dépêches*, I, 62. See *Razoumowski*, II, Part 3, 142–152, 207–215, 261–263. Andrei Kirillovich was the son of an eminent field marshal; his brother Aleksei (1748–1822) served as minister of education under Alexander (1810–1816).

dence," appointed him his chief plenipotentiary for the Congress of Châtillon in early 1814.[47]

Although he did not support all the emperor's ideas on the future government in France, Alexander valued his assistance and later used him for many key conferences during the Congress of Vienna, where his home — until its destruction by a spectacular fire in December — was one of the main centers of congress social life. With the eclipse of Nesselrode in December, Razumovskii was made the chief plenipotentiary for many of the official negotiations, and, as Capodistrias informed him, "His Majesty . . . has confided to Your Excellency the major affairs that hitherto have been treated confidentially." Lacking personal and intellectual congeniality with Alexander, Razumovskii had never been a favorite, but in Vienna there was rumor of his appointment as Chancellor of the Russian Empire. That appointment never materialized, however, according to one account because Razumovskii "was concerned over the difficulties of the post, his age, and his anxiety at the unsystematic manner in which the emperor conducted affairs."[48] Certainly, too, Razumovskii was not eager to leave Vienna for St. Petersburg. He continued to represent the Russian court in various negotiations, but he is more often remembered as patron of three Beethoven quartets than as a man of real influence in Russian diplomacy.

Charles André Pozzo di Borgo also attained a large degree of responsibility in carrying out the emperor's policies when his ideas meshed with the emperor's. A Corsican by birth, with a family vendetta against Bonaparte, Pozzo had served England before joining the Russian service in 1805. At that time Alexander recognized his talents and valued his outlook as a "sworn enemy" of Napoleon. He was sent on a special mission to Vienna in 1806 and then to Turkey in 1807.[49] One of the strongest advo-

[47] Razumovskii to Alexander, [Feb. 7, 1814], *Razoumowski*, II, Part 3, 178. Alexander to Razumovskii, [ca. Jan. 24, 1814], *ibid.*, p. 175.

[48] Capodistrias to Razumovskii, Dec. 24, 1814, Gosarkhiv XV, TsGADA, 15/626. Stein, "Tagebuchaufzeichnungen," March 11, 1815, *Briefe*, V, 373.

[49] Alexander to Chichagov, March 19, 1806, Schilder, *Aleksandr*, II, 350–351. Pozzo di Borgo was in Russia as early as 1804 and made his political debut as an acknowledged Russian agent during the abortive Russian occupation

cates of renewed war with Napoleon, he advised Alexander in 1806 that "those who have thought that Russia could isolate herself and wait for the enemy on her own frontiers have fallen into an error which will become fatal if it is invariably adopted." His advice was respected in St. Petersburg. "Next to the force of circumstances which has implicated every party in the warlike schemes against France," the British ambassador stated, "his conversations have produced the greatest effect, not only on Budberg, but on Alexander Paulowitch himself." Despite Pozzo's warnings, the Russian cabinet failed to move until the fall of Berlin. Because his position in the Russian service was anathema to Napoleon, after Tilsit Pozzo spent most of his time abroad, but continued to inform and advise the Russian court through a variety of intermediaries.[50] He joined the emperor again after the start of the war against Napoleon and performed several important missions for Alexander during the campaign years, representing him, for example, as a special envoy to Sweden in 1813 and to England in 1814.

One of the strongest opponents of any peaceful accommodation with Napoleon and a champion of the principle of legitimacy, Pozzo was the most important spokesman in the Russian service for the restoration of the Bourbons to the French throne. Alexander had been very skeptical about restoring the Bourbons, being personally unimpressed with the future Louis XVIII; for a while he was apparently more enthusiastic about Bernadotte. Most important, he believed that the French people should be given the right to choose their new ruler and hence that final decision should be withheld until the armies entered Paris and a constitutional assembly could be called. Pozzo's heartiest efforts went into convincing his sovereign to support the

---

of Naples in December 1805. For his activities in Austria and Turkey in 1806 and 1807, see his instructions and his reports to Budberg in *VPR*, III, 375–380, 433–435, 540–545, 550–553, 595–611. His mission to Austria is described by Stuart to Howich, No. 56, Nov. 19, 1806, PRO/FO 65/64.

[50] Pozzo di Borgo, "Opinion sur la conduit que la Russie devrait suivre," Aug. 18, 1806, Budberg Papers, Ts GAOR, 860/1/36. Stuart to Leveson-Gower, Oct. 12, 1806, Lord Granville Leveson-Gower, *Private Correspondence, 1781–1821*, ed. Castalia Countess Granville (2 vols.; London, n.d.), II, 228.

Bourbons. Yet, while he did much to pave the way for the return of the French dynasty, he does not deserve principal credit for the restoration. In the long run Talleyrand's activities were more influential in securing allied support, and for Alexander the indication of support for the Bourbons within France was the most crucial element.

Although Pozzo was summoned to the Congress of Vienna, he hardly saw the emperor during his six months there. He was outspoken for a favorable treatment of post-Napoleonic France and its restoration to great-power status. He agreed with Stein's proposals for the establishment of a German federation and remained strongly opposed to Alexander's Polish policies.[51] In short, his policies and his strong advocacy of them were hardly appealing for the emperor at the congress, although his influence on French affairs remained significant. Pozzo's efforts bore more fruit in 1815 when he worked with Capodistrias, partly in defiance of the emperor's instructions, to secure better terms for France after the final defeat of Napoleon at Waterloo. He continued to play an important role in implementing his sovereign's plans for France throughout the Restoration as Russian ambassador to the court of Louis XVIII. His later importance derives chiefly from his machinations in French internal politics and financial affairs and his forcefulness in representing — or overrepresenting — Russian interests in Western Europe.

Of the many individuals surrounding Alexander, the most important and successful during these years was Prince Adam Czartoryski, who had been out of office since 1806. The position and favor which Czartoryski enjoyed in 1814 and 1815 stemmed in part from his background and close friendship with the emperor and was nourished by their similarity in outlook and ideals. Most

---

[51] His recommendation about France and his isolation from the Russian sovereign were noted by Talleyrand to Louis XVIII, Jan. 6, 1815, *Correspondance inédite du prince de Talleyrand et du roi Louis XVIII pendant le Congrès de Vienne*, ed. M. G. Pallain (Paris, 1881), pp. 216–217. Pozzo's memorandum against the establishment of a kingdom of Poland under Russia, dated Oct. 20, 1814, was printed by N. I. Turgenev, *La Russie et les russes* (3 vols.; Paris, 1847), I, 443–461. A memorandum written with Laharpe (July 7, 1814) called for a German federation and expressed his stand firmly against Alexander's ideas about Poland (printed in Schilder, *Aleksandr*, III, 534–537).

important, Czartoryski supported Alexander's strong commitment to the Polish cause; he was the chief spokesman for the emperor's "favorite idea" of a Polish kingdom.

When Czartoryski left the Russian foreign ministry in 1806, he was discouraged about Alexander's intentions toward the war effort and particularly toward Poland. By that time Czartoryski was openly recommending the regeneration of Poland under Russian auspices, with Alexander assuming the Polish crown and granting the Poles a constitution and a reasonable degree of autonomy. "It is the only solution," he urged the Poles, "that will promise not only . . . success, but lasting well-being for the country." The emperor gave him some encouragement in a series of conferences and in their correspondence before 1812. As Alexander procrastinated, however, Czartoryski began to have some doubts about the Polish reactions to such a project. He wrote a friend in 1811, "I can not permit myself to give [Alexander] hopes which will not be realized or to promise him the immediate reunion of government and army; the unceasing animosities and suspicions will not suddenly change into enthusiasm and attachment."[52]

With the turn of events in 1812, however, Czartoryski felt that the auspicious moment had arrived. He was greatly encouraged in the spring when, after a long silence, Alexander assured him that as soon as "circumstances were ripe," he would turn his attention to "my favorite ideas for the regeneration of your country." When Napoleon had left Russia and the Russian troops were approaching Poland at the end of 1812, Czartoryski was full of what would prove to be naïve optimism, believing "that a new period for humanity will be dated from the present moment; that it will be the reign of justice, of great and liberal ideas, of generous and well-meaning sentiments."[53] He assured Alexander that the reestablishment of Poland "should be one of the conditions of general peace." Alexander welcomed

---

[52] Czartoryski, "Lettre circulaire sur la Pologne," 1806, CA 5229/IV; see also his memoranda reprinted in Czartoryski, *Mémoires*, II, 148–158, 178–182. Czartoryski to Stroganov, April 2, 1811, Stroganov Papers, TsGADA, 1278/1/62.

[53] Alexander to Czartoryski, April 13, 1812, Czartoryski, *Mémoires*, II, 281.

Czartoryski's views and encouragement, despite the widespread and firm opposition to the plan, and in a letter of January 1813 lamented the difficulties involved, as he put it, "in making my favorite ideas on Poland succeed." Alexander reassured Czartoryski of his intentions: "As the military results unfold, you will see to what point the interests of your country are dear to me and the extent to which I am faithful to my early ideas; as to the former, you know that I have always preferred the most liberal ones." During the next couple of years Czartoryski was actively seeking support for Alexander's Polish project in Poland itself and even more in England.[54] By the spring of 1814 he was working as an intimate adviser of the emperor and accompanied him to London in July 1814.

By the opening of the Congress of Vienna in the fall of 1814, all of the allied statesmen and virtually all of Alexander's advisers had expressed their opposition to the Polish project, but to no avail. Alexander turned to his childhood friend, who almost blindly supported the project. Czartoryski was invited to Vienna where he found himself unofficially in a position similar to the one he had enjoyed in Russia up to September 1805. "The Emperor has latterly, on the question of Poland, ceased to act through his regular servants," Castlereagh could report. By October Czartoryski was editing Alexander's memoranda to Castlereagh on Polish affairs without even consulting Nesselrode.[55] Not

Czartoryski to Robert Wilson, Dec. 25, 1812, in Wawrzkowicz, *Sprawa Polska*, p. 288. Czartoryski to Novosiltsev, Dec. 25, 1812, *Russkii arkhiv*, XXII (1884, No. 2), 280–281. Czartoryski was distressed to learn that Novosiltsev and Stroganov had turned against the plan, as evidenced in the letter of Czartoryski to Stroganov, June 1, 1812, Stroganov Papers, TsGADA, 1278/1/62.

[54] Alexander to Czartoryski, Jan. 13, 1813, Chodzko, *Pologne*, p. 586. See Czartoryski's memorandum, "La politique de la Grande Brétagne, mémoire présenté au cabinet anglais en faveur de la Pologne," Sept. 9, 1813, in Wawrzkowicz, *Sprawa Polska*, p. 314, and the additional materials in the English edition, *Memoirs of Prince Adam Czartoryski and his Correspondence with Alexander I* (London, 1888) II, 247–282. Czartoryski detailed his recommendations for Poland in "Note du Prince Adam Czartoryski présentée à l'Empereur Alexandre Ier à Chaumont en 1814," March 19, 1814, CA 5239/IV, fols. 207–230; an additional note on the same subject in draft form follows in this collection (fols. 233–241).

[55] Castlereagh to Liverpool, Nov. 5, 1814, *British Diplomacy*, p. 222; Alexander to Castlereagh, Oct. 30, 1814, *ibid.*, pp. 224–225. The copy of the memorandum in Stein's papers (Stein, *Briefe*, V, 180–183) showed it to be edited by

only was Czartoryski consulted frequently by his sovereign, but he did most of the paper work with regard to Poland. In many instances, his advice and active participation extended to other important affairs of state, particularly during periods when Nesselrode was pushed into the background. The extent of his participation in the Russian negotiations led many to suggest that it was Czartoryski, "who ought, at this time, to be considered as the veritable Minister of the Emperor." There were some rumors that he had actually been offered and had declined the position of chief of the foreign ministry.[56]

Although Czartoryski had an important role and was in a key position of influence during the congress, "it was the emperor himself," as one perceptive observer remarked, "by his own will, who created the Kingdom of Poland" against the opposition of his other advisers, his allies, and even many Polish leaders, bringing the congress to the brink of war over the issue.[57] It was only later that Czartoryski himself came to realize that the Kingdom of Poland which he so enthusiastically had helped create in 1815 was far from the reconstituted nation he had visualized. To his deep regret, Poland soon was subjected to Russian military rule under Grand Duke Constantine. That "liberal constitution," which Alexander so heartily supported, was a step in the right direction for Czartoryski, but its implementation provided little satisfaction; Poland was reunified, but popular liberties and national independence were progressively circumscribed. Alexander's closest adviser of these years left Vienna in profound disappointment and spent the rest of his life trying to remedy the worsening situation which he had so optimistically sanctioned for his native country.

As Joseph de Maistre remarked toward the opening of the

Czartoryski; Stein noted Czartoryski's role and Nesselrode's exclusion in his diary (Oct. 13 and 16, 1814, ibid., pp. 322–323).

[56] Münster to Prince Regent, Nov. 27, 1814, Political Sketches of the State of Europe from 1814–1867, p. 195; Castlereagh to Liverpool, Dec. 24, 1814, British Diplomacy, p. 269; Gentz to Karadja, Jan. 4, 1815, Gentz, Dépêches, I, 140–141; Rozenkrantz, diary entry for Jan. 10 and 11, 1815, Journal du congrès de Vienne 1814–1815, pp. 123–124.

[57] Turgenev, La Russie et les russes, pp. 57–62.

Congress of Vienna, Alexander was to see "men arrive from a thousand places who wanted to lead him this way or that." Nevertheless, Maistre continued, "I believe that he will remain completely independent and intractable." [58] The conservative publicist, then serving as a Sardinian diplomat, was right. Stein, Anstedt, Razumovskii, Pozzo di Borgo, Czartoryski, as well as the Greek patriot Capodistrias were all part of the emperor's entourage, trying to influence him on behalf of a variety of causes. What they held in common was the fact that all were men of foreign background or at least foreign upbringing and commitments who wanted to involve Russia deeply in continental affairs. But beyond that they looked to Alexander in friendship and in respect as the leader of the triumphal coalition who would have much to say about the subsequent settlement of European affairs. In their diverse ways, they were all concerned about the reconstruction of Europe, and they all sought to advance their own ideas and commitments. Alexander encouraged them or utilized their knowledge, commitment, or service as he saw fit. Their success on the whole, however, was meager.

By their role and the confidence which the emperor accorded them, they often eclipsed the influence of Nesselrode. At times their ideas more closely coincided with the emperor's aims than did those of his chief spokesman for conservative reaction, and when those ideas were important to him, Alexander used their services, confided in them, and counted on their support. Their presence was significant, but in the final analysis they were little more effective than Nesselrode. While other monarchs turned over many of the negotiations to their ministers during the campaigns and at the Congress of Vienna, and while Castlereagh, Metternich, and Talleyrand were in a position to put forth their own plans and policies, Alexander's minister and chief Russian plenipotentiary for the congress remained in the background and could only serve his sovereign — when the emperor's confidence permitted — as his secretary or diplomatic spokesman.

[58] Maistre, letter of Oct. 8, 1814, *Correspondance*, II, 27–28.

## Chapter 7

# CAPODISTRIAS: A SPOKESMAN FOR LIBERAL CAUSES

Nesselrode returned to St. Petersburg after the Congress of Vienna with neither the ministerial title nor the sole directorship of the Russian foreign ministry. From 1816 to 1822, he shared the functions of the office with a young aristocrat from Corfu, Ionnes Antonios Capodistrias. Later to be first president of the Greek republic from 1827 until his assassination in 1831, Capodistrias greatly overshadowed Nesselrode during his years in the Russian foreign office. The irony of a Greek patriot's serving as Russian foreign minister recalls the earlier situation of Czartoryski; and in fact, many aspects of Capodistrias' ideas and commitments, like his career in the service of Russia, paralleled those of the Polish prince. Close to the emperor in friendship and intellectual outlook, he was one of the most able and influential men who served Alexander I as minister for foreign affairs. While Nesselrode was a willing spokesman for Austria-oriented policies, Capodistrias brought to the Russian cabinet a progressive alternative to the Metternich system. In his successes and failures in implementing his ideas lie many of the keys to Russian diplomacy in the early Restoration.

Personally, Capodistrias was at home in the diplomatic world of the early nineteenth century; he "was justly held in high esteem by all the statesmen whose opinions were valued in Europe" and was even regarded by some as "the paragon of diplomacy." [1] With "a handsome Greek profile" and with "a look of

[1] *Personal Recollections of the Late Duc de Broglie, 1785–1820*, tr. and ed. R. de Beaufort (2 vols.; London, 1887), II, 245. Pictet de Rochemont to Turrettini, Oct. 24, 1815, in *Genève et les traités de 1815; Correspondance diplomatique de Pictet de Rochemont et de François d'Ivernois; Paris, Vienne, Turin, 1814–1816*, ed. Lucien Cramer (2 vols.; Geneva, 1914), II, 171.

pure intelligence, gracious simplicity of manners, and spontaneous elegance of speech in all languages," he was credited even
by his political adversaries as "a man of honor, of integrity," and
"a sincere friend of all that is beautiful and good in human nature." He was a relatively good administrator, and his subordinates sensed his "true zeal for the service combined with a
friendliness which is rarely found." [2] He inspired confidence and
respect in his associates to the extent that most diplomats in
St. Petersburg preferred dealing with him rather than Nesselrode.
Even Metternich's envoy Lebzeltern, who politically had more
in common with Nesselrode, had to admit that Capodistrias
usually explained political issues much more informatively and
clearly than his colleague.[3]

Aligned with men of wealth, background, and privilege, Capodistrias was as much at home in the aristocratic social worlds
of Geneva and London as in Paris and St. Petersburg. Yet he had
an antagonism to the Restoration political system which was accompanied, if not induced, by some degree of personal alienation
from the world of which he was a part. The introspection or
"speculative turn of mind" [4] to which he was inclined was apparently a psychological reaction to his frustrations in life and to his
political milieu. His distress at the "dancing congress" of
1814/1815 was typical of the melancholic reactions to the diplomatic world which cloud his personal correspondence: "The
most important affairs, the affairs of the world, are treated as one
treats amusements — by whims, by fits and starts." "The same
levity has been adopted everywhere by everyone, and becomes
the spirit of the century," he lamented. "Diplomats are not the
best sort of men," he confided to his friend Friedrich von Stein,

[2] *Souvenirs de la baronne du Montet, 1785–1866* (Paris, 1904), p. 186. Abel
François Villemain, *Souvenirs contemporains d'histoire et de littérature* (Paris,
1866), I, 478–479. Gentz to Soutsos, Oct. 30, 1820, Gentz, *Dépêches*, II, 89.
N. M. Longinov to S. R. Vorontsov, July 24, 1822, *AKV*, XXIII, 455.

[3] For example, Lebzeltern to Metternich, Jan. 1, 1818, HHS/Russ. III, 24; La
Ferronnays to Pasquier, July 6, 1820, AE/CPR, 161; Report of General Steigentesch, Sept. 13, 1819, HHS/Russ. III, 78.

[4] Philip von Neumann, entry for Sept. 1–2, 1819, *The Diary of Philip von
Neumann, 1819–1850*, ed. E. B. Chancellor (2 vols.; London, 1928), I, 2.

with whom he had a personal and political bond.[5] In Capodistrias, a real sense of involvement and serious concern with political issues did not negate self-conscious detachment.

Capodistrias' alienation, heightened by his personal frustration
in his relations with Alexander and with the woman he had
wanted to marry, may have encouraged "the spiritual dimension
in his soul" which enabled him to sympathize with some of Alexander's religious concerns. Despite a nominal commitment to
to the Orthodox church, which deepened in later life, Capodistrias had contact with some of the religious mystics who interested
Alexander, for example, the noted spiritual luminary Madame
Julie de Krüdener.[6] He often found his "soul had need of a moment's rest" with the Bavarian theologian Franz Xavier von
Baader or at the Fellenberg Institute in Switzerland.[7] However,
in neither contact nor absorption was Capodistrias ever carried to
Alexander's extremes of religiosity. The tragic resignation which
pervaded Capodistrias' attitudes never betrayed psychological
imbalance, but only suggested a faith in "that Providence
which alone is the arbiter of nations," somewhat reminiscent of
Greek tragedy.[8]

Although his associates sometimes dubbed him "more a phi-
losopher than a statesman," Capodistrias was by no means primarily an ideologue or social theorist.[9] He made no systematic
attempt to come to terms with the political issues of his day, nor
was he a man who actively read political literature or searched
for theoretical answers. It is thus hard to pigeonhole Capodistrias'
outlook, because the complexity of his ideas reflects the ironies of

[5] Conversation reported to F. A. Hager, Jan. 11, 1815, Weil, Congrès, II,
32. Capodistrias to Stein, July 28, 1815, Stein, Briefe, V, 404.

[6] Edling, Mémoires, pp. 42–43, et passim. Alexander Sturdza mentioned to
his sister Roxandra that Capodistrias had visited Madame de Krüdener with
him (Heidelberg, June 19, 1815, Sturdza Papers, PD, 288/1/86); such visits
are also recorded in the diary of Juliette de Krüdener, as quoted by Francis Ley,
Madame de Krüdener et son temps, 1764–1824 (Paris, 1961), pp. 456–458.

[7] Capodistrias to Stein, Vienna, Dec. 28, 1815, Stein, Briefe, V, 450.

[8] Capodistrias, "Address from Count Capodistrias to the Greeks," April 18,
1819, Portfolio: A Collection of State Papers, IV (London, 1836), 292–294.

[9] The Diary of Philip von Neumann, 1819–1850, I, 2. See also, Pasquier,
Histoire, V, 25; Lebzeltern to Metternich, Feb. 23, 1817, HHS/Russ. III, 21.

his personal position. His stance on many issues grew out of the ambiguity of his social, national, and political identity. The conflicts in his outlook were to be found in many enlightened men of high social and political position in the early nineteenth century; his tensions were familiar to the reforming aristocrats or men of privilege in Germany, France, and Russia, who were sensitive to historical change, yet eager to preserve the best of their world in the face of the upheavals which were sweeping the European continent. The tensions were even more familiar to progressive leaders in suppressed nations, who wished to promote their own national self-determination without violent revolution and without seeing their patriotic efforts fail before bids for hegemony on the part of the great powers.

Although Capodistrias, like the emperor, liked to use the term "liberal" in reference to his ideas, it is confusing to identify those ideas closely with European liberalism, particularly in its classical identification with bourgeois interests. Yet his ideas were progressively reformist, especially within the Russian political spectrum. However vague and ineffectual they often were, they suggested a viable alternative to the "Metternich system," with which Nesselrode was basically sympathetic. Alexander's continued preference for Capodistrias' solutions clearly demonstrates that he had not closed the door on his reforming goals.

Both Capodistrias' personal disaffection from the diplomatic world and his concern for moderately liberal political policies developed out of his early experiences and especially from his intense involvement with his native Greece. Cosmopolitanly European in background and attitudes, Capodistrias nevertheless had a primary identity with his native land. "The affair of my heart and of my mind — the affair of the Ionian Isles," he considered to be his deepest personal and political commitment. "I will never renounce the first and most sacred of my needs, that of serving my fatherland," he assured a friend in 1815. [10] Born into one of the oldest noble families of Corfu in 1776, he had seen

[10] Capodistrias to Stein, June 11, 1815, Stein, *Briefe*, V, 389; Capodistrias to Pozzo di Borgo, June 17, 1815, *SIRIO*, CXII, 263.

the Ionian Islands the prey of a series of great powers. He and his family had bitterly opposed the Venetian rule, but the first French occupation from 1797 to 1799 was even more distasteful. Capodistrias' early education in Padua qualified him as a physician, and he served briefly as an army doctor, but he abandoned medicine for politics at an early age. With his father he was closely involved in events leading to the creation of the Septinsular Republic under the suzerainty of Turkey and the guaranty of Russia in 1800 and became active in the new government. Recognizing the impossibility of complete independence at that time, Capodistrias supported the Russian protectorate of the Ionian Islands (formalized by the Treaty of Amiens in 1802), arousing strong opposition among many of his more radical compatriots. He was involved in drawing up the constitution of 1803 and became Secretary of State of the islands once it was enacted. From his own experience, he believed his native islands were best off during the period of effective Russian control from 1800 to 1807, an attitude which was reinforced for him by his position as the favorite of the Russian viceroy Count Mocenigo.[11]

The stage was well set for his transfer to Russia when the French overran the Ionian Islands in 1807. Capodistrias entered the Russian service in 1809; and after brief assignments in Vienna and with the Russian army in the Danube area, he came to the emperor's personal attention during the continental campaigns following Napoleon's invasion of Russia. It was Capodistrias' "republican sympathies," to quote the emperor, which made Alexander choose for a delicate mission to Switzerland in 1813 and 1814 this "very commendable man, by virtue of his enlightenment and his liberal views."[12] The emperor — exactly Capodistrias' age — was attracted to the count's colorful yet sensitive personality, and he admired his pleasing manner and diplomatic talents. Alexander was impressed also by the extent to which Capodistrias shared and reinforced many of the political, humanitarian, and even religious concerns which were important to him

[11] For example, see Mocenigo's high recommendation of Capodistrias to Czartoryski, May 24, 1805, CA 5502/II, fols. 68–69.

[12] Alexander to Laharpe, Jan. 3, 1814, NM, *Alexandre*, I, 340.

during those years. Capodistrias' accomplishments in Switzerland having "surpassed [the emperor's] expectations," Alexander summoned his young Greek friend as one of his close advisers during the Congress of Vienna.[13] Following the Paris settlements in the fall of 1814, in which Capodistrias had been Alexander's key negotiator, he returned to Russia with the title of State Secretary for Foreign Affairs and served as Russian foreign minister until the summer of 1822.

The personal protection he found in the service of the Russian emperor reinforced Capodistrias' hope that Alexander would be "the veritable protector of the Greeks," just as Czartoryski had hoped the emperor would ameliorate conditions for the Poles. Reestablishing its earlier protectorate of the Ionian Islands, Capodistrias believed, would give Russia reason and opportunity to support the Greeks in their desire for freedom from the Turkish yoke. "If this opportunity is neglected, if the islands are abandoned to the English or to the absolute sovereignty of any other power foreign to our interests," he argued in a flattering memorandum presented to the emperor in 1814, "it will only be by force that Russia will be able to forge a road to Greece to renew her ties there and to consolidate that beneficent system of influence through which she has long regulated the destinies of the Ottoman Empire." [14]

Alexander had promised that "he was well disposed never to abandon the Ionian Islands," [15] but having brought the Congress of Vienna to the point of war over a Russian Kingdom of Poland, he was hardly ready for a similar display over Greece and so raised scant objection to the proposal of a British protectorate over the Ionian Islands. Capodistrias was forced to rationalize British rule as being best able to guarantee the people enlightened constitutional government and "best able to secure to them

---

[13] Edling, *Mémoires*, p. 146.

[14] Capodistrias to Alexander in 1808/1809, in "Aperçu," *SIRIO*, III, 167; see also Capodistrias to R. Sturdza, June 26, 1814, *Vestnik vsemirnoi istorii* (Jan. 1900), No. 2, p. 181. Capodistrias, "Mémoire sur les Isles Ioniennes" [late 1813], Gosarkhiv XV, TsGADA, 15/537.

[15] Capodistrias to Razumovskii, Zurich, Jan. 31, 1814, Gosarkhiv XV, TsGADA, 15/537.

the advantage of their flag and the freedom of their commerce," although inwardly he bemoaned Alexander's failure to fulfill his earlier guarantees.[16] Yet rather than turn to the British or to the Greek underground, he remained in the Russian service with "the hope of employing myself for the good of my country," because Alexander assured him that "nothing could be more just and more advantageous for the Greeks than having you near me as their advocate." [17]

Throughout his years in the Russian service, Capodistrias' political outlook and activities were closely linked to his hopes for his native Corfu, which, in turn, were linked to his desire for an independent, constitutional government for all of Greece. Even as he took the office of Russian foreign minister, he kept "the hope of going to die honorably in my country." In St. Petersburg his closest friends and associates were of Greek background, as was the woman he wished to marry, Roxandra Sturdza, a lady-in-waiting to the Empress Elizabeth and a personal friend of the emperor.[18] During the Congress of Vienna he was actively soliciting support for a Greek education society, *Philomouson Etairia.* Convinced that the improvement of education constituted the best road to the betterment of conditions in Greece, he continued

[16] Castlereagh to Liverpool, Dec. 24, 1814, Castlereagh, *Correspondence,* X, 226; see also Capodistrias to Clancarty, April 9, 1815, in Emmanuel Rodocanachi, *Bonaparte et les Iles Ioniennes. Un épisode des conquêtes de la République et du Premier Empire (1797–1816)* (Paris, 1899), pp. 256–260, and Anon. report to Hager, Oct. 12, 1814, Weil, *Congrès,* I, 277–278. Capodistrias gave his private opinion in personal letters to Czartoryski (Oct. 16, 1815, CA 5444/IV, fols. 409–410) and to Pozzo di Borgo (June 17, 1815, *SIRIO,* CXII, 263–265).

[17] Capodistrias to R. Sturdza, May 20, 1814, *Vestnik vsemirnoi istorii* (Jan. 1900), No. 2, p. 189; Capodistrias, "Aperçu," *SIRIO,* III, 303.

[18] Capodistrias to Pozzo di Borgo, June 17, 1815, personal, *SIRIO,* CXII, 263. The Sturdzas — a Fanariot family from Moldavia and leaders of the Greek colony in St. Petersburg — were Capodistrias' closest friends. Roxandra described his overtures in a series of letters to her brother (May 22, June 11, and July 6, 1814; Sturdza Papers, PD, 228/1/112), explaining that she thought her mother intended him for her sister. Roxandra was married a year later to a minor German noble, Count Edling, while her sister married one of Capodistrias' secretaries, Dmitrii Severin. Alexander Sturdza worked for the foreign ministry, often on Bessarabian affairs; an ardent publicist, he wrote many articles and memoranda under orders from Capodistrias and the emperor and later developed into a religious writer and literary critic of some importance.

to promote the society throughout his years in the Russian foreign ministry. After visiting the Ionian Islands in 1819 and observing the difficulties under British rule, he returned more adamant than ever in his commitment. "I have made up my mind never to abandon the interests of my country. No consideration whatsoever could make me lax in the duties that honor prescribes. . . . Of what use to me is the high favor with which Emperor Alexander honors me, if I did not take the occasion to come to the help of those people to whom at heart I belong exclusively." [19] The division of his loyalties became increasingly difficult in his position as foreign minister.

Capodistrias' devotion to the Greek cause was in itself enough to arouse Metternich's ire because it implied the necessity for radical change in the status quo in the Balkans, with all the explosive ingredients of the Eastern Question which were to plague diplomats throughout the nineteenth century. Furthermore, Capodistrias' devotion to Russian support — and even a Russian protectorate — for Greece had the ominous implication of Russian expansionism. His policy thus stood as a direct threat to Austrian interests in the area, and meant a complete overthrow of the delicate balance of power. But, as if this was not enough, Capodistrias' opposition to Metternich went much deeper than overt political goals in the Balkans. When Metternich contrasted himself with Capodistrias by explaining that "he is all and always in the realm of ideas, while I am firmly anchored in reality," the truth was that the two men's policies were anchored in different concepts of political reality; [20] Capodistrias eschewed the "reality" of Austria-dominated European power politics. As a

[19] Capodistrias to Lieven, Jan. 19, 1820, TsGIA, 1101/1/359. For some details of Capodistrias' work in connection with *Philomouson Etairia*, see Capodistrias, "Aperçu," *SIRIO*, III, 195; Report to Hager, Feb. 5, 1815, Weil, *Congrès*, II, 142–143; Capodistrias to Stein, Dec. 28, 1815, and April 3, 1816, Stein, *Briefe*, V, 450, 480; "Pis'mo Grafini Edling k Grafu Kapodistrii," Jan. 8, 1818, *Russkii arkhiv*, XXIX (1891, No. 11), 419–423. In a letter to Alexander Sturdza, Jan. 20, 1820 (Sturdza Papers, PD, 288/1/86), Capodistrias discussed the work of the society and hoped Sturdza would assume the presidency.

[20] Metternich to Countess Lieven, Dec. 29, 1818, *Lettres du prince de Metternich à la comtesse de Lieven (1818–1819)*, ed. Jean Hanoteau (Paris, 1909), p. 96.

partisan for a new order for Greece, he was committed to a new order for Europe, founded on national states, constitutional government, and a more broadly based international system. Although these liberal sympathies were moderated and his basic outlook rendered more ambiguous by his commitment to work within the established political order as foreign minister for Russia and the aristocratic nostalgia with which he viewed the passing of the *ancien régime*, he nonetheless worked for a progressive alternative to the Metternich system, tactically as well as intellectually.

Capodistrias' central argument was that it was folly for Restoration leaders to try to turn the clock back. As he complained bitterly in 1820, "Since 1815, the cabinets have obstinately failed in their judgment of men and events of our time. . . It is as if the events of the past twenty-five years had not transpired. Such is undoubtedly the principal source of all the misfortunes with which the world is stricken. . . We made peace [in 1815]. One might as well say that we signed treaties stipulating, not the intention of constructing a social order anew, but of reproducing the ancient one." Social change was inevitable in Capodistrias' view, but he hoped it could come peacefully, gradually, and without further revolutionary cataclysms. Contemptuous of the revolutionary agitators of the Restoration period, he held no sympathy for their tactics, whether in Spain, Naples, or Greece. "These men, formed in the school of popular despotism during the French Revolution and perfected in the art of overthrowing governments by the despotism of Bonaparte, are working with fatal perseverance to regain the power which was taken from them by the reestablishment of order in Europe," he wrote in 1820, echoing Alexander's fears.[21]

Metternich might well have agreed when Capodistrias stated, "We are no longer in an age when we can be prevented from hoping that reason will direct men, that experience will be their torch, justice their rule of conduct." But for Capodistrias reason

[21] Capodistrias to G. A. Stroganov, Oct. 2, 1820, personal, Stroganov Papers, TsGADA, 1278/1/181; Capodistrias to Richelieu, Sept. 3, 1820, personal, *SIRIO*, LIV, 548.

and justice led to different — and more liberal — conclusions. Capodistrias' main dispute with Metternich was not about the desirability of revolution, but rather over the question of what should be done to prevent radical activity. If revolution arose, in Capodistrias' view, it should be answered by moderate reform and not by conservative repression. "Everywhere that factions have triumphed . . . government is isolated by an absurd and arbitrary administration," he explained; and factions "have been repulsed everywhere that wise institutions have opposed their seductions with the invincible power of law — laws that guarantee, with the existence of a strong and necessary authority, the rights and legitimate interests of the people." Gentz was right in his explanation, if not in his evaluation, that Capodistrias "mistakenly believes that the maintenance of order is compatible with the ascendency of liberal ideas." [22] Capodistrias, like many reforming aristocrats, foresaw the need for moderate, rational reform in order to preserve what could be preserved of the order to which they were socially attached. His political alienation, while strong in such realms as the Greek question, was nevertheless incomplete: Retaining many ties of identity with the old order, his alienation was not strong enough to lead him to radicalism and revolution; it was sufficient, however, to direct his hopes toward progressive development of national independence and constitutional government.

Capodistrias' personal sense of identity as a Greek and his distress at the Restoration handling of the Greek question obviously colored his thinking on the general issue of national self-determination. He sensed that the nation had replaced the sovereign as the focus of men's loyalty in the nineteenth century. Those who fought against Napoleon were, he explained, "called to arms in the name of the *fatherland*, and not in the name of the *sovereign*." [23] He came to feel, in contrast to Metternich, that ultimately national groups had a basic right to self-government. If

---

[22] Capodistrias to Richelieu, Sept. 27 and 3, 1820, *SIRIO*, LIV, 553, 548; Gentz to Soutsos, Feb. 14, 1820, Gentz, *Dépêches*, II, 13.

[23] Capodistrias to G. A. Stroganov, Oct. 2, 1820, personal, Stroganov Papers, TsGADA, 1278/1/181.

the diplomatic context of the early nineteenth century did not provide full autonomy for national units, at least the basic national aspirations should not be repressed. Typical of his attitude were his recommendations for the reorganization of Russian-controlled Bessarabia, where he affirmed that the government should be based on "the conservation of the laws and the customs, of the languages and privileges of the country" and should "conform to the national spirit of the inhabitants, to their needs and to their habits." [24] Too often statesmen "since Napoleon has been overthrown . . . have forgotten the interests of nations and occupied themselves only with the interests of princes as in former wars; thus everything has been reduced to confusion, to conflict of interests, and to the impossibility of contenting the people," Capodistrias believed. He was not advocating full self-determination, but government of the kind "which all enlightened men will most approve." [25] It was thus well within the province of established powers or their "enlightened" leaders to decide what government would be best for another country, he argued, adhering to the basic Restoration principle of the right to intervene in the domestic affairs of foreign countries. His sentiments, like Czartoryski's, were far from the full-blown nationalism of the later nineteenth century; yet they were much more nationalistic than were the feelings of most European leaders in the Restoration, including Alexander I.

Constitutionalism was one of the most important "liberal ideas" in Capodistrias' political system, but there was considerable vagueness about what he actually meant by a constitutional regime. Like Alexander I, he subscribed to the early-nineteenth-century view of a constitution as a safeguard against despotism. He sensed that during the Napoleonic wars people "fought for independence founded on laws and institutions, and not for passive obedience." Henceforth he believed, "Enlightenment and civilization require that an administrative regime be based on the au-

---

[24] Capodistrias, "Rapport à S. M. l'Empereur," March 17, 1822, TsGIA, 1308/1/8; "Projet d'Instruction pour le Général Inzoff," June 27, 1820, TsGIA, 1308/1/55.
[25] Report to Hager, Oct. 12, 1814, Weil, *Congrès*, I, 276; Stewart to Castlereagh, Nov. 3, 1820, appendix in Webster, *Castlereagh, 1815–1822*, 526.

thority of manners and customs and on the power of law." [26] Yet a "liberal" or "constitutional" regime meant more to him than mere government by law instead of decree; he wanted to see a consultative, if not actually legislative, body representative of the "enlightened" segments of the population, which would consider popular problems and govern for the benefit of the people or the "general welfare," as he often put it. Although he bitterly criticized the Venetian rule of the Ionian Islands for "elevating the privileges of the nobility and putting them in opposition to the pretentions of the bourgeoisie and the legitimate rights of the people," [27] there is much evidence that in practice he tended to expect aristocratic predominance. He foresaw that the future would bring a more broadly based popular government, but this could only be instituted, he believed, where "enlightenment" had raised the cultural and moral level of the population. Hence, his constant concern for education. Just as he believed that an improved situation for the Greeks —"the progressive amelioration of our kind" — could be realized only through an extended and invigorated education system,[28] so he believed that Russian diplomacy would improve with his projects for educating young diplomats in the foreign ministry.

In recommending what he considered to be the "best" type of government, ideally, Capodistrias would have suggested a republican regime. "The Swiss find me somewhat according to their way of thinking and a good republican," he confided to a friend in 1814. "You know that is the role which I can sustain with the least difficulty. It is my own." Yet the lack of enlightenment among the populace, he believed, often put "rightful limits" to the "active influence of republican institutions." [29] Like Alexan-

[26] Capodistrias to Stroganov, Oct. 2, 1820, personal, Stroganov Papers, TsGADA, 1278/1/181; Capodistrias, "Projet d'Instruction pour le Général Inzoff," June 27, 1820, TsGIA, 1308/1/55.
[27] Capodistrias, "Observations sur l'Etat Intérieur des Iles Ioniennes," April 12, 1816, BM/Add. MSS. 27.937.
[28] Capodistrias, "Address from Count Capodistrias to the Greeks," Corfu, April 18, 1819, *Portfolio*, IV (London, 1836), 289.
[29] Capodistrias to R. Sturdza, April 1, 1814, *Vestnik vsemirnoi istorii* (Jan. 1900), No. 2, p. 184; Capodistrias to Castlereagh, Sept. 23, 1815, in Rodocanachi, *Bonaparte et les Iles Ioniennes*, p. 270.

der, he dreamed of republican regimes for future enlightened societies, but was more often ready to recommend constitutional monarchy in the early nineteenth century. In France, for example, he thought the country should be "pacified with herself under legitimate kings" and a firmly established constitutional charter to ensure social stability. "The question is not to conserve tranquillity in France because fifteen thousand bayonets speak in favor of legitimacy, but to put legitimacy in a state to do without the foreign bayonets." Conscious of "all the influence on the rest of Europe which would result from the success of representative government in France," he wanted France to "persuade the world, that in being constitutional and highly constitutional, you obey a lasting conviction and not a passing necessity." [30]

Capodistrias supported similar constitutional regimes elsewhere in Europe when troubles arose because he believed that reform in the direction of constitutional government would guarantee legitimate political rights, provide a bulwark against revolutionary activities, and hence obviate the need for reactionary repression. He deeply feared, as he wrote in 1820, that the "social order is menaced with a frightful upheaval" because Metternich's "solutions" only put off and made more difficult any real solutions for the future. To avoid future turmoil and revolution, statesmen had to make concerted efforts "to render the reign of legitimacy compatible with the mass of illegitimate interests represented by a generation of men accustomed to govern Europe." [31]

Capodistrias looked also to reform of the European states system. As a native of one of the smallest countries of Europe, which had frequently been a prey to power struggles on the continent, he wanted machinery established to maintain the territorial integrity of weaker nations, to prevent any bids for hegemony by the great powers, and to insure the popular rights and national

[30] Capodistrias to Pozzo di Borgo, April 3, 1816, Pozzo, *Correspondance*, I, 323; La Ferronnays to Pasquier, March 1, 1820, *SIRIO*, CXXVII, 321; Capodistrias to Richelieu, Oct. 30, 1820, *SIRIO*, LIV, 564.

[31] Capodistrias to G. A. Stroganov, Oct. 2, 1820, personal, Stroganov Papers, TsGADA, 1278/1/181.

self-determination of smaller countries. He opposed Metternich's domination of European diplomacy, not just because he differed politically with Metternich's policies, but because in principle he opposed the arbitrary action of Austria as the head of a multinational empire and its unilateral action on behalf of the European powers. He contested many policies of the alliance system, because, as the Austrian ambassador explained, "His republican maxims are ever repugnant to the dictatorship of the four powers who, according to him, will accustom themselves to this reign and one day will extend it too far to the prejudice of the smaller states."[32] He worked hard for the return of France to great-power status in 1818, viewing France as an important counterweight to Austria. Yet, for Capodistrias, even the innovation of having the five major powers united in an alliance system which provided for periodic congresses to carry out the Paris treaties and to regulate the problems of the continent was not enough.

In contrast to this Restoration "congress system," Capodistrias saw the need for a more extensive, federative international organization, in keeping with many of the contemporary idealistic plans for international law and organization. He objected to many provisions of the 1814/1815 settlements which the great powers sought to preserve, but, more fundamentally, he objected to what he termed the reactionary, repressive spirit with which allied statesmen sought to carry out the treaties and preserve the status quo. Viewing the European international situation in 1820, he saw two alternatives: "On the one side there is the consoling perspective of a real brotherhood between all the states and of a progressive perfection of social institutions; on the other side appears the terrible empire of anarchy and revolutionary despotism with all the horrors of the *divide et impera* of the old diplomacy."[33] There was no doubt about which possibility Capodistrias was advocating.

Although the contrasts in general political outlooks and alter-

[32] Lebzeltern to Metternich, Aug. 28, 1816, HHS/Russ. III, 20; the appraisal of Capodistrias' view was developed further in Lebzeltern's dispatch of April 2, 1817, in the same carton.

[33] Capodistrias to Richelieu, July 27, 1820, *SIRIO*, LIV, 544.

native policies advocated by Nesselrode and Capodistrias were relatively clear-cut, the difference in their functions during the years following the Congress of Vienna was never clear or stable; in effect they jointly held the office of foreign minister. Foreign diplomats found that they had to "avail themselves to one as well as the other, but particularly to Count Capodistrias," who, the French ambassador noted, "holds a great deal of influence and entirely sets aside his rival." [34] From all reports, Capodistrias was one of Alexander's most influential advisers during this period. His influence resulted from several factors. Certainly the personal attachment between the two men was important, for, as one diplomat noted, Capodistrias was "an instrument that his master likes well enough not to force him to serve blindly." [35] Alexander held the young Greek count in high personal regard, and Capodistrias returned his sentiments: "I ask myself if it is the man I love so tenderly or, in fact, the sovereign whose thoughts and influence could do so much for the welfare of the world. It would seem that it is one as well as the other." [36] During a period when Alexander often kept away from the regular conduct of business for weeks at a time, there were many indications that "it was only the insistence of Capodistrias that could reverse this tendency." Capodistrias was in fact the man who, in Gentz's words, "best knew the principles, the political views, and even the most secret thoughts of his sovereign." [37]

Their friendship, and hence Capodistrias' influence, was founded on a general agreement in political outlook. Although contemporaries were rightly impressed at the extent to which "generous and liberal ideas had him as their advocate near the emperor Alexander," it is clear that Capodistrias was never so far to the left as his detractors — especially Metternich — pictured him; nor were his views as different from the emperor's as many

[34] Noailles to Richelieu, Dec. 13, Sept. 28, 1816, *SIRIO,* CXII, 707–708, 635.

[35] Report of Count Wallmoden to Metternich, Vienna, Oct. 28, 1816, HHS, Gesandtschaft Archiv: St. Petersburg, 36.

[36] Capodistrias to R. Sturdza, Vienna, Dec. 23, 1818, *Vestnik vsemirnoi istorii* (April 1900), No. 5, pp. 157–158.

[37] Lebzeltern to Metternich, Sept. 7, 1817, HHS/Russ. III, 23; Gentz to Soutsos, March 17, 1819, Gentz, *Dépêches,* I, 401.

reactionary statesmen wanted Alexander to believe. Capodistrias' "enlightenment and his liberal views" — those qualities which the emperor stressed in commending Capodistrias to Laharpe — kept alive for the emperor the hopes and projects for reform which had long been a major attraction to him.[38] Capodistrias appeared as a most appropriate spokesman for liberal-sounding measures abroad at a time when Alexander, discouraged at not having realized them in Russia, was eager to promote his image abroad as an "enlightened," liberal-minded sovereign. "[Capodistrias] uses the frankest language with the emperor," reported Metternich's ambassador, "rectifies his opinions, speaks to him only of justice, equity, generosity, and maintains in this monarch the principles which today offer him a new type of attraction." [39] Capodistrias intellectually supported Alexander's liberal hopes and politically served him as a strong arm against domination by Metternich, who clearly threatened the accomplishment of such goals abroad.

The imagination, initiative, persistence, and real diplomatic ability which Capodistrias brought to the Russian foreign office were other factors which led Alexander to turn to his Greek friend for many important assignments. Capodistrias devised and implemented a training program for young Russian diplomats.[40] He was charged with supervising the French-language newspaper *Le Conservateur impartial.*[41] He was usually the first to be con-

[38] Pasquier, *Histoire*, V, 25; Alexander to Laharpe, Jan. 3, 1814, NM, *Alexandre*, I, 340.
[39] Lebzeltern to Metternich, Feb. 23, 1817, HHS/Russ. III, 21; Lebzeltern made a similar report in his dispatch of April 20, 1817 (HHS/Russ. III, 22), but then added the supposition that Alexander would probably soon tire of control.
[40] The project was described by Lebzeltern in a report to Metternich (April 25, 1820, HHS/Russ. III, 29): About six pupils each year — to be chosen from the best graduates of the Lycée at Tsarskoe-Selo — were to be assigned to Capodistrias' personal supervision. They began by making summaries from newspapers and gradually worked up to editing reports and drafting dispatches; later they served an apprenticeship in the foreign ministry before assignment as assistants or secretaries in Russian missions abroad. In a letter to A. Sturdza (Jan. 20, 1820, Sturdza Papers, PD, 288/1/186), Capodistrias recommended a good library — possibly named after Rumiantsev — to instruct young employees of the chancellery and discussed remodeling the foreign ministry to improve service.
[41] Capodistrias wrote A. Sturdza (Nov. 11, 1819, Sturdza Papers, PD,

sulted about major policy statements and often was in charge of editing or drafting them. For example, in Paris in the fall of 1815 Capodistrias was the first person to see Alexander's draft of the Holy Alliance and unsuccessfully urged that it be issued as a proclamation or declaration of faith rather than a formal treaty. He was himself so sympathetic to the principle of basing international relations on moral precepts, that when the text of the Holy Alliance later came under attack in Europe for its allegedly ultraconservative tendencies, Capodistrias was put in charge of drafting an explanation that it was meant as "the surest guarantee of a well-ordered liberty, the true safeguard of law, and the most implacable enemy of arbitrary power."[42] When Alexander wanted the document resurrected before the conference of Troppau in 1820, he again turned to Capodistrias, who at that juncture was critical of the emperor's tendency to rely on "annual declarations or charters" rather than concrete proposals for action.[43]

Capodistrias, like most of the emperor's other advisers at the Congress of Vienna, split with Alexander on the issue of Poland. Strongly opposed to the creation of a Russian kingdom, Capodistrias initially was critical of the limited constitutional regime that Alexander wanted to establish.[44] Disagreement on this issue, however, did not occasion a major break, because there were enough points of agreement and enough other problems where Alexander wanted Capodistrias' support. Once Alexander's constitutional Polish kingdom was established, Capodistrias strongly supported the "liberal" measures proposed by the emperor and

---

288/1/186) that he was concerned with what he termed "the nothingness" of the journal and was looking for an able editor.

[42] Capodistrias, "Aperçu," *SIRIO*, III, 201; Sturdza, "Souvenirs du règne d'Alexandre Ier," 1837, Sturdza Papers, PD, 288/1/4. *Conservateur impartial*, No. 36 (May 16, 1817). The article was unsigned, but, according to Lebzeltern, it was the work of Capodistrias (Lebzeltern to Metternich, May 26, 1817, HHS/Russ. III, 22). Although Capodistrias undoubtedly furnished the specifications under order from the emperor, the apology itself may well have been written by Alexander Sturdza.

[43] Capodistrias to Sturdza, Oct. 17, 1820, Sturdza Papers, PD, 288/1/186b; Sturdza, *Vospominaniia o zhizni i delianiakh grafa I. A. Kapodistrii, pravitel' Gretsii* (Moscow, 1864), p. 94.

[44] Stein, diary entries for Nov. 18 and Dec. 17, 1814, Stein, *Briefe*, V, 336–337, 346–347.

counseled against repressive policies and Russification measures. Capodistrias was the first to be consulted about Alexander's most liberal speech to the Polish diet in 1818; apparently the count made no real contribution to the text, but his enthusiastic support may well have been decisive in encouraging its presentation.[45]

Not only did Alexander consult Capodistrias regularly about crucial policy issues, but he gave the count an unusual degree of responsibility in many affairs. At the Congress of Vienna, Capodistrias' influence was most discernible in the case of Switzerland, a country for which the emperor had a deep-seated regard, enhanced by his friendship for his liberal Swiss tutor, Laharpe. Capodistrias' efforts "to lead this fine country to the fulfillment of her peace and happiness" won him acclaim as "the warmest and most able of all the good friends of Geneva" and honorary citizenship in the cantons of Geneva and Vaud,[46] Capodistrias often disagreed with the emperor about details of the Swiss settlement, but he was able to utilize his position of confidence and Alexander's special long-term concern for Switzerland to advance what he considered to be the best interests of the country.

Capodistrias' efforts with respect to France were among his most successful in the years immediately after the Congress of Vienna. In the fall of 1815 Capodistrias' policy of restoring the Bourbons with the protective constitutional guarantees of the Charter coincided so completely with Alexander's views that the emperor gave him much of the responsibility for negotiating the Second Peace of Paris. The young count was eager to ease the terms the allies were imposing on France and, with Pozzo di

[45] Gentz (to Metternich, March 15, 1819, Gentz, *Briefe*, III, Part 1, 362) emphasized the count's editorial work on the Polish speech and "the skill and influence of Capodistrias which induced [Alexander] to adopt it against his better conviction." According to Capodistrias (Schilder, *Aleksandr*, IV, 495–496), he was shown the penciled, completed draft in the emperor's hand and asked to make some stylistic corrections; when he attempted a new version, his draft was not accepted, but a few of his suggestions were incorporated into the finished speech.

[46] Capodistrias to R. Sturdza, June 26, 1814, *Vestnik vsemirnoi istorii* (Jan. 1900), No. 2, pp. 190–191; Pictet de Rochemont to Turrettini, Feb. 25, 1815, Rochemont, *Genève et les traités de 1815*, I, 373; S. T. Lascaris, *Capodistrias avant la révolution grecque. Sa carrière politique jusqu'en 1822* (Lausanne, 1918), pp. 89–90.

Borgo, had such remarkable success in this regard that the French leader Baron de Barante spoke of him as "the man who contributed the most to render the treaties less oppressive for France and to inspire relative moderation in the allies." The French minister Richelieu implored Alexander "not to disavow" Capodistrias "for exceeding his instructions" on behalf of France in pressing the actual terms of settlement.[47] Following this groundwork by Capodistrias and Pozzo di Borgo in 1815, the latter continued to be an important influence on the new French government in his position as Russian ambassador to Paris; Capodistrias on the home front worked closely with Alexander on French affairs, often appearing "overloaded with tasks and more employed than ever by the emperor in editing all the papers relating to high politics." [48]

The Congress of Aix-la-Chapelle and the settlement of French affairs in 1818 climaxed Capodistrias' career in Russian foreign affairs. Recognizing the need for a strong France to offset Metternich's bid for Austrian domination even before the congress, he had been promoting the equality of France vis-à-vis the four main powers of Europe. In formulating a plan for removing foreign troops from France and for liquidating French war debts, he was supported by Pozzo di Borgo and Richelieu, with whom he worked closely on it. At first Alexander seemed inclined toward the British declaration at the opening of the congress which would have maintained the Quadruple Alliance with the exclusion of France. But, according to Richelieu, Capodistrias and Pozzo di Borgo together, "charged with refuting this piece of eloquence, pulverized it." That their goals were mostly realized in the final protocols of the congress and that France emerged with great-power status owed much to Capodistrias' influence over Al-

[47] *Souvenirs, mémoires et correspondance du baron de Barante, 1782–1866,* ed. Claude de Barante (8 vols.; Paris, 1890–1901), II, 225. Richelieu to Alexander, Oct. 17, 1815, *SIRIO,* LIV, 451. Pasquier (*Histoire,* III, 429) also praised Capodistrias' service to France, as did Alexander Sturdza (to R. Sturdza, Oct. 2, 1815, Sturdza Papers, PD, 288/1/86).

[48] Noailles to Richelieu, Nov. 30, 1817, *SIRIO,* CXIX, 483. The nature and importance of Capodistrias' involvement in Russia's relations with France in the early Restoration is apparent in his personal correspondence with Pozzo di Borgo during these years, preserved among the Pozzo di Borgo Papers in Paris.

exander, who "granted his undivided confidence to Count Capodistrias, allowing himself to be enlightened by the judgment and guided by the counsels of this minister." [49]

Despite this apparent triumph of Capodistrias' influence, all was not smooth in his relationship with the emperor, particularly after the Congress of Aix-la-Chapelle. Alexander's emotional instability and religious excesses made life difficult for even such a trusted adviser. Besides, Capodistrias was pressing for a more basic change in the structure of the alliance system than Alexander and his Eastern allies were ready to endorse; differences of opinion and "lively discussions" about important policy decisions were not infrequent. He felt inadequately reassured by second-hand accounts of the emperor's willingness "to honor my conduct . . . and what I have done for his service." As he confided to a friend, "how agreeable it would be to me to have some gauge of this opinion myself from His Imperial Majesty. I like to believe it just and sincere. But I repeat to you — I am not completely convinced of it, and, I must admit, I am grieved." [50]

Capodistrias' eight-month leave for travels to Greece and western Europe during the winter of 1818/1819 pointed up many of the tensions in his position, although it by no means marked the complete break with Alexander for which Metternich hoped. The initiative was Capodistrias', but his eagerness to visit his family and observe the situation in Corfu was indicative of his deep loyalties; his hope that a winter's relief from the rigors of the Russian climate might help to restore his "weakened health," however sincere, did not fully mask the "deep melancholy" and

[49] Richelieu to Louis XVIII, Oct. 12, 1818, in Raoul de Cisternes, *Le duc de Richelieu. Son action aux conférences d'Aix-la-Chapelle. Sa retrait du pouvior, 1818–1824* (Paris, 1898), 78–82. La Ferronnays, "Réflexion sur la situation actuelle de la France, dans le système politique de l'Europe," April 1822, AE/MD: France 699; see also Gentz to Soutsos, March 17, 1819, Gentz, *Dépêches*, I, 401.

[50] Gentz to Metternich, March 15, 1819, Gentz, *Briefe*, III, Part 1, 362–363; Capodistrias to R. Sturdza, Vienna, Dec. 23, 1818, *Vestnik vsemirnoi istorii* (April 1900), No. 5, pp. 157–158. Capodistrias expressed more confidence in Alexander's good intentions toward him in a personal letter to Pozzo di Borgo written December 25, 1818 (Pozzo di Borgo Papers); he described the great reciprocal emotion he felt at the time of his departure from Alexander.

discouragement he felt in the Russian service.[51] His observations in Greece, Italy, France, and England went directly to the emperor, but correspondence was hardly a substitute for close contact with Alexander. His "pious pilgrimage" to his homeland at such a critical time in European affairs proved, as one of his friends later pointed out, "one of the greatest errors he committed from a standpoint of politics" and foreshadowed the deterioration of his position in the Russian cabinet.[52]

Capodistrias returned to find the Russian sovereign increasingly fearful of the revolutionary rumblings throughout Europe and more discouraged than ever about threats to the world in which his liberal plans could be realized. Capodistrias' firsthand reassurances about the stability of the French political situation were not adequate to allay the emperor's concern. Differences between emperor and minister became more frequent because Capodistrias was unprepared to modify his liberal goals and continued to "fight against many of the opinions of his master and against those of general society." [53] Alexander's alarm at radical movements in Germany which culminated in the assassination of August von Kotzebue, who had been serving as Russian consul, prepared him to accept Metternich's proposals for the Carlsbad decrees. Sanctioned by the Prussian king and the German diet in 1819, these decrees abolished student societies, abridged university freedom, and imposed strict censorship; they came to symbolize the repressive policies of the three eastern courts. The extent to which Capodistrias may have condoned these measures once the emperor agreed to them is difficult to determine, but he successfully dissuaded Alexander from more active

[51] Gentz to Metternich, March 15, 1819, Gentz, *Briefe*, III, Part 1, 363. See also Capodistrias to Nesselrode, June 12, July 14, and July 20, 1819, personal, Gosarkhiv III, TsGADA, 3/57; Capodistrias to Lieven, Aug. 5, 1819, personal, Lieven Papers, BM/Add. MSS. 47284.

[52] Sturdza, "Notice biographique sur le comte J. Capodistrias, président de la Grèce," in *Oeuvres*, III, 360–361. His weakened health was a reality, and he was seriously ill at several points during his travels. See also Malvirade to Dessolles, Oct. 18, 1819, *SIRIO*, CXXVII, 197, and Malvirade to Dessolles, April 6, April 17, Oct. 26, and Nov. 15, 1819, AE/CPR, 159.

[53] Lebzeltern to Metternich, Dec. 17, 1819, HHS/Russ. III, 27; see also Malvirade to Dessolles, Nov. 15, 1819, AE/CPR, 159.

intervention in Germany. His continued influence was apparent — much to Metternich's distress — in the extent to which he convinced Alexander to agree to the principle of nonintervention. "The emperor of Russia is himself of very good principles," wrote the German statesman Hardenberg, "and it is only the erroneous notions and opinions of Count Capodistrias which led him to act in a certain manner in opposition to his own sentiments." [54]

While Capodistrias had weakened his position and influence through his travels and his preoccupation with Greek affairs, Metternich had been strengthening his own. The climax came in the series of crises and congresses initiated by the Neapolitan Revolution in 1820, in which Capodistrias faced his most decisive struggle with Metternich and, as it turned out, with Alexander. Capodistrias won the initial round by securing Alexander's support for calling a congress when revolution struck Naples. "I believe we must regard it as most fortunate that Capodistrias was alone with this prince when he received the news about the revolution in Naples," the French ambassador reported. Capodistrias was largely responsible for the emperor's decision to act only in conjunction with all the allies and to prevent unilateral action by Austria to suppress the uprising and restore the king.[55] Capodistrias upheld Alexander's resolve to establish the general principle of joint allied intervention in any revolutionized country.

When the diplomats assembled at Troppau in the fall of 1820, Capodistrias was at Alexander's side in a position of relatively high confidence. Assigned to draw up the initial Russian communication, he was careful to press his own goals in terms which would be as acceptable as possible to the assembled leaders. His proposals for the general principle of intervention by the allies in any revolutionized lands and his recommendation for joint allied

[54] Hardenberg to Castlereagh, Dec. 30, 1819, Castlereagh, *Correspondence*, XII, 163; Capodistrias, "Aperçu," *SIRIO*, III, 250. Capodistrias' views and his split with the emperor on German policy were outlined by Gentz to Soutsos, Dec. 17, 1819, Gentz, *Dépêches*, I, 450–453, and Lebzeltern to Metternich, Dec. 15, 1819, HHS/Russ. III, 27.

[55] La Ferronnays to Pasquier, Sept. 25, 1820, AE/CPR, 161. The same ambassador mentioned that Capodistrias strengthened Alexander's disagreement with Metternich in a later dispatch (Oct. 4, 1820, AE/MD: France, 716).

action in Naples to restore the king were virtually agreed upon before the assembly opened.[56] Capodistrias pressed further for his policy of attempting mediation before making any display of force; but his statement "that the first drop of blood spilt in the cause against Jacobinism might prove as prejudicial to nonrepresentative governments as the bursting forth of many Revolutions," met with some disbelief. Yet, at the end of the sessions he was relatively pleased by the allied agreement to see "that the King of Naples returns to his states peacefully, that is to say without being obliged to be proceeded by a roaring cannon or by an Austrian bayonet tinted with Neapolitan blood." [57]

What Capodistrias considered his most important proposal for Naples was the provision for a new national constitution following the model of the French Charter. This general principle was of vital significance to him because he believed "the cause of constitutions" was at stake, as it was "the wise and reasonable establishment of liberal ideas or the reversion to old institutions which must be decided." He had no sympathy for the revolution, but neither did he want to see it repressed under the Austrian proposal, which he said showed "a pitiful opinion about the means to liberate Naples from the grip of revolution." [58]

Capodistrias' enthusiasm for "national constitutions" fell on deaf ears among the Austrian chancellor and his associates. The count's memoranda were severely dissected and criticized. Alexander initially supported his proposals, but as he worried more and more about the growing unrest on the continent, especially as deceptively embellished for him by Metternich, he became unwilling to insist on a constitution for Naples, over Metternich's strong opposition. "The will of the emperor is stronger than my

[56] Capodistrias, "Travaux de Troppau, Agende," Oct. 17, 1820, Sturdza Papers, PD, 288/1/186b. The proposals were formalized in the memorandum of November 2; Capodistrias' draft that he forwarded to Sturdza is filed with his correspondence: "Réponse du cabinet de Russie, aux communications faites par les cabinets d'Autriche et de Prusse, dans les conférences du 11/23 et du 17/29 octobre," Troppau, Nov. 2, 1820, Sturdza Papers, PD, 288/1/186b.
[57] Stewart to Castlereagh, Nov. 21, 1820, PRO/FO 7/154. Capodistrias to A. Sturdza, Dec. 28, 1820, Sturdza Papers, PD, 288/1/186b.
[58] La Ferronnays to Pasquier, Oct. 4, 1820, AE/MD: France, 716. Capodistrias to A. Sturdza, Nov. 2, 1820, Sturdza Papers, PD, 288/1/186b.

opinion," Capodistrias lamented. "Rather than expose himself to active resistance [from the allies], he prefers to make concessions and bring himself around to the way of thinking of others." Even the British were a bit incredulous about Capodistrias' insistence on a constitution, because it came "from a Member of the three allied Cabinets, whose interests and views have been developed to us in the very opposite strain of *Anti-Liberalism*." [59] By the time that he was required to draft the preliminary protocol for the congress, there was little left of his constitutional plans except a vague provision with regard to the restoration in Naples, to create "an order of things which may be able to maintain itself on its own foundations, to guarantee itself against any new revolutionary shock and assure tranquillity and happiness to the nation." When he left Troppau he lamented that "the illness with which the old Europe is stricken does not reside in Naples . . . and all men who bother to think agree. But what deplorable nuances there were among the opinions of the doctors — stricken themselves — who comprised the consultation of Troppau and who are going to comprise the one at Laibach." [60]

If the Congress of Troppau was a disappointment to Capodistrias, the Congress of Laibach during the winter and spring of 1821 proved even more disheartening. As Metternich skillfully effected an agreement between himself and Alexander, the emperor became less willing to support even the most moderate liberal or nationalistic proposals. Once again Capodistrias condemned both the revolutionary activity in Italy, Spain, and Greece and the severely repressive measures with which European leaders responded. But the emperor accepted Metternich's measures rather than risk disharmony among the allies or the rupture of the alliance system. "Capodistrias twists around like a devil in holy water; but he is in holy water and can do nothing," Metternich remarked triumphantly. "The chief cause of our ac-

[59] La Ferronnays to Pasquier, Nov. 20, 1820, AE/MD: France, 717. Stewart to Castlereagh, Nov. 21, 1820, PRO/FO 7/154.

[60] The preliminary protocol, dated Nov. 19, 1820, is printed in Martens, *Recueil*, IV, Part 1, 281–286. Capodistrias to A. Sturdza, Dec. 28, 1820, Sturdza Papers, PD, 288/1/186b.

tivity today comes out of my thorough agreement with Emperor Alexander." [61] Although the emperor still sought Capodistrias' advice and used his talents for drafting key memoranda and other documents during the congress, Capodistrias found it necessary to modify his own recommendations in face of the emperor's fears of "the revolutionary menace" and his desires to compromise with allied statesmen.

By the end of the congress the French ambassador La Ferronnays, distressed that Capodistrias appeared "reduced to a colorless role," remarked sympathetically, "Circumstances have well served the one against whose system he chose to fight. Imprudence and folly have so frequently won out over good sense and reason that he is reduced to silence." The breach between Alexander and Capodistrias did not, however, result in an immediate complete eclipse of the count. "Since Laibach Count Nesselrode continues to be in charge of the principal work," Metternich's ambassador reported, but he had to admit that in some major affairs, "the opinions of Capodistrias . . . have prevailed." [62] Although Capodistrias was still consulted regularly and played a major role in the diplomatic affairs of the empire, the breach between emperor and minister was never healed; it widened until the summer of 1822, when Capodistrias left Russia.

To say simply that Capodistrias failed to maintain his position of influence when his policies diverged from Alexander's would ignore the complexities both in Capodistrias' political relationship to Alexander and in Alexander's foreign policy during the period. Also, Capodistrias' problems as foreign minister tell much about the limitations of Alexander's liberalism. On the whole, Capodistrias urged a more fundamental change in attitudes toward such political developments as constitutionalism, national identity, and a more broadly based continental power

---

[61] Personal letter dated Jan. 10, 1821, Metternich, *Mémoires*, III, 449–450. See by contrast the continuing indications of Capodistrias' influence expressed by La Ferronnays to Pasquier, Feb. 20, 1821, AE/MD: France, 719, and F. Lamb to Castlereagh, Feb. 24, 1821, Castlereagh, *Correspondence*, XII, 367–369.

[62] La Ferronnays to Pasquier, Milan, May 23, 1821, AE/CPR, 161. Lebzeltern to Metternich, July 20, 1821, HHS/Russ. III, 31. See also La Ferronnays to Pasquier, July 18, 1821, AE/CPR, 161.

structure than most European statesmen of the period would support. Alexander himself had been drawn to Capodistrias and his constitutional goals in the early years of the Restoration in connection with his policies toward France and Poland, but he had never been prepared to push for a fundamental change in the international power structure beyond his own vague religious goals as expressed in the Holy Alliance. He sympathized with the national goals of the Greeks and the Poles, for example, but never recognized the right of national identity as a general principle.

Alexander had pursued his French and Polish projects unilaterally in 1814 and 1815, but after the fall of 1815 he was unwilling to pursue liberal concepts alone, nor was he willing to align himself bilaterally with France, the one country which might have supported such views. However deep his hope for the success of the Restoration in France as an initial model of constitutional government, Alexander was not ready to revive the ill-fated Franco-Russian alliance. Only after some hesitation did he agree to the reestablishment of France as one of the major powers of Europe in order to maintain the balance of power and counter Austria, but he was less ready than Capodistrias to bring the smaller powers to the conference table. Once France was restored to great-power status in 1818 and when it became apparent that the French constitutional regime did not have the political stability he had hoped for, Alexander was even less ready to commit himself to policies which would align Russia with France. He became apprehensive about Capodistrias' "noticeable predilection for France." [63] Much as Czartoryski had failed to appreciate Alexander's commitment to Prussia in 1805, Capodistrias failed to take adequate account of Alexander's commitment to cooperation with Austria, which the presence of Nesselrode reinforced and which a firm alignment with France would have compromised.

Capodistrias was balked by Alexander's passivity in the face of Metternich's determined stance and by the vagueness of the em-

---

[63] La Ferronnays to Pasquier, March 13, 1820, *SIRIO*, CXXVII, 321. See also Capodistrias to La Sensée, Sept. 22, 1820, included by Pasquier, *Histoire*, IV, 534–536.

peror's commitment to liberal policies. Alexander's prime diplomatic goal during the last ten years of his reign was the preservation of the "alliance system," the maintenance of the European balance of power, in which he was willing to include France but which depended on cooperation with both France and Austria. The simultaneous retention of Nesselrode and Capodistrias in his cabinet showed how much Alexander wanted both doors open for friendship. His exertions to maintain personal friendship with the French ambassador, La Ferronnays, even when he seemed to align himself with Metternich, well demonstrates his primary concern. Metternich was a determined exponent of a clear policy; his tenacity eventually caused Alexander to believe that further support for Capodistrias' proposals could endanger the alliance system. As the emperor assured La Ferronnays at Laibach, "I have said everything, tried everything to make the means of conciliation prevail. I have met resistance which it is impossible to vanquish. . . . For five months you have been in a position to judge the personalities with whom it was necessary to deal. Their wills were too pronounced to combat; it was necessary to cause a schism or to cede. In this real alternative, you must understand all the reasons which finally forced me to follow a line of conduct contrary to my manner of thinking." [64] Such confidences to La Ferronnays well demonstrate that Alexander's agreement with Metternich was not as "thorough" as Metternich believed. Nevertheless, Alexander's desire to maintain the alliance and his fear of the revolutionary menace proved stronger than his devotion to the more liberal and more French-oriented program of Capodistrias.

Psychologically Alexander was not prepared to embrace Capodistrias' proposals because he was not prepared for the type of active commitment they entailed during this time of relative religious withdrawal. He recoiled in fear of new European disorders and his paranoid vision of the revolutionary conspiracy. The spread of uprisings in southern Europe, ministerial unrest in

[64] Conversation recorded by La Ferronnays to Pasquier, Feb. 27, 1821, AE/MD: France, 719.

France, difficulties in Poland, the mutiny in his own Semenovskii Regiment, the defection of his aide-de-camp Alexander Ypsilanti, and the outbreak of the Greek revolt were all interpreted by the emperor as parts of the conspiracy of the forces of evil against that European peace and order which he was committed to preserve.

Such conspiratorial connections were made for Alexander with increasing effect by the Austrian chancellor, whose diplomatic triumph was directly linked to the failure of Capodistrias. Metternich devoted his efforts during these years to gaining Alexander's assent to his reactionary, repressive measures, part of his broader system of enhancing and conserving the Austrian position in Europe, and Metternich recognized his major opponent. Capodistrias "is not a bad man, but honestly speaking, he is a complete and thorough fool, a perfect miracle of wrong-headedness," Metternich wrote in 1820. "He lives in a world to which our minds are often transported by a bad nightmare." Capodistrias' world was a nightmare for the Austrian chancellor because it held possibilities of domestic and international reform and suggested a degree of Russian influence which clearly threatened Metternich's aims. If Metternich were to succeed, he recognized that he must undermine Capodistrias' position as the only man of real influence in the Russian cabinet who presented a progressive alternative to his own system. "The struggle between Capodistrias and myself is like the conflict between a positive and a negative force," exclaimed Metternich. "[His] most eloquent phrases will never shelter anyone from the rain though he may take refuge under a whole thesis. . . . Capodistrias, too, will be soaked to the skin — that I will answer for." [65]

At the congresses of Troppau and Laibach where Capodistrias so strongly opposed Metternich's plans for the Neapolitan restoration, the Austrian chancellor used every possible means to drive a wedge between Alexander and Capodistrias. "More than anyone else," remarked La Ferronnay of Metternich's tactics, "he

---

[65] Fragments of personal letters, Nov. 27, 1820, and Feb. 22, 1822, Metternich, *Mémoires*, III, 379, 535.

possesses the art of devaluating opinions that are not his own; the most honorable life, the purest intentions are not sheltered from his insinuations. It is thus with profound ingenuity that he knew how to neutralize the influence of Count Capodistrias, the only one who could counterbalance his own." From 1818 until he at last boasted about provoking Capodistrias' departure in 1822, Metternich "left no effort unessayed to ward off all doctrines" of Capodistrias. Even Metternich's love affair with Countess Lieven, the wife of the Russian ambassador in London, had in its political dimension a "joint interest in seeing the Russian cabinet rid of the revolutionary influences of Capodistrias." [66]

The extensive Austrian police system was kept busy intercepting Capodistrias' correspondence to find incriminating phrases to send to St. Petersburg. For example, Metternich sent several reports implicating Capodistrias in revolutionary agitation in Italy. The proof of this accusation rested on a letter Capodistrias had written to the Duke of Brindisi accepting several reports and requesting additional information on the Italian situation. According to Metternich, Brindisi — one of "the worst scoundrels" — was in contact with many men of questionable political aims; Capodistrias, by implication, was supporting his activities and was thus linked to revolutionary agitators in Italy. Most particularly, Metternich tried to show that "The Greek revolution is a Russian work in all its antecedents; the role which Capodistrias assumed in all the preparatory periods is impossible to deny." As to proof, however, Metternich could show little more than letters from Capodistrias' brother and several friends supporting the revolution and seeking Capodistrias' support.[67]

[66] La Ferronnays to Pasquier, Feb. 6, 1821, AE/MD: France, 718. Stewart to Castlereagh, Troppau, Dec. 21, 1820, PRO/FO 7/154. Capodistrias, "Aperçu," *SIRIO*, III, 243–245. *Lettres du prince de Metternich à la comtesse de Lieven (1818–1819)*, passim.

[67] Metternich to Lebzeltern, Dec. 15, 1819, HHS/Russ. III, 78; Metternich to Lebzeltern, July 18, 1821, HHS, Gesandtschaft Archiv: St. Petersburg, 40. The accusatory dispatches, with multiple enclosures, were increased after the congresses of Troppau and Laibach; the slanderous campaign reached its greatest intensity in the spring of 1822, with long dispatches sent on March 31, April 22, and May 7 and 22. (Originally kept by Lebzeltern but later returned to HHS, most of these documents are filed in a separate carton marked "Interzepte,"

Since the Greek revolution was linked by Metternich to a general revolutionary conspiracy in Europe, Capodistrias, who was "preaching belief in the phrases of the false liberals," was accordingly one of the key figures causing social and political unrest on the continent. Metternich always wrote in the most flattering terms about the Russian sovereign and his policies and kept emphasizing — without any real proof — that "Capodistrias . . . has been separating the intentions of His Imperial Majesty from the correspondence of his office." Hence he demanded the dismissal of Capodistrias, "who can no longer be tolerated in office." Even when Capodistrias had the ostensible sympathy of Alexander, Metternich knew well how to capitalize on Capodistrias' shortcomings as a practical politician and raise doubts about his integrity.[68]

Although Metternich's gross exaggeration and underhanded tactics were readily apparent, Capodistrias' outspoken advocacy of Russian support of Greece even to the extent of making war on Turkey, seemed to confirm Metternich's accusations that he was "more Greek than Russian," with "his eyes only on the Hellenic cause."[69] In fact, Capodistrias might have remained in a much stronger position vis-à-vis Metternich had not his preoccupations with the Greek cause brought him so far from Alexander's aims. Capodistrias' prime political goal remained the independence for the Ionian Islands as a first step toward independence for all of Greece, but during his years in the Russian foreign office he failed to exert any significant influence in that direction.

Capodistrias' difference with the emperor over the Greek ques-

---

Russ. III, 78; they were summarized by Grand Duke Nicholas Mikhailovich in his edition of Lebzeltern, *Doneseniia*, pp. 337–401). The relatively harmless character of most of the intercepted letters leaves little doubt of their authenticity.

[68] Metternich to Lebzeltern, Feb. 23, 1820, May 20, 1822, and Oct. 6, 1821, HHS/Russ. III, 78. By Dec. 15, 1819, Metternich had been playing up "the extreme difference of opinion between the turn of mind of Capodistrias and that of his master." Long summaries of Capodistrias' opposition to Alexander's aims — at least, in Metternich's version — were given in dispatches of December 3, 23, and 31, 1821.

[69] Marginal comment on dispatch, Metternich to Francis, Aug. 18, 1818, Metternich, *Mémoires*, III, 146–147.

tion dated from the Congress of Vienna. He vigorously opposed
Alexander's Polish plan, perhaps astutely realizing that a Russian
extension into Poland could be won only by compromise with
Austria and England elsewhere. To retain Alexander's support,
however, he had to rationalize the emperor's willingness to allow
a British protectorate over the Ionian Islands. By 1816 Capodistrias, echoing Rumiantsev's earlier expansionist demands, voiced
his opposition to the 1812 Treaty of Bucharest, which he believed compromised Russia's position in regard to Turkey. Like
later nineteenth-century Russian expansionists, he advocated
Russian annexation of Moldavia and Wallachia. Furthermore, he
wanted to use Russia's treaty right to protect the Orthodox subjects of the Porte as a wedge for political control. "The immense
authority of the Church" should "become the safeguard of the
nation," he argued. Russia, for example, could legitimately support education in Greece through the Orthodox church and thus
further the aim of "preparing the Greeks for the advantages of a
moral Christian civilization." [70] Alexander was flattered by Capodistrias' arguments that support for the persecuted Christians
in Turkish lands would make an example to the world of "the
justice and liberality of Russia." But Alexander's smiles and assurances that "all that is very well thought out," were accompanied by an "intractable" rebuff: "To implement it, it would be
necessary to draw the cannon and that I do not wish to
do. . . . For good or evil, the transactions of Bucharest must be
maintained." [71]

Capodistrias' sympathies for the Greeks were deeply aroused
by renewed Turkish atrocities against Greek Christians, but he
resigned himself to a moderate path toward national regeneration. In response to some deputies from the provinces of Molda-

[70] "Address from Count Capodistrias to the Greeks," *Portfolio*, IV (1836),
292–294, 283–284. See also Capodistrias to Petro Bey, *SIRIO*, III, 297–303.
As shown in Capodistrias to A. Sturdza, Jan. 20, 1820 (Sturdza Papers, PD,
288/1/186), Capodistrias' education society contributed indirectly, apparently
through the Patriarch of Constantinople, to an elementary school that Petro
Bey founded — Alexander I was sending 3,000 Turkish piasters a year (see
Capodistrias to A. Sturdza, Jan. 20, 1820, Sturdza Papers, PD, 288/1/186).
[71] Capodistrias, "Aperçu," *SIRIO*, III, 209–213.

via and Wallachia, he expressed the two-pronged policy which his ambiguous position prescribed: "In my position as a Greek, I can only desire that liberty which the Greeks acquire by their own efforts and by the means of their initial advance in true civilization. . . . In my position as servant of His Imperial Majesty, I declare to you that his firm and invariable intention is to cement peace with the Turks on the basis of existing treaties." [72] Personally uninclined and temperamentally unprepared to identify himself with the Greek revolutionary movement, he also did not want to lose the potential influence of his position in Russia. When approached by Nicholas Galatis in 1816 to assume leadership of the radical society *Philike Etairia* — which his conservative opponents insisted on confusing with the educational society he patronized, *Philomouson Etairia* — he strongly disavowed the group and equivocated only to the extent of arranging safe conduct out of Russia for Galatis when he was imprisoned by tsarist police. [73] He sensed the full irony of his position when he observed at first hand "the evils which weigh on the unfortunate countries that England protects," during his "pious pilgrimage" to Corfu in 1818 and 1819. "Imagine the situation of the man who is considered here as the author of the treaty that relegated this country to British protection," he lamented to the Russian ambassador in Constantinople. "Whatever is said I try to remain neutral in the midst of this world. . . . I try to calm some and I give some measure of help to others." [74] Trying to tone down the nascent revolutionary movements, he emphasized to his compatriots that "it is the moral and literary efforts of Greece with which the Greeks must uniquely preoccupy themselves; any other object is vain; any other efforts are dangerous." [75]

---

[72] Quoted from an earlier letter, Capodistrias, "Aperçu," *SIRIO*, III, 228–229.

[73] There is evidence that Capodistrias was not acting clandestinely, as Alexandros Soutsos, *Histoire de la révolution grecque* (Paris, 1829), 16–18, suggests that the emperor himself secretly gave Galatis 5,000 francs when he received grace to return to his associates; see also the account of Capodistrias, "Aperçu," *SIRIO*, III, 254–255.

[74] Capodistrias to Nesselrode, June 12, 1819, Gosarkhiv III, TsGADA, 3/57; Capodistrias to Stroganov, April 3, 1819, Stroganov Papers, TsGADA, 1278/1/181 (see also his letter to Stroganov of April 23, 1819).

[75] "Address from Count Capodistrias to the Greeks," Corfu, April 18, 1819,

After his return from Corfu in 1819, Capodistrias redoubled the efforts which, as he put it, "This magnanimous sovereign . . . permits me to devote . . . to the fate of my country," and this new pressure did bring a few appeals from Alexander and his London ambassador, Count Lieven, on behalf of the Ionian Islands. But, despite his reassurance to critics that "Citizen of the Ionian Islands, I do not confuse the obligations that such a title imposes on me with those that I have contracted with the Emperor of Russia," clearly his intense preoccupation with the Greek cause decreased the security of his position in Russia.[76] As the crisis in the Orient deepened, Capodistrias began to sense that the problem of negotiation with the Turks "is quite as insoluble as that of the trisection of an angle." Since "mechanics can trisect an angle, even if it is rationally impossible," he believed that if diplomats "would leave the realm of abstractions" and "consider the Turks such as they are," they would soon realize that "reason for essentially unreasonable beings, is only force; and force alone, whatever may be its nature, can bring the Turks to agreeing to the final arrangement we would like to propose." Although he concluded in 1820 that Russia was "far from being ready to use force," his policies and recommendations took a less compromising line.[77]

Capodistrias' readiness to take a firm line against Turkey did not, however, make him any more willing to support Greek revolutionary activity. He firmly rebuffed the entreaties of Xanthos, a second member of *Philike Etaria*, who sought military and financial aid in St. Petersburg and who tried to enlist Capodis-

---

*Portfolio*, IV (1836), 290; the editor of *Portfolio*, David Urquart, a strong Russophobe, interpreted this speech and provided a doctored English translation to demonstrate Russian support for the Greek revolution; the original French text as printed, however, demonstrates Capodistrias' strong opposition to revolution and his support for a policy of religion-oriented education to effect the moral improvement of his people.

[76] Capodistrias to Bathurst, June 1820, draft, Gosarkhiv III, TsGADA 3/55. The type of appeal Capodistrias tried to get Alexander to make is evident in a draft of a letter in the hand of Capodistrias from Alexander to Wellington from late 1819 or early 1820, Gosarkhiv V, TsGADA, 5/221. See also, Capodistrias to Lieven, Jan. 19, 1820, TsGIA, 1101/1/359.

[77] Capodistrias to Stroganov, Oct. 2, 1820, Stroganov Papers, TsGADA, 1278/1/181.

trias' leadership.[78] As his friend Alexander Sturdza accurately wrote later, "Capodistrias sensed the imminence of an imprudently provoked crisis; he neglected nothing to ward off the storm, for the Greek nation did not seem to him sufficiently prepared for political independence." But try as he might to dissuade him, he could not prevent the emperor's aide-de-camp Alexander Ypsilanti from accepting the presidency of *Philike Etairia* in 1820 and obtaining, under the pretext of taking a health cure, a passport for foreign travel.[79] General Ypsilanti's activities culminated in an open revolt in the province of Moldavia in March 1821, which quickly spread to Greece proper.

Capodistrias had met with Ypsilanti several times, he knew the reason for his departure, and he did not prevent it; but beyond that there is no evidence of his support or of any implied promise of Russian aid. Ypsilanti had been trying to persuade Capodistrias and Alexander to support the Greeks and may well have departed with the hope that Alexander would take action once the revolt occurred. But such hopes — or Ypsilanti's later claims that Alexander gave reason for such hopes — could only show his blindness to the European diplomatic situation and to Alexander's own fears about revolution at the time. Capodistrias was quite opposed to the Ypsilanti venture; he well knew that Alexander would never support the revolution even if he sympathized with its aims. He realized that such an abortive revolt could not succeed. And, given the European diplomatic situation, a revolt at that time might even work against the Greek cause.

Even had he been willing or found it politic to do so, it is doubtful that Capodistrias could have prevented Ypsilanti's departure, and certainly his influence in Greece could not have prevented the abortive Greek revolution of 1821, which inauspiciously coin-

---

[78] Soutsos, *Histoire de la révolution grecque*, pp. 32–33; Notis Botzaris (*Visions balkaniques dans la préparation de la révolution grecque, 1789–1821* [Geneva, 1962], pp. 95–100), describes the episode based on the manuscript account by Xanthos in the archives of the Greek National Library, Athens, "Apologie d'Emu Xanthos."

[79] Sturdza, "Notice biographique sur le comte J. Capodistrias, président de la Grèce," *Oeuvres*, III, 355–356. Capodistrias, "Aperçu," *SIRIO*, III, 255–257; Capodistrias to Stroganov, March 26, 1821, Stroganov Papers, TsGADA, 1278/1/181.

cided with the Congress of Laibach, where the leaders of the major European powers were deciding on measures to be taken against revolutionary uprisings in southern Europe. "As if the follies and idiocies of the civilized world were not sufficient to give one bad blood, here is another sort on the part of the Greeks," Capodistrias wrote a friend on hearing the news. "Judge the deplorable events that have just announced themselves to us in the person of a man [Ypsilanti], who wants the best but who does not want it through the only means by which it could be achieved." Although the emperor inwardly shared some of the count's sympathy for the Greek cause, Capodistrias was enough of a political realist to understand that Alexander would tend to view the uprising as one more manifestation of the "subversive principles" menacing "all of Europe with revolutionary explosions." Capodistrias admired the flowery declaration with which Ypsilanti appealed for imperial support and was distressed that he was the one "condemned to reply to him." He disavowed the revolution publicly and appealed to Ypsilanti not to abandon the real interests of the country by rash moves at such a time of crisis, adding in a postscript, "I will do all that I possibly can. . . . It is only the hand of the Lord that can *make* the cause of our unfortunate country triumph." [80]

Capodistrias was upset at how much "People obstinately suppose that I have at least tacitly encouraged the Greek insurrection," and facts appear to confirm his denial. "I have a clear conscience, and I know all that I have said and done for a number of years to convince the Greeks to support the yoke that suppresses them with a Christian resignation. . . . In the present events, I fear no kind of reproach, as I believe that I may not be charged with any kind of responsibility." [81] But there is no denying his

---

[80] Capodistrias to R. Edling, March 26, 1821, *Vestnik vsemirnoi istorii* (April 1900), No. 5, 171; Capodistrias to A. Sturdza, March 30, 1821, and Capodistrias to Ypsilanti, April 27, 1821, Sturdza Papers, PD, 288/1/185. Capodistrias' official dispatches to Ypsilanti and to Stroganov, March 26, 1821, are printed in Prokesch-Osten, *Geschichte*, III, 65–70. Capodistrias' public censure of the uprising was reported from the Congress of Laibach by La Ferronnays to Pasquier, March 19, 1821, AE/MD: France, 719.

[81] Capodistrias to Stroganov, March 26 and April 15, 1821, Stroganov Papers, TsGADA, 1278/1/181. For an additional most explicit denial, see George

distress at the brutal suppression of the premature revolution: "If the Lord, who alone is the arbiter of the destinies of people and nations has decided in His impenetrable decrees that Europe must save herself in this moment of universal crisis by the sacrifice of our unfortunate fatherland, or by resurrection, the will of God be accomplished." [82]

Capodistrias was quite prepared to join the emperor in "disapproving of the fact of the revolution," but he did all he could to prevent Turkish reprisals against the Greeks. "In any case we will maintain a strict neutrality except in the case where the friendly intervention of Russia could spare Greece from the misfortunes of a Turkish reaction." As reaction did set in, he hoped that the Greek uprising would trigger a war between Russia and Turkey, so that Russia could go to the aid of her Orthodox brethren. "Possible negotiation or compromise with the Turks . . . are not for us; at least so I hope," he wrote in June 1821. He was willing to try to work things out peacefully, but he viewed war as inevitable. "If, when the time comes that . . . Russian troops *must march* and they still remain immobile, it is then myself who will be immobilized. And I will be dead for politics." As reports of Turkish atrocities increased, Capodistrias became more adamant. "I wanted to carry out the orders of His Majesty," he recalled, "but my pen refused to trace a plan for new explications with the Porte, with the result that my work served once more to demonstrate the necessity and urgence of action." [83]

Alexander did finally break Russian diplomatic relations with the Turks, but that was far short of Capodistrias' goal. Capodistrias first wanted Russia, on the grounds of protecting Moldavia and Wallachia, to display an imposing military force on the Danube, which he hoped would encourage the intervention of Euro-

Waddington, *A Visit to Greece in 1823 and 1824*, 2nd ed. (London, 1825), pp. xii–xiii.

[82] Capodistrias to A. Sturdza, March 30, 1821, Sturdza Papers, PD, 288/1/185.

[83] Capodistrias to R. Edling, March 26, 1821, *Vestnik vsemirnoi istorii* (April 1900), No. 5, p. 171. Capodistrias to A. Sturdza, June 30, 1820, Sturdza Papers, PD, 288/1/185; Capodistrias, "Aperçu," *SIRIO*, III, 274. See also Capodistrias to R. Edling, June 30, 1821, *Vestnik vsemirnoi istorii* (April 1900), No. 5, pp. 172–173.

pean allies. In other words, he really wanted Russia, supported by other European powers, to declare war on Turkey to protest Turkish atrocities against the Greeks. His idea, rarely openly expressed, was that a successful war against Turkey would secure the Danubian provinces for Russia and win Greek independence or at least a Russian protectorate. He wanted Alexander to appeal to his allies to "do all that is within [their] power . . . to bring the Turks to justice and reason." If such efforts failed, other European governments should "ally with us to deliver the Orient from the double scourge that devastates it — the scourge of the Turks and the scourge of revolution." [84] Capodistrias had an elaborate set of arguments in support of war, and, using his winning way with Alexander, he did much to arouse the emperor's Hellenic sympathy. But the achievement of moving Alexander to demonstrate support vocally or even to write Castlereagh and Francis I expressing disgust at "the deplorable affairs in Turkey," fell far short of Capodistrias' goals.[85] Although he well recognized that his very presence at the Russian court was a step ahead for the cause of his homeland, tension mounted as he became unable to endure the emperor's passive attitude.

Although Capodistrias appealed less overtly than Czartoryski had to Russian expansionism, he found many more sympathizers. The Russian army, still in wartime strength, was eager for action. Conservative Russian Orthodox circles, appalled by the Turkish atrocities, wanted to go to the aid of their Greek Christian brethren. The development of "New Russia" and its port of Odessa turned many eyes toward the south. Expansionist elements in society and at court, still recalling Catherine the Great's abandoned Greek project and the disappointments of the Treaty of Bucharest, which had renounced Russian claims to the Danubian principalities, were pressing for renewed hostilities with their eyes firmly focused on the advantages of direct Russian access to the Mediterranean. Diplomats in St. Petersburg were alarmed by

[84] Capodistrias to Pozzo di Borgo, Aug. 30, 1821, Sturdza Papers, PD, 288/2/9.
[85] Capodistrias, "Aperçu," *SIRIO*, III, 276; Alexander to Francis I, June 11, 1821, HHS/Russ. III, 47.

"the very strong public feeling in favor of the war which has been expressed and alluded to even by the Emperor in a very unusual manner, for a Government such as this where a public opinion can scarcely be said to exist." [86] But, while Capodistrias wanted to encourage such sentiments and "to do all he can to make war necessary," it was obvious that "the Emperor holds the Sword" and was not about to use it.[87] Capodistrias acutely realized that passivity was Alexander's dominant sentiment, and that he must speak of "the mode in which the Eastern Question will decide itself, and not the mode in which it will be decided. This distinction gives you the key to our system," he explained to Pozzo di Borgo. "In our system, a question will be resolved by the force of events." [88]

By 1822 Capodistrias' role had been drastically minimized. Alexander wanted him to continue in the foreign office, but he wanted him to modify his stand on the Eastern crisis. Capodistrias' proposals for Greece, especially his advocacy of a Russian war with Turkey, combined and magnified the various strands of his divergence with Alexander. Most especially, his policies spelled war at a time when the emperor frequently affirmed, "Heaven is my witness, that my only wish, my sole ambition, is to conserve that peace which cost the world so much to attain." [89] His proposals aroused the strong opposition of Austria at a time when Alexander was more ready to side with Metternich; they aroused the animosity and suspicions of the British at a time

[86] Cathcart to his father, Sept. 27, 1821, Cathcart Papers, D-105. Other indications of public support for the Greek cause and Capodistrias' position were noted by La Ferronnays to Montmorency, Feb. 20, 1822, AE/CPR, 163, and Strangford to Maitland, Constantinople, Nov. 30, 1821, Heytesburg Papers, BM/Add. MSS. 41530.

[87] La Ferronnays to Pasquier, Nov. 26, 1821, AE/CPR, 162; Bagot to Castlereagh, Oct. 20, 1821, PRO/FO 65/129; Strangford to Maitland, Constantinople, Nov. 30, 1821, Heytesburg Papers, BM/Add. MSS. 41530.

[88] Capodistrias to Pozzo di Borgo, Aug. 30, 1821, Sturdza Papers, PD, 288/2/9. In a letter to Sturdza at the same time (Aug. 29, 1821, Sturdza Papers, PD, 288/1/185), he mentioned his distress that "they do not want to act at the moment," but added that he would keep his position for the present. "Believe me that I will stay no longer, than the moment that it be demonstrated to me that they do not want to do what they must."

[89] Quoted by La Ferronnays to Pasquier, July 19, 1821, AE/CPR 161.

when Alexander hardly wanted further tension among the great powers.[90] More basically, they threatened a split in the alliance system and a diversion from its present aims at a time when the preservation of that system was Alexander's most sacred goal. Support for Greece, especially after the uprisings in 1821, however well justified by atrocities to the Orthodox subjects of the Porte, could be seen as support for revolution at a time when Alexander's fears of conspiracy led him to fear that "Ypsilanti has gone to Paris for his orders." [91] Fundamentally, Capodistrias' proposals meant an active involvement, possibly unilateral, at a time when Alexander was inclined toward a relatively passive diplomatic role.

More dangerously, Capodistrias' policies in the East implied an aggressive Russian expansionist role to which Alexander had never been inclined. In many ways it was the same policy which he had rejected with Rumiantsev and overlooked with Czartoryski; Capodistrias' views on Russia's role in Greece had all the difficulties of Czartoryski's attempts to link moral, liberal concerns with a great role for Russia, in that they could too easily degenerate into aggressive Russian nationalism. Capodistrias' patriotism thus left his handling of the Eastern Question fraught with contradictions. For even as he looked to "the beneficient enlightenment" of Alexander I to provide for Greek independence and Bessarabian rights, he was quite prepared to commit Russia to dangerously expansionist policies in the Balkans. His deep patriotic hopes for Greece, his moralistic cosmopolitanism, and his personal regard for Alexander I, seemed to blind him to the explosive potential of the Greek situation. The link which he naïvely made between expansionism and "liberal ideas" proved to be the fatal flaw in his political outlook, as far as his position in Russia was concerned.

[90] The British ambassador, Bagot, had a particularly strong hatred for Capodistrias and engaged in many intrigues against him; see La Ferronnays to Pasquier, Nov. 26, 1821, AE/CPR, 162, and Jan. 13, 1822, AE/CPR, 163. British suspicions, especially Maitland's, about Capodistrias' activities are revealed in the collected correspondence of A'Court with Maitland from 1819 and 1820 in the Heytesbury Papers, XX, BM/Add. MSS. 41530. See also Wellington to Bathurst, June 21, 1826, Wellington, *Despatches*, III, 341–342.
[91] La Ferronnays to Pasquier, July 19, 1821, AE/CPR, 161.

Alexander was prepared for a Polish protectorate — he had had his heart set on it as a "favorite idea" for years. But at the Congress of Vienna he had too much trouble winning his constitutional monarchy for Poland to divert his attention elsewhere. Poland was much closer to his heart than the Ionian Isles; the restoration of that nation was much more important to him than preserving the earlier Russian protectorate in the Mediterranean, let alone using the Ionian Islands as a wedge for setting up a protectorate in Greece. Later, Polish developments brought nothing but complaints, even from Czartoryski, his great friend and supporter. The Eastern Question was potentially even more explosive, and Alexander had scant sympathy for Capodistrias' pleas "to consolidate that beneficent system of influence through which [Russia] has long regulated the destinies of the Ottoman Empire." [92] Support for Greece and war with Turkey might bring the collapse of the Ottoman Empire and a hopelessly complex power struggle. If Russia "forged a road to Greece," what of the Slavs, to whom there were ethnic and linguistic ties, as well as the religious ones? Capodistrias' proposals were a direct threat to Austrian and British interests in the area and implied a complete upsetting of the delicate balance of power. His hopes were too narrowly linked to the Greeks and lacked even Czartoryski's conceptualization of the broader problems and implications of the Eastern Question. The liberal cast of Alexander's Polish project was inappropriate in the Balkans, where even Capodistrias recognized that the people were less prepared for independence and constitutional government. Besides, by 1821 the European situation had cooled the liberal sympathies which might have moved Alexander to support the Hellenic cause, while his pietism had cooled his personal commitment to Orthodoxy. Capodistrias thus failed most substantially because his outspoken advocacy of the Greek cause demanded a more aggressive role in the Balkans than Alexander was ready to undertake for his empire.

As with other men who had held the ministerial position during his reign, the emperor was willing to give Capodistrias a large

[92] Capodistrias, "Mémoire sur les Isles Ioniennes," Gosarkhiv XV, TsGADA, 15/537. This statement certainly justified British fears.

degree of influence only insofar as his policies corresponded with his own. As Gentz once explained, what brought Capodistrias together with Alexander I was "the dream of a better order of things executed on a generation which is totally perverted." It was as unfortunate for Europe as for Russia that the dream could not be implemented. During his years in the Russian foreign ministry, Capodistrias reinforced the emperor's goals, but he had scant opportunity, if indeed the capacity, to turn Restoration politics toward his policies for moderate reform. Diplomats often noted that "except when Alexander had strong opinions, he leaves his work to him." [93] Like few of Alexander's advisers, Capodistrias exerted a relatively strong influence over the diplomacy of his period because of Alexander's basic sympathy with him and his ideas. Perhaps Capodistrias might have contributed more to effective reformist tendencies in the Restoration alliance system had his preoccupation with Greece and his attempt to push Alexander into war with Turkey not made his position untenable. He had yielded or modified his stand on many issues, but could not on this one. He was willing to stay on in the foreign office as long as he felt there was some chance of the emperor's turning more to his point of view.[94] But on the explosive Greek issue, by 1822 Alexander neglected Capodistrias' advice and looked elsewhere for diplomatic assistance.

When Alexander sent Dmitri Tatishchev to Vienna in the spring of 1822 to try to reach a closer understanding with Metternich on the Greek crisis, most aspects of the meetings were initially "kept as a mystery" from Capodistrias. Capodistrias disapproved of the appointment and openly expressed opposition to the mission. When he realized that a new system had been drawn up with Metternich of which he did not approve, he refused to

[93] Gentz to Soutsos, Oct. 30, 1820, Gentz, *Dépêches*, II, 89; Lebzeltern to Metternich, July 20, 1820, HHS/Russ. III, 29.

[94] Lebzeltern wrote Metternich, July 25, 1822 (HHS/Russ. III, 57), "This minister senses the false and difficult position in which he finds himself; he always hopes that events will themselves be the apology for his line of conduct, and that by consequence, My Prince, that your [approach] will prove to be faulty. It is this hope which he nourishes today and which replaces all his earlier illusions."

have anything further to do with Eastern affairs, declaring himself "dead for those aspects of the service relating to the Eastern Question." Nesselrode warned his associate, "Try to satisfy the emperor; you see that his resolutions are irrevocable. . ." To that Capodistrias replied, "Yes, without doubt, I see it as well as you, but it will not be I who will execute them." [95] Alexander may not have wanted "to distress unjustly, nor perhaps even relegate from personal contact, a man who during eight years was the depository of his secrets and the organ of all his resolutions," but when he definitely decided that Capodistrias should not accompany him to the scheduled conference in Vienna in the summer of 1822, he was willing to agree to his withdrawal "to take a cure" at the German resort of Ems in mid-August. Having eschewed the Greek revolutionary cause and having been deserted by his Russian protector, Capodistrias could well feel, as he wrote a friend, "alone in my carriage, and never could solitude be a better companion." [96]

Although he retained his title in the Russian service until his formal dismissal by Nicholas I in 1827, he had nothing further to do with Russian diplomacy while Alexander was on the throne. He retired to Switzerland where he devoted the next few years to gaining support for the moderate Greek cause before returning to his homeland in 1827 as the first president of the short-lived first Greek republic. While Alexander's sympathy for Capodistrias never entirely cooled, [97] he had no use in the foreign ministry for

---

[95] Capodistrias to Pozzo di Borgo, May 29, 1822, personal, Pozzo di Borgo Papers; Capodistrias, "Aperçu," *SIRIO*, III, 283–284. See also Lebzeltern to Metternich, May 16 and 30, 1822, HHS/Russ. III, 56, and La Ferronnays to Montmorency, Feb. 20, 1822, AE/CPR, 163.

[96] La Ferronnays to Montmorency, May 27, 1822, AE/CPR, 163; Maria Nesselrode to N. Gur'ev, July 21, 1822, Gosarkhiv III, TsGADA, 3/43. Capodistrias to R. Edling, Aug. 18, 1822, *Vestnik vsemirnoi istorii* (June 1900), No. 7, p. 105. See also Capodistrias' state of resignation as revealed in the letter dated July 31, 1822. That he was expecting to leave soon was already apparent in the disappointment with which he described his situation in January (Capodistrias to R. Edling, Jan. 20, 1822, *ibid.*, p. 101).

[97] Capodistrias was assured by a letter from Karamzin in 1825 that Alexander retained to the end a warm sympathy for his former minister (see Capodistrias to R. Edling, Jan. 21, 1826, *Vestnik vsemirnoi istorii* [June 1900], No. 7, p. 115). Capodistrias explained his lasting devotion to Alexander and his belief in Alex-

a man who was unwilling to submit to the imperial will and who
continued to support a policy opposed to his own decided intentions.

---

ander's "angelic goodness" in a letter to his Swiss friend J. G. Eynard (Jan. 31,
1826, *Allelographia I. A. Kapodistria kai I. G. Eonardou, 1826–31* [Athens,
1929], p. 6).

---

## Chapter 8

# NESSELRODE: A SPOKESMAN
# FOR THE STATUS QUO

Metternich's recognition of Capodistrias as the chief impediment in the Russian cabinet to his diplomatic triumph proved to be basically correct, for with the decline of Capodistrias' influence Russia shifted to a more passive involvement in European affairs. Upon Capodistrias' departure, direction of the foreign ministry fell to Karl Robert Nesselrode, who had remained mostly in the background since 1815. Much more than Capodistrias, he stood ready to be the emperor's mouthpiece. Alexander's tendency to consult several advisers and to pursue different policies simultaneously was institutionalized, so to speak, in the joint ministry of Capodistrias and Nesselrode from 1816 to 1822, a somewhat haphazard arrangement where neither man held the ministerial title and where relative position and function varied considerably. Although Capodistrias usually overshadowed Nesselrode during this period, the presence of both men in the foreign office gave Alexander the flexible alternatives of the policies they advocated, while leaving the emperor in the predominant position of correlating and supervising Russian foreign policy.

It would be hard to imagine two more different men working together on foreign affairs. Divergent in character and basic political ideology, they were diametrically opposed in their approach to foreign policy and in their recommendations for Russian maneuvers in the years following the Congress of Vienna. To be sure, both were interested in preserving the peace and order established in Europe by the settlements of 1814 and 1815. Both were eager to avoid further revolutionary agitation which might throw Europe into more of the wars and social turmoil

which they hoped had ceased with the overthrow of Napoleon
Bonaparte. But there agreement stopped. While Capodistrias advocated moderate liberal reform, self-determination of national
entities, and gradual extensions of republican and constitutional
government, Nesselrode favored strict repression of progressive
elements, preservation of legitimate monarchical authority, and
the dynastic and territorial integrity of the great powers; in short,
as a conservative reactionary he wanted to maintain the status
quo. The cool moderation with which Nesselrode approached political affairs nonetheless kept him from being an alarmist about
the revolutionary menace. When his wife was upset about the
unrest in France, for example, Nesselrode reassured her: "That
evil exists I do not have the slightest doubt, but I do not think
that the consequences could become so immediately dangerous
and of a nature to justify the intervention of foreign powers." [1]

Nesselrode differed most completely with Capodistrias in regard to the Eastern Question. With none of his colleague's religious and patriotic ties to the Greeks, he showed no sympathy
whatsoever for the Hellenic cause, particularly as exemplified in
the Greek revolutionary movement. He was appalled at the prospect of a war against Turkey or a change in the Balkan power
structure. In 1821 the French ambassador noted that Capodistrias "desires to do all that he can to make war necessary," while
Nesselrode showed himself "most anxious to avoid war." By
1825 the British ambassador was reporting that Nesselrode was
more eager to preserve peace in the Levant than Alexander himself. "You know very well that during the last four years, I am
the one who has been the apostle of peace," Nesselrode assured
the French ambassador early that year. "I swear by my honor that
my only desire is still to avoid this war." When Alexander was
himself beginning to turn toward the possibility of war and public pressure was mounting in favor of arming against the Turks,
Nesselrode stood firm. Gentz believed that if Nesselrode had

[1] Karl to Maria Nesselrode, April 25, 1819, *LPN*, VI, 56. The contrast in
political orientation between Nesselrode and Capodistrias was well presented
by Gentz to Soutsos, Oct. 30, 1820, Gentz, *Dépêches*, II, 89–90.

enough influence, "the chapter of coercive means against the Porte would soon be reduced to a few lines." [2]

Gentz's praise for Nesselrode's intentions suggests another point of division between the two foreign ministers. While Metternich was doing all he could to effect Capodistrias' dismissal, he found Nesselrode "a very useful man at all times" and worked to maintain Nesselrode's favor with the emperor. Unlike Capodistrias, whose political bent was more towards France, Nesselrode was closely allied to the Austrian chancellor in principles, goals, and political outlook, and he generally approved of Metternich's means of resolving the issues of foreign affairs. Nesselrode's support for the Austrian position at the time of the Vienna congress continued throughout the remainder of Alexander's reign. His "reputation of being strongly carried by Austria" was enhanced by the warm welcome which Lebzeltern, the Austrian ambassador, whom critics called "the devilish soul of Prince Metternich," found in Nesselrode's home and in the house of his father-in-law, the Russian finance minister Count Gur'ev.[3] "Nesselrode, from the start, has given the energetic measures of Metternich enough praise to remove all doubts whatsoever about his manner of thinking," remarked the French ambassador in 1820. "Through interests as well as affections, Monsieur de N[esselrode] remains entirely open to Austrian views," the same ambassador reported in 1823. "And what little influence that he may be able to exert on the mind of the emperor will always be used to maintain and increase the influence of Prince M[etternich]." [4]

[2] La Ferronnays to Pasquier, Nov. 20, 1821, AE/CPR, 162. Strangford to Canning, Nov. 27, 1825, PRO/FO 65/149. La Ferronnays to Damas, Feb. 23, 1825, AE/CPR, 167. Gentz to Lebzeltern, Aug. 7, 1825, Lebzeltern Papers. See Nesselrode's policy on the Eastern Question as outlined in his "Mémoire du Cabinet de Russie sur la pacification de la Grèce," Jan. 9, 1824, Prokesch-Osten, *Geschichte*, IV, 62–73.

[3] Metternich, personal letter, Nov. 1, 1820, *Mémoires*, III, 375. Noailles to Richelieu, Sept. 19, 1817, *SIRIO*, CXIX, 364. Longinov to S. R. Vorontsov, Sept. 16, 1821, and Feb. 4, 1822, *AKV*, XXIII, 439–440, 444. According to the French ambassador, Lebzeltern arranged to lease a dacha belonging to Gur'ev and occasionally occupied by Nesselrode (Noailles to Richelieu, Sept. 28, 1816, *SIRIO*, CXII, 635).

[4] La Ferronnays to Pasquier, Sept. 16, 1820, and Feb. 22, 1820, *SIRIO*, CXXVII, 451, 292–293. La Ferronnays to Chateaubriand, Oct. 1, 1823, AE/

Nesselrode and Capodistrias personally got along together much better than the divergence of their political aims might suggest. Capodistrias never had a very high regard for Nesselrode; he associated him scornfully with the "bureaucratic diplomats." But despite his feelings about the shortcomings of Nesselrode's personality and intellect, he found working with him pleasant and easy; after returning to St. Petersburg in 1816, Capodistrias recalled, "We fell into perfect agreement as to procedures and the nature of service that had been confined to us." "The loyal friendship of Capodistrias himself, who constantly pleaded his cause," as Gentz put it, may well have helped Nesselrode retain his position.[5]

Nesselrode had the highest regard for his colleague, whom he considered "a delicate man with such a perfect character." He was most distressed by the pressure to have Capodistrias removed from office because there was no other man with whom he could work so closely and whom he would rather have as a friend: "If our compatriots complain about Capodistrias, they are wrong and truly ungrateful." Nesselrode had originally subscribed to Capodistrias' Greek education society, hoping "that the most fortunate success may crown an enterprise the results of which will be advantageous not only for the Greeks, but for all of Europe." Later, however, he had strong reservations about his colleague's Greek interests and sought to modify his position to better conform with the emperor's wishes.[6]

Although Nesselrode was himself favorably disposed to Metternich and felt by the spring of 1822 that "things could not go on with the tendencies, opinions, and methods of his colleague," he would have nothing to do with Metternich's plots to overthrow Capodistrias and refused to show the emperor Metternich's re-

CPR, 165; see also La Ferronnays to Chateaubriand, Aug. 29, 1823, AE/CPR, 165.

[5] For example, Capodistrias to Stein, June 11, 1815, Stein, *Briefe*, V, 388–389; here Nesselrode was mentioned by name as one of those diplomats who, he explained, "are not the best sort of men." Capodistrias, "Aperçu," *SIRIO*, III, 207; Gentz to I. Karadja, Jan. 1, 1816, Gentz, *Dépêches*, I, 205–206.

[6] Karl to Maria Nesselrode, Jan. 9, 1821, *LPN*, VI, 115–116. Nesselrode to Capodistrias, Feb. 3, 1815, Weil, *Congrès*, II, 136. Capodistrias, "Aperçu," *SIRIO*, III, 283.

ports about Capodistrias' alleged revolutionary activities. Not believing Metternich's accusations, "the good and honest Nesselrode," Lebzeltern reported, "could not resolve to act so clandestinely against a man with whom he had been associated for several years on a footing of confidence and friendship; it was repugnant to his loyalty." If Nesselrode depended on Capodistrias for support, the obverse was also true. At the height of the Eastern crisis, for example, when Nesselrode "by conviction was in full agreement with the emperor" and "at odds with his colleague," he still tried to assume an attitude of moderation during joint sessions with Alexander. When Capodistrias "would often utter phrases objecting to the adopted system, Nesselrode would discuss, or dispute what little he dared, always trying to avoid strong disagreements with him." [7] Rather than argue with his colleague, he might turn to one of the foreign ambassadors to relay his views to Capodistrias, reducing himself to the weak role of "presenting the diplomatic corps with the arguments of his colleague that are opposed to his own opinion, and in turn searching for the success of his own opinions with his colleague through the intervention of the diplomatic corps." [8]

At least part of Nesselrode's strong support for Capodistrias stemmed from his own deep "fears of the responsibilities which outweigh his strength" and his disinclination to assume the sole responsibility for Russian diplomacy. Metternich, although he tried to sustain Nesselrode, believed "he has not the constitution of the captain of a ship in the middle of a tempest," which coincides closely with Nesselrode's own admission that "if ever Capodistrias should leave the emperor, I would not stay an instant myself for the very simple reason that I do not feel that I have the strength myself to conduct the ship alone." [9] During the final years of Alexander's reign, Nesselrode did gain experience and self-assurance, but essentially little changed. "Count Nesselrode

[7] Lebzeltern to Metternich, May 20, 1822, HHS/Russ. III, 55a. Maria Nesselrode to N. Gur'ev [June 1822], Gosarkhiv III, TsGADA 3/43.
[8] La Ferronnays to Montmorency, Jan. 13, 1822, AE/CPR, 163.
[9] Lebzeltern to Metternich, Sept. 4, 1823, HHS/Russ. III, 61. Metternich to Lebzeltern, Feb. 22, 1826, HHS/Russ. III, 78. Karl to Maria Nesselrode, Jan 9, 1821, *LPN*, VI, 115.

is as your highness has known him," Lebzeltern reported in
1816; "he has the same attitudes, the same passivity, the same
displaced modesty, the same manner of conducting business superficially and with terror of finding some difficulties." But "if he
is too weak for the weight he bears, it is not his fault," affirmed
Gentz after Nesselrode's appointment to remain in office under
Nicholas I. "Man is not responsible for the faculties that the
heavens dispense to him. I could not even reproach him for having remained in a position evidently above his level. A minister,
when his conscience so dictates, could and should resign, but the
secretary of state of a sovereign who believes himself to be his
own master has not this resource." [10]

Nesselrode's characteristic attitudes led him to a very different
type of relationship with Alexander than his colleague assumed.
Capodistrias was always eager to put his own opinions forward
and try to influence Alexander. Nesselrode, by contrast, was willing to submit to a relatively "passive and somewhat mute
role . . . never trying in any way to make his opinions prevail."
His personal views, "known only by his intimate friends," he was
"always disposed to sacrifice for personal considerations"; reportedly, the emperor appreciated his "conciliatory character" and
"always rendered him justice . . . for avoiding disagreeable
discussions." [11] Later, when he no longer had to contend with
"the ascendancy in the cabinet of . . . a man such as Capodistrias," and when he began to have misgivings about Austrian interests, associates still found him "in such an attitude of fear toward his master that he had never dared to discuss the probity of
Metternich" and "was a little frightened at the boldness" of those
who spoke out to the emperor. Clearly, Nesselrode was not the
man to take initiative. "It is not that he lacks the judgment necessary to direct important affairs," foreign diplomats observed,
"but he prefers to content himself with acting under the direction
of the emperor." [12]

[10] Lebzeltern to Metternich, Aug. 23, 1816, HHS/Russ. III, 20. Gentz to Lebzeltern, Aug. 18, 1826, Lebzeltern Papers.
[11] La Ferronnays to Pasquier, Sept. 25, 1820, AE/CPR, 161. Maria Nesselrode
to N. Gur'ev [June 1822], Gosarkhiv III, TsGADA 3/43.
[12] La Ferronnays to Pasquier, Sept. 25, 1820, AE/CPR, 161. *The Unpublished*

During the time when both were in St. Petersburg, much of the work of the ministry was handled by Capodistrias and Nesselrode together; they held joint conferences with Alexander and often both signed official papers. Sometimes, when a foreign diplomat addressed a matter to one, the other would answer. There was no rhyme nor reason to the division of work between them, a situation which added immeasurably to the inefficiency of the chancellery and made it "rather difficult for the members of the diplomatic corps to know to which of these chiefs of the College of Foreign Affairs it is best to present oneself when there is business to be done." Yet, while they "share the work in foreign affairs" and "live in the best harmony," diplomats found "the most important questions are ordinarily incumbent on Count Capodistrias." Since more often than not, Capodistrias was "kept in charge of all the delicate aspects of diplomacy," while Nesselrode was left "with the routine . . . supervision of the work of the chancellery," foreign diplomats most often tried to avoid Nesselrode, a trend increased by those who found that he did "not keep up well of affairs which he does not like." [13] Nesselrode was shown "personal esteem and confidence . . . but in infinitely more cases, His Majesty works with Count Capodistrias, who agrees more with his principles." When Capodistrias was away, Nesselrode appeared reassured that "the emperor seems satisfied and does not appear to notice the absence of the eighth sage," as his colleague was sometimes called. When Capodistrias accompanied the emperor, however, as he did to Poland in the spring of 1820, Nesselrode could give Russian diplomats little more than "a few words of friendship." "I will have to limit myself strictly to that," he explained in a personal postscript to a dispatch to Count Lieven in London. "For as to business and high politics, you will find that I am completely in the dark. It is from Warsaw that you will receive enlightenment." [14]

---

*Diary and Political Sketches of Princess Lieven*, ed. Harold Temperley (London, 1925), p. 89. Lebzeltern to Metternich, Sept. 4, 1823, HHS/Russ. III, 61.

[13] Noailles to Richelieu, June 3, 1816, *SIRIO*, CXII, 525; see also La Moussaye to Richelieu, Feb. 4, 1816, *SIRIO*, CXII, 395. Gentz to Karadja, Jan. 16, 1817, Gentz, *Dépêches*, I, 276; Noailles to Richelieu, Dec. 13, 1816, *SIRIO*, CXII, 708.

[14] Lebzeltern to Metternich, Aug. 23, 1816, HHS/Russ. III, 20. Karl to Maria

When Nesselrode assumed the sole direction of the foreign ministry in the summer of 1822, he became neither a minister by official title nor "a minister in the accepted sense of that title." His position was more crucial as Alexander withdrew more from active participation in governmental affairs, since Nesselrode was one of the few officials with whom the emperor continued to deal with any regularity. The foreign diplomatic corps had to deal with him, particularly as they found that "approaching the emperor directly becomes more difficult each day." [15] Initial assumptions that "Nesselrode will henceforth have more influence" when he was promoted to the grade of Intimate Councillor at the end of 1823 were soon proved wrong. In most instances where decisions were made, "the emperor's resolution was taken spontaneously; Count Nesselrode was not able, or rather knew not how, to oppose it." His role remained essentially stable. "It is true that he could not take the place of his imperial master in everything, but within the context of his instructions, he strove to carry out His intentions with that hearty loyalty we know in him." [16]

Rather than a change in Nesselrode's role following Capodistrias' departure, there was a change in Russia's role. While still deeply committed to a preponderant position on the European scene, in the final years of Alexander's reign Russia's diplomatic role was almost as passive as that of her foreign minister. With Alexander's frustrated withdrawal from affairs of state went the withdrawal of Russian initiative in European affairs. Nesselrode's name is hardly remembered in this period, because there were no significant new diplomatic developments to which his name might have been attached. With the departure of Capodistrias, there was little further Russian opposition to Metternich's diplomatic leadership, and what opposition there was did not come from the foreign minister.

---

Nesselrode, March 28 and April 25, 1819, *LPN*, VI, 32, 58. Nesselrode to Lieven, April 25, 1820, TsGIA 1101/1/360.

[15] Lebzeltern to Metternich, Sept. 4, 1823, HHS/Russ. III, 61. Lebzeltern to Metternich, Aug. 2, 1823, HHS/Russ. III, 58.

[16] Metternich, personal letter, Jan. 8, 1824, *Mémoires*, IV, 88. Lebzeltern to Metternich, Feb. 9, 1824, HHS/Russ. III, 62. Metternich, personal letter, Nov. 8, 1823, *Mémoires*, IV, 24.

Nesselrode's importance during the period was as a staunch defender of the alliance system drawn up by the Congress of Vienna as interpreted by Metternich. Insofar as his opinions were requested, he remained the advocate of the status quo, "the friend of order and peace," the real spokesman for the "Metternich system" in the Russian court. Metternich's ambassador had achieved his goal of persuading "Count Nesselrode that the Austrian system is the only good one, certainly the only one which the autocratic sovereign of Russia should and can really follow today." [17] Accordingly, the fluctuation of his favor corresponded closely with Alexander's attitude toward the Austrian chancellor and his diplomatic system.

Alexander's vacillations were apparent in Nesselrode's changing position before, during, and immediately after the Congress of Vienna. Between 1816 and 1820 Alexander retained a degree of distrust for Metternich and consequently for Nesselrode, with the result that it was to Capodistrias more than to Nesselrode that he turned for advice. Yet the retention of Nesselrode during this period gave Alexander more room to maneuver, and in satisfying Metternich, it helped promote the solidarity of the alliance system. Metternich's "conversion" efforts were more successful during the congresses of Troppau and Laibach when he was able to incite Alexander's deep fears of the revolutionary disturbances. As Alexander's visions of the "empire of evil," which he considered to be "more powerful than the might of Napoleon," approached paranoid dimensions, he was ready to send Russian troops to suppress "those secret and impious enemies," because he believed "that all is legitimate, all is legal, all is right and duty when it is a question of annihilating a sect whose progress is terrifying, the success of which would infallibly bring . . . the entire ruin of Europe." [18] Having "this type of rapprochement between his opinions and those of Metternich," which so amazed foreign diplomats, Nesselrode was given the responsibility of

[17] Lebzeltern to Metternich, Sept. 13, 1825, HHS/Russ. III, 68. La Ferronnays to Pasquier, Sept. 25, 1820, AE/CPR, 161.
[18] Alexander to Golitsyn, March 10, 1821, NM, *Alexandre*, I, 535; Alexander, quoted by La Ferronnays to Pasquier, Jan. 14, 1821, AE/MD: France, 718.

working secretly with Metternich to edit a declaration against
revolution at the end of the Congress of Laibach, which was
shown to Capodistrias only after being approved. [19]

The "remarkable change" which had taken place in Alexander
proved to be more "in appearance" than Metternich liked to
think. While he was ready to support Metternich's measures
against the revolutionary uprisings, Alexander was not in full
agreement with the Austrian chancellor in regard to constructive
measures for a new government in Italy. As far as Alexander's
sympathy was concerned, Nesselrode still had to contend with
Capodistrias' proposals for establishing a constitutional government in Naples. That Alexander ended by supporting Metternich
was in Nesselrode's favor, although it was hardly due to his influence. That the emperor ended by feeling "forced to follow a
line of conduct contrary to my manner of thinking" [20] clearly
showed that his support of the policies of Metternich and Nesselrode was not unilateral nor wholehearted enough to promote a
creative relationship with Nesselrode. Not wanting to rupture
the alliance system and risk a complete break with Austria by
pressing a more liberal policy, Alexander was willing to agree
with Metternich. Nesselrode was on hand, ready and willing to
second his master, but as to bringing about Alexander's support
for the Austrian position, even Metternich had to lament, "It is a
shame that Nesselrode is so much in the background." [21]

Alexander's views on the Eastern crisis were equally unsettled.
He was horrified by the Turkish atrocities against the Orthodox
population, feeling that "Russia no more than any other European power can remain an immobile spectator to these sacrileges
and cruelties." Nevertheless, he was willing to give his "Sacred
Word of Honour . . . that there is nothing which I desire so

[19] La Ferronnays to Pasquier, Jan. 4, 1821, AE/MD: France, 718. See also
Caraman to Richelieu, Nov. 21, 1821, Richelieu Papers, 83; Caraman to Pasquier, May 9, 1821, AE/MD: France, 719.

[20] La Ferronnays to Pasquier, Feb. 27, 1821, AE/MD: France, 719, and Jan. 4,
1821, AE/MD: France, 718. It was clear from these conversations that Alexander
wanted to retain the friendship of the French ambassador and the close ties
with France promoted by Capodistrias.

[21] Metternich, personal letters, Dec. 5 and Nov. 4, 1820, Mémoires, III, 381,
376.

much as peace," because he would not risk war to defend the
Greeks, most particularly when Russia might not be joined by
the allies and might be strongly opposed by Austria. Metternich
did his utmost to convince Alexander that the dangers of a Turkish war included the prospect that it could "assist the game of the
revolutionaries of every country in Europe." "It is certain," reported the British ambassador, "that the nearer the supposed season of hostilities approaches and the more menacing appearances
become, the more the Emperor shrinks from the idea of
War." [22] Metternich's boast of "perhaps the greatest victory that
one cabinet has ever gained over another" was somewhat exaggerated. But Metternich could claim a victory over Alexander on
the Eastern Question because the chancellor's policy best accorded with Alexander's own desire to preserve the alliance system, to avoid war, and to prevent the spread of revolution.[23] The
decision against a Turkish war implied a less expansionist role
for Russia in the East and again reinforced Nesselrode's position
in the Russian cabinet, where he was a perfect spokesman for
the policy adopted.

On a deeper level, Alexander's support for Metternich and his
consequent retention of Nesselrode arose from his growing aversion to taking an active role in foreign affairs. Metternich was
most perceptive when he noted that Alexander "has withdrawn
from all positive action and thrown himself morally upon
me." [24] Subservience to Metternich's policies gave Alexander
freedom from the responsibilities of pursuing his own. The position of Nesselrode reinforced this attitude, because Nesselrode,
unlike Capodistrias, was not trying to force Alexander into tak-

[22] Alexander to Stroganov, June 28, 1821, Prokesch-Osten, *Geschichte* III,
91. Bagot to Castlereagh, Sept. 17, 1821, PRO/FO 65/129, and May 6, 1822,
PRO/FO 65/132.
[23] Metternich to Francis I, May 31, 1822, *Mémoires*, III, 587. Joseph Villèle
suggested that Metternich had deceitfully played on Alexander's fears of revolution in the West and South in order to get his policy in the Orient, "in making
him forget the true interests of his own country and the inspiration of a wise
policy to give him the role of the gendarme of civilized Europe" (*Mémoires et
correspondance du comte de Villèle* [5 vols., Paris, 1888–1890], V, 170).
[24] Metternich, personal letter, July 23, 1821, *Mémoires*, III, 473; Metternich
then went on, "This explains my cobweb. Such webs are pretty to look at,
cleverly spun, and will bear a light touch, but not a gale of wind."

ing initiative; his passivity coincided with the passivity which Alexander wished to follow in his state of mind which called increasingly for psychological withdrawal and political isolation. Nesselrode thus found his strongest support, as the French ambassador noted, in the fact that "the emperor was long habituated to working with him," as well as in "this complete abnegation of will which makes it convenient for him to make the Austrian government his strongest crutch." Nesselrode's characteristic lack of initiative thus contributed to his position at the same time that it curtailed what influence he might have exerted. As one diplomat put it, "To be truthful, when the master does not speak, what could the minister say?" [25]

The fact that Nesselrode did not assume a very significant role nevertheless did leave a power vacuum in diplomatic affairs which, when not filled by Capodistrias, was often filled by pressures from different directions and by Alexander's continuing policy of conducting diplomatic affairs through diverse channels. Unlike earlier key domestic advisers, who were usually involved in foreign affairs, Alexander's de facto prime minister in the last part of his reign, General Alexis Arakcheev — the person "to whom the Emperor professes to give the greatest share of his confidence" — clearly "was not involved with diplomatic business." [26] Lacking any distinctive foreign policies himself, Arakcheev gave no evidence of strong commitments on the diplomatic scene, nor did he show marked allegiance to either Capodistrias or Nesselrode. His often ruthless and usually repressive activities, seemingly dominated more by devoted obeisance to his sovereign than by any real political convictions or constructive policies, left their unenlightened mark on the domestic scene after the Congress of Vienna and gave a real stamp of despotism to the period. Left to his own devices by Alexander's growing frustration and disinterest in domestic affairs, Arakcheev became associated with the darkest and most repressive aspects of Alex-

[25] La Ferronnays to Chateaubriand, Oct. 1, 1823, AE/CPR, 165; Lebzeltern to Metternich, Nov. 27, 1824, HHS/Russ. III, 63.

[26] Cathcart to Castlereagh, July 13, 1816, Castlereagh, *Correspondence*, XI, 264; report of Major de Clam Martinez, May–June 1818, Wellington, *Supplementary Despatches*, XIV, 695.

ander's reign. The emperor, however, took more interest in international developments during that time, with the result that Arakcheev's activities had minimal repercussions on diplomacy, despite the fears of foreign diplomats.

In foreign affairs the independence and activity of Russian diplomats abroad often severely limited the role of the minister in St. Petersburg. Nowhere was this problem more apparent than in the case of the illustrious native of Corsica, General Pozzo di Borgo, whom Alexander considered "one of the most distinguished among those in his service." [27] Pozzo had risen in the Russian service through relatively minor anti-Napoleonic activities before and during the Russo-French alliance to being one of the leading spokesmen for the Bourbon cause before the Congress of Vienna. With the return of the Bourbons to the French throne, he was assigned the important — and somewhat ironic — position as Russian ambassador to France. Never very close to Alexander, Pozzo, a master of political intrigue, officially communicated to the Russian court through normal diplomatic channels, sending only occasional secret reports on special instruction directly to the emperor. Ties with his home court were kept secure through his close friendships with both Capodistrias and Nesselrode, which gave considerable leverage to his incessant activity. While augmenting his own wealth, he contributed much to the Russian position in Paris and in western Europe, although his precise diplomatic achievements are rather hard to pinpoint.

Whatever the real extent of his influence, his intrigues had their most severe repercussions in arousing the suspicions of the allies about the overextension of Russian influence. Canning was convinced "that Russia governs Continental Europe through Pozzo, now, nearly as absolutely as she heretofore governed Poland through Poniatowski," and the British cabinet sent Canning to Paris with the express purpose of defeating "the influence of Pozzo di Borgo, not only in France but throughout the south of Europe." [28]

---

[27] Capodistrias to Pozzo di Borgo, July 22, 1818, *SIRIO*, CXIX, 776.
[28] Canning to Wellington, Oct. 8, 1824, Wellington, *Despatches*, II, 316; Wellington to Canning, Oct. 10, 1824, *ibid.*, p. 318.

The British attempts to undermine Pozzo were outdone —
also without success — by Metternich, who was alarmed by the
extent to which "Russian tutelage has succeeded everywhere
it had means of exercising itself" through the influence of
Pozzo. Aware that "so much has been done in France which
will now be so difficult to undo," Metternich conducted the same
sort of slanderous campaign against that "infernal intriguer" that
he had waged earlier against Capodistrias. He considered Pozzo
"a permanent obstacle to the viability of the alliance" and made
every effort to secure his dismissal. Metternich denounced Pozzo
in words which were intended to reach the ears of the Russian
court. His remarks also give some measure of Pozzo's importance: "Blinded by his fortune, knowing neither limit nor rule to
his ambition," Pozzo considers himself "placed above all control
by his cabinet; he mows all the fields around him with all the
freedom of action which he willingly draws from the independence of his diplomatic position." Pozzo, Metternich concluded, is
"in a word an obstacle to everything and a useful instrument to
none." Complaining that "it is in large part the ideas of General
Pozzo which create the point of view and the judgment of the
Russian cabinet," Metternich chided Nesselrode for accepting his
reports uncritically: Nesselrode's "confidence in the superiority of
the genius of Pozzo deprives him of all facility of extending his
view to even the most immediate future."[29] Metternich's campaign against Pozzo backfired; ironically, it undermined Alexander's confidence in Metternich and thereby weakened Nesselrode's position.

Other ambassadors also worked with great independence, and
Alexander frequently worked directly with foreign diplomats or
heads of state and independently of his ministers through special
emissaries. During Nesselrode's later period in office, Dmitri
Tatishchev was the most prominent of these. After the Congress of
Vienna, Tatishchev gained an unpleasant reputation for his intrigues on behalf of Russia — many in conjunction with Pozzo di

---

[29] Metternich to Lebzeltern, June 5, 1820, HHS, Gesandtschaft Archiv: St.
Petersburg, 39. Metternich to Lebzeltern, Aug. 11 and Feb. 7, 1824, HHS/Russ.
III, 78.

Borgo — while he was serving as Russian minister to Spain.[30] At the height of the Eastern crisis in the last months of 1821 and the first half of 1822, when Alexander was cautiously resisting the recommendations of Capodistrias for active Russian support of the Greeks, it was to Tatishchev not to Nesselrode that he turned, even though Nesselrode's policy was much closer to Alexander's. It may have been partly Nesselrode's unwillingness to turn against Capodistrias that led the emperor to select Tatishchev for the delicate secret mission to Vienna in the spring of 1822 to work toward some resolution of the Eastern crisis with Metternich. Capodistrias had nothing to do with the mission, and Nesselrode had little more, because while Tatishchev ostensibly was cooperating with the Russian ambassador Golovkin in Vienna, he was in fact working independently and sending his most important reports directly to the emperor. Ambivalent or undecided himself about policies, Tatishchev continued to play a major role in Eastern affairs in the following years. Although he was evidently unable to influence the emperor significantly in cases where he did have some conviction, there were rumors that Tatishchev might replace Nesselrode in the ministry, and certainly his place in Alexander's confidence limited Nesselrode's responsibility as foreign minister.[31]

At least at this stage of his career Nesselrode made no attempts to increase his own prestige or to prevent the influence of

[30] The complaints about his activities and Pozzo's direction of them, particularly from Austrian and British diplomats, equaled in intensity the complaints about Pozzo di Borgo in Paris. That he had influential connections in the Spanish court seems well established, but Metternich was exaggerating when he spoke of Spain as "the country which [Tatishchev] had governed during four years" (Metternich to Lebzeltern, June 5, 1820, HHS, Gesandtschaft Archiv: St. Petersburg, 39).

[31] Bagot to Castlereagh, May 6, 1822, PRO/FO 65/132; Metternich to Lebzeltern, April 22, 1822, Prokesch-Osten, *Geschichte*, III, 365–366, and Metternich to Lebzeltern, April 22, 1822, personal, HHS/Russ. III, 53. La Ferronnays to Chateaubriand, Oct. 1, 1823, AE/CPR 165. A French diplomat of the period suggested that Tatishchev hesitated to join either those favoring war or those favoring peace, and that, accordingly, Alexander used him when he was tired of intrigues and party disagreements (Charles-Joseph-Edmond Boislecomte, "Précis des négociations relatives aux affaires d'Orient depuis l'insurrection des Grecs, jusqu'au départ de l'Empereur de Russie pour le Congrès de Vérone," appendix to dispatch of Aug. 18, 1822, AE/MD: Russie, 40).

others who happened to be in the emperor's favor. Lacking emotional rapport with Alexander and increasingly insecure about dealing with the emperor during his frequent periods of emotional instability and religious withdrawal, Nesselrode chose to remain in the passive role which had insured his position for so long. Reports about how much "Nesselrode lets himself be influenced increasingly by Pozzo on the Occident and by Tatishchev on the Orient" were not without foundation because Nesselrode's opinions were "easily influenced by people." [32] When Metternich complained that one of Nesselrode's greatest faults was his "letting himself be led by a predilection for such individuals without scrutiny as to what they offer of real value," he might have well been describing Nesselrode's attitude toward himself, too. [33]

The basic disparity in the characters, attitudes, and political principles of Alexander and Metternich had always precluded full accord; toward the final year of Alexander's reign, a major split was again apparent. Alexander seemingly was resuming the role that he had assumed in his earlier alliance with Napoleon. He followed an overt policy of complete agreement with Metternich, while he was also pursuing a usually covert policy of opposition to the Metternich system through such agents as Pozzo di Borgo, who continued some of Capodistrias' policies, and through direct relationships with such French leaders as Chateaubriand and La Ferronnays. There is no doubt that by the beginning of 1825, if not earlier, Alexander had come to believe "that the system of Austria, however useful and commendable during the greater part of the transactions of the last few years, is now run out and worthless, and must be replaced by one more likely to produce more real and permanent results." Before his death Alexander had already charted the policy which led Russia to war in support of Greece in 1827. In fact, in November 1825 the British ambassador reported that the emperor was "now perfectly

---

[31] Lebzeltern to Metternich, Sept. 4, 1823, HHS/Russ. III, 61; see also La Ferronnays to Pasquier, Sept. 25, 1820, AE/CPR, 161; Pasquier, *Histoire*, V, 24–25.

[33] Metternich to Lebzeltern, May 22, 1823, HHS/Russ. III, 78; Metternich was here complaining about his reliance on Pozzo di Borgo.

habituated to the Idea of War, as the only means of compelling
Turkey to enter into an arrangement respecting Greece. . . He
considers himself abandoned by His Allies to whose counsels he
has hitherto yielded." According to this report, Alexander believed that "He has thus acquired the *right* of acting for himself,
and of pursuing His own views, without any further reference to
Their opinions or advice." [34]

Despite such change in Alexander's attitude, Nesselrode clung
strenuously to the policy of peace; even though he too had doubts
about some of Metternich's motives and policies, he was not the
one to speak out against the Austrian chancellor. Rumors multi-
plied that Nesselrode might be replaced by Tatishchev as foreign
minister, but time seemed to be on his side. It was noted that during the emperor's final voyage to Taganrog in the late fall of
1825 Nesselrode, "the only one of the cabinet adverse to hostile
maneuvers, has not been ordered to accompany the Emperor." [35]
Had Alexander lived, Nesselrode possibly would have been replaced, but the emperor's death saved the foreign minister's position. At the advent of the new reign, Nesselrode was immediately
assured his place by Nicholas I, whose attitudes and principles he
found more congenial.

The length of Nesselrode's tenure under Alexander and during
most of the long reign of Nicholas I suggests much about his success: He at no time presented a threat to the imperial authority.
Most observers felt during the joint ministry that "everything
must assure the triumph of Count Capodistrias," but the French

---

[34] Strangford to Canning, Nov. 27 and 22, 1825, PRO/FO 65/149. The ambassador added that Alexander seemed eager for an understanding with England
as "the only one of the Great Powers on whose justice and impartiality in the
Greek Affair, the Emperor had the slightest reliance." Alexander's readiness
to support the Greeks and break with Metternich is confirmed by reference to
other documents in the period presented in Harold Temperley, "Princess Lieven
and the Protocol of 4 April 1826," *English Historical Review*, XXXIX (Jan.
1924), No. 153, 55–62. See also Lebzeltern to Metternich, July 30, 1825,
HHS/Russ. III, 68; Fontenay to Damas, Oct. 22, 1825, AE/CPR 169; Canning
to Wellesley, March 1826, *The Diary and Correspondence of Henry Wellesley,
First Lord Cowley, 1790–1846*, ed. F. A. Wellesley (London, n.d.), p. 142; *The
Unpublished Diary and Political Sketches of Princess Lieven*, pp. 90–92.

[35] *The Unpublished Diary and Political Sketches of Princess Lieven*, p. 89;
Strangford to Canning, Nov. 27, 1825, PRO/FO 65/149.

ambassador's doubts were revealing: "This triumph would not even seem doubtful to me, were it not known that the emperor, wishing to conduct affairs for himself, could forget the good of his service to satisfy his pride, could fear the nearness of a superior man and search for a mediocre one who would never be able to share his glory." [36] The French ambassador may have overemphasized the emperor's pride and failed to mention other factors in Nesselrode's triumph, but the main thrust of his prediction was borne out. Nesselrode's long term as minister was significant not for his substantive influence on diplomacy, like Canning's, Metternich's, or even Chateaubriand's, but rather for his singular ability to reflect and support the will of his sovereign.

[36] Noailles to Richelieu, Sept. 28, 1816, *SIRIO*, CXII, 635–636.

## Chapter 9

# DIPLOMATIC SPOKESMEN AND THE TSAR-DIPLOMAT

Russian foreign relations during the first quarter of the nineteenth century were conducted within the context of the European states system, in which Russia stood as the one power capable of counterbalancing Napoleonic France. It was a cosmopolitan age which inherited a strong sense of a European balance of power and sought to secure a peaceful European community. But it was also an age in which that community was shattered to its core, first by having witnessed the vulnerability of the French ancien régime to revolution and the rise of Bonaparte, and more recently by witnessing the defenselessness of countries great and small against the Napoleonic bid for European hegemony. The zenith of Russia's power and prestige in Europe did not mean the end of its vulnerability to the challenge of Napoleonic France, a challenge which came on military, political, and social levels.

Foreign policy during the period was determined largely by the responses Russian leaders made to Napoleon's challenge. The alternations between war and peace, the equivocation between involvement and noninvolvement, the conflicts of national interest with international concerns were all aspects of that response. The extent to which Russia increased its commitment to the European community greatly enhanced Russian prestige and demonstrated its potential for arbitrating the destinies of the entire continent. But it resulted also in the neglect of its own internal reform and modernization, reflecting in a sense the real ambivalence of its commitment to the West. In succeeding generations this neglect and ambivalence would result in a disparity between Russia's commitments abroad and its ability to sustain those commitments, forcing it into the disastrous position of being one of the most backward of the great powers on the continent.

This commitment to great-power status in the European community in the early nineteenth century was the strongest characteristic of Russian foreign policy. Such a commitment hardly distinguished Russian foreign policy from that of other major powers, but at least at that time it was founded on diplomatic and military realities. This commitment carried with it an eighteenth-century sense of a balance of power in Europe, which was characteristic of European statesmen with the exception of Napoleon.

At the same time, Russia was not entirely immune from the urge for expansion which characterized Napoleonic France and which was expressed in the overseas growth of other powers. Although the extent to which Russia increased its empire during Alexander's reign never matched the type of expansionist policies of the reign of Catherine the Great or of the later Pan-Slavist movements, there were many undercurrents of expansionism in Russian foreign policy, particularly with regard to Poland and the Balkans. Both the problem of Poland and the Eastern Question were carried over from the eighteenth century, but both were given new nineteenth-century directions during the reign of Alexander I.

No single all-embracing expansionist policy was argued, nor were any official policies voiced which were aimed at increasing Russian frontiers; rather there were a variety of proposals, often made by the same person and at times even in conflict with one another. In fact, except for Nesselrode and Kochubei, all Alexander's foreign ministers in one way or another cast their influence in the direction of potentially expansionist designs. In most cases, the ministers, much more than the emperor, were the driving force behind expansionist proposals or activities.

The most frequent justification for Russian expansion during the period, and one argued loudly by Czartoryski, Budberg, and Rumiantsev, was that it was a reaction to Napoleonic designs and that it was necessary — as in the Balkans — to maintain the balance of power in an area where Napoleonic inroads threatened to overthrow that balance. This argument clearly was in defensive reaction to European developments, but it was often accompanied or reinforced by more ulterior motives. Relatively conservative Russians of nationalist pride like Rumiantsev and Budberg sought expansion and "Russian glory" through greater influence and territory at the expense of the decaying Ottoman Empire; Rumiantsev and Czartoryski, as proponents of commercial development who were anxious to compete economically with England, perceived the potential of Black Sea commerce and sought further advances in that area; Rumiantsev also sought trading colonies farther afield in the Far East and North America. The most vehement arguments for expansionist policies for Russia ironically came from foreigners: Capodistrias and Czartoryski, as representatives of repressed nations, saw Russia as the protector of their national rights and the promoter of their national revivals.

Even to the extent that these multi-faceted elements of expansionism ran through Russian policies, they hardly added up to a dominant current in Russian foreign policy or a prime determining factor underlying Russian diplomacy. The main reason is that such arguments for expansion were never really adopted by the emperor and never really became an official policy; even Alexander's ambition to reunify Poland and assume the Polish crown stemmed less from any thought of increasing his empire than from a genuine humanitarian concern to right the wrong of his grandmother's partitions.

What overall consistency there was in Russian foreign policy in the early nineteenth century resulted much more from the political outlook of Alexander I and his own individual response to international developments than from any predetermined patterns of Russian foreign-policy objectives. This fact stemmed as much from the decision-making process in the state as it did from the particular character and outlook of the emperor. In the great age of Weberian "traditional authority" in Russia, the concept of state was scarcely differentiated from the personal, patriarchal authority of a charismatic sovereign. With bureaucracy and institutional controls inadequately developed, decision-making in

Russian foreign policy devolved on the emperor and his chosen advisers. That policy in both its formative and functional aspects was determined by their highly personal idiosyncratic responses to the challenges from the West and to the political context. Russian diplomacy at that time, for all its formalities and conventions, was still a highly personalized business where individual reactions and personal attitudes counted far more heavily than institutional and ideological patterns or self-conscious broad economic, social, or geographic concerns.

Not that ideas or political concerns were unimportant; the foreign policy of Alexander and his ministers was definitely idea-oriented. Ministers rose or fell from favor more because of their personal commitments and political attitudes and their relative energy in pursuing them than because of their administrative or diplomatic abilities. However, it was not ideas per se which determined policy, but ideas as embedded in the social attitudes and the outlooks of individuals which made the period one of personal, as opposed to institutional or ideological, diplomacy. To be sure, the similar aristocratic backgrounds of most leading diplomats gave an esprit de corps to diplomatic circles and a common denominator to social assumptions. But there was nothing distinctively Russian in such assumptions, and there was neither party nor stable political faction to demand loyalty or to focus political concerns. Furthermore, the individual interests and political commitments of those who served as Russian foreign minister varied too extensively for them to fit the mold of any one political or class ideology. Under Alexander's successor "Official Nationality," comprising the triad of "Autocracy, Orthodoxy, and Nationality," became a state creed to a degree which justifies considering it an ideology. During the first quarter of the century, however, not one of those elements was a prominent consideration in foreign policy. There was no such clear-cut formula underlying political decisions.

Although Alexander himself lacked the well-developed creed which his brother Nicholas was to embrace in Official Nationality, the complex of hopes and ideas which characterized Alexander's outlook were as important for Russian diplomacy as the more consistent policies of his successor. Alexander's real devotion both to the encouragement of enlightened reform and to the maintenance of social order gave his policies a consistency which is not often recognized. The enthusiasm with which he could both insist on constitutions for France and Poland and condone Metternich's suppression of revolutions in southern Europe is understandable in terms of these contradictory aims, which he was never really able to reconcile. The contradictions stemmed from basic dilemmas in Alexander's character and situation; the result was the peculiar blending of enlightenment and despotism which pervaded his reign.

Alexander was a master diplomat — however difficult he may have been to work with — in his ability to pursue rival policies simultaneously, leaving various possibilities open for diplomatic maneuver. The type of duplicity which could allow him to profess his allegiance to the Napoleonic alliance strongly between 1807 and 1812 and at the same time pursue diplomatic and military preparations for a renewed struggle against Napoleon was repeated later in his ability to work closely with Capodistrias on behalf of some of his liberal goals while keeping Nesselrode on hand to maintain close ties with Metternich's Austria. This is not to credit the emperor with a completely rational plan and a consistent foreign policy, for Alexander's diplomatic maneuvers seem to have come almost naturally and circumstantially; they seem less the result of foresight than of the fear of closing the door on political possibilities.

As important in the determination of policy as his pursuit of seemingly rival aims were the alternating enthusiasm and hesitation with which Alexander followed his ideas. His personal and psychological reactions were intricately involved in his public and political activities. His extremes of emotional withdrawal from and commitment to various projects, and of enthusiasm and irresolution on specific programs had constant political repercussions, as did his shifting image of himself as liberal political reformer, as defiant defender of social order, as traditional military leader, as enlightened constitutional monarch, or as inspired spiritual crusader. The ambivalence toward the West which was to characterize Russian policy throughout the century seems to have followed the vacillating pattern of Alexander's personal reactions; he himself did not pose "Russia" against "the West" as did his brother Nicholas I, but that opposition was latent in his search for his own and his country's political identity and in his attempts to realize his own vague reformist ideals on the political scene.

Alexander's ideas and character were crucial to Russian diplomacy during this perod because, whether active in European affairs or withdrawing from international leadership, Alexander kept the reins of diplomacy in his own hands. More than any other contemporary head of state — with the possible exception of Napoleon — he was his own foreign minister; even Talleyrand under Napoleon had a more creative role than did any of Alexander's foreign ministers. His reign brought the zenith of Russian power in Europe, and, to an extent unprecedented among Russian sovereigns, the tsar-diplomat gave international developments his strong impress: He decided for peace with Napoleon in 1807; Europe bore the brunt of the Franco-Russian Alliance. He decided to pursue Napoleon to Paris in 1812; the European statesmen joined him in war. He insisted on a constitutional charter for France; the Bourbon Restoration was a constitutional monarchy. He underwrote a neutralized republic for Switzerland and a moderate constitution for Finland. He insisted on returning France to great-power status in 1818. The tenacity with which he stood by his cherished dream for a reunited, constitutional Kingdom of Poland at the Congress of Vienna in the face of opposition from most of his advisers and all the leaders of Europe well illustrates the extraordinary extent to which personal preferences could be carried into international politics.

Polish developments also illustrate Alexander's basic failure to reconcile his liberal goals with his desire for social order and stability: his genuinely humanitarian motives were transformed into one of the most oppressive regimes in the history of Poland. At the Congress of Vienna, when all eyes were turned toward the monarch who had victoriously led the European armies into Napoleon's Paris, Alexander tragically disappointed those who expected so much from him. Had he been more steadfast in pursuing his professed liberal goals, the results of the congress might have been very different; but he danced, and the congress danced with him. He abandoned the practical implementation of his ideals in the extremely complex situation and settled for the, to him, comforting vision of a Christian community in the Holy Alliance. The vision and his intentions may have been noble, but the European heads of state who endorsed his treaty with bewilderment and disdain realized how sentimental and meaningless the document was to a Europe that had been shaken to its foundations by the French Revolution and Napoleon. In some sense, however, the results of the Congress of Vienna corresponded with his ideals. He had advocated the restoration of equilibrium in Europe and the establishment of an alliance system. He wanted peace and order for Europe, and the settlements of 1814 and 1815 brought Europe an extraordinarily long period without major war. While the Concert of Europe was not really his work, it corresponded with one part of his goals, and he did much to make it last until the end of his reign.

But the preservation of those goals of peace and order through the maintenance of the alliance system resulted in the tragic eclipse of Alexander's attempts to realize his liberal and humanitarian ideals. The existing system became an end in itself, and its perpetuation became more important to him than much-needed reforms. The religious enthusiasm and humanitarian concern with which he had campaigned against Napoleon found their tragic counterpart later in his paranoid fears of revolutionary conspiracy which in the end motivated his acquiescence to Metternich's reactionary campaign and in his personal religious withdrawal from worldly affairs, which left him scarcely attentive to similar reactionary developments on the home front.

Alexander himself recognized that in diplomacy it was "necessary to deal with the weakness and even with the faults of men." In words all too applicable to his own shortcomings, he was conscious that personal feelings, even "those of a petty nature," often influenced great events so that "the most important interests are sacrificed to miserable considerations."[1] Alexander's own unstable personality revealed itself in his day-to-day conduct, as well as in his major diplomatic decisions. His personal discouragements, suspicions, conflicts, and guilts, all had their parts in the frustrations he experienced in trying to govern the largest empire in Europe. His periods of actively supervising the minutest details of diplomacy countered periods of great withdrawal. His reluctance to extend confidence to his subordinates matched boundless outflows of confidence, and his dealings were complicated by the inner duplicity with which he could honestly and sincerely extend confidences to rival individuals or causes simultaneously. Though his diplomatic successes were often a result of his personal manner of dealing with people, that manner often meant that personal emotion could outweigh more rational political calculations.

In a period of transition from the extremely personal absolutism of eighteenth-century Russia to the more bureaucratic absolutism of Nicholas I, individual personality and personal relationships still exerted a strong influence on the affairs of state. The position of the emperor, his manner of governing, and his own character and attitudes remained the most important determinants of the role of any foreign minister. Alexander's attitudes and personality thus largely determined his choice and the functions of his foreign ministers. These men served Alexander more as personal advisers than as institutional ministers; and his favor and their influence depended largely on their personal relationships with the sovereign. There was no coincidence in the fact that his most successful ministers, Czartoryski and Capodistrias, were those to whom he felt closest personally and politically. They were given more responsibility than other ministers largely because they were idealists and reformers like the emperor and were willing and able to exert more initiative. Alexander had a deep personal regard for these men, and he wanted his friends in office; but he also wanted his friends to agree with him. They ultimately failed in their relations with the emperor and had to re-

---

[1] La Ferronnays to Pasquier, Dec. 9, 1820, AE/MD: France, 717.

sign from office because sooner or later they outspokenly pursued policies which disagreed with the emperor's aims and were unwilling to implement policies which conflicted with their own ideals. Their failures and their importance as foreign ministers were due to their unwillingness to serve as mere instruments of the imperial will.

None of Alexander's other foreign ministers held the same degree of personal confidence as Czartoryski and Capodistrias, and their careers in the foreign office all reflected that fact. The terms of Panin, Kochubei, Vorontsov, and Budberg were short. Panin's ambitions for Russia contrasted sharply with the emperor's and those of his circle of young advisers, and Panin also had been associated with the group which staged the coup against Alexander's father in March 1801. Kochubei was much closer to the emperor in confidence and was a member of the Secret Committee, but he served in the foreign office against his will, and his denunciation of Alexander's Prussian ties at the time of the Memel interview produced a degree of personal antagonism. Vorontsov, who had been at the periphery of Alexander's inner circles since 1801, lent his name and dignity to the office of foreign minister, but his failing health soon gave Alexander the excuse to let him retire and to turn to the counsels of his close friend Czartoryski, who was much more sympathetic to the emperor's attitudes. Budberg had been one of Alexander's early tutors; in 1806 he was helped by not having been involved in Alexander's early failures at home and abroad, but he never established the personal rapport which Alexander wanted with his close advisers. He served little more than a year.

Rumiantsev lasted longer and held an important position in the Russian government, combining the offices of minister of commerce and minister for foreign affairs and later of state chancellor. Without enjoying the emperor's close friendship or confidence, he was retained to preserve the French alliance, but Alexander at the same time was working secretly through other men on contrary policies. The minister who lasted longest through the greatest number of shifts of policy was Count Karl Robert Nesselrode, who was best able and most willing to subordinate himself to the emperor. Nesselrode survived so long because he challenged the emperor neither psychologically nor politically, because he was always willing to conform to the emperor's point of view even when he disagreed.

The very lack of closeness between Alexander and many of his ministers suggests an institutionalization of the office of foreign minister. During the thirty-year reign of Alexander's successor, when only Count Nesselrode served as Russian foreign minister, the office became part of a thoroughly elaborated bureaucracy. During the shorter reign of Alexander, of the eight men of diverse background, character, and persuasion who occupied this office, only three — Vorontsov, Budberg, and Rumiantsev — held the official title of Foreign Minister. It was clear, however, that there was always one man (if not two) who occupied the ministerial office, headed the chancellery, and was recognized as the effective foreign minister of the Russian Empire. Often he was not, to quote the Austrian ambassador, "a minister in the accepted use of the term," [2] but he was, like his foreign counterparts, a man with a definite function in the state, to whom the emperor turned to administer the business of diplomacy and to carry out the current official foreign policy line.

Although personal diplomacy was the rule, the office was sufficiently institutionalized to give truth to the comment that "a great deal is . . . in the power of the ministers." Whereas Alexander's own diplomatic policies usually prevailed, they were developed and implemented in close collaboration with his acting foreign ministers, who discussed, edited, elaborated, and interpreted the policies in the course of conducting the business of foreign relations. "All those with whom His Imperial Majesty personally and habitually transacts business have more influence than he is aware of," remarked the British ambassador, "by the manner in which their reports are worded, and the moment when they are made . . . it must frequently happen that business will assume a very different form after it has gone through this proc-

[2] Lebzeltern to Metternich, Sept. 4, 1823, HHSRuss. III, 61.

ess, from what is promised in the first audience." [3] Some at times even succeeded in pressing particular lines of policy; the influence of others was less direct. But in all cases, while they acted in the name of the emperor and usually under his close orders, each gave his own personal stamp to his work. Much as Alexander may have wanted to be his own foreign minister, the functioning of his subordinates was often crucial.

In some ways, the position of foreign minister in Russia had as much potential responsibility as in other European states, but in other ways it was peculiarly limited. The Russian foreign ministers had potential power because, unlike their British and French colleagues, they were not answerable to any legislative body. Neither were they beholden to a political party nor limited by a cabinet or executive council having any policy-making function; even the early limitation of Panin's effectiveness by the Secret Committee really resulted more from Alexander's loss of confidence in him than from the executive function of that committee. Although ministers had much to gain from the lack of parliamentary or cabinet limitations, obversely, they did not have such institutions to support them and therefore were more directly dependent on the personal confidence of their sovereign. Even the bureaucratic inefficiency and poor organization of the ministry, which forced the minister to oversee the work of his subordinates personally, usually proved to be more of a drain on his strength than a real source of bureaucratic power. Under Alexander I the foreign ministers suffered much less from the interference of court or camarilla than was usual in absolute monarchies. Neither were their policies affected by the pressures of commercial interests. They were, however, limited by military pressures, but this was because Russian diplomacy of the period was much more intricately tied to war than to commerce. Potentially, one of the severest limitations on the effectiveness of the foreign minister was the independence of Russian diplomats abroad; but, while Stackelberg, Anstedt, Razumovskii, Simon Vorontsov, and

---

[3] Cathcart to Castlereagh, July 13, 1816, Castlereagh, *Correspondence*, XI, 264, and No. 42, July 12, 1816, PRO/FO 65/104.

especially Pozzo di Borgo can all be cited as ambassadors who sometimes overshadowed the foreign ministers at home, such independence and initiative usually resulted either from the weakness of a particular foreign minister or from a special responsibility of confidence bestowed on the ambassador by the emperor.

The complete personal control over diplomacy which the emperor may have lost through the institutional development of the office or through the personal initiative of some ministers was frequently regained by other procedures. Most notably he limited his ministers' effectiveness by secretly promoting unofficial or rival policies simultaneously with the policy being conducted by the acting official minister. At times Alexander chose to bypass the minister and deal directly with Russian diplomats abroad; at other times he chose to handle diplomatic business with the help of other ministers, officials, aides-de-camp, or occasionally through court figures or friends who were in a position to discuss particular lines of policy with him. The practice of employing special emissaries became a standard procedure, whereby Alexander chose a friend or trusted individual for a special errand or negotiation, often unknown — or only subsequently revealed — to the official foreign minister.

Often, too, Alexander dealt directly with foreign heads of state or their chief advisers, especially at the many international conferences and on state visits; the King of Prussia, Napoleon, and Metternich are but a few of the individuals with whom Alexander's personal relationships had a direct and overpowering effect on the course of Russian diplomacy. In such instances, the initiative was not always Alexander's, but the effect nonetheless drastically curtailed the influence of his foreign ministers. Direct dealings with foreign diplomats in St. Petersburg had the same result; the success with which they found access to the emperor varied considerably in the course of the reign and generally depended on the personal regard Alexander had for specific individuals or on the course of policy he was pursuing at a particular moment.

Such procedures through which Alexander usually carried out his policies — like those policies themselves — were seldom well coordinated, nor did they always result from a rational plan or from foresight. They produced haphazard and inefficient administration because, as contemporaries so often complained, it was "unfortunately all too true that the ministers recently created to be in charge of the different departments do not always know what is going on." The characteristic diffusion of confidence through which Alexander tended "to surround himself with mutually hostile opinions and systems," generally insured that no one was fully informed about all diplomatic proceedings. Contemporaries were concerned by the unpredictable nature of his executive actions: "He listens to all sides, and then more or less mysteriously follows the route corresponding to the ideas dominating him at the moment."[4] But the most important result of these procedures was the concentration of power and decision-making in the hands of the sovereign; while everyone consulted with him, he alone held all the threads and controlled the power, and thus he could circumvent institutional patterns and deal with individuals as he saw fit.

The mystery which contemporaries saw in the process rightly emphasized the personal, idiosyncratic nature of many of Alexander's policy decisions, and the attribution of those decisions to "the ideas dominating him at the time" perceptively exposed the real significance of his political attitudes. For all the importance of personal relationships in the conduct of government during Alexander's reign, there was usually a political rationale — even when it was embedded in emotion — in Alexander's ministerial appointments and in his choice of individuals for diplomatic functions. Foreign ministers held or lost office and gained and lost influence, not with fluctuations of personal regard like Catherine the Great's lovers, but as spokesmen for specific foreign policies or for general political orientations.

Ministerial changes often came in response to major diplomatic or military crises — the defeat of the Third Coalition at Austerlitz, the conclusions of peace with Napoleon at Tilsit, the invasion of Russia in 1812. And such changes occurred as major

---

[4] Hudelist to Colloredo, Dec. 26, 1802, HHS/Russ. II, 95. La Ferronnays to Montmorency, No. 12, May 27, 1822, AE/CPR, 163.

alliances shifted, since ministers were often identified with particular allies. Such was the case with Panin, the instrument of peace
with England in 1801 who was not prepared to sign a new rapprochement with France later, and Kochubei, who was content
with the French agreements but was unsympathetic to renewing
ties with Prussia in 1802. Budberg was pleased to work with
Prussia in opposing Napoleon in 1806 but was hardly an appropriate figure to renew ties with France, whereas Rumiantsev was
the perfect spokesman for complete alliance with Napoleon. Capodistrias was eager to promote French-oriented policies during
the early Restoration, and his strong opposition to Metternich led
to his demise once Alexander had decided on closer friendship
with the Austrian court, supported by Nesselrode.

Ministers changed, more fundamentally, as the pendulum
swung between war and peace, between involvement and noninvolvement on the continent. Panin, who stood for grand and active policies for Russia abroad, was replaced by Kochubei whose
advocacy of withdrawal corresponded with Alexander's early desires to concentrate on internal reform. Vorontsov was a transi-
tional figure who corresponded with Alexander's desire for more
cautious involvement abroad, while Czartoryski, already working
with Alexander, stood for complete involvement as the Russian
architect of the Third Coalition. Following the failure of the coalition, Czartoryski found himself in the background for another
period of Alexander's hesitancy and vacillation until Budberg
emerged to represent Czartoryski's earlier call for renewed war
with Napoleon. With the failure at war in 1807 came the most
ostensible attempt at peace, with Rumiantsev as the spokesman
for the unpopular French alliance of 1807 to 1812. Nesselrode,
who had been one of Alexander's agents in the covert preparation for further war with Napoleon, came to the fore after Napoleon's invasion of Russia; he, by background and outlook very
much tied to anti-Napoleonic Europe, became Alexander's chief
diplomat during the Fourth Coalition against Napoleon. Then,
during the early Restoration, Capodistrias pursued an active,
progressive policy for Russia on the continent until Alexander
reached a point after 1820 where the more passive foreign policy

so well represented by Nesselrode came to conform to his current attitudes.

For Alexander, ministerial changes, like political shifts, were not cut and dried. Periods of hesitation or ambivalence often kept a minister in office after his real usefulness was over because the emperor wished to keep open the possibility of resuming an earlier policy or moving toward an alternate orientation. Two ministers might be in office at once, like Capodistrias and Nesselrode, when Alexander wanted to pursue rival policies simultaneously. Or he might turn to new advisers even while maintaining an official policy under the ostensible minister; thus, he was working with Czartoryski while Vorontsov still remained in office, and with Koshelev, Nesselrode, and others in preparation for war with France while Rumiantsev, the official minister, was still preaching peace.

In looking back on Alexander's reign, we see that there was much political reason behind the apparent madness with which Russian diplomacy proceeded. There was even stability behind the changing nameplate on the office of the foreign minister. The ostensible "mysteriousness" with which Alexander's confidence shifted from one man to another proved to be an effective diplomatic tool in the hands of an emperor who sought to match the personal attitudes of individuals to specific foreign policies. In a period when bureaucratic procedures counted for much less than the personal action of individuals, when the diplomat was far from the civil servant of today, Alexander found it most effective to work with individuals who were personally committed to the policies they were promoting. When their commitments corresponded to policies he wished them to pursue, he could trust them to assume a high degree of responsibility; but when their commitments exceeded the desired bounds, he singled out other individuals whose convictions better corresponded to his current wishes. Thus, Rumiantsev was given a great deal of responsibility in carrying out the policy of alliance with France, to which he was committed more sincerely than Alexander was; but when Rumiantsev's ambitions for Russia in the Balkans made him unwilling to negotiate peace with the Turks in 1812 and his desire to preserve an understanding with Napoleon prevented his wholehearted switch to war, Alexander turned to Nesselrode and others. "I have had the pleasure to repeat to you several times," Alexander warned Rumiantsev in 1811, "that I will conduct myself according to my own point of view and not that of others, and you as well as the others would please conform to it." [5]

Alexander wanted political commitment from his ministers, but he wanted them also to conform to his decided policies. In a revealing comment to Panin after his banishment, Alexander expressed dismay that Panin's actions in office were being held against him personally because, as the emperor put it, "during your ministry, you could only have been the organ of my will." [6] Capodistrias and Czartoryski succeeded so well in their ministries because they pursued policies which had the emperor's support as well as their own commitment. But they failed when they urged policies which would have committed Russia to a more expansionist, aggressive course than Alexander was ready to pursue. Their policies — Czartoryski's in Poland and the Balkans, and Capodistrias' in the West and in Greece — left their mark on Russian foreign policy throughout the nineteenth century, but they terminated the ministers' usefulness as Alexander's officials.

The office of foreign minister was one of the most important in the Russian government in the first quarter of the nineteenth century. Although it hardly proved a place for long, brilliant careers or lasting influence, the men who served often had a crucial role in the shifting pattern of Russian foreign policy and bore much of the responsibility for the day-to-day conduct of diplomacy. The role and responsibility of the minister were naturally most important when his policies were being followed, and he usually became extraneous when the emperor's attitudes and the march of diplomacy brought new policies to the fore. Some, like Czartoryski and Capodistrias, were able to exert significant influence on diplomatic proceedings or were given some responsibility for the administration of diplomacy. The importance of individual min-

---

[5] Alexander to Koshelev, Oct. 11, 1811, NM, *Alexandre*, II, 4.
[6] Alexander to Panin, June 24, 1802, *NPP*, VII, 26.

isters varied with their personal relationships to the emperor, with their affinity to his own political ideals, and with the importance of the particular line of policy they represented. When Alexander supervised matters closely, they could only be his faithful secretaries. When he abandoned affairs or had confidence in their commitment, they could assume more responsibilities. When his ideas were vague, they could provide substance; when he was determined, they might try to dissuade him, but in the end they could only follow or resign.

The functions and roles of the men who served as Alexander's foreign ministers were circumscribed by vague institutional patterns. Their position and influence, at the same time, always depended on their personal idiosyncrasies and their interpersonal relations with the emperor. Their influence resulted largely from their personal and political commitments, their willingness and ability to pursue them, and the correlation of their attitudes with those of Alexander I. They all were caught in the unreconciled dilemma between Alexander's enlightened aims, with which they had to sympathize to succeed, and his fundamental quest for peace and social stability — in whose interest he might pursue the most despotic conduct — to which they had to be willing to submit.

# REFERENCE MATERIALS

# BIBLIOGRAPHICAL NOTE

The study of the Russian foreign ministers in the early nineteenth century is still fraught with the difficulty of getting at all the sources. Many of the potentially most important materials, of course, are forever lost, as Metternich remarked in his memoirs, in the unrecorded conferences, debates, and informal discussions of a period when diplomacy was often conducted in meetings between heads of state and in the tête-à-tête sessions of audience chamber or drawing room. Many other records have been destroyed through accident or war, and some have been done away with intentionally, as were some of Alexander's personal papers which were destroyed by order of Nicholas I. Those which remain have been scattered so widely in different state and private collections that even the scholarship of the last century and a half has not succeeded in cataloging or even finding them all. Many still are unfortunately not available to the public because they remain in private ancestral collections or in the uncataloged inner recesses of such state archives as the Quai d'Orsay or because they are not available for full scholarly use in the foreign ministry archives in Moscow.

Such documentary shortcomings are rendered less frustrating, however, by the tremendous volume of materials which are available. The inaccessibility of the Russian foreign ministry chancellery files, for instance, was less crucial than it might have been for my undertaking because many important documents or copies of them, which might normally be supposed to be there, have been published or can be found in other archives in the Soviet Union and Western Europe. In fact, the diffusion of manuscripts relevant to this study was one of the most difficult problems of research.

Nowhere was that problem more apparent than in the Soviet Union itself, where my search for correspondence and papers relating to the foreign ministers led me to eight different archival repositories, and even then I hardly exhausted the possibilities. For a general discussion of the organization of Soviet archives and manuscript collections and a bibliography of published guides and catalogs which yield further information about the holdings, see my article, "Soviet Archives and Manuscript Collections: A Bibliographical Introduction," in the *Slavic Review*, XXIV, No. 1 (March 1965), 105–120.

Foreign diplomatic reports and the private correspondence of foreign diplomats from St. Petersburg also proved to be of tremendous value in assessing the role and attitudes of the ministers. By following and comparing the reports regarding a given foreign minister and the emperor by several foreign diplomats who knew and worked with the minister — and often the emperor — personally in St. Petersburg, it was possible to reconstruct a much more detailed picture than would emerge from official papers in the Russian foreign ministry or even from the minister's own papers. In addition, foreign diplomatic correspondence often contains copies of important Russian dispatches, memoranda, and other documents, which supplement materials available elsewhere. The nature and importance of these materials in the French, Austrian, and British foreign-office archives for the period up to 1812 is described briefly in an article by R. E. McGrew, "A Note on Some European Foreign Office Archives and Russian Domestic History, 1790–1812," *Slavic Review*, XXIII, No. 3 (Sept. 1964), 531–536. Whereas McGrew is concerned with the materials for Russian domestic history, his conclusions underlining their value can be further magnified when the subject concerns foreign relations. Although somewhat outdated and uneven in its coverage of specific countries, the best initial list of guides and catalogs and the best introduction to the technical details of working in these collections is the handbook edited by Daniel H. Thomas and Lynn M. Case, *Guide to the Diplomatic Archives of Western Europe* (Philadelphia, 1959).

The personal papers of the ministers themselves and of other foreign diplomats also were important sources for this study. Many key memoranda and much important correspondence remain in original or contemporary copy among the personal papers of diplomats. It was customary then for officials to explain their reactions and to offer their own private reflections in personal or secret appendixes to diplomatic dispatches, in separate enclosures, or in personal letters. Although some are available in special files in foreign ministry archives, in many cases this type of correspondence was retained among private papers, some of which are still available. Because of the greater degree of honesty or openness with which diplomats might speak in their personal letters, this material often proved more important than official diplomatic correspondence.

An attempt to cover all the archival sources bearing on Russian diplomacy during Alexander's reign would be practically limitless by the time both public and private holdings in large and small countries were considered. My choice of sources was dictated in part by the availability of the holdings and in part by their suspected importance, which was most often determined by significant lacunae or by other indications in related published documents.

The bibliography which follows is highly selective and emphasizes the unpublished or little-known materials used in this study. No attempt has been made to include all works cited in the notes, nor has justice been done to the plethora of secondary literature on which any scholar must certainly depend. The first part of the bibliography discusses the general archival materials and the major published collections of documents on which the study is based. This is followed by chapter bibliographies, which briefly discuss the important manuscripts and publications used for each chapter.

## Russian Sources

Potentially the most valuable sources for this study would be in the voluminous chancellery files and the fonds covering the diplomatic correspondence with Russian missions abroad in the archives of the Russian foreign ministry, now contained in Arkhiv Vneshnei Politiki Rossi (AVPR) under the foreign ministry. However, although I was admitted to this archive, these files were not available to me, nor was it possible to see any catalog or inventory from which the full extent of the contents could be determined or from which specific items could be requested. I was able to work with only a limited number of documents from section four of the archives (Razriad IV: Administrativnye dela), consisting only of official administrative documents about minor and usually routine matters of no political or diplomatic significance. As to the other, more politically important sections of the archives, I had to rely on published documents, copies of documents found elsewhere, or on gleanings from published studies based on research there by other historians.

The Soviet Foreign Ministry initiated the publication of a foreign policy document series from these archives in 1960, under the editorship of a distinguished group of Soviet scholars (*VPR*). The series does increase the availability of documents from the chancellery files; however, because of the necessary selectivity and because many of the documents had been published before, it serves more to whet than to satisfy the appetite of the specialist. Although all the published documents are from AVPR, no specific archival designations are given which might help scholars locate contiguous materials. Series 1 is to cover the period from 1801 to 1815, but at the time of this writing only the first six volumes have appeared: Vol. 1 (March 1801–April 1804), Vol. 2 (April 1804–Dec. 1805), Vol. 3 (Jan. 1806–July 1807), Vol. 4 (July 1807–March 1809), Vol. 5 (April 1809–Jan. 1811), and Vol. 6 (1811–1812). Unfortunately, reports from the Soviet Union indicate that work on subsequent volumes has been at least temporarily delayed. For further discussion of this series, see my review of the first four volumes published, in the *Slavonic and East European Review*, XLIV (Jan. 1966), 227–228. Each volume has a very helpful bibliography of previous publications containing diplomatic documents for the years covered.

All the treaties and many of the official protocols from the period have been published in a fifteen-volume collection edited by Fedor Fedorovich Martens (Martens, *Recueil*). Relations with Austria are covered in Vols. 2–4, with Germany in Vols. 6 and 7, with England in Vol. 11, and with France during Alexander's reign in Vols. 13–15. Although specific references to these volumes do not always appear in the notes, they were of fundamental importance throughout my study. Running commentary and introductory sections which accompany the successive treaties detail relations between the countries; these textual discussions, drawing heavily as they do on unpublished Russian diplomatic papers, would augment the value of the series were they not often lacking in adequate annotation and marred by many mistakes and by misleading and inaccurate interpretations.

Several important collections of documents from the archives of the Ministry for Foreign Affairs were published before the Revolution by the Russian Imperial Historical Society, among the 148 volumes of its major publication series (*SIRIO*). Most useful were the multivolume collections of French-Russian diplomatic correspondence and related documents drawn from the archives of the French and the Russian foreign ministries. Four volumes edited by Aleksandr S. Trachevskii cover 1800 through 1807: *Diplomaticheskie snosheniia Rossii s Frantsiei v epokhu Napoleona I, SIRIO*, Vols. 70, 77, 82, and 88. For the later part of the period only three of the projected volumes, covering the years 1814 to 1820, were published, edited with annotations by A. A. Polovtsov: *Doneseniia frantsuzskikh predstavitelei pri russkom dvore i russkikh predstavitelei pri frantsuzskom dvore,*

*SIRIO*, Vols. 112, 119, and 127. (Some of these volumes also bore French title pages, *Correspondance diplomatique des ambassadeurs et ministres de Russie en France et de France en Russie de 1814 à 1830 [1820] avec leurs gouvernements.*) Other scattered volumes in the *SIRIO* series include additional important documents. Many of the unpublished Papers of the Russian Imperial Historical Society are now housed in the manuscript division of the Leningrad branch of the Institute of History of the USSR Academy of Sciences (LOII, Fond 113); included there are copies of some documents, collected but never published.

A separate seven-volume publication of official French-Russian diplomatic correspondence from 1808 to 1812, edited by Grand Duke Nikolai Mikhailovich (*DSRF*), fills part of the gap in the above collections; the editing leaves something to be desired, but the contents, drawn from French and Russian foreign ministry archives, make it a major source.

Among the rich collections in other Soviet archives, the most important, although miscellaneous, materials are in the former State Archives of the Russian Empire, now in TsGADA. A concise description of this collection appears included in the guide to the archives, *Tsentral'nyi gosudarstvennyi arkhiv drevnikh aktov. Putevoditel'*, Vol. 1, ed. S. K. Bogoiavlenskii *et al.* (Moscow, Glavnoe arkhivnoe upravlenie, 1946), pp. 160–179. The use of these materials was impeded because it was not possible to use any catalog or detailed inventories, and by the apparent unavailability of some of the documents described in the guide. Among the documents used for this study, Section III (Gosarkhiv III): "Materials Pertaining to Foreign and Internal Politics of Russia" contains some folders of documents relating to the congresses of Laibach and Aix-la-Chapelle and some personal correspondence of the Nesselrode family and of Capodistrias. Section V (Gosarkhiv V): "Letters of Sovereigns to Private Persons" includes some correspondence of Empress Maria Feodorovna and Empress Elizabeth Aleksevna with Rumiantsev, some letters and notes from Alexander I to Rumiantsev, and some correspondence of Alexander I with Shuvalov, Gur'ev, and others. Some interesting miscellaneous correspondence, especially of Rumiantsev, was consulted in Section XI: "Correspondence with Various Persons." Section XV: "Diplomatic Section" contains some materials pertaining to the Congress of Vienna, and miscellaneous diplomatic reports and correspondence of Czartoryski, Anstedt, Razumovskii, and Capodistrias.

The collected papers of the prerevolutionary Russian historian N. K. Schilder, now available as Fond #859 in the manuscript division of the M. E. Saltykov-Shchedrin State Public Library in Leningrad (GPB), provide important sources for the historian of the reign of Alexander I. Schilder, while writing his monumental four-volume court history of Alexander I, *Imperator Aleksandr Pervyi, ego zhizn i tsarstvovanie*, 2nd ed. (St. Petersburg, 1904–1905), had access to a wide range of archival materials in Russia and abroad, including materials stored in the archives of the Russian Foreign Ministry. His clippings, copious notes, and full transcripts of important documents (many from foreign ministry files) provide much material for the historian who may not have access to the originals, as well as giving bibliographic indications of materials concerning the period in various archives and in little-known publications. A comprehensive inventory of the collection, which is still used, was published in a 1910 supplement to the periodical journal of the library, *Otchet Imperatorskoi Publichnoi biblioteki: Opis' bumag N. K. Shil'dera postupivshikh v 1903 godu v Imperatorskuiu Publichnuiu biblioteku*, ed. V. V. Maikov (St. Petersburg, 1910).

The papers of the Vorontsov family deserve special note, particularly for the early years of Alexander's reign. Alexander Romanovich and his brother Simon, the Russian ambassador in London, themselves had key positions in Russian foreign affairs, and both had voluminous correspondence with many of the most important figures of the period. A brief description of selected portions of their archives, which includes notes on their organization, was published by Marc Bouloiseau, "Les archives Voronzov," in *Revue historique*, CCXXX (July–Sept. 1963), 121–130. Significant portions of their personal and official correspondence appear in a forty-volume publication from their archives edited by P. I. Bartenev (*AKV*). Although many of the letters there are rather sloppily edited, poorly arranged, and leave significant gaps, the richness and variety of correspondence included makes it an invaluable collection. A most useful table of contents and index of proper names for the forty volumes was published subsequently: *Rospic soroka knigam arkhiva kniazia Vorontsova s azbuchnym ukazatelem lichnykh imen* (Moscow, 1897).

The manuscripts themselves are now divided and are to be found in several archives in the Soviet Union. The portion of these papers now in TsGADA (Fond #1261) is fully described in an article by V. Z. Dzhincharadze, "Obzor fonda Vorontsovykh khraniashchegosia v TsGADA," *Istoricheskie zapiski*, No. 32 (1950), pp. 242–268. Among the many documents consulted in the TsGADA collection that were of particular interest in this study were registers from the Russian foreign ministry for the years 1801 to 1803 (1261/1177). The portions of the papers remaining in the manuscript division of the Leningrad branch of the Institute of History of the Academy of Sciences (LOII) were very difficult to use, because they have never been adequately inventoried; but a full inventory is now projected which should make them much more easily accessible. They are described in an article in the Institute of History series: V. A. Petrov, "Obzor sobraniia Vorontsovykh khraniashchegosia v arkhiv Leningradskogo otdela Instituta istorii Akademii nauk SSSR," *Problemy istochnikovedennia*, V (Moscow, 1956), 102–145, and, with slightly less detail, in the guide to the archives published by the Institute of History, *Putevoditel' po arkhivu Leningradskogo otdeleniia Instituta istorii*, ed. A. I. Andreev *et al.* (Leningrad, Akademiia nauk SSSR, 1958), pp. 264–285.

Another important collection of private papers is that of the Stroganov family, now situated in TsGADA (Fond #1278). Some of the papers relating to the career of P. A. Stroganov — one of the emperor's "young friends" and a close adviser early in his reign — appeared under the editorship of Grand Duke Nicholas Mikhailovich in his three-volume study published in St. Petersburg in 1903 and in a French edition in 1905 (*Stroganov*). Volume II contains Stroganov's minutes of the meetings of the Secret Committee and other materials relating to that group; important selections from his correspondence continue into Volume III. The remaining manuscripts are described briefly in the general guide to TsGADA, but the more detailed hand-written inventory was unavailable for research purposes. Included in the manuscript collection, and particularly important for this study, is Stroganov's correspondence with the emperor, Stroganov's wife, and Czartoryski; there is also correspondence from Kochubei, Richelieu, Bogdanovich, Novosiltsev, and S. R. Vorontsov among others, and a group of bound volumes relating to the affairs of the foreign ministry and containing a large collection of memoranda by Czartoryski and others. In addition to the materials concerning P. A. Stroganov, there are many important papers of his younger brother, G. A. Stroganov, including some of his private correspondence with Capodistrias while Stroganov was Russian ambassador to Constantinople later in the reign; unfortunately, all these latter papers were not readily available.

Other manuscript collections in the Soviet Union which were of value for my study included the Novosiltsev Papers (GPB, Fond #526), which contain materials relating to Novosiltsev's missions in 1804 and 1805, notes from the emperor, and correspondence from S. R. Vorontsov, Capodistrias, Pozzo di Borgo, Rumiantsev, and Czartoryski. The Divov Papers (TsGAOR, Fond #917) include letters of Anstedt, Capodistrias, Nesselrode, and Rumiantsev, but they mostly concern formalities of the foreign ministry, where Divov was Nesselrode's assistant. The Benckendorff Papers (TsGAOR, Fond #1126) include the correspondence and diplomatic dispatches of Alopeus with Budberg, Czartoryski, Rumiantsev, and the emperor. The Gur'ev Papers (TsGIA, Fond #746) contain correspondence of Alexander I with Gur'ev, who was finance minister and Nesselrode's father-in-law. The papers of the Imperial Chancellery (TsGIA, Fond #1409) include correspondence of the emperor and others with Divov, Budberg, Czartoryski, and Kochubei.

Among the many published memoirs, diaries, and letters of Russian leaders of the period, of general interest in this study were those of Gen. L. A. von Bennigsen, A. P. Butenev, P. V. Chichagov, E. R. Dashkova, P. G. Divov, N. V. Dolgorukii, Prince A. N. Golitsyn, N. B. Golitsyn, V. N. Golovina, F. G. Golovkin, I. V. Lopukhin, Baron Woldemar de Löwenstern, Dowager Empress Maria Feodorovna, A. I. Mikhailovskii-Danilevskii, A. I. Morkov, I. M. Muraviev-Apostol', Prince N. V. Repnin, F. V. Rostopchin, P. A. Shuvalov, P. K. Sukhtelen, N. I. Turgenev, Princess V. I. Turkestanova, and I. V. Vasilchikov.

## British Sources

In Great Britain the most important collection used was the archives of the Foreign Office now housed among the state papers in the Public Record Office in London. This collection has been indexed for the period in the *List of Foreign Office Records to 1878 Preserved in the Public Record Office* (London, 1929; "Lists and Indexes," Vol. 52); while this catalog is in many libraries, the copy in the PRO reading room has been updated with handwritten additions and corrections. Most relevant in the Foreign Office series was the file titled "General Correspondence: Russia," PRO/FO 65, Vols. 48–151; the diplomatic reports *from* St. Petersburg (most bound separately) were more useful than instructions to British diplomats in Russia and correspondence with the Russian embassy in London. Other scattered volumes were also helpful, for example, the private reports from Lord Cathcart to Castlereagh during the Napoleonic campaigns when he was with the Russian emperor (Russia: Supplementary, PRO/FO 97/343) and the reports from Lord Stewart during the Congress of Vienna (General Correspondence: Austria, PRO/FO 7/117); many of the interesting reports from these latter two volumes were published along with other important documents for the period under the editorship of C. K. Webster in *British Diplomacy, 1813–1815: Select Documents Dealing with the Reconstruction of Europe* (London, 1921). The reports from Stewart to Castlereagh which cover the period of the congresses of Troppau and Laibach, are also of interest; they are in later volumes of the "General Correspondence: Austria" files (PRO/FO 7/152–154, 158–160). Also consulted were materials on the Congress of Aix-la-Chapelle in the "General Correspondence: Continent" series (PRO/FO 139/44–48). The archives kept by the British Legation in St. Petersburg (PRO/FO 181) consist predominantly of registers containing only copies of correspondence, which closely duplicate the reports in PRO/FO 65. The private papers in the PRO were of less value and often duplicated the PRO/FO 65 files. Those consulted included the Jackson Papers (PRO/FO 353), the Stratford Canning Papers (PRO/FO 352), and the Stuart de Rothesay Papers (PRO/FO 342).

Selected papers from the archives of many major British foreign ministers of the period are published in extensive editions. Most important are the papers of Robert Stewart, Viscount Castlereagh, *Correspondence, Despatches and other Papers of Viscount Castlereagh, Second Marquess of Londonderry,* ed. Charles W. Vane (12 vols.; London, 1848–1853). Many additional materials regarding Castlereagh are analyzed in that most impressive two-volume biography by C. K. Webster, *The Foreign Policy of Castlereagh, 1812–1815: Britain and the Reconstruction of Europe* (London, 1931) and *The Foreign Policy of Castlereagh, 1815–1822: Britain and the European Alliance,* 2nd ed. (London, 1934). Less extensive are the publications from the Canning Papers, *Some Official Correspondence of George Canning,* ed. Edward J. Stapleton (2 vols.; London, 1887), but there is an excellent biography, *The Foreign Policy of Canning, 1822–1827: England, the Neo-Holy Alliance and the New World* (London, 1925), by Harold Temperley. Important diplomatic correspondence of the Duke of Wellington is published as *Supplementary Despatches, Correspondence, and Memoranda of Field Marshal Arthur, Duke of Wellington, K. G., edited by his Son* (15 vols.; London, 1858–1872), and some additional materials are in the first three volumes of *Despatches, Correspondence and Memoranda of Field Marshal Arthur, Duke of Wellington, K. G.,* New Series (7 vols.; London, 1867–1880).

Among the contemporary British ambassadors to St. Petersburg, Lord Cathcart served the longest and won the greatest favor from Alexander I. The papers of Sir William Schew, tenth lord (first earl) Cathcart, were consulted in London and Cornwall, where they remain in the custody of his descendants; a typed inventory is in the files of the Historical Manuscripts Commission in London. Many of his "Letterbooks" duplicate material in the PRO, but some of his private and family correspondence was of interest. Also of value was the journal of Cathcart's son, who served with him during part of his term, "Record of the Principal Events of My Life Commencing with My First Appointment as Aide de Camp to the Duke of Wellington in 1815 to the end of 1837," by Sir George Cathcart; another box contained letters of Sir George to his father.

The papers of the Lieven family, most particularly of the Russian ambassador to England after 1815, are now in the manuscript division of the British Museum (BM/Add. MSS. 47236–47435), but at the time of writing they were difficult to use because large portions were uncataloged. Of great interest was the wide variety of personal and official correspondence of Lieven with Alexander I, Kochubei, Czartoryski, Panin, Vorontsov, Rumiantsev, Budberg, Cathcart, Bagot, A. C. Benckendorff (Lieven's brother-in-law), and Metternich. Of special note was the diplomatic and personal correspondence between Lieven and Capodistrias and Nesselrode, and some miscellaneous collections of diplomatic dispatches and other documents.

Also consulted in the British Museum were the papers of Sir Robert Thomas Wilson, a British general sent on several important missions to Russia between 1807 and 1813. Most of Wilson's revealing diaries and some of his other correspondence during these missions have been published in several editions, but some material of interest was found in his correspondence with Castlereagh, Czartoryski, Stein, Metternich, Cathcart, and others (BM/Add. MSS. 30106–30107).

Many of the published diaries, memoirs, and correspondence of British diplomats and other important figures shed light on various aspects of this study. Among those consulted were those of Sir Robert Adair, Sir George Cathcart, Thomas Clarkson, Sir Edward Gibbon, Lord Granville Leveson Gower, James Harris (first earl of Malmesbury), Sir George Jackson, Sir Arthur Paget, Sir Charles Vane, Henry Wellesley (first lord Cowley), and Martha and Catherine Wilmot. Also of note are scattered issues of the *Annual Register* and volumes of the *British and Foreign State Papers* and the *Parliamentary Debates*, all of which contain occasional diplomatic papers and other documents of interest.

## French Sources

The most important French sources for this study were in the foreign ministry Archives of the Ministry of Foreign Affairs at the Quai d'Orsay. These were more difficult to use than the British documents, because of the less-detailed catalog descriptions of the contents of volumes, but two recent publications will aid future researchers in this respect: the article by Michel Lesure, "Aperçu sur les fonds russes dans les archives du ministère des affaires étrangères français," *Cahiers du monde russe et soviétique*, IV (July–September 1963), 312–330, and Basile Spiridonakis' guide, *Mémoires et documents du Ministère des Affaires Etrangères de France sur la Russie* (Quebec, 1962). Of principal value was the "Correspondance Politique: Russie" series (AE/CPR), with reports from French diplomatic envoys in St. Petersburg and drafts of the instructions to them. Extensive publications have been made covering parts of the period in the collections published by the Imperial Russian Historical Society and Grand Duke Nicholas Mikhailovich (see "Russian Sources," above). Accordingly, most of my attention was spent on the volumes from the years after 1820, Nos. 159 to 169 (now available on microfilm in the library of the University of California in Berkeley), containing many revealing dispatches of La Ferronnays.

The diverse "Mémoires et Documents" series (AE/MD) at the Quai d'Orsay also provided much important material, including the historical summaries of the congresses of Aix-la-Chapelle, Troppau, Laibach, and Verona, compiled by Charles-Joseph-Edmond Boislecomte; additional memoranda by Boislecomte, Bechu, Bray, and La Ferronnays; collections of correspondence, protocols, and other documents relating to those four congresses, including the personal correspondence of La Ferronnays and Caraman; and a collection of émigré correspondence copied by and/or for Ernest Daudet from Moscow and

St. Petersburg archives, including correspondence of Louis XVIII with Alexander and Russian ministers and reports to the Russian government by émigrés.

Unfortunately, many other documents in the Quai d'Orsay — those from the archives of the French embassy in St. Petersburg, for example, and from many private collections which have been presented to the foreign ministry — have not been cataloged and are not available for research. The state and availability of public documents in France are, however, far better than those of private papers, despite the vigorous special committee for private archives at the Archives Nationales. Because in Alexander's time official documents were often kept among personal papers and because the most important diplomatic concerns were often discussed in private correspondence between ambassadors and ministers, especially when they were personal friends, private papers of diplomats often are extremely important historical sources. But unfortunately many families refuse to make these papers available to scholars.

Whereas I was not permitted to do any direct research among the Pozzo di Borgo Papers, through the kindness of Professor John M. P. McErlean of York University, Toronto, I was able to consult microfilms of some of the important correspondence of Capodistrias and Nesselrode with Pozzo, when he was serving as Russian ambassador to France. Neither was I permitted to consult the private papers of La Ferronnays, either those still in the hands of his descendants or those in the custody of the Quai d'Orsay; nor was it possible to see those of Nesselrode, also presumably extant in France.

The papers of Caulaincourt, Napoleon's ambassador to Russia from 1808 to 1811, are available at the Archives Nationales, but they were relatively unimportant for this study because of the many scholarly and documentary publications covering his years in office. Caulaincourt's memoirs are available in a good edition by Jean Hanoteau, *Mémoires du général de Caulaincourt, duc de Vicence, grand écuyer de l'empereur* (3 vols.; Paris, 1933), and in several condensed English translations; the correspondence relating to his embassy is well covered in other documentary publications such as *DSRF*.

The papers of Armand-Emmanuel du Plessis, duc de Richelieu, who as an émigré served as governor of Odessa and who also served as a key French statesman during the Restoration until his death in 1822, were consulted in the Bibliothèque Victor Cousin at the Sorbonne. The unpublished private letters from La Ferronnays and Caraman to Richelieu, which remain among his papers, were of special interest. The most important parts of Richelieu's correspondence relating to Russia — the letters to and from Alexander, Kochubei, Capodistrias, and Nesselrode, among others — have been published as Volume 54 of the Imperial Russian Historical Society collection, *Gertsog Armand-Emmanuil Rishele. Dokumenty i bumagi o ego zhizni i deiatelnosti, 1766–1822*, ed. A. A. Polovtsov, *SIRIO*, LIV. The volume by Raoul de Cisternes, *Le duc de Richelieu. Son action aux conférences d'Aix-la-Chapelle, sa retraite du pouvoir* (Paris, 1898), contains many documents from the Richelieu Papers and the Quai d'Orsay archives, including the series of letters from Richelieu to King Louis XVIII during the Congress of Aix-la-Chapelle.

Napoleon's own correspondence with Alexander and his other correspondence relating to Russia are available in several well known collections; of particular relevance are the personal letters included by Sergei Tatishchev in *Alexandre 1er et Napoléon d'après leur correspondance inédite, 1801–1812* (Paris, 1891). Primary materials utilized from French sources include the published memoirs, diaries, and correspondence of such leading figures as Baron G. P. B. Barante; Nicolas Bergasse; Louis de Bignon; A. L. V., Duc de Broglie; Vicomte F. R. A. de Chateaubriand; S. de Tisenhaus, Comtesse Sophie de Choiseul-Gouffier; Comte Edouard de Colbert-Chabanais; Joseph Fouché, Duc d'Otrante; Auguste Charles de Messence, Comte de la Garde-Chambonas; Comte Auguste de La Ferronnays; King Louis XVIII; Baron C. F. de Méneval; Comte L. M. de Molé; A. de la Boutetière de Saint-Mars; Baronne M. H. du Montet; Baron (later Duc) E. D. Pasquier; Madame Julie Récamier; A. E. du Plessis, Duc de Richelieu; Louis Victor Léon, Comte de Rochechouart; Comte A. A. R. de Saint-Chamans; Comte Pierre de Serre; Comte P. P. de Ségur; Madame Germaine Necker de Staël; Prince C. M. de Talleyrand-Périgord; Comte Joseph de Villèle; and A. F. Villemain.

## Austrian Sources

Of the archives of the three major powers I consulted, the Austrian state archives were the most fruitful. The tremendous volume of relevant material in Vienna's Hof-, Haus-, und Staatsarchiv (HHS) could only begin to be explored. There, although there are some catalogs and general guides, the researcher must depend very much on the archival staff.

A manuscript catalog of many of the diplomatic holdings from the *Staatskanzlei* (State Chancellery) files does exist: "Archivbehelf 200/2: Acten und Urkunden betreffend die Staaten und Länder in Ost-Europa, Asien, Afrika," which must be used with a revised typewritten list indicating new numbers and nomenclature. Most of the important material for this study was found in the two Russian series which cover the period. In the first group "Staatenabteilung Russland II," Cartons 95–111 hold the *Berichte* (reports) from St. Petersburg from 1801 to 1806. Other important documents in this group were the scattered cartons of *Weisungen* (instructions), and several cartons marked *Varia* which contain many of the more private letters of the envoys. Cartons 211 and 212 hold the personal correspondence between Alexander and Francis up to 1806; Carton 238 has the valuable "Journal du Colonel Baron de Stutterheim pendant sa mission à St. Pétersbourg" (1804–1805); Carton 227 contains some material on the Wintzingerode missions, and Carton 240 is devoted to the war of 1805.

The second series, "Neuere Akten Staatskanzlei: Russland III," covers the remaining years of Alexander's reign. The reports from St. Petersburg during this period occupy Cartons 1, 3, 5, 7, 9–16, 18–31, 56–59, 62, 63, 67, and 68. Drafts or copies of the instructions fill many of the intervening cartons, while many of the originals of the instructions were consulted in the Austrian embassy archives, "Gesandtschaft Archiv: St. Petersburg" (covered by a separate catalog); Cartons 36–43 cover the period after the Congress of Vienna. The court correspondence — personal and official letters between Alexander and Francis — are available in Russland III, Cartons 46 and 47. Some of the private diplomatic correspondence of officials and many related papers are in the *Varia* files, Cartons 49–53, 55, 61, and 72. Carton 78 contains, under the rather misleading title, "Interzepte (1818–1824)," many originals of the most significant dispatches from Metternich to Lebzeltern, which were apparently acquired later from the Lebzeltern family papers; these were summarized in the volume edited by Grand Duke Nicholas Mikhailovich, (Lebzeltern, *Doneseniia*). This volume also contains selections from Lebzeltern's dispatches from St. Petersburg, drawn from the HHS files; because many included are carelessly edited or are incomplete, citations are given to the original manuscripts.

The "Kongressakten" series, including cartons of materials from Aix-la-Chapelle, Troppau, Laibach, and Verona, contain mostly official papers, protocols, and the journals of the important international congresses of that time. Other scattered volumes were consulted, but they proved to be more tangential.

The papers of an important and relatively unstudied figure, Ludwig von Lebzeltern, Metternich's close confidant and ambassador to Russia, remain in the hands of his descendants in France. There, through the courtesy of Countess de Lévis-Mirepoix, princesse de Robech, I consulted them in the family archives at Brûmare (Eure). Although the gaps in the HHS holdings might lead one to expect more official dispatches and correspondence between Lebzeltern and Metternich, only several drafts were found. There were scant remains of Lebzeltern's private and official correspondence during his period in Russia. Of most interest for this study were some letters from Gentz to Lebzeltern (1821–1828), a private journal from his first mission to Russia (1811–1813), and some of his other diaries, memoirs, and miscellaneous correspondence. A highly selective version of Lebzeltern's fragmentary memoirs, principally containing unidentified fragments of his correspondence and other papers was published by a descendant, Emmanuel de Lévis-Mirepoix, prince de Robech, *Un collaborateur de Metternich. Mémoires et papiers de Lebzeltern* (Paris, 1949).

Metternich's own private papers that are now in Czechoslovakia appear from the bibliographic information at the HHS in Vienna to be tangential to this study. His more important political writings are available in the Vienna archives, and a good selection of his papers appears in the eight volumes edited by his son, Prince Richard Metternich, *Aus Metternichs nachgelassenen Papieren* (Vienna, 1880-1884); a complete French edition was published simultaneously, *Mémoires, documents et écrits divers laissés par le prince de Metternich, chancelier de cour et d'état* (Paris, 1880–1884), but the English version, *Memoirs of Prince Metternich, 1773–1829* (2 vols.; New York, 1881), is abridged, and the translation by Mrs. Alexander Napier is often awkward.

The correspondence and dispatches of Friedrich von Gentz that are most relevant to this study appear in several editions, mostly drawn from the files of the Vienna archives. Particularly revealing are the letters edited by Anton Prokesch von Osten, *Dépêches inédites aux hospodars de Valachie pour servir à l'histoire de la politique européenne (1813 à 1828)* (3 vols.; Paris, 1876–1877), and the three volumes devoted mostly to his correspondence with Metternich, edited by F. C. Wittichen and E. Salzer, *Briefe von und an Friedrich von Gentz* (3 vols.; Munich and Berlin, 1909–1913). In addition to the large amount of published material relating to Metternich and Gentz, the published sources relating to such Austrian leaders as Philipp von Stadion, Ludwig Fürst Starhemberg, Philip von Neumann, and Archduke John of Austria have also been consulted. The historical works by Anton Prokesch von Osten and Adolf Beer, also contain abundant Austrian diplomatic documents.

## *German Sources*

A descriptive survey of the Prussian archives in East Germany is provided in an article by G. Castellan, "Les archives de la République démocratique allemande," *Revue historique*, CCXXI (January–March 1959), 56–89, but there is no reference to diplomatic papers for 1801–1825. Recent published studies do indicate that many diplomatic documents have been preserved from this period in the Deutsches Zentralarchiv in Merseburg and in the Sächsisches Landeshauptarchiv in Dresden, but it was not possible for me to arrange to consult them.

Copies of some important Prussian dispatches from St. Petersburg during Alexander's reign were found among the Papers of the Imperial Russian Historical Society, now in the manuscript division of the Leningrad branch of the Institute of History of the Academy of Sciences (LOII–Fond #113, Carton 17, No. 90); the package is dated "1801–1824," but the fragmentary extracts, apparently part of a publication project never completed, are predominantly from the early years of that period.

Several published collections present important archival materials regarding leading Prussian statesmen. Leopold von Ranke's edition of Hardenberg's papers, *Denkwürdigkeiten des Staatskanzlers Fürsten von Hardenberg* (5 vols.; Leipzig, 1877), was helpful, as were the published papers of Wilhelm von Humboldt, *Gessammelte Schriften*, ed. Albert Leitzmann (19 vols.; Berlin, 1903–1936), especially Vols. 11–13, *Politische Denkschriften*, ed. Bruno Gebhardt, and Vols. 16–17, *Politische Briefe*, ed. Wilhelm Richter, and *Wilhelm und Caroline von Humboldt in ihren Briefen*, ed. Anna von Sydow (7 vols.; Berlin, 1906–1916). Most valuable among the German documents are the published volumes of Stein's papers, particularly because Stein also served as adviser to the emperor Alexander I between 1812 and

1815. The extensive edition by Erich Botzenhart in the 1930's, *Brief-wechsel, Denkschriften und Aufzeichnungen im Auftrag der Reichs-regierung der preussischen Staatsregierung und des deutschen und preussischen Stadtetages* (7 vols.; Berlin, 1931–1937), has now been superseded by the edition of Walther Hubatsch, *Briefe und amtliche Schriften* (6 vols.; Stuttgart, 1957–1965), although the new edition omits some of the letters from Capodistrias to Stein which were important for this study.

## Diplomatic Sources of Lesser Powers

The published reports of several diplomats who represented lesser powers in St. Petersburg during this period enriched my study. Among the most valuable were those of the Swedish minister, Curt von Stedingk, published as *Mémoires posthumes du feld-maréchal comte de Stedingk redigés sur les lettres, dépêches et autres pièces authentiques laissées à sa famille par le général comte de Björnstjerna* (3 vols.; Paris, 1844–1847). A particularly perceptive but biased observer was Joseph de Maistre, the Sardinian minister in St. Petersburg during the early part of the period. His correspondence from that time was published in two editions; *Mémoires politiques et correspondance diplomatique de Joseph de Maistre*, ed. A. Blanc (Paris, 1858), covers the early years 1803–1810, while the later period is covered by *Correspondance diplomatique de Joseph de Maistre, 1811–1817*, ed. A. Blanc (2 vols.; Paris, 1860). Of lesser interest were the reports of the Dutch envoy represented in the volume *Mémoires du général Dirk van Hogendorp, comte de l'empire, publiées par son petit-fils M. le comte D. C. A. van Hogendorp* (The Hague, 1887).

Thanks to the very extensive microfilming project at the United States National Archives, complete files of the ministerial and consular correspondence with the American envoys in St. Petersburg are now readily available. Most important are the ministerial files: United States Department of State, "Despatches from United States Ministers to Russia"; Reels 1–10 cover the period from the establishment of diplomatic relations in 1808 through 1826. Of lesser interest are the first two reels titled "Consular Letters. St. Petersburg," covering from 1794 to 1830.

Of the American ministers during the period, John Quincy Adams was the most important because of his voluminous correspondence and the closeness of his description and observations of the Russian scene. Most of his official reports are available in the Department of State files, and many are published in Volumes 3–5 of *Writings of John Quincy Adams*, ed. Worthington C. Ford (7 vols.; New York, 1913–1917). Some of his private correspondence in St. Petersburg is also published in this edition of his *Writings* and in the collection edited by Charles Francis Adams, Jr., "Correspondence of John Quincy Adams, 1811–1814," *Proceedings of the American Antiquarian Society*, N. S. XXIII (April 1913), 110–169. However, many of his revealing letters from Russia remain in manuscript, now available in *The Adams Papers on Microfilm*; "Letterbooks" of interest include those on Reels 135–141 and 144. His voluminous diary for the period was only partially published in Volumes 2 and 3 of Charles Francis Adams' edition, *Memoirs of John Quincy Adams Comprising Portions of His Diary from 1795 to 1848* (12 vols.; Philadelphia, 1877). The complete manuscript version of his "Diary" from 1809 to 1816 was consulted on Reels 31 and 32. Among other portions of his papers on microfilm, Reels 201 and 202, "Miscellany," contain some material of interest — mostly memoranda from his stay in St. Petersburg, including a description of his library and lists of books purchased. Also of interest in this collection is Reel 329, the diary of Adams' nephew and private secretary, William Steuben Smith, who was left in charge of the legation in St. Petersburg during 1814.

# CHAPTER BIBLIOGRAPHIES

## Chapter 1: The Context of Diplomacy

General characteristics of diplomacy in the early nineteenth century are discussed in several pieces by Harold Nicolson: *Diplomacy*, 3rd ed. (London, 1963), *The Evolution of the Diplomatic Method* (New York, 1954), his published lecture *The Old Diplomacy and the New* (London, 1961), and two volumes by C. K. Webster, *The Art and Practice of Diplomacy* (New York, 1962), and *The Study of Nineteenth-Century Diplomacy* (London, 1915). Also helpful are the essays by Sir E. Satow, "Peacemaking, Old and New," *Cambridge Historical Journal*, I, No. 1 (1923), 23–60; Franz Schnabel, "Bismarck and the End of Classical Diplomacy," *Measure*, II, No. 4 (Fall 1951) 376–385; and the book by Peter Richard Rohden, *Die klassische Diplomatie von Kaunitz bis Metternich* (Leipzig, 1939). Felix Gilbert's article, "The 'New Diplomacy' of the Eighteenth Century," *World Politics*, IV, No. 1 (Oct. 1951), 1–38, discusses some of Woodrow Wilson's 1919 diplomatic ideals in terms of their derivation in the eighteenth-century rational thought of the philosophes. The first volume of Albert Sorel's *L'Europe et la Révolution française*, 4th ed. (8 vols.; Paris, 1897–1906), gives a good picture of many of the diplomatic practices of the early nineteenth century.

The first few chapters of C. K. Webster's two-volume biography of Castlereagh and Harold Temperley's study of Canning present much information about the institutions and the conduct of diplomacy at that time. Both authors also carefully consider the extent to which British procedures presented an exception to the classical "monarchical diplomacy" of the period. On that point, C. K. Webster's essay, "The Machinery of British Policy in the Nineteenth and Twentieth Centuries," in *The Art and Practice of Diplomacy* (New York, 1962), presents a helpful perspective.

Edward Vose Gulick's study, *Europe's Classical Balance of Power: A Case History of the Theory and Practice of One of the Great Concepts of European Statecraft* (Ithaca, 1955), is an admirable analysis of one of the most important concepts behind the diplomacy of the period. Although it is weakest in its treatment of Russian materials, it provides many insights helpful for further analysis of the diplomatic background and aims of the Vienna settlements in 1815. Also concerned with conceptual problems of international relations at that time is B. S. Mirkin-Getsevich's "L'influence de la Révolution française sur le développement du droit international dans l'Europe orientale," *Recueil des cours de l'Académie de Droit International*, XXII, No. 2 (Paris, 1920), 295–457, and Baron Michel de Taube, "Etudes sur le développement historique du droit international dans l'Europe orientale," in the 1926 volume of the same *Recueil*, XI, No. 1 (1926), pp. 341–533. Additional perspective on the development and implementation of plans for international relations in the period is presented by F. H. Hinsley in *Power and the Pursuit of Peace: Theory and Practice in the History of Relations Between States* (Cambridge, 1963); this study also analyzes many of the contemporary ideas on international relations, thus putting some of the views of Alexander I, Czartoryski, and Capodistrias into their historical context.

Charles de Martens' *Manuel diplomatique, ou Précis des droits et des fonctions des agents diplomatiques, suivi d'un recueil d'actes et d'offices pour servir de quide aux personnes qui se destinent à la carrière politique* (Paris, 1822) is an important source for the study of the customs and diplomatic procedures of that period; this volume, published in many subsequent nineteenth-century editions, usually under the title *Guide diplomatique*, was a basic handbook for diplomats. Many of the formulas of diplomatic precedence were outlined in the regulation of March 19, 1815, annex No. 17 to the Treaty of Paris of June 9, 1815; the original text and most of the other official pronouncements of the congress are in L. J. B. Chodzko (Count d'Angeberg), *Le Congrès de Vienne et les traités de 1815* (4 vols.; Paris, 1864), Vol. III. See also the English version in E. Hertslet, ed., *The Map of Europe by Treaty, Showing the Various Political and Territorial Changes which have taken place since the General Peace of 1814* (4 vols.; London, 1875–1891), I, 62–63. From the standpoint of ideas and procedures, it is interesting to compare the influential book by François de Callières, *De la manière de négocier avec les souverains . . .* , originally published in Amsterdam 1716, and available in an able English translation by A. F. Whyte: *On the Manner of Negotiating with Princes; on the Uses of Diplomacy; the Choice of Ministers and Envoys; and the Personal Qualities Necessary for Success in Missions Abroad* (New York, 1919). The training and ideals for diplomats are suggested in a document written by an official in the French foreign office, Comte d'Hauterive, "Conseils à un élève du ministère des relations extérieures," printed as part of "L'éducation d'un diplomate," in *Revue d'histoire diplomatique*, XV, No. 2 (1901), 161–224, suggesting the reading for young members of the French diplomatic service in the early nineteenth century. A brief memorandum for Russian diplomats by an influential publicist in the Russian foreign ministry is revealing, as well: Alexander Sturdza, "Avis aux jeunes diplomats," in Volume 3 of *Oeuvres posthumes, religieuses, historiques, philosophiques et littéraires d'Alexandre de Stourdza* (5 vols.; Paris, 1858–1861).

There is no adequate study of the development of the Russian foreign ministry or the function and role of the foreign minister. The official centennial history of the foreign ministry, *Ocherk istorii Ministerstva Inostrannykh del, 1802–1902* (St. Petersburg, 1902) provides a general descriptive summary and includes two background chapters on the period before 1802. The report of V. A. Polenov, "Obozrenie prezhnego i nyneshnego sostoianiia Ministerstva Inostrannykh del" (1837), *SIRIO*, XXXI, 163–196, sketches some of the background of the ministry but emphasizes especially the reforms made in the reign of Nicholas I. Other generalized notes are in Sergei S. Tatishchev, *Iz proshlogo russkoi diplomati. Istoricheskie issledovaniia i polemicheskie stat'i* (St. Petersburg, 1890), especially in the first essay, "Russkaia diplomatiia staraia i novaia," pp. 3–71.

The severe criticism of administration in the Russian foreign ministry is well substantiated by comparison with western European governments. A survey of the situation in the French foreign ministry appears in Emmanuel de Lévis-Mirepoix's *Le Ministère des Affaires Étrangères. Organisation de l'administration centrale et des services extérieures (1793–1933)* (Angers, 1934). More scholarly and thorough is the study by Frédéric Masson, *Le Département des Affaires Étrangères pendant la Révolution, 1787–1804* (Paris, 1877); in his concluding chapter, Masson discusses the ministry under Talleyrand up to June 1807; a short appendix covering 1814 to 1877 gives only a summary of the later period. The opening chapter of Webster's *Castlereagh, 1815–1822*, as well as several sections in the preceding volume, give a very good idea of the work and function of the Foreign Office in Great Britain.

Several biographical essays on the most important chancellors and ministers appear in Constantin de Grunwald's *Trois siècles de diplo-*

*matie russe* (Paris, 1945), and Aleksandr V. Tereshchenko presents brief descriptions, particularly on chancellors before the nineteenth century, in *Opyt obozreniia zhizni sanovnikov, upravliavshikh inostrannymi delami v Rossii* (St. Petersburg, 1837). Longer biographies of many diplomats appear in the incomplete *Russkii biograficheskii slovar*. A few Russian diplomats are included with many foreign colleagues in the somewhat popularized collection by Jean-Baptiste Capefigue, *Les diplomates européens* (4 vols.; Paris, 1843–1847). On a more general level, some relevant problems of Russian officialdom are discussed in the essay by Marc Raeff, "The Russian Autocracy and Its Officials," in *Russian Thought and Politics*, ed. Hugh McLean and others (The Hague, 1957; "Harvard Slavic Studies," Vol. IV), pp. 77–91. The outlook of some of the Russian gentry prominent in the foreign office at the end of the eighteenth and early nineteenth centuries is considered in more detail by Raeff in *The Origins of the Russian Intelligentsia: The Eighteenth Century Nobility* (New York, 1966).

The best, but still incomplete, list of Russian diplomatic representatives in this period is in an appendix to the centennial history of the foreign ministry mentioned above. Consideration of this list makes clear the meagerness of the representation in non-European areas. The dissertation by John Wentworth Strong, "Russian Relations with Khiva, Bukhara, and Kokand, 1800–1858" (Harvard University, 1964), documents how extremely limited Russian contacts and interest in Central Asia were in the first quarter of the nineteenth century. George Alexander Lensen's *The Russian Push Toward Japan: Russo-Japanese Relations, 1697–1875* (Princeton, 1959) makes clear that the mission of Rezanov and Krusenstern to Japan (1804–1805) had no positive diplomatic significance. The recent study of Russian-American relations based on thorough archival research by N. N. Bolkhovitinov, *Stanovlenie russko-amerikanskikh otnoshenii, 1775–1815* (Moscow, 1966), fills in many details of Russian diplomatic activities in North America, but makes it clear that these remained dependent on or subsidiary to involvements in Europe.

The collection of essays which grew out of a 1961 conference at Yale, *Russian Foreign Policy: Essays in Historical Perspective*, ed. Ivo J. Lederer (New Haven, 1962), while concerned chiefly with post-1861 developments, presents many insights and helps conceptualize some important problems, but the essays do not give enough detail to be of much specific help for this book. Gordon Craig's essay, "Techniques of Negotiation," helps put Russian diplomatic methods of those times in a European context. Richard E. Pipes's essay, "Domestic Politics and Foreign Affairs," reinforces my conclusion of the inconsequential effect of domestic public pressures on foreign policy and the unimportance of "national interest" in the determination of policy, while Robert C. Tucker's article, "Autocrats and Oligarchs," reaffirms the importance of the autocratic personality in Russian diplomacy and emphasizes the weighty role of individuals compared to economic and other impersonal factors in the determination of foreign policy. Also of interest are Cyril Black's analysis of theoretical and strategic factors in Russian foreign policy and the specific essays on policy in action in the European political system, the Balkans, Africa, the Middle East, and the Far East, by Hajo Holborn, Ivo J. Lederer, Sergius Yakobson, Firuz Kazemzadeh, and Donald W. Treadgold, respectively. Robert M. Slusser's "The Role of the Foreign Ministry" pertains predominantly to the later period, but fails to consider the position of foreign minister adequately. Martin Malia kindly made available to me his insightful essay "Western Attitudes Towards Russia," originally presented at the same conference, which is being prepared separately for publication as a book.

There are no general treatments of Russian foreign relations during Alexander's reign which are entirely satisfactory, although a tremendous volume of material is listed in general and specialized bibliographies. The most recent textbook accounts by N. S. Kiniapina, *Vneshniaia politika Rossii pervoi poloviny XIX veka* (Moscow, 1963), and the early chapters of Barbara Jelavich's *A Century of Russian Foreign Policy, 1814–1914* (Philadelphia, 1964) tend toward oversimplification. The earlier narrative treatment by A. A. Lobanov-Rostovsky, *Russia and Europe 1789–1825* (Durham, N.C., 1947), is highly derivative and at points misleading. The relevant chapters in the latest edition of the three-volume Soviet *Istoriia diplomatii* (Moscow, 1959–1965) provide the best factual background of Russian foreign relations, but they are overshadowed from the point of view of interpretive interest by many of the general studies of European diplomacy during the first quarter of the century.

## Chapter 2: The Tsar-Diplomat

This sketch of the emperor and his attitudes is derived chiefly from published sources and from archival materials most specifically related to diplomacy. Intended only to provide general background for later discussion of his foreign ministers, it makes no attempt to cover many important aspects of his reign, particularly domestic developments.

Many of Alexander's private papers and those of several persons close to him have been destroyed — some by order of Nicholas I, some by accident, some by Alexander's own associates or their descendants; it would appear that little important correspondence and few other personal documents have still to be published. The great majority of the emperor's extant personal papers and those of his close associates, were used by N. K. Schilder in his four-volume court history, published in a second edition in 1904–1905. The notes and appendixes to this study, the fullest and most closely documented account of the reign, include much primary material. The earlier, but less well annotated six-volume account by M. I. Bogdanovich, *Istoriia tsarstvovaniia Imperatora Aleksandra I i Rossiia v ego vremia* (6 vols.; St. Petersburg, 1869–1871), also contains much primary materials. Much valuable correspondence and other unpublished materials relating to the emperor were appended to the interesting essay by the Grand Duke Nikolai Mikhailovich, *Imperator Aleksandr I. Opyt istoricheskogo issledovaniia* (2 vols.; St. Petersburg, 1912), published simultaneously in French as *L'empereur Alexandre Ier. Essai d'étude historique*; a second one-volume edition was published in St. Petersburg in 1914, and the essay itself was later translated into French by Baron N. Wrangel and published without the documentary appendixes as *Le tsar Alexandre Ier* (Paris, 1931). The first Russian edition contains the most extensive documentary appendixes; the second edition cut more than half the appendixes, but added a few documents, most notably pertaining to Alexander's death. In all cases the editing of the documents leaves much to be desired.

Additional personal correspondence of the emperor is published in widely scattered works. His correspondence with the Prussian royal family is available in the edition by Paul Bailleu, *Briefwechsel Königs Friedrich Wilhelm's III und der Königin Luise mit Kaiser Alexander I nebst ergänzenden fürstlichen Korrespondenzen* (Leipzig, 1900; "Publicationen aus den K. Preussischen Staatsarchiven, LXXV"), and with the French title, *Correspondance inédite du roi Frédéric Guillaume III et de la reine Louise avec l'empereur Alexandre Ier d'après les originaux des archives de Berlin et de Saint-Pétersbourg* (Paris, 1900). Some of Alexander's correspondence with the Austrian emperor appears as appendixes to three studies by Adolf

Beer: *Zur Geschichte der Oesterreichischen Politik in den Jahren 1801 und 1802* (Vienna, 1874), *Oesterreich und Russland in den Jahren 1804 und 1805, mit der Correspondenz zwischen Alexander I und Franz II* (Vienna, 1875), and *Zehn Jahre oesterreichischer Politik, 1801–1810* (Leipzig, 1877); but the original and complete correspondence was consulted in the Vienna archives, HHS/Russ. II, 211–212, and Russ. III, 46–47. His correspondence with his sister Catherine has been published: *Perepiska imperatora Aleksandra I s sestroi velikoi kniaginei Ekaterinoi Pavlovnoi,* ed. Grand Duke Nikolai Mikhailovich (St. Petersburg, 1910), and in an English translation by Henry Havelock, *Scenes of Russian Court Life, Being the Correspondence of Alexander I with his Sister Catherine* (London, n.d.); see also the French extracts and comment by Léonce Pingaud, "L'empereur Alexandre Ier et la grande-duchesse Catherine Paulovna d'après leur correspondance," *Revue d'histoire diplomatique,* XXV (1911, No. 3), 379–395. Some of Alexander's revealing correspondence with his mother has been published in several places: "Nakanune Erfurtskogo svidaniia 1808 goda," ed. N. K. Schilder, *Russkaia starina,* XCVIII (April 1899), 3–24; "Pis'ma imperatritsy Marii Feodorovny k imperatoru Aleksandru I-mu," ed. Grand Duke Nikolai Mikhailovich, *Russkii arkhiv,* XLIX (1911, No. 1), pp. 129–172, and duplicated in "Lettres de l'impératrice Marie Féodorowna à l'empereur Alexandre Ier," *Zeitschrift für Osteuropäische Geschichte,* I (1911, No. 4), 481–510; "Pis'mo imperatora Aleksandra I imperatritse Marii Feodorovne posle vziatia Parizha," ed. E. Shumigorskii, *Russkaia starina,* CLVII (March 1914), 483–490, the latter text is also in the appendix of N. K. Schilder, *Imperator Nikolai Pervyi, ego zhizn i tsarstvovanie* (2 vols.; St. Petersburg, 1903). Some of Alexander's letters to Arakcheev, Kutuzov, Shishkov, and others are in "Ukazy, reskripty, pis'ma, doneseniia, predaniia, zametki: Tsarstvovanie Aleksandra I-go," *Russkaia starina,* I (Jan.–June 1870), 440–513. Alexander's correspondence with Bernadotte is published in two editions: "Lettres inédites de l'empereur Alexandre Ier et de Bernadotte," *Miscellanea Napoleonica,* Ser. III–IV (Rome, 1898), pp. 679–727, and *Correspondance inédite de l'empereur Alexandre et de Bernadotte pendant l'année 1812* (Paris, 1909). Also of interest are his correspondence with Thomas Jefferson, published by N. Hans, "Tsar Alexander I and Jefferson: Unpublished Correspondence," *SEER,* XXXII (Dec. 1953), 215–225; his letters to the French conservative publicist Nicholas Bergasse, published with an introduction by Etienne Lang, *Un défenseur des principes tradition-nels sous la Révolution: Nicolas Bergasse, 1750–1832* (Paris, 1810); his correspondence with Madame de Staël: "Lettres de l'empereur Alexandre Ier et Mme de Staël (1814–1817)," *Revue de Paris* (Jan 1, 1897), 5–22, and in Russian translation, ed. N. K. Schilder, in *Vestnik Evropy*, XXXI (Dec. 1896), 570–594; several letters to Countess Edling (Roxandra Sturdza): "Pis'ma imperatora Aleksandra Pavlovicha k R. S. Sturdze (Grafine Edling)," *Russkii arkhiv*, XXVI (1888, No. 11) 373–377; and his spiritual outpouring to Princess Meshcherska revealed in "Pis'mo imperatora Aleksandra Pervogo k kniagine Sofii Sergeevne Meshcherskoi," *Russkii arkhiv*, XXIV (1886, No. 3), 403–408. A manuscript collection of drafts of his letters to various women is in TsGAOR, 728/1/1008.

The most scholarly single volume on Alexander's reign is Theodor Schiemann, *Kaiser Alexander I und die Ergebnisse seiner Lebensar-beit* (Berlin, 1904), published as *Geschichte Russlands unter Kaiser Nikolaus I*, Vol. I, and subsequently translated into Russian. Aside from Schilder, Bogdanovich, and Grand Duke Nikolai Mikhailovich, few published studies of Alexander I, have used any additional origi-nal sources. The extensive treatment by K. Waliszewski, *La Russie il y a cent ans. Le règne d'Alexandre Ier* (3 vols.; Paris, 1923–1925), is helpful for some of its French documentation and bibliography, but it tends to be overly colorful in its approach. Other interpretive essays of particular interest include A. E. Presniakov, *Aleksandr I* (Petro-grad, 1924), S. M. Solov'ev, *Imperator Aleksandr Pervyi, politika, diplomatiia* (St. Petersburg, 1877), A. A. Kizevetter, "Aleksandr I," in *Istoricheskie siluety, liudi i sobytiia* (Berlin, 1931), pp. 124–145, and A. Fateev, "Le problème de l'individu et de l'homme d'état dans la personalité historique d'Alexandre I, empereur de toutes les Rus-sies," *Zapiski nauchno-issledovatel'skogo ob"edineniia, Russkii svo-bodnyi universitet v Prage*, New Series, III (1936), 139–178; V (1937), 1–36; VI (1938), 1–42; and IX (1939), 1–47.

The correspondence and other papers relating to Alexander's wife, Empress Elizabeth, are presented with a brief sketch about her by Grand Duke Nikolai Mikhailovich in *Imperatritsa Elisaveta Alek-seevna, supruga imperatora Aleksandra I* (3 vols.; St. Petersburg, 1908–1909), also published in a French edition, *L'impératrice Elisa-beth, épouse d'Alexandre Ier* (3 vols.; Paris, 1908–1909). Many de-tails of Alexander's relationship to Elizabeth and her reactions to the

Russian court are available there, especially in Elizabeth's revealing letters to her mother.

For a statement of the mysterious facts supporting the legend of the religious hermit, Feodor Kuzmich, who was supposed to have been Alexander I, see the appendix in Leonid I. Strakhovsky, *Alexander I of Russia: The Man Who Defeated Napoleon* (New York, 1947). One of the important links in Strakhovsky's version was the assertion that Alexander was taken from the Crimea to the Holy Land in 1825 on a yacht belonging to the British ambassador, Lord Cathcart; proof of the voyage was supposed to lie in the unopened Cathcart Papers, but my thorough examination of the family papers in London and Devon uncovered no clues whatsoever. For a summary of recent discussion of the legend in Soviet historical circles, see S. B. Okun and N. N. Belianchikov, "Suschestvuet li 'Taina Fedora Kuzmicha'?" *Voprosy istorii*, 1967, No. 1, pp. 191–201.

Alexander's tutor, Frédéric-César Laharpe, has been the subject of numerous studies: Those of particular note include Charles Monnard, *Notice biographique sur le général Frédéric-César de La Harpe, Précepteur de l'empereur de Russie, Alexandre Ier* (Paris, 1838), and two articles by L. Mogéon: "Frédéric-César de la Harpe, précepteur," *Revue historique vaudoise*, XLVI (May–June 1938), 83–102, and "L'influence de Laharpe sur Alexandre avec des témoignages de souverains et écrivains russes," *ibid.*, pp. 129–145. Many Laharpe papers relating to Alexander and Russia have been published. Much of Alexander's correspondence with Laharpe is printed in "Pis'ma imperatora Aleksandra I-go i drugikh osob tsarstvennogo doma k F. Ts. Lagarpu," *SIRIO*, V, 1–121. Some is in Schilder's appendixes, and other letters are scattered. Some of Laharpe's reflections and attitudes on Russia are revealed in the publication of N. P. Durov, "Zapiski Lagarpa o vospitanii velikikh kniazei Aleksandra i Constantina Pavlovichei, 1786–1794," ed. N. P. Durov, *Russkaia starina*, I (Jan.–June 1870), 152–205, and II (July–Dec. 1870), 161–174, 253–266. Some of his memoranda, a few hitherto unpublished, remain among Alexander's papers in TsGAOR, 728/1/536.

Alexander's relations with Napoleon, which so dominated the diplomatic stage in the first half of his reign, are covered in many studies. Most important for my purposes because of the many documents they contain were Sergei Tatishchev, *Alexandre Ier et Napoleon d'après leur correspondance inédite, 1801–1812* (Paris, 1891), and Albert Vandal, *Napoléon et Alexandre Ier. L'alliance russe sous le Premier*

*Empire*, 2nd ed. (3 vols.; Paris, 1900). These two studies are discussed by Albert Sorel in "Napoléon et Alexandre — L'alliance et le conflit," *Lectures historiques* (Paris, 1894), pp. 169–196. More recent, and the result of extensive archival research, is the short monograph by V. G. Sirotkin, *Duel' dvukh diplomatii. Rossiia i Frantsiia v 1801–1812gg.* (Moscow, 1966), a study which sheds important light on Alexander's simultaneous policies of war and peace.

There has not been any completely successful appraisal of Alexander's relationship to Metternich despite several attempts, such as Léonce Pingaud's "Alexandre Ier et Metternich d'après les rapports de Lebzeltern (1816–1826)," *Revue d'histoire diplomatique*, XXVIII (1914, No. 2), 161–177, and Constantin de Grunwald's "Metternich et Alexandre Ier," *Monde Slave*, XV (1938, No. 1), 29–64.

Many phases of Russia's relations with Italy throughout Alexander's reign are treated by Giuseppe Berti in *Rossiia i ital'ianskie gosudarstva v period Risordzhimento* (Moscow, 1959; the original Italian edition, *Russia e stati italiani nel Risorgimento,* was published in Rome in 1957); this lengthy, closely documented study devotes considerable detail to several of the foreign ministers, notably Czartoryski and Capodistrias.

Relatively little work has been done on general social and political activities during Alexander's reign. The recent study by A. V. Predtechenskii, *Ocherki obshchestvenno-politicheskoi istorii Rossii v pervoi chetverti XIX veka* (Moscow, 1957), is helpful but adds little documentation. Also of interest is the prerevolutionary study by the liberal Westernizer, A. N. Pypin, *Obshchestvennoe dvizenie v Rossii pri Aleksandre* I, 3rd ed. (St. Petersburg, 1900). The thorough, scholarly study by Marc Raeff, *Michael Speransky: Statesman of Imperial Russia, 1772–1839* (The Hague, 1957), discusses Speranskii's reform projects. Raeff's chapter on Alexander's "constitutionalism" presents a debatable interpretation of the emperor's political ideals, overemphasizing its legalistic basis; the bibliographies are extremely helpful for published materials. See also Raeff's article on early attempts at reform, "Le climat politique et les projets de réforme dans les premières années du règne d'Alexandre Ier," *Cahiers du monde russe et soviétique*, II (Oct.–Dec. 1961), 415–433, and his more general remarks in "Some Reflections on Russian Liberalism," *Russian Review*, XVIII, No. 3 (July 1959), 218–230. George Vernadsky analyzes some of the sources of Alexander's ideas in "Reforms Under Czar Alexander I: French and American Influences," *Review of Poli-*

*tics,* IX (Jan. 1947), 47–64; and he analyzes Alexander's later ideas and reform projects in *La charte constitutionelle de l'Empire russe de l'an 1820* (Paris, 1933), where in the course of presenting the text and an analysis of the 1820 Novosil'tsev constitution, he further documents Alexander's continuing interest in enlightened reform.

A well researched and highly readable biography, *Arakcheev: Grand Vizier of the Russian Empire* (New York, 1968), by Michael Jenkins, has just been published to fill a significant gap in the literature on major figures of Alexander's reign. Unfortunately the author was not permitted to utilize the extensive archival holdings in the Soviet Union related to Arakcheev which must be tapped for a definitive work on the subject, but he has done an admirable job of analyzing his role and relationship to the emperor based on extensive published sources. I appreciate the kindness of the Dial Press in making an advance copy of this book available to me. For a more complete bibliography on the subject, however, one should also consult the earlier unpublished dissertation by Kenneth R. Whiting, "Aleksei Andreevich Arakcheev" (Harvard University, 1951). Both Jenkins and Whiting substantiate my own findings which demonstrate Arakcheev's complete disassociation from foreign policy. See also the interesting essay by A. A. Kizevetter, "Imperator Aleksandr I i Arakcheev," in *Istoricheskie ocherki* (Moscow, 1912), pp. 287–401.

Alexander Koyré's *La philosophie et le problème national en Russie au début de XIXe siècle* (Paris, 1929) gives some background on intellectual currents of the times as well as posing the problem of national attitudes. George Vernadsky in "Alexandre Ier et le problème Slave pendant la première moitié de son règne," *Revue des études Slaves,* VII (1927), 94–111, deals more specifically with Slavic national aspirations and the ideas of uniting the Southern Slavs to support their liberation. This issue in the year 1812 is discussed in a more recent dissertation and subsequent article by V. V. Pugachev, "K voprosu o planakh Aleksandra I otnositelno slavianskogo i nemetskogo natsional'no-osvoboditel'nogo dvizheniia v 1812 godu," *Uchenye zapiski molotovskogo gosudarstvennogo universiteta,* VI, No. 4 (1951), 116–120.

The general problem of Russia's interests to the south is treated in an unpublished dissertation by Norman Saul, "Russia and the Mediterranean, 1797–1807" (Columbia University, 1965), which plays up the role of the threat to Russia in the Mediterranean in the Third Coalition. The patterns of trade development in this area and the lack of political support for it in the early years of the nineteenth century is well demonstrated in the dissertation by Patricia M. Herlihy, "Russian Grain and Mediterranean Markets, 1774–1861" (University of Pennsylvania, 1963). Among the recent published literature on the Eastern Question, of particular note is the study based on documents in the Russian foreign ministry archives by A. M. Stanislavskaia, *Russko-angliiskie otnosheniia i problemy sredizemnomor'ia, 1798–1807* (Moscow, 1962), which deals with the Eastern Question in the context of Anglo-Russian relations; in the course of her study, Stanislavskaia assesses much of the important historical literature on the subject.

Many aspects of Russian economic development in the early nineteenth century are covered in the recent volume by William L. Blackwell *The Beginnings of Russian Industrialization, 1800–1860* (Princeton, 1968); what this admittedly derivative volume lacks in structural analysis and interpretive nuances it makes up for in abundant details culled from a wide variety of published sources.

Documents relating to the Polish problem are collected by L. J. B. Chodzko (Comte d'Angeberg) in *Recueil des traités, conventions et actes diplomatiques concernant la Pologne, 1762–1862* (Paris, 1862). Alexander's Polish projects and policies are summarized by Léonce Pingaud, "L'empereur Alexandre Ier, Roi de Pologne — La 'Kongressovka' (1801–1825)," *Revue d'histoire diplomatique*, XXXII, No. 4 (1918), 513–540, by Pierre Morane, "Alexandre Ier, Constantin et la Pologne (1815–1825)," *Revue des études historiques*, LXXVI (1910), 264–289, and more recently by William Leslie Blackwell, "Alexander I and Poland: The Foundations of his Polish Policy and Its Repercussions in Russia, 1801–1825" (unpublished dissertation, Princeton University, 1959); in the latter, the scope and problems are too loosely defined and the sources too limited to make a significant contribution.

Earlier studies of Russian religious movements during Alexander's reign by A. N. Pypin and S. R. Tompkins were less helpful for this work than the recent unpublished dissertation by Judith C. Zacek, "The Russian Bible Society, 1812–1826" (Columbia, 1964), from which a most helpful article, "The Russian Bible Society and the Russian Orthodox Church," was published in *Church History*, XXXV, No. 4 (Dec. 1966), 411–437. The article by E. J. Knapton, "The Origins of the Treaty of Holy Alliance," *History*, new ser. XXVI (Sept. 1941), 132–140, summarizes much of the earlier literature on the background of the Holy Alliance and provides a helpful bibliography, but it only partly clarifies the thorny issue. Of particular significance are the studies by Werner Näf, *Zur Geschichte der Heiligen Allianz* (Bern, 1928; "Berner Untersuchungen zur allgemeinen Geschichte," Vol. 1), analyzing Metternich's "corrections," and Hildegard Schaeder, *Autokratie und Heilige Allianz* (Darmstadt, 1963), an only slightly revised edition of the much criticized 1934 study *Die Dritte Koalition und die Heilige Allianz.*

Madame de Krüdener and her alleged influence on Alexander are treated in a host of literature. H. L. Empaytaz, *Notice sur Alexandre, empereur de Russie,* 2nd ed. (Geneva, 1840), is an account by a man who officiated in the household of Madame de Krüdener, recording several interviews with the emperor. The two-volume account by Charles Eynard, *Vie de Madame de Krüdener* (Paris, 1849), contains the texts of many letters, especially the correspondence with Roxandra Sturdza through whom Alexander first met Madame de Krüdener. In his extensive scholarly biography, *The Lady of the Holy Alliance: The Life of Julie de Krüdener* (New York, 1939), E. J. Knapton demonstrates conclusively that she had nothing to do with drafting the Holy Alliance. The more recent study by her descendant Francis Ley *Madame de Krüdener et son temps, 1764–1824* (Paris, 1961), which uses many hitherto unpublished manuscripts from family archives, further substantiates the same point and provides an extensive bibliography on the subject. There is also abundant literature on many of the other mystical figures who were in touch with the emperor. *Madame Swetchine. Sa vie et ses oeuvres,* 4th ed. (2 vols.; Paris, 1861), by Count Alfred Frédéric Pierre Falloux, details the life of this admirer of Saint-Martin, who was close to Alexander and others of the emperor's associates. See also Ernest Seillière, *Le coeur et la raison de Madame Swetchine d'après des documents inédits,* 2nd ed. (Paris, 1924). Eugene Susini analyzes the thought of the Catholic mystic Baader, who had some connections with the emperor and several of his entourage, in his detailed study *Franz von Baader et le romantisme mystique* (2 vols.; Paris, 1942); these two volumes titled *La Philosophie de Franz von Baader* constitute parts 2 and 3 of a projected study. Susini has also published a comprehensive and carefully edited collection of Baader's correspondence: *Lettres inédites de Franz von Baader* (3 vols.; Paris, 1942–1951); the second and third volumes consist entirely of notes and commentary. The relations of the emperor with the lesser-known Madame La Bouche are explored

in an article based on some of her letters found among the Richelieu
Papers by Guillaume de Bertier de Sauvigny, "L'extravagante equipée
de la prophétesse marseillaise à la cour extravagante du tsar Alexandre Ier," *Le Figaro littéraire* (Dec. 10, 1960), pp. 5–6.

## Chapter 3: Panin, Kochubei, and Vorontsov

A brief outline of the life of Panin written by A. G. Brückner, "Nikita Petrovich Panin," is found in *Russkii biograficheskii slovar*, XIII,
205–211. Brückner was the editor of the seven-volume collection
of Panin's papers *Materialy dlia zhizneopisaniia grafa Nikity Petro-
vicha Panina, 1770–1837* (St. Petersburg, 1888–1892). A brief essay on
his life based on the Brückner collection was published in German by
J. Engelmann, "Vice-Kanzler Graf Nikita Petrowitsch Panin," *Bal-
tische Monatsschrift*, XLI (1894), 199–226, 261–282. The first five
volumes of the Brückner collection document Panin's activities before
1801. Panin's term in the foreign ministry under Alexander I is covered by Volume 6, and Volume 7 contains materials from his retirement years. Panin's correspondence with S. R. Vorontsov, much of it
duplicating letters in the Brückner edition, is published in *Arkhiv
kniazia Vorontsova*, Vol. 11. Panin sketched his early life in a letter
to S. R. Vorontsov dated February 30, 1799 (*AKV*, XI, 69–77). Additional papers, again with much duplication are available in *SIRIO*,
Vol. 77, and *VPR*, Vol. 1. Most of the manuscript Panin Papers are
now in TsGADA in Moscow, where they have been gathered from
several holdings; but all the manuscripts shown to me there had been
published in Brückner's collection.

There is no adequate study of Kochubei. A helpful description of
his life was published by N. D. Chechulin, "Viktor Pavlovich Kochubei," in *Russkii biograficheskii slovar*, IX, 366–382; approximately
the same essay was published separately as *Kniaz Viktor Pavlovich
Kochubei, 1768–1834. Ocherk zhizni i deiatelnosti* (St. Petersburg,
1900). A eulogy published the year of his death by Remi Gillet, *A la
mémoire du prince Kotseubey, chancelier de l'Empire de Russie* (St.
Petersburg, 1834), sketches his life briefly with only scant detail. His
early diplomatic background is summarized in a letter by S. R. Vorontsov to N. P. Panin (Oct. 23, 1798, *NPP*, III, 628–629), and Tatishchev
treats his service as foreign minister in a short section of his essay on
Czartoryski "Vneshnie dela v upravlenii grafa Kochubeia," *Iz proshlogo russkoi diplomatii*, pp. 295–307.

Kochubei's early relationship with the emperor is explored, and extracts from their personal correspondence published, in an article by T. Bogdanovich, "Iz perepiski Aleksandra I s V. P. Kochubeem," *Russkoe proshloe*, 1923, No. 5, pp. 101–111. Selections from Kochubei's correspondence with the Vorontsov brothers are published in the Bartenev collection; correspondence with Simon Romanovich is printed in *AKV*, Vol. 18, and with Alexander Romanovich in *AKV*, Vol. 14. His views on reform and on foreign policy can be followed in Stroganov's abbreviated minutes of the Secret Committee meetings, published in the second volume of Grand Duke Nicholas' edition, *Graf P. A. Stroganov (1774–1817). Istoricheskoe issledovanie epokhi imperatora Aleksandra I* (3 vols.; St. Petersburg, 1902). A few of his letters to A. K. Razumovskii are included in the Vasilchikov publication, *Les Razoumowski*, Vol. 2; additional diplomatic materials pertaining to his ministry are included in *SIRIO*, Vols. 77 and 82, and in *VPR*, Vol. 1.

The Kochubei family papers are now in TsGADA in Moscow; however, a careful check of the two-part inventory for Fond #1445, "Kochubei," revealed nothing of interest for Victor Pavlovich during his year in the College of Foreign Affairs. The fond contains mostly the papers of earlier or later members of his family. It has not been possible to locate copies of his important memoranda on foreign policy from 1801 and 1802 (possibly in AVPR), nor have I found any remains of his personal papers from this period, although they may turn up elsewhere.

Unfortunately, there is no published study of Alexander Romanovich Vorontsov. Vorontsov started writing his autobiography shortly before his death in 1805, but he only reached 1760: "Avtobiograficheskie pokazaniia grafa Aleksandra Romanovicha Vorontsova: Notice sur ma vie et les événements différents qui se sont passés tant en Russie qu'en Europe pendant ce temps-là" (*AKV*, V, 1–87). Selections from his correspondence and papers have been published in the forty-volume collection from the Vorontsov family archives edited by Bartenev (see above). The portions of the collection comprising his archives are described in the final index volume *AKV, Rospic,* pp. 31–45; for his letters from the period in the foreign ministry, see especially Volumes 5, 28, 30, and 32. Several reports, memoranda, and general declarations on foreign policy were printed in *AKV*, XI; several more appeared in *SIRIO*, Vols. 77 and 78, and a few additional documents have recently been published in *VPR*, Vol. 1. But it is difficult to reconstruct Vorontsov's views during his ministry because many of his papers and crucial parts of his correspondence are not available and could not be found among the manuscript papers in TsGADA and LOII; neither could it be determined whether important papers relating to his ministry were to be found in *AVPR*.

Several important sets of papers relating to Vorontsov are in the Czartoryski Papers in the National Museum in Cracow. These include two large bound volumes of letters from Vorontsov to Czartoryski: CA 5529/IV, covering 1804, and CA 5530/IV, covering 1805, which contain drafts in his own hand and copies by a secretary. A large volume of letters from Count S. R. Vorontsov to Czartoryski and A. R. Vorontsov from 1801 to 1807, CA 5528/IV, mostly contains personal letters in his own hand, but they have little bearing on the ministry of Alexander Romanovich. Another volume "Worontzoff-1804," CA 5531/IV, contains additional miscellaneous materials, including an interesting collection of memoranda drawn up by Vorontsov on the eve of his retirement — fols. 1–63, "Quatre notices pour Mr. le Prince Adam Czartoryski."

Vorontsov's connections with Radishchev and his role in drafting the so-called "Charter for the Russian People" are discussed in Georg Sacke, *Graf A. Vorontcov, A. N. Radiščev und der "Gnadenbrief für das Russische Volk"* (Emsdetten, 1937), and D. M. Lang, *The First Russian Radical, Alexander Radishchev* (London, 1959). An English translation of the Charter, edited by Marc Raeff, is included in *Plans for Political Reform in Imperial Russia, 1730–1905* (Englewood Cliffs, N.J., 1966), pp. 75–84.

More work needs to be done on the background of diplomatic developments during the reign of Alexander's father, Paul I. The dissertation by Clara J. Tucker "The Foreign Policy of Tsar Paul I" (Syracuse University, 1965) is more satisfactory than most standard text accounts, but it is based on limited published sources and lacks depth in places. Hugh A. Ragsdale investigated "Russian Diplomacy in the Age of Napoleon: The Franco-Russian Rapprochement of 1800–1801," in his dissertation (Virginia, 1964), from which he drew the article , "The Origins of Bonaparte's Russian Policy," *Slavic Review*, XXVII (March 1968), 85–90, but the subject needs further archival investigation. A helpful analysis of the abortive expedition to India in 1801 is provided by John. W. Strong in "Russia's Plans for an Invasion of India in 1801," *Canadian Slavonic Papers*, VII (Toronto, 1965), 114–126.

For a recent Soviet discussion of relations with England during the early years of Alexander's reign, especially for background on the Russian-British convention in the spring of 1801, see Stanislavskaia, *Russko-angliiskie otnosheniia i problemy sredizemnomor'ia, 1798– 1807*. The 1802 overtures toward forming an Anglo-Russian alliance are documented by Harold Beeley in "A Project of Alliance with Russia in 1802," *English Historical Review*, XLIX (July 1934), 497–502. For Russian relations with Prussia and the background and effects of the Memel interview in the spring of 1802, the most thorough study remains that of Heinrich Ulmann, *Russisch-Preussische Politik unter Alexander I und Friedrich Wilhelm III bis 1806* (Leipzig, 1899), especially pp. 32–47.

# Chapter 4: Czartoryski, Spokesman for Concerted Action

There is extensive literature on Czartoryski. The biography by the Polish émigré Marian Kukiel, *Czartoryski and European Unity, 1770–1861* (Princeton, 1955), contains an extensive but yet incomplete bibliography. While extremely sympathetic to his hero, Kukiel presents the most complete study available on Czartoryski's life and political activities. The author directed the Czartoryski Museum in Cracow before 1939, but unfortunately he wrote the book in exile, and therefore was not able to draw on the Cracow manuscript material when writing. He used the British Foreign Office archives and, for the later periods after 1831, some of the Czartoryski Papers available in the West; Kukiel's chapters on Czartoryski's role under Alexander I are thus much less adequately documented, and they are generally weak in their presentation and analysis of Czartoryski's political attitudes.

Much more satisfactory on Czartoryski's political outlook during his service as Russian foreign minister is the article by Polish historian Jerzy Skowronek "Le programme européen du Prince Adam Jerzy Czartoryski en 1803–1805," *Acta Poloniae Historica*, No. 17 (1968), pp. 137–159. This article, which became available to me just as my own study was going to press, is based on a careful analysis of Czartoryski's 1803 memorandum "Sur le systéme politique que devroit suivre la Russie" and supporting materials from the Czartoryski Papers and other manuscripts in the USSR. It makes an admirable attempt to consider his ideas within his own intellectual and political context.

The three-volume biography by Marceli Handelsman, *Adam Czartoryski* (Warsaw, 1948–1950; "Rozprawy historyczne," Vols. 23–25), written in wartime conditions and published posthumously, devotes only a small portion of Volume 1 to Czartoryski's Russian service. Kukiel set forth his disagreements in his review of Handelsman's book in the *Journal of Central European Affairs*, XIII (July, 1953), 187.

Charles Morley has written two articles dealing specifically with Czartoryski's period in Russia and his connection with Alexander's Polish policies, "Alexander I and Czartoryski: The Polish Question from 1801–1813," *SEER*, XXV (April 1947), 405–426, and "Czartoryski's Attempts at a New Foreign Policy under Alexander I," *ASEER*, XII (Dec. 1953), 475–485. Morley based his analysis on published sources, which were thus more limited than Kukiel's, and he trusted Czartoryski's memoirs too much in some places. The study by S. S. Tatishchev, "Kniaz Adam Chartoryiskii," in *Iz proshlogo russkoi diplomatii*, 155–342, presents a Russian nationalist interpretation. Among the general articles summarizing his life, see Louis de Viel-Castel, "Le prince Adam Czartoryski," in *Le Correspondant*, new ser. XIX (1862), 625–680, and V. Novodvorskii, "Kniaz Adam Adamovich (Adam Iurii) Chartorizhskii," in *Russkii biograficheskii slovar*, XXII, 38–56. J.-B. Ostrowski's *Adam-George Prince Czartoryski. Fragment de l'histoire de Pologne au XIXe siècle* (Paris, 1845) is a bitter polemic against Czartoryski, which argues that by supporting Russian interests Czartoryski sealed the doom of Poland. I. P. Kornilov, *Kniaz Adam Chartoryiskii* (Moscow, 1896), is little more than a Russian translation of significant portions of Czartoryski's memoirs and some contemporary appraisals of him. Ludwik Debicki's *Puławy (1762–1830). Monografia z zycia towarzyskiego, politycznego i literackiego na podstawie archiwum ks. Czartoryskich w Krakowie* (4 vols.; Lwow, 1887–1888) gives many extracts from the Czartoryski family papers.

M. Lempitskii, "Aleksandr I v Pulavakh. Ego otnosheneniia k semeistvu Chartoryskikh, 1805–1825," *Russkaia starina*, LV (July 1887), 165–182, details Alexander's visits to the Czartoryski family estate. For Czartoryski's educational activities, see the summary regarding the University of Vilna in the unpublished dissertation by James T. Flynn, "The Universities in the Russia of Alexander I: Patterns of Reform and Reaction" (Clark University, 1964), and N. A.

Hans, "Polish Schools in Russia, 1772–1831," *SEER*, XXXVIII (1960), 394–399.

Czartoryski's plans for the restoration of Europe and his proposals for an international league as set forth in the Novosiltsev instructions of 1804 have received a variety of comment, particularly after 1919: Charles Dupuis, "Les antécédents de la Société des Nations. Le plan d'Adam Czartoryski et d'Alexandre," *Séances et Travaux de l'Academie des Sciences Morales et Politiques* (1929, No. 4), pp. 25–54; B. S. Mirkin-Getsevich, "Russkii proekt mezhdunarodnoi organizatsii Evropy 1804 goda," *Sbornik statei, posviashchennykh Pavlu Nikolaevichu Miliukovu, 1859–1929* (Prague, 1929), pp. 435–449, and a French version, "Un projet de fédération Européenne en 1804," *Mélanges offerts à M. Nicolas Iorga par ses amis de France et des pays de langue française* (Paris, 1933), pp. 677–694; and Marian Kukiel, "Ligue des Nations, Union Européenne et la troisième coalition," *Teki Historyczne*, IV, No. 2–3 (1950), 127–133. The two sketchy articles by M. K. Dziewanowski, "Czartoryski: European Federalist," *Current History*, XIX (July 1950), 21–28, and "La vertue de la politique," *Journal of Central European Affairs*, V (Oct. 1945), 281–287, both emphasize aspects of his later *Essai sur la diplomatie*. All of these studies tend to abstract Czartoryski from his intellectual and political context in glorifying him unduly as a precursor of Woodrow Wilson. The cursory summary by P. S. Wandycz, "The Polish Precursors of Federalism," *Journal of Central European Affairs*, XII (Jan. 1953), 346–355, gives more of the Polish intellectual background.

Henryk Batowski's "Un précurseur polonais de l'Union balkanique, le prince Adam Czartoryski," *Revue internationale des études balkaniques*, II (1936, No. 1/3), 149–156, summarizes some of Czartoryski's published ideas on a Slavic federation, although Batowski tends to take them out of context. Frank Fadner devotes the early part of his study, *Seventy Years of Pan-Slavism in Russia; Karazin to Danilevskii, 1800–1870* (Washington, 1962), to such concerns. Czartoryski's views and policies for the Balkans are discussed by Stanislavskaia in *Russko-angliiskie otnosheniia i problemy sredizemnomoria (1798–1807)*; this study is based upon some of the unpublished material in AVPR, but it does little to analyze Czartoryski's complicated political views beyond associating them with class interests of the Russian gentry. Two other Soviet articles bear on Czartoryski's activities: V. G. Sirotkin, "Iz istorii vneshnei politiki Rossii v sredizemnomor'e v nachale XIX v.," *Istoricheskie zapiski*, LXVII (1960), 211–233, and I. V. Evstigneev, "K voprosy o tseliakh vneshnei politiki Rossii v 1804–1805 godakh," *Voprosy istorii* (1962, No. 5), pp. 203–210. Many important dispatches from the British files relating to the Third Coalition were published by J. H. Rose, *Select Despatches from the British Foreign Office Archives Relating to the Formation of the Third Coalition Against France, 1804–1805* (London, 1904; Camden Series, Vol. 7). The role of P. P. Dolgorukii in the Third Coalition and many relevant documents are set forth in the volume by Grand Duke Nikolai Mikhailovich, *Kniazia Dolgorukie, spodvizhniki imperatora Aleksandra I v pervye gody ego tsarstvovaniia. Biograficheskie ocherki*, 2nd ed. (St. Petersburg, 1902).

Among primary materials, Czartoryski's memoirs covering his time in the Russian foreign office and his association with Alexander I were published with several important memoranda and his correspondence with the emperor by Charles de Mazade in *Mémoires du prince Adam Czartoryski et sa correspondance avec l'empereur Alexandre Ier* (2 vols.; Paris, 1887). This edition includes the materials published earlier as *Alexandre Ier et le prince Czartoryski. Correspondance particulière et conversations, 1801–1823*, ed. Charles de Mazade (Paris, 1865). The English version, *Memoirs of Prince Adam Czartoryski and his Correspondence with Alexander I*, ed. Adam Gielgud, 2nd ed. (2 vols.; London, 1888), is somewhat abridged and badly translated; but it contains some material not in the French edition, particularly pertaining to Czartoryski's relations with England. Czartoryski's memoirs, written in the 1820's and 1830's, are factually accurate, for the most part, although the discussion does not follow a strict chronological pattern, which makes it sometimes difficult to date attitudes and events. His memoirs reveal his bitter disappointments with many developments; they tend toward self-justification and self-glorification in some parts, which is shown particularly by his idealization of his role in Russia and in Polish policies.

Some of Czartoryski's attitudes toward political morality and international relations were set forth in a rambling, speculative treatise written in 1823 and published in Marseilles in 1830 as *Essai sur la diplomatie par un Philhellène*; the 1864 Paris edition bore the author's name. This work is very revealing of Czartoryski's discouragement at the establishment of Alexander's "Congress Kingdom" of Poland, and of his idealistic intellectual gropings toward fanciful schemes for the future of diplomacy.

Czartoryski's attitudes and some of his foreign policy plans which he sought to realize while he was foreign minister are set forth in his important 1803 memorandum "Sur le système politique que devroit suivre la Russie" (Czartoryski, "Système"), found bound in a volume of his personal diplomatic papers in the Czartoryski Library in Cracow (CA 5226/IV, folios 13–138). The authorship of this memorandum has been the subject of some dispute, but, although Czartoryski is undoubtedly indebted to others for some of the ideas, he adopted the proposals as his own and presented them as such to the emperor. The memorandum is now published in the original French with my introduction, analysis, and commentary, in the *California Slavic Papers*, Vol. 5 (Berkeley, in process): "Principles of Russian Foreign Policy: An Early Nineteenth-Century Version of Prince Adam Czartoryski."

Many of Czartoryski's other memoranda, reflections, and correspondence during his Russian residence have been published. The Novosiltsev instructions have been reprinted and some additional secret instructions published for the first time in Vol. 2 of the *VPR* series. The first three volumes of this series contain additional correspondence and important memoranda of Czartoryski. Many of his political dispatches and memoranda are included in the earlier collection of diplomatic documents for the period in *SIRIO*, Vols. 77 and 82. Some correspondence with the Vorontsov brothers is printed in *AKV*, especially Volume 15, pp. 151–430, while his correspondence with Stroganov is available in the third volume of Nicholas Mikhailovich's *Stroganov*. Some of Czartoryski's correspondence with A. K. Razumovskii can be followed in Vol. 2 (4 parts) of A. A. Vasilchikov's *Les Razoumowski*. His correspondence with Constantin Ypsilanti on the Danubian provinces is published in the original French from the manuscripts in his archives by P. P. Panaitescu, *Corespondenta lui Constantin Ypsilanti cu guvernul rusesc 1806–1810, pregătirea eteriei și a renașterii politice românești* (Bucarest, 1933; "Așezământul cultural ion C. Bratianu," Vol. 20). Additional materials published include, "Zapiska kniazia A. A. Chartorizhskogo podannaia imperatoru Aleksandru I, 26 iiuna 1808 g.," *SIRIO*, VI, 372–386; "Zapiski kniazia Adama Chartoryzhskogo" (June 20, 1810), *Russkii arkhiv*, XIV (1876, No. 1), 418–436; "Pis'ma kniazia A. A. Chartorizhskogo k N. N. Novosil'tsevu," *SIRIO*, IX, 431–443; "Pis'mo kniazia Adama Chartoryzhskogo k N. N. Novosil'tsevu" (Dec. 12, 1812), *Russkii arkhiv*, XXII (1884, No. 2), 280–282; and "Tri pis'ma kniazia Adama

Chartoryskogo k N. N. Novosil'tsevu," *Russkii arkhiv*, XIII (1875, No. 3), 325–328.

Manuscripts I consulted include the political memoranda and correspondence for 1804 to 1806 and some additional private correspondence in the Stroganov Papers, TsGADA, Fond #1278, Nos. 40, 41, 42, 45, and 62.

The Czartoryski family papers are now in the Czartoryski Library, which forms part of the National Museum in Cracow, Poland. Apparently some of the papers were destroyed in 1939. The typewritten inventory for most of the collection (The New York Public Library possesses a partial microfilm) is badly organized and difficult to use. Among the materials in this collection which were consulted for this study were volumes of his political correspondence from 1802 to 1805 (5214–5220/IV), diplomatic papers and memoranda, 1802–1806 and 1813–1815 (5226–5230/IV, 5238–5239/IV), memoranda and papers on Polish affairs (5222/V–5231/IV), correspondence arranged alphabetically in bound volumes, including letters of interest from Capodistrias, Novosiltsev, and Oubril (5444–5470), correspondence on educational affairs (5476–5477/IV), letters of Count de Mocenigo, 1804–1807 (5502/IV), letters and memoranda of Piattoli (5508/IV), letters of Pisani to Czartoryski, Budberg, and others, 1806–1808 (5509/IV), letters of the Potocki family to Czartoryski (5512/IV), letters of Duke de Serracapriola and his memoranda on Naples, 1806–1807 (5513/IV), correspondence of Stroganov with Czartoryski (5516/IV), letters and drafts of letters from Czartoryski to A. K. Vorontsov, 1803–1805 (5533/IV), letters from Gentz, 1805–1806 (5534/III), correspondence with Razumovskii (ew XVII/605), letters of Czartoryski to his father, 1789–1821 (ew XVII/819) and his sister Marie, 1781–1815 (ew XVII/823–824), correspondence with his mother, Isabelle (ew XVII/1036 and 1039), and letters from his father, Adam Kasimir (ew XVII/1046).

## Chapter 5: Budberg and Rumiantsev

The only available summary of Budberg's life and background is the article by V. Fursenko, "Baron Andrei (Gotthard) Iakovlevich Budberg," in *Russkii biograficheskii slovar*, III, 431–435. Texts of some of his diplomatic correspondence during his mission to Sweden in 1796 are published in *SIRIO*, IX, 195–398. What remain of Budberg's papers are now in TsGAOR in Moscow, Fond #860, but it was impossible to appraise the contents because an inventory was not available. There were a few letters of Pozzo di Borgo to Budberg (860/1/77) and a folder of letters from Dowager Empress Maria Feodorovna, 1806–1809 (860/1/72). Most important of the papers consulted were some memoranda, and letters of Alexander I to Budberg (1794–1807) including a series of penciled notes in the emperor's hand written during Budberg's ministry (860/1/7) and some drafts of Budberg's letters to the emperor, especially concerning his retirement (860/1/621).

Much more has been written about Nikolai Petrovich Rumiantsev, although there is no adequate coverage of his role as foreign minister. A summary of his life with extensive bibliography is given by N. Maikov in "Graf Nikolai Petrovich Rumiantsev," in *Russkii biograficheskii slovar*, XVII, 493–521. For more detail, see the biography by A. D. Ivanovskii, *Gosudarstvennyi kantsler graf Nikolai Petrovich Rumiantsev. Biograficheskii ocherk* (St. Petersburg, 1871), which describes some of his political activities as well as his cultural contributions. Most studies emphasize his cultural role, as do the early articles by A. V. Starchevskii, "O zaslugakh grafa Rumiantseva okazannykh otechestvennoi istorii," *Zhurnal Ministerstva Narodnogo Prosveshcheniia*, XLIX (1846, Nos. 1–3, Part 5), 1–50, and "Sodeistvie kruga kantsleru grafu Rumiantsevu v pol'zu russkoi istorii," *ibid.*, LXV (Jan. 1850, Part 5), 1–34. An able analysis and some correspondence was presented by A. A. Kochubinskii in *Nachalnye gody russkogo slavianovedeniia. Admiral Shishkov i kantsler graf Rumiantsov* (Odessa, 1887–1889). V. S. Ikonnikov's closely documented article, "Graf Nikolai Petrovich Rumiantsev. Deiatelnost ego na pol'zu razrabotki russkoi istorii i arkheologii," *Russkaia starina*, XXXII (Sept. 1881), 47–74, and (Oct. 1881), 225–250, was included with some modification and extensive bibliography in the same author's lengthy *Opyt istoriografii* (2 vols.; Kiev, 1891–1908), I, Part 1, 132–243. The latter volume also gives a detailed description of his library, established after his death as the Rumiantsev Museum, *ibid.*, pp. 841–882. See also Pavel N. Miliukov, *Glavnye techeniia russkoi istoricheskoi mysli*, 3rd ed. (St. Petersburg, 1913), pp. 178–210; and the recent summary by Frank Fadner, *Seventy Years of Russian Pan-Slavism*, pp. 29–31, 37–41. A Soviet *kandidat* dissertation was devoted to his political role in the French alliance — Tatiana Mikhailovna Iagodina, "N. P. Rumiantsev i russko-frantsuzskie otnosheniia, 1807–1812 gg." (Moscow, 1948)—but I was unable to see the text since it has been officially withdrawn from the Lenin Library.

In addition to the materials in Nicholas Mikhailovich's *DSRF* and in *VPR*, some of Rumiantsev's diplomatic correspondence with A. B. Kurakin was published in *SIRIO*, Vol. 21, pp. 351–410. A selection of his correspondence, mostly preceding his period in the Foreign Ministry is available in scattered volumes of the published Vorontsov Papers (*AKV*). His published correspondence from the period mostly involves his scholarly activities, for example, *Perepiska gosudarstvennogo kantslera grafa N. P. Rumiantseva s moskovskimi uchenymi*, ed. N. D. Chechulin (St. Petersburg, 1893), and "K biografii grafa N. P. Rumiantseva," ed. M. A. Venevitinov, *Russkaia starina*, LXXXIX (Mar. 1897), 573–580.

Rumiantsev's archives are available in the manuscript division of the Lenin Library, Fond #255, and a complete inventory has been prepared by K. Maikov (1952), "Opis'arkhiva Rumiantsevykh." The correspondence preserved there from his time in the foreign ministry is almost entirely personal or scholarly and therefore provides scant documentation for his political attitudes and activities. A few of his letters to Admiral P. V. Chichagov in 1812 are preserved in the Chichagov Papers (Fond 333/Chichag. 24) in the same repository. Many of Alexander I's penciled personal notes to Rumiantsev during his ministry are preserved in TsGADA, Gosarkhiv V (5/209); those written during 1812 are published in the second part of S. Goriainov, *1812. Dokumenty Gosudarstvennogo i S.-Peterburgskogo Glavnogo arkhivov* (2 parts; St. Petersburg, 1912). Part 2 also includes some of Alexander's correspondence with P. Chichagov. One of the most revealing of Alexander's personal letters to Rumiantsev was printed earlier with analysis: "Pis'mo imperatora Aleksandra Pavlovicha k gosudarstvennomu kantsleru grafu N. P. Rumiantsevu," *Russkii arkhiv*, VII (1869, No. 4), 609–614.

The memoirs and correspondence of General Savary, Napoleon's first envoy to St. Petersburg during the alliance, are published: *Mémoires du duc de Rovigo pour servir à l'histoire de l'empereur Napoléon* (8 vols.; Paris, 1828), and *La mission du général Savary à Saint-Pétersbourg. Sa correspondance avec l'empereur Napoléon et les ministres des relations extérieures, 1807* (St. Petersburg, 1892; *SIRIO*, Vol. LXXXIII); part of this was published earlier as "La Cour de Russie en 1807–1808; Notes sur la Cour de Russie et Saint-Pétersbourg, écrites en décembre 1807 par le général Savary," ed. A. Vandal,

*Revue d'histoire diplomatique,* IV (March 1890), 399–419. The sources on P. A. Tolstoi's mission to Paris are available in a companion volume, *Posol'stvo grafa P. A. Tolstogo v Parizh v 1807 i 1808 gg. Ot Til'zita do Erfurta,* ed. N. K. Schilder (St. Petersburg, 1893; *SIRIO,* Vol. 89). Many of the source materials for subsequent years were published by Grand Duke Nicholas Mikhailovich, *DSRF;* and some have been published elsewhere, for example: "Les instructions données par Napoléon à M. de Caulaincourt après la paix de Tilsit," ed. Albert Vandal, *Revue d'histoire diplomatique,* IV (Jan. 1890), 54–78; "Documents rélatifs au partage de l'Orient négocié entre Napoléon et Alexandre Ier (janvier–juin 1808)," ed. Albert Vandal, *Revue d'histoire diplomatique,* IV (March 1890), 421–470; "Correspondance inédite de Napoléon avec le général Caulaincourt, 1808–1809," ed. Albert Vandal, *Revue Bleue,* III, Nos. 13–16 (March–April 1895), 386–392, 418–426, 455–459, and 487–491; and René Bittard des Portes, "Les préliminaires de l'entrevue d'Erfurt, 1808," *Revue d'histoire diplomatique,* IV (Jan. 1890), 95–144. Some of Kurakin's reports and correspondence with Rumiantsev and Alexander were published in *Russkii arkhiv,* VIII (1870), 1–162, and many were included in *SIRIO,* XXI, 329–410. Some of Chernyshev's reports were also published in the latter volume, and others were included in *SIRIO,* Vol. 121 — *Bumagi A. I. Chernyshev za tsarstvovanie imperatora Aleksandra I, 1809–1825 gg. (Arkhiv kniazia A. I. Chernysheva)* (St. Petersburg, 1906). On Chernyshev see also *SIRIO,* Vol. CXXII — *Zhizneopisanie vsepoddanneishie doklady i perepiska kniazia Aleksandra Ivanovicha Chernysheva* (St. Petersburg, 1905).

Speranskii's activities during this period are covered in Raeff's biographical study, but the early work by Modest Andreevich Korf, *Zhizn' grafa Speranskogo* (2 vols.; St. Petersburg, 1861), is also important. Several of Speranskii's memoranda on foreign affairs have been published: "Zapiska M. M. Speranskogo o veroiatnostiakh voiny s Frantsieu posle Til'sitskogo mira," ed. N. Dubrovin, *Russkaia starina,* CI (Jan. 1900), 57–65, and "Dve zapiski M. M. Speranskogo po politicheskim delam," *Russkaia starina,* CIV (Nov. 1900), 429–440.

Among the voluminous historical literature on the period consulted, the studies by S. Tatishchev, A. Vandal, E. Driault, H. Butterfield, V. Puryear, E. V. Tarle, and V. G. Sirotkin, provided the best background and the most extensive documentation on Franco-Russian relations at that time. Studies of the Russo-Turkish war consulted included those by N. F. Dubrovin, B. Muraviev, A. F. Miller, A. Pe-

trov, P. F. Shupp, and A. M. Stanislavskaia. New light on the thorny
subject of the Continental Blockade is shed by the posthumously
published study by M. F. Zlotnikov *Kontinental'naia blokada i Rossiia* (Moscow/Leningrad, 1966), but this does not undermine the importance of the earlier work by E. Heckscher, E. V. Tarle, and F.
Crouzet; the chapter by V. G. Sirotkin (*Duel' dvukh diplomatii*, pp.
134–162) is currently the best starting point for this subject and the
controversy which surrounds it.

This study does not begin to do justice to the fascinating and controversial subject of the diplomatic background and conduct of the
war resulting from Napoleon's 1812 invasion of Russia. For a starting
point in the rich bibliography and for some of the recent controversy
on this subject, particularly in the sesquicentennial publications, see
the article by Barry Hollingsworth, "The Napoleonic Invasion of Russia and Recent Soviet Historical Writing," *Journal of Modern History*, XXXVIII, No. 1 (March 1966), 38–52.

# Chapter 6: Nesselrode
# and the Congress of Vienna

There is no adequate study of Nesselrode's long career, most particularly for the period of his association with Alexander. Constantine
de Grunwald devoted a chapter to him, mostly dealing with the period
of Nicholas I, "Nesselrode et le 'Gendarme de l'Europe,'" in *Trois
siècles de diplomatie russe* (Paris, 1945), pp. 173–197. Louis de Lo-
ménie's popularized essay, *M. de Nesselrode* (Paris, 1844), appeared
in Volume 8 of *Galerie des contemporains illustres, par un homme de
rien* (10 vols.; Paris, 1840–1847), and Jean Baptiste Capefigue included a chapter on Nesselrode in Volume 1 of *Les diplomates européens* (Paris, 1843–1847). But essentially Nesselrode has been a forgotten figure in the scholarship on the period.

Significant portions of Nesselrode's papers have been published in
an eleven-volume edition by his grandson A. de Nesselrode, *Lettres et
papiers du chancelier comte de Nesselrode, 1760–1850 (Extraits de
ses archives)* (Paris, [1908–1912]). The second volume includes his
fragmentary "Autobiographie," which was published in Russian as
"Zapiski grafa Karla Vasilevicha Nesselrode" in *Russkii Vestnik*,
CLXXXVI (Oct. 1865), 519–568, and in a somewhat different version, "Vospominaniia grafa K. V. Nesselrode," *Russkii arkhiv*, XLIII

(1905, Part 2, No. 8), 491–534; written when he was seventy-eight, this piece, which covers the period to 1815, is marred by some vagueness and inaccuracy. Some of his diplomatic correspondence, particularly with Pozzo di Borgo, is in *SIRIO*, Vols. 112, 119, and 127; some of his correspondence with Pozzo di Borgo, including some private letters, was published from the Pozzo di Borgo Papers as *Correspondance diplomatique du comte Pozzo di Borgo et du comte de Nesselrode depuis la restauration des Bourbons jusqu'au congrès d'Aix-la-Chapelle, 1814–1818*, ed. Charles Pozzo di Borgo, 2nd ed. (2 vols.; Paris, 1890–1897). The subsequent unpublished series of private letters from Nesselrode to Pozzo di Borgo was made available to me on microfilm from a manuscript volume in the Pozzo di Borgo Papers. A few manuscript letters of Nesselrode to Kochubei in 1821 were found in some of the Kochubei Papers in the Saltykov-Shchedrin Library in Leningrad (GPB 387/42). Some further pieces of his correspondence and that of his wife with her family was found among state papers in TsGADA (Gosarkhiv III, Fond 3/43), and his correspondence with Lieven was consulted in the Lieven Papers in the British Museum (Add. MSS. 47251–47253), and a few of his letters to Lieven in 1820 were in a miscellaneous fond in TsGIA (1101/1/360). It has not been possible, however, to consult the main collection of Nesselrode Papers, presumably extant in France.

Literature on Stein is abundant. An early biography by Georg Heinrich Pertz, *Aus Stein's Leben* (2 vols.; Berlin, 1856), includes large extracts from his papers. The two editions of his correspondence and papers, edited respectively by Erich Botzenhart and Walther Hubatsch, have been described above. An early essay on Stein and Pozzo di Borgo by the Russian publicist Sergei S. Uvarov, *Stein et Pozzo di Borgo* (St. Petersburg, 1846), was also translated into English by D. F. Campbell as *Stein and Pozzo di Borgo* (London, 1847). Some of his letters and papers from 1812 were published with Russian commentary by Aleksandr Nikolaevich Popov, "Baron Shtein v Rossii v 1812 godu," *Russkaia starina*, LXXVII (Feb. 1893), 383–404. An unpublished doctoral dissertation by Oswald P. Backus, "Stein and Russia's Prussian Policy from Tilsit to Vienna" (Yale University, 1949), analyzes Stein's role in Russia thoroughly on the basis of available published sources and gives a particularly valuable summary of his policies. Hans A. Schmitt, "1812: Stein, Alexander I and the Crusade Against Napoleon," *Journal of Modern History*, XXXI (Dec. 1959), 325–328, gives an incisive and well-documented summary of interpretations of Stein's influence on Alexander, concluding that he provided support and implementation more than he influenced the emperor.

The recent Soviet documentary publication on the war in Germany in 1813, edited by L. G. Beskrovnii, contains some materials of interest to this study, *Pokhod russkoi armii protiv Napoleona v 1813 godu i osvobozhdenie Germanii* (Moscow, 1964). This volume along with other recent Soviet analyses of the war of the Fourth Coalition against Napoleon are considered in the article mentioned earlier by Barry Hollingsworth, "The Napoleonic Invasion of Russia and Recent Soviet Historical Writing," *Journal of Modern History*, XXXVIII (March 1966), 49–51.

The colorful diplomat from Corsica, Pozzo di Borgo, has been treated in a variety of literature, but his career still awaits a full scholarly analysis. Pozzo di Borgo summarized his early career himself in a memorandum presented to the Russian government in 1804, "Sobstvennoruchnaia zapiska G. Potstso di Borgo o nem samom," *SIRIO*, II, 158–163, and many of his subsequent memoranda and correspondence have been published in collections listed above. His voluminous, inadequately inventoried, family papers remain in the custody of his descendants in Paris, where I was not permitted to see them. His activities as a secret agent against Napoleon from 1804 to 1812 have been studied from his personal papers and other archival sources by J. M. P. McErlean, to whom I am grateful for availing me of a copy of his article on the subject to be published soon in *Canadian Slavic Studies*.

Little has been published regarding Razumovskii, aside from one multivolume study by A. A. Vasilchikov containing many extracts from his papers and correspondence edited by A. Brückner, *Les Razoumowski*; the most specifically useful for my study was Vol. 2, *Le comte André Razoumowski* (4 parts; Halle s/Saale, 1893–1894). The study was originally published in Russian as *Semeistvo Razumovskikh* (4 vols.; St. Petersburg, 1880–1887).

The early attitudes of the allied leaders toward France in 1814 are well revealed in the large documentary appendixes to August Fournier's study, *Der Congress von Châtillon. Der Politik im Kriege von 1814* (Vienna and Prague, 1900). Eugenius Wawrzkowicz, *Anglia i sprawa Polska, 1813–1815* (Cracow and Warsaw, 1919; "Monografie w zakresie Dziejow nowozytnych"), includes many of the documents which have been helpful for the study of Czartoryski's role. A good idea of the attitudes of Alexander's brother Grand Duke Constantine toward Poland can be learned from his letters to V. F. Vasilev — "Pis'ma velikogo kniazia Konstantina Pavlovich k grafu Vladimiru Fedorovichu Vasilevu, 1812–1814," *Russkii arkhiv*, XX (1882, No. 1), 125–159.

The treaties and official documents of the Congress of Vienna are conveniently published in L. J. B. Chodzko (Comte d'Angeberg), *Le Congrès de Vienne et les traités de 1815* (4 vols.; Paris, 1864). A very revealing collection of police reports, which include transcripts of conversations and copies of correspondence of delegates, during the Vienna congress were published by Maurice-Henri Weil, *Les dessous du Congrès de Vienne d'après les documents originaux des archives du Ministère Impérial et Royal de l'Intérieur à Vienne* (2 vols.; Paris, 1917), which is more comprehensive than the later German edition by Fournier.

The massive literature on the Congress of Vienna cannot be summarized here. Some of the well-known work on the period is listed in the updated bibliography to the 1963 reprint edition of C. K. Webster's classic treatment, *The Congress of Vienna, 1814–1815*. The first study in many years to draw on Soviet and Prussian archival sources is the monograph by Leonid Abramovich Zak, *Monarkhi protiv narodov. Diplomatischeskaia bor'ba na razvalinakh napoleonovskoi imperii* (Moscow, 1966); in addition to his interesting but debatable interpretation, the author analyzes the historiography on the subject and includes an extensive multilingual bibliography covering 1813 to 1815.

## Chapter 7: Capodistrias, A Spokesman for Liberal Causes

Although it was not available at the time of writing, the best starting point for the sources and literature on Capodistrias is the article by Domna N. Dontas "John Capodistrias and the Greek Historians: A Selective Bibliographical Review," *Balkan Studies*, VII (1966, No. 2), 411–422; it is strongest, but not complete, on the published sources for Capodistrias and, as its title would indicate, on secondary and related writings by Greek authors; it does not include the sources from Soviet archives used in this study, nor does it mention some of the other published sources and secondary literature used here. My discussion will accordingly emphasize materials not covered in this article by Dontas.

BIBLIOGRAPHY

A short sketch of Capodistrias' life, "Graf Ioann Antonovich Kapodistriia," is available in *Russkii biograficheskii slovar*, VIII, 479–481. A longer article by Joseph Arthur Gobineau, "Capodistrias," appeared in *Revue des Deux Mondes* XXVI (1841), 234-271, and was reprinted in the author's *Deux études sur la Grèce moderne* (Paris, 1905). His early life and Russian service are treated only briefly in the study by V. Teplov, *Graf Ioann Kapodistriia, prezident Gretsii. Istoricheskii ocherk* (St. Petersburg, 1893); that study was criticized by P. A. Pogodin in *Graf Ioann Kapodistriia, prezident Gretsii. Istoricheskii ocherk V. Teplova. Retsenziia P. A. Pogodina* (St. Petersburg, 1896).

Most of the many studies of Capodistrias' role as the first president of Greece are discussed by Dontas. Recently in English William P. Kaldis has published *John Capodistrias and the Modern Greek State* (Madison, 1963); based chiefly on published sources, narrative in approach with minimal analysis of his ideas, it emphasizes the Greek Revolution and the presidency of Capodistrias, but adds little to our understanding of the man and his role. On this later period in his life see also the article by P. A. Argyropoulo, "Capodistrias et la constitution de l'état hellénique (1827–1832)," *Les Balkans*, XII (1940, No. 1), 1–20.

The only full-length study of Capodistrias in Russia, Stamati Lascaris' *Capodistrias avant la révolution grecque. Sa carrière politique jusqu'en 1822* (Lausanne, 1918), is most valuable for the 1813–1815 period for which the author utilized Swiss archival sources. The authoritative article by C. W. Crawley, "John Capodistrias and the Greeks Before 1821," *Cambridge Historical Journal*, XIII (1957, No. 2), 162–182, provides a most helpful account and a penetrating analysis of his attitudes and activities. Capodistrias' mission to Switzerland in 1813 and 1814 is covered briefly in an essay by Emmanuel Lévis- Mirepoix, prince de Robech, *Une mission diplomatique austro-russe en Suisse* (Angers, 1931), based on materials in the Lebzeltern Papers.

Portions of this chapter draw on ideas developed more extensively in my analysis of Capodistrias' political attitudes during his Russian service, "Capodistrias and a 'New Order' for Restoration Europe: The 'Liberal Ideas' of a Russian Foreign Minister, 1814–1822," *Journal of Modern History*, XL (June 1968), 166–192, which should also be consulted for additional documentation.

A thorough study of Capodistrias' role as Russian foreign minister must await free access to documents in the Russian foreign ministry archives and auxiliary repositories, but the documents available at present in manuscript or in published form add much to our understanding. Most of Capodistrias' personal papers for the period of his Russian service have been either lost or destroyed. The few relevant manuscripts from this period which remain in his family papers in the archives of Corfu are in the process of publication by the Institute of Balkan Studies in Thessalonika, edited with a lengthy introduction by C. W. Crawley.

Most subsequent work on this period of Capodistrias' career draws heavily on his self-justifying account of his Russian service which he presented to Nicholas I with his request for formal retirement in 1826, "Aperçu de ma carrière publique depuis 1798 jusqu'à 1822 (Mémoire à S. M. l'Empereur Nicholas)," Dec. 12/24, 1826, *SIRIO*, III (St. Petersburg, 1868), 163–292. (Dontas names the Greek editions.) An additional fragment was printed in Schilder, *Aleksandr*, IV, 495–496. Portions of the original in his own hand and copied portions in the hand of a secretary are among the Sturdza Papers in Leningrad (PD 288/2/35 and 37).

Capodistrias' important memorandum, "Mémoire sur les Isles Ioniennes," which had been forwarded to Razumovskii with his letter of Jan. 31, 1814, was found with some of his other letters to Razumovskii in TsGADA (15/537 and 626). His report to the emperor on the Fellenberg school system was printed in several editions, *Rapport présenté à Sa Majesté l'Empereur Alexandre, par le comte de Capo d'Istria, sur les établissements de M. de Fellenberg à Hofwyl, en octobre 1814*, ed. Charles Pictet (Geneva, 1817; English translation, London, 1820). A copy of his memorandum, "Observations sur l'état intérieur des Iles Ioniennes," dated April 12, 1816, was found in a collection in the British Museum, "Original papers and letters, chiefly addressed to the family of Slade, 1783–1862, with some additional papers interspersed," (BM/Add. MSS. 27,937).

The important speech Capodistrias gave in Corfu, dated April 18, 1819, was printed later with a misleading English translation and commentary, "Address from Count Capodistrias to the Greeks," in *The Portfolio: A Collection of State Papers, and other Documents and Correspondence, Historical, Diplomatic, and Commercial*, IV (London, 1836), 282–301; it was printed earlier as "Observations sur les moyens d'améliorer le sort des Grecs," in George Waddington's *A Visit to Greece in 1823 and 1824*, 2nd ed. (London, 1825), pp.

xxxiv–xlv, with the author's insightful comments on Capodistrias and his attitudes on restraining revolution in Greece. The address (or paper, as it has been referred to here) has recently been republished along with an explanatory letter from British Consul William Meyer to Castlereagh (Prevesa, May 20, 1821) by the Greek historian Eleutheriou Prevelake in *Triton panionion sunedrion. Praktika* (Athens, 1967), pp. 298–328; the article includes an analysis of the text and a comparison of earlier textual variations.

The article by Emmanuel G. Protopsaltis, "Ypomnemata synaphe Ignatiou Metropolitou Oungrovlachias kai Jo. Kapodistriou peri tes tyches tes Ellados (1821)," *Athena*, LX (1956), 145–182, includes a Greek translation of Capodistrias' long letter to Metropolitan Ignatius setting forth his views on the regeneration of Greece after the failure of the 1821 revolution (it was rendered into English for me by Dia Phillipides); a copy of the French original remains in TsGADA, but was unavailable to me there.

Several of Capodistrias' reports to the emperor are also in the Sturdza Papers, including his "Rapport à S. M. l'Empereur" (March 17, 1822) on Bessarabia (PD 288/2/48); a copy of that report, with several others from 1820 to 1822, appeared in the files of the Ministry of the Interior, among the papers of the chancellery of the government of the Bessarabia in TsGIA (1308/1/8, 9, and 55). An article on Greece attributed to Capodistrias' brother from the *Gazette de Brême* (July 8, 1822), was published in pamphlet form with remarks of refutation possibly by Capodistrias himself, *Remarques politiques sur la cause des grecs* (Paris, 1822).

Some of Capodistrias' diplomatic correspondence from 1816 to 1820 was published in *SIRIO*, Vols. 112, 119, and 127; his correspondence with Richelieu was published with other documents from the Richelieu Papers in *SIRIO*, Vol. 54, and several of his private letters to Nesselrode, Pozzo di Borgo, and Stein, are in published collections of their correspondence. Most of Capodistrias' personal letters to Roxandra Sturdza (Countess Edling) during his period in Russia were published, but have gone unnoticed by scholars, despite their important political contents. They were edited with an introduction by A. F. Shidlovskii: "Perepiska grafa I. A. Kapodistriia: Pis'ma grafa I. A. Kapodistriia grafin Edling," *Vestnik vsemirnoi istorii. Ezhemesiachnyi zhurnal istoricheskoi literatury i nauki* (Jan. 1900), No. 2, 176–195; (Feb. 1900), No. 3, 199–217; (April 1900), No. 5, 151–174; (June 1900), No. 7, 98–123. A few of her letters to him were published, for example, "Pis'mo grafini Edling k grafu Kapodistrii" (1817/1818), *Russkii arkhiv*, XXIX (1891, No. 11), 419–423, and a few others from 1817 are among her family papers (PD 288/1/110).

A four-volume collection of Capodistrias' correspondence from 1827 to 1831, edited by his brothers, *Correspondance du comte J. Capodistrias, Président de la Grèce* (Geneva, 1839), is too late in his life to be of direct value for this study, but contains much interesting material for background, as does his French correspondence with his close friend, the Genevese philhellene Jean-Gabriel Eynard, *Allelographia I. A. Kapodistria kai I. G. Eonardou, 1826–31* (Athens, 1929).

The secret letters of Capodistrias to his friend Foscolo regarding complaints against the British administration in Corfu in 1819 and some letters to Lieven and others published by C. Mertzios in the Greek periodical *Parnassos*, II (1960), 445–472, and III (1961), 103–126 and 207–238, further substantiate my interpretation of his attitudes and activities on behalf of Greece from 1819 on.

Capodistrias' very revealing private letters to his friend and secretary Alexander Sturdza (mostly from 1819 to 1821) are preserved in the Sturdza Papers in Leningrad with many copies of other important letters, evidently sent with them (PD 288/1/185, 186, 186a, and 186b). A few manuscripts of personal letters to Nesselrode during Capodistrias' travels in southern Europe in 1818 and 1819 are in TsGADA, Gosarkhiv III (3/57). A very important collection of Capodistrias' personal letters to Pozzo di Borgo during the period from 1815 to 1822 were found in the Pozzo di Borgo Papers in Paris and made available to me on microfilm. Also of prime importance is a collection of private letters from Capodistrias to the Russian ambassador in Constantinople, his friend Grigorii Aleksandrovich Stroganov, in the Stroganov Papers (TsGADA, 1278/1/181). Capodistrias' private correspondence with the Russian ambassador in England, Lieven, is partially preserved among the Lieven Papers in the British Museum (Add. MSS. 47,284), and a few letters written to Lieven during 1820 are in a miscellaneous collection in TsGIA (1101/1/359). Some additional correspondence of Capodistrias was found in TsGADA, including his letters to Anstedt in 1814 and 1815 (15/277 and 281), his correspondence with Petro Bey from 1818 to 1820 (15/288), some letters to Razumovskii (15/537 and 626), and some drafts of his letters to Lord Bathurst, 1819–1820 (3/55) to the Duke of Wellington, 1819–1820 (3/56), and to Metternich, 1819–1820 (3/58).

Alexander Sturdza introduced the 1839 edition of Capodistrias' correspondence with an interesting and sympathetic essay on his friend's life, "Notice biographique sur le comte J. Capodistrias, Président de la Grèce," a version of which was also published in the posthumous edition of Sturdza's writings, *Oeuvres posthumes, réligieuses, historiques, philosophiques et littéraires d'Alexandre de Stourdza* (5 vols.; Paris, 1858), III, 312–430; the original manuscript is in his papers. A somewhat different version of Sturdza's life of Capodistrias was published in Russian, *Vospominaniia o zhizni i delianiakh grafa I. A. Kapodistrii, pravitel' Gretsii* (Moscow, 1864), parts of the French original of which are preserved in his papers, "Souvenirs de la vie et carrière du comte Jean Capodistrias" (PD 288/2/36; 288/1/4). Sturdza's other memoir account of that period, "Souvenirs du règne d'Alexandre Ier," dated 1837 (PD 288/1/4), was partly published in his *Oeuvres posthumes*, III, 71–124. The published memoirs of Roxandra Sturdza (Countess Edling), *Mémoires de la Ctesse Edling (née Stourdza)* (Moscow, 1888), are very important for a study of Capodistrias and his position vis-à-vis the emperor, and they are extremely revealing of the character of Alexander I and of many contemporary political developments; a Russian edition, "Iz zapisok grafini Edeling, urozhdennoi Sturdzy, s neizdannoi frantsuzskoi rukopisi," was published in *Russkii arkhiv*, XXV (1887, Nos. 2–4), 194–228, 289–304, and 405–438.

Much other correspondence and some additional manuscripts in the Sturdza Papers had direct bearing on this study because of the close association of Capodistrias with members of the Sturdza family. These materials included Alexander Sturdza's letters to his sister Roxandra (PD 288/1/86, 90, and 100) and her husband, Count Edling (288/1/89), to his mother and sisters (288/1/86), and to his mother (288/1/85); Roxandra's letters to her brother (288/1/121), her mother, and other members of the family (288/1/123, 124, 125); Alexander Sturdza's letters to his brother-in-law and Capodistrias' secretary, D. P. Severin (288/1/83, 84, and 98); and Severin's letters to Alexander and Roxandra (288/1/221). There are additional letters of interest, some of them published, from Joseph de Maistre and Madame de Krüdener to Roxandra Sturdza (288/1/285 and 273). Also informative are the manuscripts by Sturdza, "Ma Vie" (288/1/2), "Considérations sur l'acte de l'alliance fraternelle et chrétienne" (dated 1815) (288/1/21), and his report "Revue de l'année 1819" (288/1/5). Also important is the published version of Sturdza's controversial *Mémoire sur l'état actuelle d'Allemagne* (Paris, 1818). Sturdza's published diplomatic history of Romania includes an appendix of some of Roxandra's letters to Alexander I, letters to her from Joseph de Maistre, and other selected family correspondence — *De l'histoire diplomatique des roumains 1821–1859. Règne de Michel Sturdza, Prince regnant de Moldavie, 1834–1849, précédé d'un exposé historique des événements de 1821 à 1834 et suivi d'un aperçu historique sur les événements de 1849 à 1859, d'actes et documents diplomatiques inédits* (Paris, 1907).

Some important material on developments regarding the Ionian Islands with references to Capodistrias' interests was found in the PRO, the French Foreign Ministry files, and the Heytesburg Papers in the British Museum, Volumes 19 and 20, "Correspondence of A'Court with Lt. Gen. Sir Thomas Maitland, 1815–1822" (BM/Add. MSS. 41,520 and 41,530).

The study by Anton Prokesch von Osten on the Greek Revolution, *Geschichte des Abfalls der Griechen vom Türkischen Reiche im Jahre 1821 und der Gründung des Hellenischen Königreiches aus diplomatischem Standpuncte* (6 vols.; Vienna, 1867), ranks as a primary source because Volumes 3 and 4 are totally devoted to diplomatic documents from the period, mostly from the Vienna archives. See also Alexandros Soutsos, *Histoire de la révolution grecque* (Paris, 1829). Other general histories of the Greek Revolution provided me with background. The recent study of Greek revolutionary plans by Notis Botzaris, *Visions balkaniques dans la préparation de la Révolution grecque 1789–1821* (Geneva, 1962; "Etudes d'histoire économique, politique et sociale sous la direction de Jacques Freymond et Jacques l'Huillier," XXXVIII), was very helpful, particularly for its treatment, based on Greek archival sources, of Capodistrias' disavowal of revolution and his refusal to become involved in Greek revolutionary activities. The Soviet point of view on Russian policy in the Balkans is expressed by A. V. Fadeev in "Sotsialno-ekonomicheskie predposylki vneshnei politiki tsarizma v period 'vostochnogo krizisa' 20-kh godov XIX v.," *Istoricheskie zapiski*, LIV (1955), 327–342, and in his book, *Rossiia i vostochnii krizis 20-kh godov XIX veka* (Moscow, 1958).

For a recent statement of the implication of Alexander I and Capodistrias in the Greek Revolution of 1821, see the article by the Romanian historian André Oretea, "L'Hétairie d'il y a cent cinquante ans," *Balkan Studies*, VI (1965, No. 2), 249–264. Oretea had access to some Soviet documents not available to me, but his conclusions appear to have been read into the materials; they do not seem to result from a careful consideration of the documents and of countervailing evidence, nor do they account for the attitudes of the persons involved and for subsequent diplomatic developments. The article is convincingly refuted by Alexandre Despotopoulos, "La Révolution grecque, Alexandre Ypsilantis, et la politique de la Russie," *Balkan Studies*, VII (1966, No. 2), 395–410. See also Oretea's article "Les grandes puissances et le mouvement hétairiste dans les principautés roumaines," *Balkan Studies*, VII (1966, No. 2), pp. 379–394, and the recent study by the Soviet specialist, G. L. Arsh, *Tainoe obshchestvo "Filiki Etairia"* (Moscow, 1965).

Among recent works on diplomatic developments I would single out Paul W. Schroeder's *Metternich's Diplomacy at Its Zenith, 1820–1823* (Austin, Tex., 1962), which carefully reconsiders Metternich's role at the crucial congresses; based mainly on documents from the Vienna archives, it is weakest in its consideration of Alexander and its lack of French and Russian documentation. Its treatment, particularly of the congresses, is helpful however, particularly in conjunction with C. K. Webster's earlier studies of Castlereagh and many of the more general works on the period for filling in the background of European diplomacy.

## Chapter 8: Nesselrode, a Spokesman for the Status Quo

The biographical and source materials on Nesselrode were discussed in connection with Chapter 6. Many of the primary sources and secondary accounts mentioned for Capodistrias in connection with Chapter 7 pertain also to Nesselrode's role during his co-ministry with Capodistrias and his own ministry after 1822. One further document of importance is his long memorandum concerning the Eastern Question, presented to Nicholas I in 1826. A copy of this from the archives of the Polish Library in Paris was published by Grégoire Yakschitchas, "La Russie et la Porte ottomane de 1812 à 1826," *Revue historique*, XCI (July–Aug. 1906), 281–306, XCIII (Jan.–Feb. 1907), 74–89, and (March–April 1907), 283–310.

# INDEX

Adams, John Quincy, 16, 19, 22, 33, 177, 179
Aix-la-Chapelle, Congress of, 14, 244–245
Alaska, 175
Alexander I: character of, 34–42, 63–65, 74–75, 194–196, 286, 291–292; attitudes toward, 34–35, 49, 70–71, 74, 110, 139–140, 173, 286; enlightenment ideals, 47–57, 59, 63–65, 70–71, 82, 113, 174, 241; ideas of European community, 3, 5, 9–10, 33, 45–46, 56–61, 117, 194–196 (*See also* Alliance system; Holy Alliance); legend of Feodor Kuzmich, 37; military enthusiasms, 3, 6–7, 22–23, 35, 37–38, 44–45, 139–140, 194–195, 204, 207–208; personal relations, 36, 108–109; relations with advisers, 28, 39–42, 101–103, 182–186, 191–192, 196, 280–283, 290, 291, 297–299, 301; religious concerns of, 36–39, 56–60, 62–64, 117, 140, 194, 228, 293; role in diplomacy, 4–7, 11–14, 18, 21, 23–24, 30–34, 42–69, 75–80, 87–90, 95, 101–106, 114, 128–129, 131, 133–149, 159, 160–167, 169, 174, 180–183, 188–196, 197, 204–214, 215, 225, 269, 280–283, 289–290, 296–303; and Budberg, 152–155, 158–159, 160, 162–164, 167, 295; and Capodistrias, 29, 50, 60–61, 62, 212, 226, 228–233, 236, 240–253, 255–256, 258–268, 269, 274, 277–280, 291, 294–295, 302; and constitutions, 49–55, 195, 208–209, 210, 242–243, 248–249, 250–251, 291–293; and Czartoryski, 40, 48, 75, 98–100, 103, 106–113, 120–122, 124, 133, 135–153, 221–225, 294–295, 302; and Eastern Ques-

tion, 43, 44, 128, 156, 173–174, 231–232, 255–267, 278–279, 284–285, 301; and foreign diplomats, 22–23, 180, 183, 192, 213–214, 298; and French Restoration, 50, 52–54, 208–209, 216, 220–221, 243–244, 251–252, 292, 300; and Kochubei, 75, 80–81, 82–83, 85–91, 101–103, 193, 295; and Metternich, 14, 46, 53, 59–63, 207, 212–214, 218, 240–241, 248–255, 263, 266, 276–280, 284–286, 293, 298, 300; and Napoleon, 9, 14, 44, 46, 67–68, 163–168, 173–174, 178–182, 186–189, 190, 194–195, 207–208, 214–215, 217–220, 298; and Nesselrode, 29, 192, 193, 196–199, 203–214, 225, 250, 252, 274–276, 278, 280, 283–286, 291, 295–296; and Panin, 69–71, 74–80, 101–103, 295, 297; and Poland, 44, 47, 50, 54–56, 61–62, 119–122, 134–139, 195, 210–212, 216, 217, 218, 221–224, 231, 242–243, 251, 253, 265, 288, 292–293; and reform, 7, 10, 32, 39–40, 47–57, 62–65, 70–71, 75–76, 82–84, 104, 109–111, 114, 124, 240–242, 291; and revolutionary menace, 52–53, 61–63, 246–250, 252–254, 259–261, 277–278, 291, 293; and Rumiantsev, 169–170, 173–174, 179, 180–181, 183, 186–193, 204, 295, 301–302; and A. R. Vorontsov, 98–99, 101–103, 295
Alliance system, 33, 59, 60–62, 238–239, 244–245, 252, 266, 277–279, 293
Alopeus, Maxim, 137, 138, 141
Amiens, Treaty of, 67, 104, 230
Anglo-Russian Convention of 1801, 72, 101, 139
Ancillon, Friedrich, 201

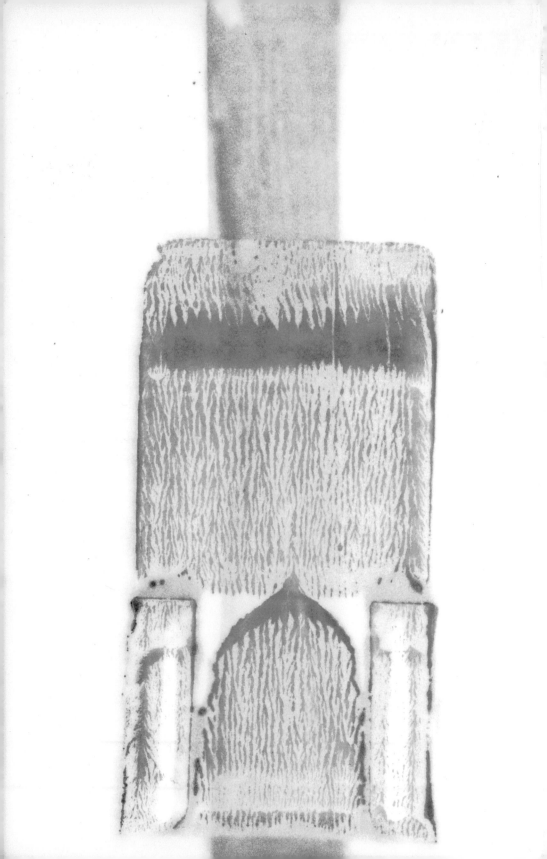